I need that pioneering spirit.

© Pascal Gertschen, Stellisee, Matterhorn

I need Switzerland.

Switzerland.

THE
ALPINE JOURNAL
2021

Doug Scott, among the best and most influential mountaineers of the post-war era, and a former president of the Alpine Club. His obituary appears on p361.
(Bernard Newman)

THE
ALPINE JOURNAL
2021

The Journal of the Alpine Club

A record of mountain adventure
and scientific observation

Editor: Ed Douglas

Production: Rosie Edwards

Volume 125

Number 369

Supported by the
MOUNT EVEREST FOUNDATION

Published by
THE ALPINE CLUB

© 2021 by the Alpine Club

THE ALPINE JOURNAL 2021
Volume 125 No 369

www.alpine-club.org.uk

Address all editorial communication to the Hon Editor:
Alpine Club, 55 Charlotte Rd, London, EC2A 3QF

Address all sales and distribution communications to:
Cordee, 11 Jacknell Rd, Dodwells Bridge Ind Est, Hinckley, LE10 3BS

Back numbers:
Apply to the Alpine Club, 55 Charlotte Rd, London, EC2A 3QF or, for
1969 to date, apply to Cordee, as above.

First published in 2021 by The Alpine Club
Typeset by Rosie Edwards, Vertebrate Publishing
Printed and bound by Novoprint SA, Barcelona

A CIP catalogue record for this book is available from The British Library

ISBN 978-1-7399535-0-8

Front cover: Uli Biaho Tower, Karakoram. This image as well as the two
endpapers, are taken from *The Karakoram: Ice Mountains of Pakistan,* the
sumptuous new book from mountain photographer Colin Prior. See p320.
(Colin Prior)

Endpapers
Front: Colin Prior's shot of Lobsang Spire, above the Baltoro glacier.
The first ascent was made in 1983 by Greg Child, Pete Thexton and Doug
Scott, whose obituary appears on p361. *(Colin Prior)*
Back: Sokha Lumbu glacier, north-west of the village of Askole. *(Colin Prior)*

Foreword

What constitutes mountaineering success? Even with obviously significant achievements, like the first winter ascent of K2, that's not an easy question to answer. Leading alpinists offered radically views of the success of Nirmal 'Nimsdai' Purja, Mingma G and eight more Sherpas who reached the summit on 16 January, as we report in the Area Notes for Pakistan in this issue of the *Alpine Journal*. As for the rest of us, with ambitions that are a little more modest, the answer is even more difficult. Summits can be important, but not if they're too easily won; perhaps it's better to see them as inflection points in a long and continuing story. Ron Kauk once said that the best climber in the world is the one having the most fun. But while climbing is also remarkably easy when it's fun, annoyingly, this isn't always our experience. Then some gentle self-interrogation is worth the trouble, since we all calibrate success differently.

The ubiquity of social media has made that process harder: trusting your own judgement gets more difficult when the opinions and experiences of a thousand other people who seem more self-assured and happy are filling up your timelines. Then the absence of like-minded souls can be rather dispiriting, creating barriers others simply can't see. For that reason, it's a pleasure to celebrate the centenary of the Pinnacle Club in this issue of the *Alpine Journal*, and the 150th anniversary of the first female ascent of the Matterhorn, in words and pictures.

Among those female artists Robin Campbell celebrates in his frontispieces and his notes about them on p56, he includes the mountain-loving heiress Una Cameron. This sent me back to the *Alpine Journal* of 30 years ago, to read Janet Adam Smith's review of Cameron's climbing life. (That any of us could have such an elegant writer putting our lives in order.) Adam Smith, who had encountered Cameron at school, made the point that beyond a few pieces in the *Ladies' Alpine Club Journal*, her friend had left little trace of her exceptional climbing record. She was, for example, the only British climber, male or female, to repeat two of T Graham Brown's triptych on the Brenva face of Mont Blanc before the war: the *Red Sentinel* and *Route Major*. She also made daring expeditions to the Caucasus and the Rwenzori. But it's the joy and pleasure she took from her life in the mountains that resonates in Janet Adam Smith's telling of her. She was marvellously self-deprecating too, describing her skiing technique as 'stately and slow, rather like a mother on a bicycle', and cheerfully recalled how on Monte Viso a local had observed: 'I had no idea that a great fat person like you could go so well.' Cameron described herself as 'a rich Eastern potentate with my red flannel waistband round the bulging middle and a shirt on my ski-sticks keeping the sun off.' All this, and we haven't yet mentioned her art.

The truth is, as I discovered in David Smart's recent biography of Emilio

Comici, that the 1920s and 1930s were full of outstanding female climbers, very few of whom have any kind of profile today. The reasons for that are complicated. Of course, men often wrote the history and felt disinclined to judge female achievements fairly. (Cameron was wealthy and could hire top guides, and so on.) But I wonder if Cameron would have cared either way. There has always been the sort of climber for whom a great ascent isn't quite complete without the recognition of his or her peers. I'm not sure Cameron was one of them. The experience itself was rich enough for her, and the pleasure she took in the company of friends. The historian, however, has an obligation to dig deeper, to offer fresh perspectives on the past, and not simply to follow the weight of press attention. I suspect we are still only in the foothills of mountaineering history, apart from the Everest story. I would certainly like to know more about Una Cameron and anyone else with a similar sense of fun.

The continuing Covid-19 pandemic has left a mark on so many aspects of modern life and it has been fascinating to watch how the world's climbers have responded. We have not by necessity been able to publish as many expedition reports as usual. But one of the great strengths of the *Alpine Journal* is the coverage of the Alps provided by our former president Lindsay Griffin, who remains for many the world's leading authority on new climbs past and present. As he notes, the presence of so much talent confined to their local mountains saw a sudden increase in hard new routes in the Alps. Where there's a will. The Club is very grateful to him and all those who provide our Area Notes. We are always looking for others to contribute.

I would like to thank also Rod Smith for his help with the In Memoriam section, which this year includes obituaries for two colossal figures in the history of British mountaineering: Doug Scott and Hamish MacInnes. Although from slightly different generations, they were both giants of the post-war era, both original and creative, and yet so very different. They were in a sense privileged to find a climbing world with more space and time for true exploration, but they made the most of it. They will remain an inspiration for generations to come.

Ed Douglas

Contents

AREA NOTES

This year's frontispieces have been chosen to celebrate women's alpinism, the centenary of the Pinnacle Club and the 150th anniversary of the first female ascent of the Matterhorn by Lucy Walker (1836-1916), second president of the Ladies' Alpine Club. They are the work of Hilda Hechle (1886-1939) and Constance Gordon-Cumming (1837-1924), whose careers and those of other female mountain artists are the subject of Robin Campbell's article on p56.

Expeditions

'South side of Mont Blanc: the Brenva Glacier', Hilda Hechle, 1905, watercolour, 71cm x 49.5cm. *(Courtesy of Henry Adams, Fine Art Auctioneers)*

MÁREK HOLOČEK

Heaven's Trap

Márek Holoček on the lower section of the north-west face of Baruntse.
(All photos courtesy of Márek Holoček).

A special time: and a strange one. The future suddenly seemed a little drunk: fuzzy and a bit dull. Anxieties emerged like worms from holes. It was not the year I'd been expecting, and one that swept away all our plans. I'm not complaining about it at all because a certain amount of social chaos suits my nature. I like uncertainty. It's an environment where I thrive.

What's more, my little girl was kicked out of school, and since online attendance could be managed from anywhere with an Internet connection, we were not tied to home, free to cross the viral map of Europe. As a result, our family was all together and on parade. That's something that won't be offered in the future. So we enjoyed the time that circumstance brought us. I was able to spend many months in the famous rocky areas of Italy and Spain that are normally overwhelmed with people. Suddenly there was peace, interrupted only by the wind rubbing against the rocks. The only flowers in my garden not blooming were my expeditions to the big hills. And in that respect I began to feel great uneasiness. Fortunately, with the coming spring, snow began to melt not only on the slopes of the Himalaya, but all the bans and regulations for visiting Nepal began to dissolve.

At the moment the door to Nepal opened, I went for it. I quickly became familiar with official obstructions and embarked on the uncertain game of

3

The line of *Heavenly Trap* with the descent in blue, ending at the point where the two Czechs were evacuated by helicopter. A closer view of the route shows the dry conditions the climbers experienced and detail of the wall's upper portion shows the route's steep crux.

the lottery, where the chances of a cancelled flight significantly exceeded the chances of departure. One thing is for sure, I do not suffer from a fear of uncertainty, and if there is a chance for a meaningful attempt, I go for it. In the end, I was greeted by the familiar sweet stench so typical of the Nepali metropolis of Kathmandu. Except the pulse and vibrancy of the city had disappeared completely inside people's houses, with Covid-19 restrictions. This peace couldn't last. We had to hurry, so I quickly sent Radoslav 'Radek' Groh, my climbing partner, and other friends trekking with us to Lukla.

I had to go through inconveniences in Kathmandu: a date at the ministry of tourism, where officials graciously gave me a permit for the hill and I paid thousands of dollars to the establishment. As soon as that happened,

Above: Holoček on the first day.

Left: A similar view of the same wall from 2013 illustrates the impact recent dry years is having in this part of the Himalaya.

the door behind me closed and the whole of Nepal went into a hard lockdown. I left Kathmandu on the brink of legality with small financial incentives offered in certain places. I ran quickly to my friends in the mountains. A group of friends and porters were still waiting for me in Lukla. I knew I would be free there and that my fate would be in my hands again. Even here, at the gate to paradise, I couldn't shake the feeling that these constrictions could still thwart our departure to the mountains. As soon as the plane landed, I drank two beers at the Paradise Hotel and then we all ran further into the heart of the Himalaya.

Next day we met a bunch of friends travelling in the opposite direction: Honza Trávníček, mountain killers Zdeněk 'Háček' Hák and Jaroslav 'Banan' Bánský, who were brandishing a first-ascent scalp from Kangchung Shar.[1] They were returning to Mordor and we were ascending to Rivendell. We felt it necessary to celebrate both our chance meeting and a successful ascent, so we sat in a lodge, where the *didi* was soon rushed off her feet as we relieved her of a significant proportion of her beer supplies. Luckily for her, all of us still had commitments to move that day and a farewell was inevitable. One half of the drunken party continued in the direction of Lukla, and we climbed the slope over the cable bridges to Namche Bazaar.

The following days were filled with a trek with friends, which was also good acclimatisation for Radek and me. It led through 5,000m passes around Gokyo and then over the highest of them all, the Amphu Labsta (5845m) to the Hunku valley. The whole process took a great 15 days right across the heart of the Himalaya. We didn't have very good weather, yet every day we'd see something miraculous. From the last col, we reached base camp at Baruntse. Here, we were enveloped in complete peace and freedom. For far and wide, there was no living soul, only silence occasionally interrupted by the crack of a serac, the rumble of rolling moraine, or a falling avalanche.

Whatever we did, our goal was in sight, whether I opened the tent a little in the morning, or went to the lake to brush my teeth, or in the early evening when we watched the setting sun bathing in the bloody bath of the west wall. Unique, sculptural Baruntse (7129m) filled the entire horizon and left no doubt as to who was in charge here. I'd had the relentless look of this giantess in my memory for a few years now. It is a steep wall roughly rendered with a bit of snow and ice and it inspires fear. It's horribly compelling. You lower your eyes to the ground even as you feel an irresistible desire to keep looking at it: a mixture of monstrosity, wonder, beauty and admiration.

Right from our first encounter, when my eyes were exploring Baruntse's shape bit by bit, I was looking for her weaker points, and a clear idea of a new line stuck in my head. Then I pushed the idea away. Some ideas need time for awareness and courage to grow. I did not revive this one until 2019, when my steps led me once again into the Hunku where Baruntse smiled at me in her full beauty, with that Mona Lisa laziness. I was caught in my own nets and knew that look would haunt me in my dreams and determine my future: just one damn look. However, at that time there was another top of the list a little further along the same valley where Háček and I now went to climb a new route: the north-west face of Chamlang. Now it is May 2021 and I'm standing under Baruntse again. We arrived in base camp on 13 May. We are already well acclimatised and are just waiting for four days of continuous good weather to go to the west face. It's been a waiting game as that window refuses to open but it's no hardship because the weather allows us to run among the surrounding hills and thus shorten our sentence.

1. Hák and Bánský made the first traverse of Kangchung Shar (6030m), climbing the north face to the saddle between Kangchung Shar and Cholo, then following the north-west ridge to the top, returning to the saddle and descending the south face.

Márek Holoček digging out the first bivouac.

Thin ice and crumbly rock as the wall steepens.

Márek Holoček higher on the same pitch.

21 May. A message arrives via the satellite phone that immediately increases our blood pressure. Our moment has come. We pack our gear and food for six days and immediately run to the glacier. Our first bivouac is just below the start of difficulties, hidden under a serac that protects us from stone fall. At the same time, it must be admitted that the glacier is just a frozen river that is still rolling, albeit at the speed of a snail. We simply hope it won't move at the precise moment we are under it.

22 May. We start cutting our way up the first metres of this two-kilometre wall and immediately encounter unpleasant and difficult ground. The lower section is hard ice, often turning into mixed sections. The axes and tips of our crampons creak as though someone were scratching their nails down a board. Even at the slightest swing, did not penetrate deeper and only pinched a thousand-year-old mountain coat into a million tiny fragments that fell directly onto Radek's head.

No wonder, as the west wall has undergone a major change in the last dry years, when lots of snow and ice have disappeared from the cliffs. Only the hardest skin remained, which withstood temperature fluctuations. An ascent like the Russian expedition from 1995 led by Sergei Efimov, which climbed the pillar of the western wall, significantly to the right of our line, is unrepeatable under current conditions. Change must come again and perhaps a richer period of snowfall as well.

The difficult terrain did not allow us to accelerate; more and more difficult sections were encountered, which slowed down the way up. It was still cool, below zero, but the sun's rays managed to loosen stones in the upper section, and humming projectiles begin to fall around us. After 10 hours on the tips of our crampons and pounding axes, which bounce off ice as hard as glass, all we have to do is dig a platform into a glued-on snow ridge, reminiscent of an organ pipe. A bivouac is waiting for us, sitting all night and hanging on the rope. We use the tent without the poles to sit in. From a distance, it looks like a garbage bag with two puppets on a string. It's a desperate place, barely room for two buttocks, our legs hanging over the abyss. In addition, it's a hundred metres lower than we had originally planned: a glitch in the plan and our psyche right at the start.

'Radek, we have to catch up tomorrow,' I say, as much to myself. Calm words emerge from the twisted knot next to me. 'Márek, we'll make it.'

23 May. The weather is good. We climb to the ice field, which leads us diagonally left over more snow pipes towards the rock section. We thrash our ice axes into hard ice all day, climb from one groove, which is always bounded by a rib of loose snow, to the next. The climbing is monotonous, tiring and dangerous. My calves are on fire and with each new axe placement my hands lose a little more. This day's section costs us a lot of energy again but in the late afternoon we finish with a pleasant surprise. As light from the reddening west licks the wall, we find a space for the tent: a snow rib shaped by wind and frost, like a swallow's nest stuck to a wall. After a small adjustment, we have an excellent bivouac, where we can stretch our bodies and catch up on last night's missed sleep. I realise we have hardly exchanged a word. There has been no time to eat or even drink. We are tortured and hungry. But the place where we sleep is comfortable and in less than an hour our dry throats are moistened with the first tea.

24 May. In the morning we reach the most difficult section of the ascent. Above our head we have a 250m barrier of broken rock. It takes us a while to decide where our steps should lead. The process slows us down and the weather begins to deteriorate.

The early arrival of bad weather caught the climbers before they'd escaped the wall.

'Radek,' I say, 'the section above my head can't be protected much, and it's this crumbly layered rock, which I'll peel off like gingerbread in climbing it. I'll put one more screw into the ice so there's something between us and go to Russian roulette mode.'

'I'll be careful, but try to get a cam or peg in that pig, Márek.'

'Sure, but there'll be flying rocks, so duck and just hope I don't fly with them. I really wouldn't like that.'

In the end, using everything we've got, we climb to within 70m of the ridge. Already, it's snowing heavily. Climbing is difficult, unpleasant even, and in the end we are stopped by the weather. The rivers of snow resemble white snakes, slithering down the wall, showering us with flurries. Once more we have to find somewhere to spend a night that wasn't planned. Fortunately, we find a rocky promontory protruding above the valley, exactly large enough for our tent. We build an airy bivouac on this spot, which does not have a spare centimetre on any side before the kilometre void beyond.

This eagle's nest has one beneficial effect. Except for a narrow neck connecting us to the wall, the stream of snow goes round us. In the tent, we pull out sleeping bags, which, thanks to previous nights attracting moisture, have frozen into icy rubble. Even so, it is better to climb into them and steam. I quickly pull out the satellite phone to find a message from Alena (our friend the meteorologist) who is our guardian angel and sends me weather reports.

Above and opposite: Strong winds and heavy snow intensified as the climbers topped out turning the descent into a protracted nightmare lasting 80 hours and stretching the two Czechs to the limit.

'Damn, the weather wasn't supposed to change today, and it's going to get worse tomorrow afternoon.'

I read the message again and quickly write back with the current situation. Nature can readily invent its own story, without taking into account mathematical models and years of knowledge in weather forecasting. Nothing is ever that firm, clear or unchanging. And we cannot anticipate all variables in advance in order to prepare for them. In the mountains, it is necessary to learn to accept change and respond to it. It is true that we are half a day slower than planned, but the dramatic deterioration in weather has accelerated by a day and a half. This brought us closer to the trouble we were expecting.

I form a picture of the morning that has yet to come. As long as we're still hanging under the top of the route, we're vulnerable. We can't go down and the only way is up. We have to hope that the weather will allow us to climb those few tens of metres tomorrow and then we will descend down the ridge to safety. Another dream that does not come true. Suddenly, the satellite phone beeps with an SMS. It's Alena again.

'Tomorrow the weather will be like today and in the evening there will be a significant deterioration. And the next day, Saigon will come.'

'That means, Radek, we have to be extra fast, get to the ridge and immediately run to the top and continue down. If bad weather catches us up there, we have a big problem.'

'Tomorrow, we'll leave as fast as the martins; I don't want to be here

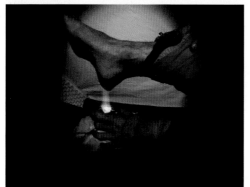

another minute, Márek.' We fall asleep in a fighting mood.

25 May. It's cloudy in the morning with poor visibility, but there is no choice. We have to climb to the ridge, get up and over the summit and down. Easy to say, but the falling snow, the wind and the last mixed sections take all day again. On one pitch, Radek climbs up to me and says through clenched teeth: 'Let it fucking end.' I try not to make the situation worse and calmly answer: 'It will be good, it will only be good.' I don't know I am lying to myself.

We reach the summit around 4pm, completely frozen, covered with hoarfrost and we can't see a step thanks to the fog. All that remains is to set up the tent with the knowledge that Wednesday with its hurricane winds and snowfall will not pass us by. As a small consolation, I keep repeating to myself, at least we have left that wall of terror behind us.

With darkness comes a strong wind, which, with the brutality of gunfire, drives snow against the thin walls of our house. At any moment, it seems, the tent will collapse and tear under this onslaught. Just before morning, it stops shaking. The wind is still shrieking, but the whole tent has been completely covered and turned into an igloo. The interior has shrunk to the barest minimum; it's impossible to move without pushing against each other. The air is heavy and it's difficult to breathe. Neither of us wants to go

Top: Climbing the last steep pitches to the ridge.

Left: Holoček packs up following the last night on the wall.

Opposite: After the punishing multi-day storm, the morning of 29 May was clear, allowing the pair to descend 1,100m before camping again. At the limit of their endurance and with deep new snow, they summoned a helicopter.

to hell yet. So there is nothing for it but to move, otherwise this place will become our grave. Here we go.

26 May. In the morning, we move the whole tent a few metres further. We perform this operation blind. I can't see the tip of my nose, let alone whether we are already too close to the edge of the overhanging ridge, beneath which is a void all the way down to the glacier. This white blankness prevents any attempt to descend. And those few minutes outside the tent seem like an eternity. The cold and wind chill us; we're shivering in our damp clothes in an instant. It takes us hours in the sleeping bag for the shivering to stop and a feeling of warmth to return. We lie side by side all day without speaking, heavy thoughts tramping through our heads, each keeping to themself. At the same time, we know very well that this is wrong. There will be no chance of better weather for the next three days. On the

contrary, it will worsen on Friday. Before us lies the prospect of 72 hours lying in wet sleeping bags, without taking a step. We are stuck on a ridge 7,000m high, in places as sharp as a knife and with slopes falling more than a kilometre either side. At night the wind comes again and strengthens to a hurricane, completely covering our tent with more new snow.

27 May. Snooping around in the morning, it's clear nothing has changed. We lie around all day.

28 May. Around ten o'clock, the wind begins to calm down. Even the thick fog melts at times. We quickly pack the tent hoping to get at least a little lower today. The light is diffused, which induces a drunken effect. We have nothing with which to contrast the view in front of us; we can't judge what it is we're stepping on. The ambient light is shimmering white and we flounder around like tangled noodles.

'Radek, we can't go on, we can't see anything.'

'But we have to keep going, or we'll die here, Márek.'

'I know it's hard to accept, but there's nothing we can do, we have to wait. We don't know if we're going to fall into the valley with the next step.'

'Come,' Radek's voice insists. 'Try again.'

'Shit, we don't even know if we're descending the ridge or just branching off on a lateral rib.'

This heated discussion continues for a moment, soaked in tension. In the end, pragmatic reason prevails. A few tens of metres below, we set up the tent and climb into it again. This time we're there for two days and two nights. The weather remains devilish, and even ordinary basic tasks, such as boiling water or going to urinate, are difficult tasks for us, costing a lot of effort. We free the tent again from the grip of the snow. We wait and pray. There is nothing more we can do. Meanwhile, our wet things freeze and the cold bites into us. Food supplies disappear. There is still a stove for boiling snow, but our tea and soluble tablets are finished.

30 May. It's a beautiful morning that promises a nice day. Yesterday we managed to descend a significant distance but now we're exhausted. We immediately take advantage of the opportunity offered to use our satellite phone and send our coordinates to our helicopter pilot. There is no desire to suffer more and risk avalanches. Last night was too much. My feet are frozen and two fingers tingle like hell.

'How are you, Radek?'

'I don't know yet. But please God, let the helicopter pick us up, I don't want to go any further.'

Fortunately, our call is heard and at 7am, a helicopter frees us from this icy hell. We fly along the western wall, which has been our home for 10 days. I stare at places already deeply etched in my memory, while at the same time glad that we're moving away with every passing second. I'm alive and can finally afford to let the rein on my emotions drop. I feel the joy of a completed dream, a rush of fatigue, the onset of pain that shoots in spasms through my frozen fingers. The machine floats like a dragonfly right in the heart of the Himalaya, around Ama Dablam, Lhotse, Everest, Pumori, Kusum Kanguru and beautiful peaks all around the horizon. The pilot moves through them in minutes and we are soon landing in Lukla, where the whole thing started. Just before landing, I turn to my friend and try to compete with the noise of the rotors.

'Thanks Radek, you were great again.'

Summary: First ascent of *Heavenly Trap* (ABO+, VI+, M6+, 80°, 1300m) on the north-west face of Baruntse (7129m), leaving base camp on 20 May and evacuated by helicopter on 30 May. The climbers dedicated their route to Petr Machold and Kuba Vanek, who disappeared attempting a similar line in 2013. The route goes to the left of the line taken by Sergei Efimov's Russian team in 1995.

SIMON RICHARDSON

The Chardonnet from End to End

Rick Allen on the lower section of the *Scottish Route* on the Grande Fourche.
(Simon Richardson)

Chamonix, July 1979. Peri-Jane Cheal and I were both 19 years old and eager to get to grips with alpine climbing. After a warm up on the Petits Charmoz traverse we made our way up to the Albert Premier hut. Our ascent of the *Forbes Arête* on the Aiguille du Chardonnet next day was a wonderful life-affirming experience. Other teams rushed past us on the glacier in the night, but unperturbed we followed their steps over the ice bulge of the Bosse and, all alone, we emerged onto the east ridge at daybreak.

The weather was a little unsettled and we followed the perfect crest of granite and snow in swirling mist. Every so often we caught tantalising glimpses of the great icy faces of the Argentière wall glistening white through the cloud. Helpful footsteps led down from the summit to a couple of abseils and we were back in Chamonix by mid afternoon. The *Forbes Arête* proved a steppingstone to bigger things and a week later we were climbing the north face of the Obergabelhorn.

I returned to the Chardonnet five years later for the popular *North Spur*. Although it is not a difficult route, some say it is one of the finest mixed climbs in the Alps. Sure enough, the route did not disappoint, but at that stage in my climbing career it was all about moving fast. My two-hour time

15

The classic view of the north face of the Aiguille du Chardonnet from the Albert Premier hut. The *Forbes Arête* follows the near left-hand ice ridge over the curved hump of the Bosse before following the skyline arête to the summit. The *North Spur* takes the central buttress right of the fluted ice face and the descent down the west ridge follows the right skyline to the sloping col Adams Reilly. The recalcitrant double bergschrund lies directly below in the shadow of Aiguille Adams Reilly. *(Simon Richardson)*

was rather average and certainly did not compare with Roger Everett and Phil Bartlett's lightning ascent in 1975 when they climbed the route so quickly that they were back in Snell's Field before breakfast.

After that, I forgot about the Chardonnet for nearly 30 years, until my interest was rekindled when Tom Prentice and I started to explore untravelled rock features in the range. On the mountain's south-west face, just north of the col du Chardonnet, there are three attractive pillars comprising perfect Chamonix granite. Jean-Franck Charlet climbed the right and left pillars in the 1970s but the central line was unclimbed. Tom and I made the long approach up the Chardonnet glacier in August 2013 and, after a bivouac, climbed the pillar in 10 sustained pitches to the summit of Pt 3660m, a prominent sub-peak of the mountain. We wore rock shoes and after tagging the top, abseiled back down to our boots and crampons on the glacier.

Our climb on Pt 3660m pointed to a forgotten side of the Chardonnet. Viewed from the Albert Premier hut, the *Forbes Arête* appears to climb the full length of the mountain's eastern crest but, hidden behind the frontier ridge, a steep extension plunges nearly 500m into Switzerland at the head of the Saleina glacier. It is a major structural feature and quite incredibly, there was no record of an ascent. Slowly a plan began to form. How about

Above: Peri-Jane Cheal climbing the *Forbes Arête* in July 1979. *(Simon Richardson)*

Right: Rick Allen on day one of the *East Ridge Integrale,* climbing the right-facing corner leading to the lower crest.

traversing the complete spine of the Chardonnet from east to west? The route would start from the Saleina glacier, ascend the unclimbed lower east ridge, continue along the *Forbes Arête* and finish by descending the west ridge. The plan had simplicity and elegance and Rick Allen was up for the challenge in early summer 2017.

I was astonished how dry the mountains looked as I travelled from Geneva to Chamonix on 22 June. It felt more like September than late spring but the weather was good, so we immediately set off for our first objective on the Grande Fourche. The south-east face of the mountain above the Saleina glacier was particularly intriguing as its 500m central spur was unclimbed and, equally important, it would give us a good view of the eastern end of the Chardonnet.

After a night in the Albert Premier hut, we crossed the Fenêtre de Saleina and started up our spur in bright sunshine next morning. The most difficult climbing was near the start where a 'sea of slabs' led to a steep tower. We expected to climb the route in a day and were travelling light but had underestimated the difficulties. By early afternoon we were only a quarter of the way up the route. Still, June days are long and the weather forecast was good, so we pressed on up easier climbing on the upper part of the spur in the full knowledge that we would be spending a night out.

We settled down on a good ledge just below the summit as dusk fell and were a little surprised when it started to drizzle. We were even more surprised when the drizzle turned to rain and we spent the night curled up in our lightweight waterproofs willing morning to arrive. It was cold, wet and miserable, but I was determined not to make a fuss. I've known Rick for over 30 years, and I knew full well that he would be the last to complain. After all, this was nothing compared to his open bivouac on Nanga Parbat after the Mazeno ridge. Cold muscles meant it was slow going next morning and we made our careful way over the summit in thick cloud to descend

Looking up the lower east ridge on day one. *(Simon Richardson)*

Left: Rick Allen climbing the
lower east ridge on day one.
(Simon Richardson)

to the Tour glacier. Next day Rick took us shopping in Chamonix to buy emergency bivouac sacks.

The weather became cold and unsettled but we made the best of it with short rock routes in the Aiguilles Rouges and a wintry traverse of the Aiguilles d'Entrèves. It started to snow on one of the Aiguilles Rouges routes and we caused consternation among neighbouring continental teams when we continued climbing rather than abseiling off. The weather was just like Scotland, so unperturbed we continued up. Finally on 3 July we had a good weather forecast so we made our way up to Albert Premier hut all set to traverse the Chardonnet from end to end.

Tuesday 4 July. We're up at 3.30am and away from the hut an hour later. The fresh snow on the glacier has consolidated quickly after the bad weather and it is quick going up to the Fenêtre du Tour. We cross into Switzerland, traverse the head of the Saleina glacier and cut across to the Chardonnet where a horizontal traverse across the bergschrund leads to a snowed-up right-facing corner leading up to the lower east ridge. The sun is rising fast but the left wall of the corner is in shade and still frozen so we make good progress in two long rope lengths to the crest.

A natural line of weakness on the right flank of the ridge leads to a snowy gully cutting through a tower. The gully walls are smooth-sided and I'm lucky to find a jammed flake belay when the rope runs out. The rock is horrible decomposing granite and the gully steepens and narrows above. But luck is on our side as the recent storms have lined the gully bed with a thin sliver of ice. Rick delicately front points up to a giant chockstone and threads his way underneath: a great lead and very Scottish.

Above, an overhanging flake-chimney leads up to a small ledge. It's rather disconcerting because the corner is formed by a giant flake of rotten granite lying against the wall and we can see daylight shining through at several points. I belay at the top and am relieved to see that our line continues up a slabby wall and rather than blank out. More importantly, the rock quality has improved, so I change into my rock shoes. The slabby wall is surprisingly awkward, but after a difficult start I reach flakes and belay below a snowy chimney.

Rick leads through and kicks steps up the left edge of the first of two slanting snow patches above that are noticeable landmarks on the route. We are making good progress but the upper ridge looms above, guarded by a smooth vertical headwall that is looking increasingly difficult as we gain height. I continue up the barrier wall separating the two snow patches. Water is dripping down from the upper patch and there are a couple of hard moves through a steep slabby section. The route is starting to put up a fight and the climbing is significantly harder than it looks.

Rick moves up to the headwall and belays on some grey flakes. The granite is more featured than it looked from below and we're hopeful of finding a way to the horizontal crest above. My pitch goes well until I reach a blank section below the first summit tower that appears to overhang in all directions. An awkward step right onto a hanging V-groove leads to a good ledge. I continue up a difficult snowed-up corner and then back and foot up a snow-choked chimney dividing the first two towers on the crest. As I reach the narrow gap at its top, I'm disappointed to see that the second tower is as monolithic as the first. There is no way of continuing so I lower off a sling back to the ledge.

My legs and right arm are dripping wet and I'm not in a good mood. We've been climbing well, but it looks like we've run out of options. The only possibility is to aid climb up an overhanging corner at the right end of the ledge but it's running with water, with a small stream pouring down its left wall. The wintry conditions that helped us lower down the climb are now conspiring against us.

Rick Allen following the smooth slab-corner above the crux corner on day two.
Grande Fourche in the background. *(Simon Richardson)*

'Hey Rick, let's bivvy here. Hopefully things will look better in the morning.'

I've played this trick several times before. The way ahead is in shadow and it is difficult to see exactly where to go, but I know that a good night's sleep will make everything look far more amenable, especially in the morning sunshine. We settle down to a comfortable bivouac and Rick melts water and feeds me bread and cheese. He is happy and calm and exudes confidence. Slowly I begin to relax. The weather had clouded in during the day,

Looking back on day two along the horizontal crest with the north face of the Aiguille d'Argentière in the background. *(Simon Richardson)*

but the sky clears through the night and it is just cold enough to freeze the drips on our ledge.

Wednesday 5 July. We wake to the pink glow of dawn over the Valais skyline and the familiar outline of the Weisshorn, Dent Blanche and Matterhorn. There is no urgency as we wait for the rock to warm up but we're packed and ready to go by 7am. As we hoped, the morning sun makes everything look far better. The overhanging corner is the only way to go, but fortunately the water has stopped running and it doesn't look verglassed.

I put on my rock boots, sort the gear and start to aid up the corner. Initially it takes small wires but higher up I leapfrog cams. And then, horror of horrors, as I pull over the bulge at the top there is a peg. The only explanation is that Charlet must have passed this way. (Later, I check the guidebook later and this is exactly what happened. Starting from France on the south side of the ridge the *Charlet-Belin* pillar gains the same notch that I reached the evening before. Unable to continue up the monolithic rock above, they crossed over to the north side of the ridge and climbed the corner to gain the crest. And like me, they used aid to climb the pitch). A few free moves gain a small flake ledge. I haul my sack and Rick skilfully follows, replacing gear where I had removed it. Above a smooth slab-corner leads to the crest. I look around the edge and the way ahead is clear. The route is going to go.

The horizontal crenelated ridge is as difficult as it is spectacular, with vertical walls plunging either side. From the summits of two successive towers we abseil into deep notches before finally gaining easier-angled ground leading to the base of Pt 3660m. The going is slow and awkward with soft snow overlying steep slabs. Eventually, Rick leads a difficult pitch down and right under Pt 3660m into the line of the east couloir. (Charlet and Belin were cannier than us. Rather than follow the exact crest they bypassed the towers on their north side before crossing back over and descending into France).

The east couloir should have been full of snow but we find instead a discontinuous ribbon of grey ice leading up the left side of the gully bed. Rick carefully picks his way up the ice to gain the col immediately west of Pt 3660m where he hesitates.

Aiguille du Chardonnet
(3824m)

P3660

East Ridge integrale (TD) (Allen-Richardson 2017)
East Pillar from the Chardonnet Glacier (TD)
(Belin-Charlet 1971)
NNE Ridge (AD) (Aubert-Aubert-Crettez 1899)
Forbes Arete (AD) (Sisley-Crettez-Crettez 1899)

Above: Rick Allen on the *Forbes Arête*. Grande Fourche in background. *(Simon Richardson)*

Left: A topo showing the *East Ridge Integrale* and how it relates to other routes on the mountain. The orange line is the *Forbes Arête*. *(Simon Richardson).*

'Er, Simon? I thought you said it would be easy from here?'

Instead of scrambling terrain, Rick is confronted by a knife-edge rocky ridge leading over big towers. This is not the easy access onto the *Forbes Arête* that I had promised so I dig into my rucksack and flick through a collection of photos of the Chardonnet that I'd downloaded from the Internet. These show that moving across to a notch on the north-north-east ridge is possibly a better way to go.

Rick reverses carefully back down and I lead across broken ground to the notch. We can see easy snow slopes leading across to the *Forbes Arête;* footsteps are only a couple of hundred metres away! We settle down on a broken ledge for an early bivouac at 5pm. I have the better position this time

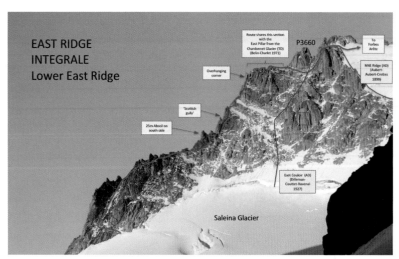

EAST RIDGE
INTEGRALE
Lower East Ridge

Another view of the *East Ridge Integrale* above the Saleina glacier. The blue central line is the *East Couloir*, climbed in 1927. *(Simon Richardson)*

so do the cooking. Unlike the night before, we're both happy and at ease. We've completed the new route part of our ascent and are looking forward to an enjoyable journey along the Forbes Arête in the morning.

Thursday 6 July. We wake early and are soon front pointing across névé slopes to join the *Forbes Arête* above the Bosse. The weather is perfect, but conditions on the ridge are lean and the climbing is more involved than we expected. The crest has lost its helpful covering of snow, so we traverse around individual towers on hard water ice. The situation is spectacular, although I'm a little disappointed that the great ice faces of the Argentière wall are dry and grey and not gleaming white like they were when Peri-Jane and I passed this way 38 years ago.

On the summit there are no friendly snowy footsteps leading down the west ridge; instead we are greeted by a long convex slope of black ice. When the ice runs out, we start abseiling. Eventually we gain the gentle slopes leading to the col Adams Reilly but the ice is so hard that we have to abseil here too.

Now on the glacier we hope for faster progress but soon encounter a huge bergschrund. We front point down this as far as we dare, skirting under smooth rock on the right until we find a spike for an anchor. A long abseil just takes us over the lower lip of this double-lipped monster; we're very grateful for our 60m ropes. We find a sling wrapped around a couple of large stones buried in soft snow halfway down and can only imagine the horror of a previous party negotiating this obstacle with a single rope.

The glacier is very crevassed and the route finding complex, so it is late when we reach the hut. The guardian has been watching out for us and saved us dinner. He said he was worried as part of the Bosse had collapsed

1 Scottish Route (TD)
2 East Couloir (AD)
3 Adams-Crettex Route (AD)
S – Sea of Slabs, T – Central Tower
R- Right-trending Ramp, C – Final Crest

Topo showing line of the *Scottish Route*.

that morning resulting in a huge avalanche that swept across the approach to the *Forbes Arête*. My holiday is nearly over. I need to travel to Germany early next morning, so we walk down to the valley through the night, happy and fulfilled after an exciting adventure.

Our difficult descent from the Chardonnet makes me reflect on how lucky we were to be able to climb in the Alps in the 1980s and 1990s. All around the world, global warming is changing glaciers fast. Even at the beginning of the summer season in the Mont Blanc range, glacier travel can be problematic. Looking back to when Peri-Jane and I climbed the *Forbes Arête* in 1979 it is inconceivable that two teenagers, on their first ever glaciated alpine climb, could have safely negotiated the terrain that Rick and I found in 2017. And as for climbing the mountain and arriving back in the valley before breakfast like Roger and Phil – we can but dream.

Summary
Scottish Route (500m, TD, 6a), Grande Fourche (3610m), Rick Allen and Simon Richardson, 24 Jun 2017.

Complete east-west traverse of the Aiguille du Chardonnet (3824m) via *East Ridge Integrale* (800m, TD), Rick Allen and Simon Richardson, 4-6 Jul 2017.

• Rick Allen died in an avalanche on K2 in July. His obituary will be published in next year's *Alpine Journal.*

DEREK BUCKLE

Seven Climbs, Seven Continents

I never set out to climb a mountain on every continent, but suddenly realised it seemed to be happening by default. Rather unusually perhaps, my first major mountain was climbed many years ago on a commercial expedition to Ecuador when our team climbed Cotopaxi and Chimborazo, but these were simply a taste of better things to come. It was several years later, when work and family commitments relaxed somewhat, that I could justifiably spend more time in the Greater Ranges, as opposed to simply fell walking and winter climbing in the more modest mountains of Britain.

It is in this context that I first spent many summer seasons in the European Alps before climbing in Africa, Asia, Australasia, Antarctica, North America and back to South America once again. Every visit was a personal adventure, with the people, culture, sights and sounds, providing an important complement to the *raison d'être* of mountaineering. Without these additional experiences mountaineering for me would lose much of its charm. This is, then, a very personal account.

Having now climbed well over a thousand mountains around the globe it is no easy task to select just one from each continent since so many have been memorable. Here, however, I have tried to pick out those that for one reason or another have left some of the most lasting impressions. They are not presented in chronological order.

Europe

I have climbed a lot in the Alps over the years, but for me one mountain in particular stands out: the Piz Badile. Seen from the Sasc Fura hut, the classic view is of the north ridge, highlighted in the photo by the intersection of light and shade and emphasised by the backdrop of an azure sky.

Ever since my first glimpse of a photo of the Badile's north ridge, bathed so entrancingly in light and shade, I knew it had to be added to my ever-increasing list of 'must do' climbs. It was not until 2000, however, that a suitable opportunity arose. That year the Alpine Club were holding their annual meet in Pontresina in the Bernina, and I managed to convince Nick King, my regular climbing partner, that we should go along too. Unfortunately, heavy snowfall that year severely limited the major Bernina climbing objectives so we eventually separated from the main group to focus on the Bregaglia, just a short drive away.

Based conveniently in a campsite at Viscosoprano, we acclimatised in the Albina valley before the draw of the Badile became irresistible. There was just one little problem: Nick and I lacked transport, having been driven from the UK by our friend Steve Humphries. After some delicate discussions,

Light and shade on the Badile north ridge from the Sasc Fura hut.
(Derek Buckle)

facilitated by copious quantities of beer and wine, we finally managed to persuade Steve that we should borrow his car while he and John Temple went on their three-day climb over the Zocca pass into Italy. It was a fine solution, with the only snag that we now had a strictly limited period in which to both climb the Badile and, more importantly, return Steve's car before he and John got back.

So, on a fine August morning Nick and I set off for the three and a half hour walk along a tree-lined path to the Sasc Fura hut. Perched on the promontory just below the foot of the north ridge the hut afforded fine views of our objective so that we too could take photos of the kind that first inspired me to want to climb this compelling line.

Unsurprisingly, we were not alone and around 6am we joined numerous other parties heading up the promontory towards the start of the route. While some teams were clearly intent on the classic *Cassin* route on the north-east face, most, like us, were hurrying to get into pole-position on the ridge proper. After the initial jostling on the easier lower section, Nick and I succeeded in getting ahead of all but one other party and were at last able to savour both the position and the excellent granite that this route provides. Foreshortening makes the north ridge considerably longer than it appears from the hut, but moving quickly reasonable progress was made by taking a line of spaced pegs and fixed belays situated mostly on the crest itself.

Seven hours after leaving the hut we finally reached the summit. From here the average party continues towards the Gianetti hut via the normal route on the south face. We, however, had a deadline to meet as Steve and John would be expecting to see their car when they returned to the valley after their climb. With little choice, we had to rappel the north ridge,

Window Route and *Diamond Couloir* on Mount Kenya. Batian is to the left and Nelion to the right. *(Derek Buckle)*

a daunting task bearing in mind that there are 700m of descent. Initially we joined forces with two German climbers who had decided not to climb the final snow section to the top, but their slow progress and the threat of an incoming storm eventually forced us to descend alone.

Some 20 rappels and five hours later we reached easy ground, but by this time rain was falling in torrents and water was forming impressive bow waves over our boots. Copious spray from our abseil devices added to the discomfort in our nether regions but fortunately, the lightning we feared most only began during the final rappels. The German pair was still high on the ridge as we ran down towards the hut and it is my suspicion that they spent an uncomfortable night on the mountain before descending the following day.

Grateful to be watching the full-blown storm from the comfort of the hut, Nick and I continued to Bondo next morning, returning the car well before Steve and John got back to the valley. So ended a memorable ascent of the Badile, although another time I'll take the normal route back.

Africa

I retired in early December 1996 but did not have too long to think about what I was now going to do. Within two weeks I received a phone call from John Temple, a longstanding friend and climbing partner. Did I fancy a trip at the end of the month to climb Mount Kenya? It took a split second to reply. Although most people mention Kilimanjaro, the highest mountain on the continent, when they think about African mountains, Mount Kenya is the mountaineer's mountain in Africa. Nelion and Batian, the two main rocky summits of this long extinct volcano rise to over 5,000m above the

African plains and offer no easy routes. By contrast, Point Lenana, the third highest summit at a little under 5,000m, is a popular and easy trekking peak.

Like Ian Howell and several other ex-pats, John had worked in Kenya for several years and knew the mountain well. As such, he was the ideal person to go with. After I arrived in Nairobi just before the start of the New Year we wasted no time in travelling to Chogoria from where a Land Rover took us to the park gates' ranger station. With no time to lose we collected our single porter for the walk into the rather decrepit Mintos hut at 4,297m. By this time my incipient headache was more insistent and I had to spend extra time acclimatising before going higher. John, on the other hand, had been guiding in Kenya for the previous few weeks and had no such problems. Still, the delay did give me plenty of time to watch the resident hyraxes scavenging for scraps around the hut and to take in the awesome scenery.

Two days later John and I walked to the Austrian hut (4790m). While John organised dinner I took the opportunity for a quick stroll to Point Lenana (4985m) for some additional, much needed acclimatisation. Our main objective was the *Ice Window* route between Nelion and Batian, but with so many new things for me to do on my first trip to Kenya we first climbed Nelion (5188m) by the normal route before camping just below the American camp in order to climb Midget Peak (4700m) and the Point John couloir. By now we were ready for the 800m *Ice Window,* which sadly rarely forms these days. Moving up to the rather primitive Black Hole bivouac we launched our attack the following day, finding the grade III route in fantastic condition with superb plastic ice. It was a true delight with both axes sinking smoothly into the ice and all protection absolutely bomber. At the only partially formed Ice Window, which gives the route its name, we crossed to the aptly named Gateway of the Mists to spend the night in Ian Howell's micro-hut near the summit of Nelion. It was cramped enough with only John and myself in residence, but when two South Africans who had had a multi-day epic on Batian's south face also moved in it was cosy indeed! The advantage was that with so much body heat we never felt cold, although if one person moved then so did all the others, so it was hardly a comfortable night's sleep.

In continuing good weather, we rose early the next morning to see Batian (5198m), the highest of Mount Kenya's tops, looking so near and inviting that it seemed rather churlish not to climb it as well. We therefore ate a hasty breakfast in the cold early morning before continuing easily to its summit. Crossing back to Nelion we descended to our camp by its *voie normale* in preparation for the long walkout to the road-head at Noro Moru. From there an uncomfortable crowded *matatu* (shared taxi) took us back to Nairobi to end a fantastic and unforgettable two weeks in the Mount Kenya National Park.

Asia

With so many attractive mountains in Asia it is difficult to know where to start when trying to pinpoint just a single memorable peak. Even limiting the options to India alone only marginally simplifies the problem. Eventually,

Thrung-ma Kangri. *(Divyesh Muni)*

however, I homed in on a peak in the East Karakoram on which we successfully made the first ascent in 2016. The party included Drew Cook, Gus Morton, Mike Cocker and myself. Apart from the peak itself, which we named Thrung-ma Kangri (6315m, 'Protector Peak'), a key motivation to visit this region was that due to its proximity to sensitive borders with Tibet and Pakistan it had received few visitors. Indeed, until relatively recently access for non-Indian nationals was highly restricted and mountaineering was virtually unknown.

After a nail-biting wait for authorisation from the Indian ministries of defence and home affairs, without which we were going nowhere, we flew to Leh on 27 August 2016. With Leh situated at 3,500m it was necessary to acclimatise for a few days visiting local monasteries and the old palace before crossing the 5,370m Kardung La into the Nubra valley. After spending a further two nights near Sumur we then trekked for three days up the Tirit valley to make our base camp a little beyond Arganglas at 4,756m. Initially our party had included a fifth member, a Norwegian friend Knut Tønsberg, but he became severely unwell at base camp and had to be evacuated home to Norway. Fortunately, he made a full recovery following a short spell in hospital.

Above Arganglas the valley divides beneath Thugu (6158m) with outflows descending from the Rassa glacier to the north and the Phunangma glacier to the south. The terminal moraine of the Rassa glacier is one of the most complex that I have even seen as it is perforated by deep, unstable depressions akin to those of an open-cast mine. The surrounding mountains, by contrast, were stunning. Several forays later we eventually identified an idyllic spot for an advance base camp at 5,100m on a sandy oasis by two attractive pools. We then moved up to two higher camps on the glacier, the first at 5,585m and the second at 5,675m. The upper camp gave access to a number of interesting objectives that we had identified during our research.

Keen to get at least one summit under our belt we first climbed the easier mountain closest to the camp, which we called Lak Kangri (6222m, 'Raptor Peak'), before returning to the comforts of base camp. Several days later we were back at the high camp with Thrung-ma Kangri in our sights. Its south face, marked by a pronounced rocky spur at three-quarters height, appeared to offer an attractive route of ascent. Leaving early, we zigzagged up the first part of the 40° snowy face until the rock spur where we roped up in two pairs. From here a leftwards traverse led to steeper, icier ground, which soon exited onto the easier summit slopes. The climb was delightful, never too hard at Alpine D, but varied and interesting. We reached the compact airy summit in seven hours to be rewarded by stunning 360° views backed by a cerulean sky. With time pressing, we returned the same way, making eight full-length abseils to reach easier ground and arrive back at camp just as night approached, some 12 hours after leaving. It was now time to return to Leh and then back home, but I am convinced that if this peak were more accessible it would undoubtedly become a sought-after classic.

See also: 'Rassa Glacier, Lak Kangri, Southeast Face; Thrung-ma Kangri, South Face', D Buckle, *American Alpine Journal* 2017, **91**, pp289-90.

Antarctica

After many decades mountaineering I had a strong urge to go to Antarctica. It has that air of mystique and otherworldliness that seemed to offer the ultimate adventure. Thus, when Phil Wickens said that he was organising an Alpine Club expedition to the Antarctic Peninsula I needed little persuasion to go. I had previously been on an expedition to the Pamirs with Phil and knew him quite well. I also knew that he had made numerous trips to the Antarctic as a polar guide with commercial cruises and that he had spent several seasons with the British Antarctic Survey. There are few, if any, better authorities on the Antarctic Peninsula, which is where he planned the 2010 ski-touring expedition. Most climbing on the peninsula was, and still is, done as part of day raids from yacht-based accommodation, but Phil was more interested in multi-day trips that ventured deep into the interior to reach hitherto unclimbed mountains that would otherwise be inaccessible.

After the usual preliminaries we flew to Ushuaia via Buenos Aires on 22 November to meet up with Phil, who was already in residence. The team was limited to seven people as our transport to Antarctica, the *Spirit of Sydney*, a 60ft aluminium-hulled yacht, had a maximum capacity of nine

The team high on the north-east ridge of Mount Cloos. *(Dave Wynne-Jones)*

people, inclusive of the then owners, Darrel Day and Cath Hew. It seemed a very small boat indeed for the task ahead, but Darrel and Cath were experienced sailors who knew the route well. We would be in capable hands.

Unfortunately, the trip did not start off well. Several key items of my luggage, including my ski boots and much of my cold-weather clothing, failed to arrive in Argentina, making it something of a disaster. Checks with the airline confirmed that the missing luggage was still in Madrid, although it was unclear if and when it would be sent on. Since many of the contents were essential, I needed to beg, borrow or buy replacements, just in case the worst happened and they never arrived. It was easy to purchase thermals, underwear, socks, toiletries and other sundry items in the local shops, but nowhere catered for people with size 11 feet. Getting replacement ski boots was therefore a problem. Darrel eventually managed to find some old climbing boots in his local stockpile that sort of fitted, but these would not be ideal footwear for a modest skier like myself.

So it was with considerable relief that two hours before we were due to sail I received a call to say that my bag was now at Ushuaia. A quick drive to the airport and a few customs formalities, then we sped back to the yacht for our departure. At least I now had everything needed for a ski tour in Antarctica.

The next four and a half days were memorable for all the wrong reasons. Darrel had said that the Drake Passage, the most notorious stretch of water on the planet, was reportedly calm, but it certainly did not look that way and nobody seemed to have told my stomach. As the boat rolled, pitched and yawed Mike Fletcher and I earned the undisputed reputation as the 'chuck-up team'. Every six hours we dragged ourselves from our bunks, dressed while being thrown from one side of the yacht to the other, in time for our obligatory three hours' stint on watch. It was all that we could do to stand, let alone keep an eye open for icebergs, growlers and other nautical hazards. The torment only ceased once we had crossed the Antarctic Convergence (the point where the Antarctic Ocean meets the warmer and more saline Atlantic and Pacific Oceans), and the turbulent seas relented. Finally, we could eat and look forward to spotting land. One can quite see why the ancient mariners valued this experience so highly, and their sea faring involved months at sea rather than our few days.

No acclimatisation is necessary for peaks on the Antarctic Peninsula; they rarely rise much above 3,000m. Nevertheless, as newcomers to the continent we needed to get a feel for conditions and regain our ski legs after almost five days at sea. A quick skin up Jabet Peak (552m) near Port Lochroy ensured we were all set before continuing to Deloncle Bay from where we planned to disembark for eight days on the Hotine glacier. Towing haul bags in preference to pulks, we made several separate camps on the glacier from which we climbed a number of virgin peaks.

The highlight was undoubtedly Mount Cloos (1200m), which we climbed on 8 December from a camp at 307m. All seven of the party first climbed the smaller, but elegant, South Peak to its compact airy summit at 935m. Then we traversed the corniced ridge over a high point at 940m to the foot of the impressive north face of the main summit overlooking Deloncle Bay. At this point three of the team decided to return to camp while Phil, Mike, Oly Metherell and myself attempted the north-east ridge.

The climb rose beneath a series of large, but seemingly stable seracs to the left of an obvious rock face before continuing up steep, icy slopes. Higher up it skirted to the right of the large overhanging ice cliff which was a major feature of the face before reaching a draughty wind scoop and short, but awkward, ice chimney. Above the chimney a relatively straightforward walk led up the upper slopes to the summit. The overall grade was Alpine D+. It took seven and a half hours to reach this point but the reward was a truly exhilarating experience in awesome surroundings with the bonus of a virgin summit with superlative panoramic views. We returned the same way in the knowledge that Mount Cloos really would take some beating.

See also: 'An Account of the 2010 AC Expedition to Antarctica', D Buckle & P Wickens, *Alpine Journal* 2012, 116, pp179-90.

South America

The Cordillera Blanca range of Peru is without doubt the jewel of the Andean mountains and a magnet for large numbers of climbers from around the world – and with justifiable reason. With a plethora of beautiful peaks,

West face of Shaqsha. *(Derek Buckle)*

often fluted and covering all range of difficulties in a relatively accessible area, its attraction is not hard to understand. Huaraz is the undisputed centre from which to explore virtually the whole range, effectively the Chamonix of Peru, but lacking the commercialism. Safe and just eight hours or so by bus from Lima, the capital, it is also very easy to get to and a place to which I have returned frequently. Escaping the crowds on many of the iconic mountains is, however, often a challenge and it is always a pleasure to visit less popular regions of the range in which to climb. Moving away from honeypots such as Alpamayo and Tocclaraju, which feature on nearly everyone's hit list (including my own, I must confess), it is still possible to find quiet areas that offer all that an enthusiast could ask for.

Several times during my visits to the Peruvian Andes I had walked past a stunning mountain called Shaqsha (5703m). It is isolated to the south of the main climbing areas and consequently less frequently attempted. By June 2018, however, it had risen to high priority on my list of key South American objectives. But before we could think about Shaqsha we needed to acclimatise. This we did with a foray to Nevando Chequaraju (5286m) followed by a splendid traverse of Vallunaraju (5686m). After returning to Huaraz for

Paul Knott on the west ridge of Mount Eaton. *(Derek Buckle)*

a short break we then drove to the road-head at Huaripampa to be met by an *arriero* and four donkeys for the trek to an intermediate camp at 4,700m: the limit to which the donkeys could go. From there a straightforward climb took us – Nick Berry, Nick Smith, Nigel Bassam and I – to a higher camp on the glacier at 5,270m, within sight of Shaqsha's impressive west face. Climbing as two roped pairs, we set off at 3.30am the next day to take a superb but rather convoluted route up the face to avoid the numerous ice cliffs and the worst of the objective danger. Several hours later we reached the steep, narrow arête that led to the airy summit. There was only room for one person at a time to sit on the highest point so we did that in rotation, making the most of the photographic opportunities that the spectacular position offered. Despite its relatively easy grade (Alpine AD), climbing Shaqsha is a true delight for those wishing to experience a rare beauty of the Peruvian Andes in the almost guaranteed absence of other climbers.

See also: 'Peruvian Andes Expedition 2018', D Buckle, *Asian Alpine e-News,* 2018, 32, pp2-8.

North America

By 2013 Alaska-Yukon was one of the last major mountaineering venues still on my radar so when I received an invitation to join Paul Knott for an attempt on the east ridge of Mount Augusta (4289m) in the St Elias range I accepted without hesitation. Paul had been to Alaska several times previously so he organised all the logistics and had strong views about what clothing and equipment to take. Despite my making a number of positive suggestions, they were all uniformly overruled and I eventually went with the flow. Having organised over 30 major expeditions myself this was an unusual approach for me, and one that I subsequently had cause to regret.

In late April I met up with Paul in Seattle before continuing on an internal flight to Juneau. At Juneau we boarded the coastal ferry to our start point at Haines. Although I knew how fickle Alaskan weather could be, it was at Haines that I experienced it first hand as we were forced to wait nine days before our pilot, Paul Swanstrom, could safely fly us to our proposed base camp at the foot of Mount Owen on the Seward glacier. It was immediately obvious that the south-west rib of Mount Eaton, by which we had hoped to access the ridge to Mount Augusta, was non-viable, but an alternative route via the much longer east ridge of Mount Eaton (3337m) appeared feasible. Having stashed most of the supplies near our landing point we set off immediately to snowshoe across the glacier and camp a little short of an obvious, left-slanting ramp near the Corwin Cliffs at 1,290m.

After a relatively late start next morning, we continued along the glacier until it was possible to access the easy-angled ramp. Stashing snowshoes where the angle of the slope noticeably increased, we then climbed to a small ledge at 2,040m to make our second camp just below the ridgeline. This site offered spectacular views of Mounts Vancouver, Queen Mary and King George, in addition to Mount Cook and Mount Owen close to where we had started. It was not as far as we had hoped, but our heavy loads were beginning to take their toll, on me at least. With only a narrow weather window open to us it was now clear that to attempt this long ridge as far as Mount Augusta was no longer an option, so we set our sights on simply making the first ascent of Mount Eaton instead. Anticipating only one or two more nights before returning we stashed all bar three days' worth of food before leaving early the following day. Gaining the ridge proper up a steep snow face, we continued along Mount Eaton's convoluted and foreshortened east ridge to establish a high camp in a depression at 2,524m, little knowing that we were later to get trapped at this height by inclement weather.

On the morning of 9 May, we set off to climb along the heavily corniced ridge, traversing numerous false summits before reaching the rounded snow dome of Mount Eaton after almost six hours at an estimated Alpine grade of AD+. At this point the sky remained clear and we had excellent views of Mount Logan and the fantastic east ridge of Mount Augusta. Heading back to high camp, however, we arrived just ahead of a storm we had expected to start a day later.

Despite extremely poor visibility and heavy overnight snowfall, we tried to descend next day having been advised that the low-pressure area developing over the region would be short-lived. Before long, however, it became evident that without a clear view a safe descent of the complex ridge was impossible. Somewhat resignedly we struggled back up through deep snow to the site of our high camp to re-erect the tent. The following three days gave consistently gusty winds, near zero visibility and dumped some four metres of new snow so that we had to dig out the tent regularly in order to prevent its collapse. We eventually decided to relocate to a snow hole.

Unfortunately, no sooner had we transferred all the gear to the snow hole than we realised we were being buried alive. It was with some effort that we re-assembled the tent yet again and moved all the gear back in. With the situation looking increasingly desperate we made one further attempt to descend on 15 May in continuing poor visibility, but the steep slopes were in such a dangerous condition that we abandoned that attempt. In our weakened state we were lucky to manage the 50m climb back to the snow dome we had so recently vacated. At this point rescue was the only option if we were to survive since we could not use the liquid fuel stove to melt water and had virtually no food.

Increasingly dehydrated and with so little food I was on the verge of hypothermia, we called the Kluane National Park. Their response was magnificent, but they could do nothing under prevailing conditions since they also required clear weather. Although in regular contact, it was a further five days with another three metres of snow before they could launch a rescue. At 5am on 19 May, after a windy and cold night, down to -12°C, we saw clear skies for the first time in eight days. A possible rescue was on! A little after 6.30am we heard the sound of a helicopter and 12 minutes later Dion Parker and Scott Stewart teetered on the three-metre square that constituted the only available landing space with the engine running to maintain stability. Although only 15m from the tent, I struggled to make the distance to the landing area, dragging my sack through the thigh-deep snow. The relief was indescribable, but we still had to get back to Kluane. With heavy cloud circling Mount Vancouver it required some skilful navigation and we made it with only 30 minutes of fuel remaining after a two and a half hour round trip. It was a close call.

Back in civilisation Paul was treated for serious dehydration and I nursed frostbitten hands and feet. Fortunately, neither of us appeared to have suffered permanent damage, but without the Kluane rescue effort it would have been a very different story.

See also: 'Survival on Mount Eaton', D Buckle, *Alpine Journal* 2013, 117, pp133-6.

Australasia
Having failed to climb Mount Cook, or indeed any other mountain, from the Plateau Hut on South Island in December 2001 on account of unstable snow conditions, I was keen to complete at least one significant climb in

Mount Taranaki. *(Derek Buckle)*

New Zealand before returning home. As Jill, my wife, and I passed through North Island on our way back to Auckland, I seriously considered Taranaki (aka Mount Egmont), a 2,518m-high dormant volcano overlooking the town of New Plymouth on the west coast. Its elegant, symmetrical cone looked inviting in the evening light as we drove up from the south, but by the following morning it was draped in heavy cloud and rain was falling in stair rods. Unfortunately, this was not the opportunity that I was looking for and I returned home rather disappointed.

A second chance to attempt Taranaki eventually arrived in January 2010, when I again visited New Zealand. This was supposed to be a sightseeing holiday for Jill, but I could not resist the opportunity to climbing something significant, and Taranaki was in pristine condition. With no climbing partner on this trip it was an ideal mountain to solo and, furthermore, could be climbed easily via the north ridge in a single day from the visitor centre at 952m. The route itself is rather convoluted but does pass a number of evocatively named features such as the Razorback, Shark's Tooth and the Lizard; all characteristics one might expect from a strato-volcano that last erupted as recently as 1775.

Soon after leaving the visitor centre on 10 January the well-defined trail followed increasingly broken ground marked by a poles until steep scoria slopes were reached. At this point the poles either no longer existed, or had been dislodged and damaged by movement of the unstable slopes. The route then continued uphill to the prominent rocky ridge (The Lizard) which exited onto the final short snow gully leading to the summit some four hours after leaving the visitor centre. An ice axe provided reassurance at this point, but it was not really necessary under the prevailing conditions. Route finding would have been considerably more challenging in cloudy conditions, but fortunately the sky was clear all day and afforded summit views that were both impressive and extensive. In a further 2.5 hours I was back at the visitor centre ready to resume my sight-seeing itinerary with Jill and happy in the knowledge that I had achieved at least one significant ascent in Australasia. Maybe one day I will return for a more demanding achievement, one never knows!

Glass Ceilings

'Alphubel, Täschhorn and Fee Glacier from the Längfluh', Hilda Hechle,
watercolour, 50cm x 36cm. *(Alpine Club Collection)*

MARGARET CLENNETT & ADÈLE LONG

A Woman's Place

The Centenary of the Pinnacle Club

Eleanor Winthrop Young. *(Pinnacle Club)*

What would Dorothy Pilley think of us? Or Lilian Bray, Len Winthrop Young and Pat Kelly, some of the founder members of the Pinnacle Club?

When I asked a former Pinnacle Club president how she thought the original members might view the club today her reaction was immediate: 'They would turn in their graves!' She was, however, thinking of how we obey the rules and accept the bureaucracy that has seeped into our sport, long before Covid-19 came along. Think of the red tape concerning huts: health and safety, water quality, fire regulations, electrical testing, child protection policies and the rest. Evelyn Leech, who turned an empty cottage into the Emily Kelly hut over six months in 1932, and was its warden for nearly 20 years, might well be aghast, though she would probably have welcomed

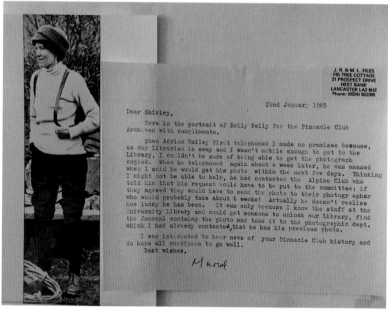

Emily Kelly. *(Pinnacle Club)*

our indoor hot and cold water supply rather than fetching buckets from the stream, and a flush loo instead of an Elsan outside. Pilley, with an attitude of 'leaping crevasses in the dark', might have rebelled against the rules, and the former president I spoke with is something of an anarchist herself. As we celebrate the club's centenary let's look at how those women climbers of a century ago might respond to the wider aspects of club life today.

When nine women gathered in the billiard room of the Pen y Gwryd in March 1921 for the inaugural meeting of the Pinnacle Club almost the same number again would have been there too if they hadn't been still out climbing. One party was simply too slow, the others just wanted to make the most of the day. Those mountain lovers would have had every sympathy for today's members, a president who wants to squeeze in an extra route at the risk of being late for a committee meeting she is supposed to be chairing, or a group reveling in a cloudless, crispy-snow day in the Helvellyn range, deliberately extending their walk to descend at dusk despite knowing they are late for the AGM. Scheduling a committee meeting for daytime on a Saturday to allow plenty of time for discussion would be anathema. Better by far to follow the 1920s women who held more than one committee meeting on Great Gable's Dress Circle, and another on Sgurr a'Ghreadaidh, Skye, the latter at 10pm 'in the sunshine' during a circuit of 14 tops on the Cuillin ridge from Bruach na Frithe to Sgurr na Banachdich.

Pilley, Bray, Kelly et al would doubtless think that Pinnaclers today have an easy time in many ways, and of course they would be right. Non-climbing family and friends may think our activities odd but we don't

Top: Pinnacle Club Easter meet, Kiln House, Rosthwaite, 1928:
From left to right, top row: Millicent Taylor, Harriet Turner, Margaret Isherwood,
Mildred Ashton, Elsie Eastwood, Lynn Clarke, Marjorie Wood.
Bottom row: E M Hobkinson, Lilian Bray, Ella Mann, Hilda Summersgill,
Dr Catherine Corbett, Madge Scott. *(Pinnacle Club)*

Lilian Bray.
(Pinnacle Club)

Gwen Moffatt.

Gill Price on *Comes the Dervish*, Vivian Quarry.

Gill Price and Jill Lawrence, two of the lynchpins of British climbing in the early 1980s.

face opprobrium for defying convention or going to the hills without a chaperone. Early Pinnaclers had to be self-confident and risk scorn, or even outrage for their 'unseemly clothing' particularly wearing trousers in public, and there are frequent mentions of mending and patching their garments. Was this because of rough rock, low abrasion resistance, thrutching up chimneys or poor climbing technique? How those ladies would have loved our lightweight, stretchy, wicking fabrics, and clothes no one in the street would pass comment on.

Modern gear would be a revelation. Lilian Bray (like Dorothy Pilley also a Ladies' Alpine Club member) instilled the need for safe practices in the novices she taught, and had been impressed by the Austrian Mauerhaken custom pitons with rings or karabiners to reduce the length of a leader fall. She would surely have been an advocate of cams, ropes that handle well in the wet and belay devices, a boon for women belaying a heavier leader, man or woman.

So far so good, but would those founder members be justified in thinking we are less adventurous? Are routes easier now, laced with runners from bottom to top and a fall no longer an automatic short cut to heaven? We have guidebooks galore, routes reliably graded with photos and topos to identify them. Climbs are scratched, polished, flecked with chalk. A GPS can navigate us off the mountain. Twenty-first century climbers are, in general, more risk averse than our forbears. Who today would accept an invitation

The Emily Kelly hut in Nant Gwynant, acquired in 1932. *(Pinnacle Club)*

from a friend to second her on a multi-pitch new route on Scafell with a novice in tow as third person in order to provide a belay, since two pitches lacked an anchor for the second? Mrs Eden Smith did just that, seconding H M Kelly on *Moss Ghyll Grooves* in 1926.

Technical standards are now so high that unless we visit a remote location or climb E5 there is less scope for exploration, new routing or first female ascents. But the spirit of adventure is still there, with Pinnaclers regularly visiting Morocco and putting up new routes in the Jebel el Kest area. In 2014 a meet on Mingulay also produced some additions to the first ascents list at what today are modest grades.

An annual Alpine season was the conventional summer holiday for those with a mountaineering inclination. In the 1920s the usual practice was to employ guides, but Pilley, Bray and the Wells sisters pioneered guideless ascents by women, though initially deliberately choosing routes well within their capabilities, not wanting to risk criticism by taking on a peak which could cause them difficulties. Pinnaclers went on to make numerous first female ascents, often guideless. They would have been disappointed that as late as the 1990s Pinnacle parties ski touring were being asked, 'where is your guide?' Or, when half a dozen topped out on a sport route at Orpierre, 'where are your husbands?' Fewer Pinnaclers go to the Alps these days. With limited annual leave they prefer clipping bolts in the sun to sitting in the rain in Chamonix, but for those who are first-timers in the big mountains there is still the timeless appreciation of scenery and the skills necessary to reach the summit.

Pinnaclers have always been travellers. Early members wrote in the Pinnacle Club journal about trips to Norway, Spain, Iceland, the Pyrenees and South Africa as well as the Alps. How they would have loved the great range of holiday options we enjoy now, thanks mainly to air travel. Eileen Healey, in the 1950s, would go out to the Alps by train, as was usual, but in 1953 her return was thwarted by a train strike. She accepted the offer of a seat in a small plane from Le Touquet to England, her first ever flight, but was worried about what her parents might think about such a dangerous means of transport. Now, thanks to long-haul flights, we can take our annual leave in the Greater Ranges if we wish or via easyJet enjoy numerous short breaks in Europe, with the proviso of 21st century challenges like climate change and all the challenges that presents to mountaineers.

One of the objectives of the club is 'to foster the independent development of rock climbing and mountaineering amongst women' and in the early years experienced members would teach rope work and leading skills to novices. Today, with plenty of courses on rock and at walls, aspiring female climbers are not hampered by a lack of opportunity to learn. Pat Kelly would have been pleased. She might, however, have been surprised and disappointed that even today, some new members still say that they have found local or university clubs 'too male oriented' but would be reassured by comments made by participants at the 2016 women's international climbing meet (WICM), most of whom had not faced prejudice or lack of opportunity. Inspiration, support and camaraderie were all pervading during that magic week in north Wales.

The club's second objective is 'to bring together those interested in the sport.' Now that car ownership is widespread, travelling to meets is easier and the two dozen meets per year we have now are a major improvement on the six or so held in the 1920s when drivers were encouraged to call at Betws-y-Coed station in case any Pinnaclers were there hoping for a lift. WICM was not the first international meet hosted by the club but was certainly high profile: not only that, but it spawned the Women's Tradfest and is a blueprint for the PC 100 meet planned for September 2021 as part of the club's centenary celebrations.

Although today we are not fighting the prejudices our predecessors faced and women are now welcomed into what were previously exclusively male clubs, the Pinnacle Club continues to provide a unique environment for women climbers, to have fun, make friends and share their enthusiasm. Pilley, Kelly and their companions would, I hope, be proud.

Looking ahead to the next 100 years, what will Pinnaclers of the 22nd century make of us today? Will they look back in surprise at our rigid definitions of male and female and see the concept of a women-only club as defunct due to gender fluidity and identity? Already the younger generation is embracing these ideas and gender discrimination is viewed as outdated. How will such views be reconciled with the continued fight for equality in, for example, the work place? Rebecca Cassells, principal research fellow at the Bankwest Curtin Economics Centre, believes that although women will have parity with men at lower management levels within the next 10 to 20 years, they won't hold the same number of CEO positions until 2100. But is this an outdated approach, the continued fight for equality, as our successors feel more advantaged and gender boundaries are flexed?

The impact on sport in general and climbing in particular may be even more striking. Trans athletes are gaining recognition in amateur and professional arenas and a number of trans women are successful in women's competitions. What will it mean to be a woman (or for that matter a man) in 100 years time? Will our Pinnaclers see the definition of a woman as part of a continuum and accept self-identification as the norm? With the current rate of change it is not beyond the realms of possibility that there will be a reversal of current attitudes and gender will become more discretely defined. Perhaps we'll see the start of matriarchal societies?

And what about climate change? Will the race to reduce carbon emissions be won or will our 22nd century Pinnaclers look back at us with envy as they watch, listen and read about our exploits using crampons and ice axes to cross long-gone glaciers? Will they wonder how we managed without the safety equipment designed to reduce the dangers associated with rock loosened by the melting of permafrost as mountain ranges become bare and suffer desertification? Will our Pinnaclers of the future be appalled at our penchant for air travel or be whizzing from country to country in machines propelled by renewable energy?

Thwarted by the pandemic, the club centenary expedition to Kyrgyzstan has been postposed and in its place is a challenge to do all of Ken Wilson's *Classic Rock* routes in one summer. In 100 years will Ken's list of climbs be worn so smooth that they are no longer classic? Will a new set of must-do climbs be the ambition for future generations? One created by a woman, even a Pinnacler?

Whether the future seems utopian or dystopian is a matter of perspective. We can only hope that women (and men) will continue to enjoy the mountains and crags and retain the ability to form friendships and bonds, something climbers have valued above all else in the past and still do today. Here's to the next 100 years.

• For more information on the Pinnacle Club's history, see the Pinnacle Club Centenary Project at *www.PC100.org*.

J G R HARDING

'A Prey to that Longing'

The Life of Freda Du Faur

Freda Du Faur (1882-1935). *(Guy Mannering)*

We reached the Hermitage the same day, and not all the luxuries of life as there enjoyed could compensate me for the knowledge that I had had my last climb for the season, and that I must now pack up my belongings, turn my back upon the mountains, and go my way, the better, happier, and stronger for my days and nights spent among them, but a prey to that longing which all the excitement, gaiety, and turmoil of city life cannot deaden, for just one glimpse of snow-clad heights, and the peace of the vast silent spaces ...

Freda Du Faur, *The Conquest of Mount Cook*

Few have evinced a deeper passion for mountaineering than the Australian Emmeline Freda Du Faur (1882-1935) who, during her four seasons in the New Zealand Alps in the early years of the 20th century, became an exemplar and inspiration for all Antipodean mountaineers. A direct descendent of the aristocratic French Huguenot family the du Faurs de Pibrac in Haut Garonne, Freda's great-great-grandfather Cyprian had emigrated to England in 1733 and married the daughter of the proctor of Rochester. The Du Faurs had long been Anglicised before Freda's father Eccleston went to Harrow. But rather than going up to Cambridge as originally intended, he joined the 1853 Australian Gold Rush and then the department of the surveyor general of Victoria to explore Australia's unchartered mountain ranges. After financing an expedition to the New Hebrides, he created his own 35,000-acre nature reserve at Cowan Creek near Sydney and established the Du Faur and Gerard Pastoral Company. A classical scholar, natural historian and photographer, he was also a founder member of the New South Wales Academy of Arts, subsequently Australia's National Art Gallery. Freda's mother Blanche was another first generation Australian, descended, in her case, from a distinguished English academic family. Her father the Rev John Woolley, had been a scholar at Exeter College, Oxford, before emigrating to Australia to become professor of classics and principal of Sydney University where he founded its School of Arts.

Freda, born in 1882 and the only girl of five children inherited the dominant genes of both her parents. Intelligent, artistic and articulate, she was only 5ft 2in tall, but spirited and courageous and never afraid to mix it with her brothers physically or intellectually. Proud of her ancestry and secure in her social status, she could be arrogant and intolerant, but was always passionate in supporting gender equality and never abashed about her incipient lesbianism.

The pattern of Freda's early life was not entirely typical of upper class Australian society. Her father Eccleston had built a fine family house named Pibrac, after the Du Faur's ancestral chateau, at Warrawee outside Sydney, but preferred to spend his time at the Bohemian art and photographic camps he organised in the Blue Mountains or in the wilds of his Cowan Creek estate. It was here that Freda, unconstrained by polite convention, explored the untrammelled bush, developed her rock-climbing skills and fostered a love of nature.

Originally set on a nursing career, she enrolled as a probationer at Sydney's Homeopathic Hospital in 1903 aged 21. Surprisingly, she failed to complete the course due to her 'sensitive and highly-strung nature' and later admitted that she found nursing 'much more stressful than mountaineering'. This combination of sensitivity and physical courage might have explained her near-mystical attachment to mountains and when the nursing experiment was terminated prematurely, she cast around for a role that would give her life new purpose.

The event that changed it forever was a trip with her father to New Zealand in 1906 to attend a photographic exhibition in Christchurch. A photographic

Mount Cook, from the Tasman glacier. *(J G R Harding)*

panorama of the Southern Alps so moved her that she resolved to see these superb mountains for herself. Travelling down to the Hermitage, her first view of Aoraki/Mount Cook from Lake Pukaki filled her 'with a passionate longing to touch those shining snows and to climb to their heights of silence and solitude'. From that moment, it became her mission to climb that shining mountain. When questioned later, 'Why take up mountaineering?' she replied: 'The true mountaineer, like the poet, is born not made.'

At this time, mountaineering was only barely recognised by alpha-male New Zealanders as a proper sport. Twenty-four years had elapsed since the Rev W S Green of the Alpine Club had travelled out to New Zealand with his Swiss guide Ulrich Kaufmann and the hotelier Emil Boss in 1882 with the avowed aim of climbing Aoraki. After two unsuccessful attempts, they got within 200 feet of the summit only to be defeated by a tremendous storm, which forced a nightmare bivouac and a desperate escape after 62 hours on the mountain. For the next 12 years, Mount Cook's summit remained inviolate despite four attempts by local New Zealander climbers Mannering and Dixon via Green's original Linda glacier route.

In 1891, the founding of the Alpine Club of New Zealand inspired a burst of activity culminating in first ascents of the Minarets, Malte Brun, Darwin and Footstool, though mainly by visiting foreign climbers. Put on notice by the arrival of the British mountaineer Edward Fitzgerald and his renowned Swiss guide Matthias Zurbriggen, the Kiwi breakthrough came on Christmas Day 1894 when Fyfe, Graham and Clark made the first ascent of Aoraki/Mount Cook's summit peak from the head of the Hooker glacier.

Freda seated between her guides Peter and Alex Graham, after her ascent of Mount Cook.
(Guy Mannering)

At last the spell had been broken, but when Fitzgerald and Zurbriggen put up a daring new route to Cook's summit and followed this with first ascents of Sefton, Hardinger, Sealy and Tasman, a gauntlet was cast. Freda Du Faur saw it as her mission to pick it up.

The place of women in the New Zealand climbing scene in this new Edwardian Age was ambivalent. Although New Zealand had given its women suffrage in 1893 (a quarter of a century before Britain) and the New Zealand Alpine Club, founded two years earlier in 1891, had been open to all who fulfilled its climbing qualifications irrespective of gender, hidebound Victorian conventions still prevailed. And while in the Alps, many women mountaineers had already exchanged skirts for breeches and had no compunction about sharing tents or bivouacs with men, when Freda proposed her first serious expedition with her guide Peter Graham, the prospect of her climbing alone with another man, let alone sharing a bivouac, aroused so much hostility at the Hermitage that she was forced to employ a porter – 'Tom' – to act as a chaperone.

Freda had first met Graham, the leading Hermitage guide, in 1906 and promptly joined his party to visit the Sealy range. Four years older than Freda, this sensitive but socially unsophisticated man of the mountains was immediately impressed by Freda's natural ability and determination. Adopting the roles of both mentor and friend, he was probably the only man she ever came close to emotionally. However, this first 1906-07 climbing season was abandoned when she had to return to Sydney unexpectedly 'to attend her dying mother at her bedside'.

In 1908 a windfall legacy of £2,000 (£80,000 today) from an aunt's estate enabled her to return to the Hermitage for the 1908-09 climbing season financially secure and on her own terms. Now aged 26, she engaged Graham full-time for what became their famous climbing partnership.

After traversing Mounts Kinsey and Wakefield (when Freda saved her chaperone Tom's life by arresting his fall with an ice-axe belay), they failed on the Minarets, but went on to traverse Malte Brun in record time. Freda's first attempt to climb Mount Cook with Graham was met with another 'storm of disapproval and criticism' at the Hermitage, but after sitting out a third bivouac in dreadful weather, they had to call it off.

In November 1910, Freda left Sydney for the Southern Alps in excellent physical shape thanks to a three-month regime of rigorous training under Muriel Cadogan, the independent-minded, deputy-head of Sydney's Dupain Institute of Physical Education. In turn, Freda introduced Muriel to mountaineering. It was a meeting of minds and bodies; in due course the two became lovers with their lives forever after intertwined. Freda's early climbs in that 1910-11 season had included a second stab at Mount Cook followed by successful ascents of De la Beche, Green and Chudleigh. But with other lady aspirants hovering in the wings, these were mere dress rehearsals for her third attempt at Cook. The weather had been uncertain, but this time nothing was going to stop her and on 30 November 1910 she reached the object of her dreams with Peter Graham and his brother Alex in the then record time of six hours up and six and a half down. It was the mountain's first ascent by a woman and instantly made Freda world-famous. Guy Mannering's iconic photograph of her gazing fixedly towards the distant peaks, with the neck of her white lace blouse demurely fastened with a brooch and one hand firmly grasping the adze of her long ice axe captured well her steely determination but also hinted at emotional vulnerability.

With Cook conquered, Freda's climbing ambitions were boundless. The following season she returned to the Hermitage and in the course of a two-month campaign accounted for Nazami and Dampier, both difficult first ascents, Lendenfeld, Muller, a new route on Sebastopol and most impressively, after narrowly failing on her first attempt, the second ascent of Tasman, the 'greatest snow climb in the New Zealand Alps'. She was now ready to attempt her most ambitious climb of all: the complete traverse of Aoraki/ Mount Cook's three peaks, reckoned to be 'impossible' by some of New Zealand's most experienced mountaineers.

At 2am on 3 January 1913, Freda, Peter Graham and Darby Thomson left their bivouac below Cook's west ridge and five hours later reached its Low Peak. Before them lay the mountain's undulating, one and a half mile-long, saw-tooth summit ridge averaging 12,000ft in height with terrifying exposure on either side. That six and a half hour traverse to the High Peak gave Freda nightmares for the rest of her life.

They summited at 1.30pm and after descending the dangerously avalanche-prone, heavily crevassed Linda glacier without mishap, reached safe ground after 24 hours of continuous climbing. Luck had been with them for without perfect weather, a storm on the ridge would have destroyed them. For the next fortnight it rained and snowed without interruption, causing the Tasman glacier's moraine to break and flood the Hermitage so badly that it had to be completely re-built.

Freda was still not satisfied. Once the weather had settled, she set forth once again with Peter Graham and Darby Thomson to make the first traverse of Mount Sefton. This time, the weather was appalling and a paralysing blizzard almost did for them on the summit. Their epic day closed with a two-hour wade down an icy, swollen creek long after dark. On returning

Freda's first view of Mount Cook's 'shining snows', from Lake Pukaki.
(J G R Harding)

to the Hermitage late that night, they were greeted with the news of Capt Robert Scott's ill-fated polar party's disaster. Before completing what was to be her last season, Freda first climbed the peak she named Cadogan, then Elie de Beaumont and finally the difficult Aiguille Rouge on Malte Brun.

Over only four seasons, Freda Du Faur had achieved an unparalleled climbing record that included the first female ascent and first ever traverses of both Mount Cook and Sefton; the first mountaineer to have climbed all three of New Zealand's highest mountains – Cook, Tasman and Dampier – as well as a score of others, many of them first ascents. Her climbs were often undertaken in typically dreadful New Zealand weather; huts were few and bivouacs many; laborious step cutting did for crampons; equipment was crude and the bulky woollen skirt she wore over knickerbockers restrictive. She had always been a natural climber, but it was her stoicism, courage and determination that most impressed her guides. Freda's climbs, modestly recorded in her mountaineering autobiography *The Conquest of Mount Cook*, published in 1915, were the touchstones of her life. Her observations on nature and her passionate feelings for the grandeur and beauty of mountains illuminate a vivid narrative, while her superb photographs provide an unrivalled record of what the peaks, snowscapes and glaciers of the Southern Alps resembled in their ice-bound prime before the advent of global warming.

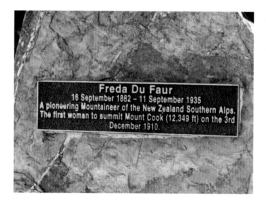

The memorial to Freda Du Faur in Sydney's Manly Cemetery, erected in 2006.

In 1914, Freda, then aged 32, was still at the peak of her powers when she and Muriel Cadogan decided to leave Australia to live and work in London prior to exploring the European Alps, the Canadian Rockies and the Himalaya together. It was a fatal decision. Deeply shocked by an avalanche accident on the Linda glacier, which killed her former guide Darby Thomson that same year, the outbreak of the First World War effectively stranded both Freda and Muriel in England for the war's duration.

Freda had always been passionate in her beliefs and determined in her views, but a vein of stubbornness now proved her worst enemy. At the urging of a young Canadian, Otto Frind, whom she had first met at the Hermitage, she had joined the Canadian Alpine Club. However, on discovering in London that the Alpine Club was a male-only preserve, she was so incensed that she refused to even contemplate joining its sister organisation the recently (1907) established Ladies' Alpine Club which included some of the era's most outstanding women climbers whose company might have given Freda the support and camaraderie that her proud yet sensitive nature craved. But she was never one compromise. As her biographer Sally Irwin[1] wrote:

> Freda underestimated the high standard of the women in the Ladies' [Alpine] Club … The members were educated women, of high social standing, artists, writers and linguists. They worked hard to maintain the club, and probably felt as put out as Freda that they'd had to form one of their own. But they'd more than made the best of the situation.

Instead, Freda Du Faur turned her back on mountaineering and threw her energies into the cause of women's suffrage. However, when that campaign achieved its initial objective in 1918, her *raison d'être* had vanished and her mountaineering triumphs were all but forgotten.

On its first publication in 1915, her book *The Conquest of Mount Cook* had received a lukewarm notice from Edward Fitzgerald. But it took the *New*

---

[1] S Irwin, *Between Heaven and Earth: The Life of a Mountaineer, Freda du Faur*, Victoria, 2000.

Zealand Alpine Club Journal another six years to publish its own more disparaging review in which Freda was accused of being 'tainted with egotism' and unfairly criticising certain New Zealand climbers. These slights would have hurt Freda deeply, but more serious was the gradual deterioration in the mental health of Muriel who, despite expensive medical treatment paid for by Freda, died in 1929 aged 44.

Freda was devastated and with her woes exacerbated by the stock market crash and an unseemly dispute about Muriel's Australian estate, she returned to Australia in 1935 a wizened, withdrawn and lonely woman, her world in ruins. On 11 September, aged 53, she committed suicide by putting her head into a gas oven. For decades, Freda's exceptional mountaineering achievements were largely forgotten but in 2006 a group of New Zealand climbers finally placed a memorial stone over her unmarked grave at Sydney's Manly Cemetery.

Only after reading Jim Wilson's monograph of Mount Cook, *Aorangi,* in 1970 did I learn about Freda Du Faur. My young family and I had emigrated temporarily to Australia and before returning to England I made my own bid to climb Mount Cook, achieving that ambition on 25 November 1970 with Mike Browne when we took 10 hours to get up and down. Our hubris was quickly dispelled on learning that Freda's great traverse had been done without crampons. Eighteen years on, in 1988, I visited the Mount Cook National Park once again for three days' ski mountaineering with Shaun Norman. We climbed Elie de Beaumont and Broderick on successive days before making our exit down the Tasman glacier. And it is here, in the shadow of Aoraki, romantically translated as the 'Cloud Piercer', Freda's mountain, that all journeys in the Southern Alps should end.

ROBIN N CAMPBELL

Hilda Hechle

and Other Women Mountain Artists

In this year of celebrating women's mountaineering, I sought to decorate the *Alpine Journal* with suitable frontispieces and to give some account of British women mountain artists. I apologise for the incomplete nature of this review but plead in my defence the inaccessibility of libraries, galleries and other institutions during the Covid-19 pandemic.

Hilda Marion Hechle (1886-1939) was born at Brassington Manor House, the home of the Breakell family, to Una Marion Breakell and Henry John Hechle. The Hechles were a Liverpool family and Henry inherited enough to spare him the trouble of working. Among the many Breakell siblings, at least one – Mary Louise – was a successful artist, and author of a watercolour 'how-to' book still read today.

In the 1890s the Hechles moved to north Wales. Hilda attended St John's Wood Art School and then the Royal Academy Schools, and eventually became a member of the Royal Society of British Artists (RBA) in 1926, and the Society of Women Artists in 1929.[1] However, before treading the beaten trails of London art education she had exhibited at Liverpool's Walker Gallery in 1903, and began to visit the Alps to climb and sketch while still a teenager. Presumably, she was accompanied by a parent or two, although her mother became ill and was confined to a Liverpool asylum by 1901, and we know from press reports that latterly her father accompanied her.[2] In 1905 she encountered William Ling and Harold Raeburn at the Montenvers and traversed the Petit Charmoz with them, Ling praising her performance in his usual paternalistic fashion 'our companion took [the awkward pitch at the summit] in good style and with plenty of pluck.'[3]

In the same year she sketched the Brenva glacier and the resulting watercolour was accepted for the Royal Academy Summer Exhibition in 1906 when she had just turned 19. She exhibited mountain watercolours throughout her life, in the annual exhibitions of the Alpine Club and the Ladies' Alpine Club, at RA, SWA and RBA annual exhibitions and in at least two solo exhibitions in the St George's Gallery in Hanover Square. As well as drawing mountains, she produced 'fairy paintings' conforming to certain Edwardian and post-war tastes and even added fairies and goblins

---

1. Hechle is a featured artist in Peter Mallalieu's *Artists of the Alpine Club* (2007), which includes basic biographical information about her.
2. *London Weekly Dispatch,* 8 Feb 1925.
3. *Ling's Diary,* Book 5, p39, AC Archives. Ling's diary records his every mountain day between 1893 and 1953, a historical record of immense value.

William Ling and Hilda Hechle at the Montenvers Hotel, 1905.

to perfectly realistic north Wales scenic postcards, as well as providing illustrations to accompany various literary works.

Her mountain works were of uneven quality, but at her best she was as good as any of her contemporaries, excelling in the depiction of glaciers, skies and atmospheric effects, and demonstrating sureness of line and colouring in all her works. Hechle joined the Ladies' Alpine Club in 1923 and her contributions to its yearbook are accessible through Johanna Merz's index, published in 2000. Among these was a lecture titled 'Mountains in Art' in 1929. The yearbook for 1929 (p40) gives some details of this, including a golden nugget of advice, valid for photographers as well as for artists, 'that the best place from which to draw one mountain is from half way up another.'

Despite my best efforts, I managed to find only eight of her mountain pictures to use as frontispieces. In the captions, I have given any existing titles in

Constance Gordon-Cumming, aged 50, from her 1904 autobiography *Memories*.

single quotes followed by descriptive titles without quotes. Three of the frontispieces deserve a little additional comment:

'South side of Mont Blanc: the Brenva Glacier' shows the part of the face containing the *Old Brenva* route. This beautiful watercolour uses portrait format to great effect, and demonstrates great precocity.

'Nocturne des Alpes', the Blumisalp group from the Oeschinen See. This large and impressive oil painting is unusual as to medium: other works in oil by her are rare. It may well be based on a watercolour of the same scene, which was sold on eBay a few years ago. There is a full description of the 'Nocturne' with a useful biography on the Maas Gallery's website.

'Weisshorner', possibly a title invented by a dealer, is probably 'Monte Rosa Group – Dawn' exhibited in 1927 and described by a reviewer as showing 'a luminous green sky with the clouds curling off the summits'.[4] Other reviews mention that she stopped at the Solvay refuge on the Matterhorn and spent the morning sketching there.[5] This impressive drawing is perfectly compatible with the view from the Solvay. One might complain about the Lyskamm, which is drawn rather undersized, but it is surely an outstanding evocation of a high Alpine dawn.

I am grateful to our members Tony Astill and Tom Smallwood for providing images, and to Rupert Maas for the 'Nocturne' and advice.

Constance Frederika Gordon-Cumming (1837-1924), known to her friends as 'Eka', was the daughter of William Gordon Gordon-Cumming, 2nd Baronet of Altyre and Gordonstoun and Eliza Maria Campbell. She was blessed with rich relatives, including 11 siblings, and well-connected friends scattered about the globe. In 1867 she visited India, which marked the start of 12 years of continuous travelling, encompassing the Himalaya, Ceylon, Fiji, Tahiti, the Californian mountains, China, and the volcanoes of Hawaii and Japan. Although not a mountaineer in the conventional sense – what club might she have joined? – Gordon-Cumming was a strong walker, an enthusiastic camper and climbed Mount Fuji, the Hawaiian volcanoes and several of the Yosemite trails to the valley rim.

Her art was self-taught but regularly exercised. She painted over a thousand watercolours and worked with the motto: 'never a day without at least one careful-coloured sketch'. She was one of a few intrepid solo women travellers of the Victorian period. Marianne North and Isabella Bird

4. *The Times*, 1 Apr 1927
5. *Western Mail*, 2 Mar 1927

Beatrice Lithiby,
c1937.

Ulrica Hyde,
self-portrait bust.

'Jungfrau from
the Eiger Glacier',
by Beatrice Lithiby,
LAC Yearbook 1938.

were two others. Although Marianne North was a better artist, Gordon-Cumming was more of a mountain artist than North. She was enchanted by Yosemite valley, extending what was intended as a three-day visit to three months, and wrote an illustrated book about it.[6] I am indebted to the very full Wikipedia entry for much of the above information.

The three watercolours used as frontispieces are more or less self-explanatory. 'The Khylas Mountains from Pangi' shows perhaps Jorkanden (6473m) and the sharp peak of Kinnaur Kailas (6050m), the object of a popular pilgrimage but not to be confused with the better known Kailas further east. In the view of Fuji, the Otome pass connects Hakone and Gotemba, which town lurks below the cloud-sea. 'Yosemite Falls', like Hechle's pictures of the Brenva and the Mischabel, shows the value of portrait format in giving

6. *Granite Crags,* Blackwood, 1884.

Mountain Hare　　　　　*Wood-engraving by* ULRICA HYDE

Ulrica Hyde's woodcut 'Mountain Hare' from the *LAC Yearbook* 1938.

full value to height. Her pictures, though carefully executed and important records of early exotic travel, perhaps lack beauty of line and colour. I am grateful to Chris Beetles Gallery, London and to PBA Galleries, San Francisco for providing the images of Fuji and 'Yosemite Falls'.

The Ladies' Alpine Club fostered women's art by mounting annual exhibitions in its clubroom in the Great Central Hotel in Marylebone.[7] Many contributors to these exhibitions were established artists, but their works have mostly vanished from public view, one would hope temporarily. **Beatrice Ethel Lithiby** (1890-1966) trained in the Royal Academy Schools, served as a war artist in Queen Mary's Army Auxiliary Corps in the Great War, and joined the RBA in 1930. She contributed some works to the LAC's yearbook, and one of these is shown below: she was clearly a very able mountain artist. **Ulrica Hyde** (1911-87) – full name Margery Ulrica Fitzwilliams-Hyde – trained at the Royal College of Art, and became a successful sculptor and wood engraver. She had the double misfortune to lose her father in the last days of the First World War and her brother in the last days of the Second,

7. A huge Victorian Gothic pile now known as The Landmark. The original Victorian restaurant survives on a basement floor.

Edouard Bareux, Una Cameron
and Elisée Croux at their Caucasus
camp in 1932, published in *A Good
Line,* Cameron's account of the
expedition.

both killed in action. She served
as a sergeant in the Royal Army
Service Corps in Cairo and met
her husband, the well-known
archaeologist Seton Lloyd there.
She contributed works to the
LAC exhibitions and yearbooks,
and one of these – an impressive
woodcut of a mountain hare – is
shown here. **Una May Cameron**
(1904-87) was the first of twins, her
sister being Bertha Dewar. Her mother Jane was one of the whisky Dewars,
so she was born with a silver spoon filled with liquid gold. She received
her art education at the Central School of Arts and Crafts, London, and in
Rome. Her favoured medium was woodcut and she exhibited these regularly
at the LAC and in the yearbooks. Unlike the other women artists reviewed
here, Cameron was a formidable climber, fortified by wealth and ambition
and armed with two guides Edouard Bareux and Elisée Croux. And she was
no ordinary woman: avoiding marriage, she cut a dash around London and
Courmayeur in powerful open-top sports cars, smoking a pipe or cigars. She
climbed all over the world, but lived latterly at La Palud above Courmayeur
whence she climbed almost every available route on Mont Blanc.[8]

8. She is featured in Mallalieu's *Artists of the Alpine Club,* 2007, p26, and was the subject of a wonderful obituary notice by Janet Adam Smith in *AJ* 1988, pp323-6. See the no less wonderful appraisal of her climbing life,
also from Janet Adam Smith, in *AJ* 1990, pp157-73.

Legends & Myths

'Fujiyama from Otome togi Pass', Constance Gordon-Cumming,
12 August 1879, watercolour, 15in x 24in. *(Courtesy of Chris Beetles Gallery)*

ALAN HEPPENSTALL

Remembering Maestri

Cesare with his wife Fernanda when they were living in Andalo during the winter of 1959-60. *(All images courtesy of Gianluigi Maestri unless stated otherwise.)*

On 19 January 2021 the Italian alpinist Cesare Maestri, 'il Ragno delle Dolomiti', died at the age of 91. He was perhaps the most controversial mountaineer of all time.

When I heard the news, I knew at once that I wanted to write an article about his life. Maestri operated mainly in Italian circles and as a result he was not widely known by the world at large. I had the opportunity to correspond with him on a number of occasions, and to meet him in person, and I felt that after his death he deserved to be better known to the outside world. I also recognised that portraying him objectively would not be an easy task, given the controversies that have surrounded him, mainly due to his activities between 1957 and 1970 on a certain remote peak in Patagonia: Cerro Torre.

Left: The famous meeting between Maestri and Bonatti near the summit of Cerro Adelas, after Bonatti pipped Maestri to the summit to claim the first ascent. *(Photo by Carlo Mauri, Folco Doro Altan collection)*

My relationship with Maestri started during the period from 1969 to 1972, when I had the good fortune to be working at the Rome office of what was then called the British Tourist Authority. Because of my love of mountains, and climbing in general, one of the first actions I took after arriving in Rome in September 1969 was to join the Rome branch of the Italian Alpine Club (CAI). This meant I could enjoy regular trips to the limestone outcrops around the city, as well as visiting the higher mountains of central Italy. It also meant I received regular journals and news bulletins from the CAI, enabling me to keep myself 'al corrente' with the doings of Italian mountaineers around the world.

During a visit to the UK I met Ken Wilson, founder and editor of *Mountain,* and asked if he would like me to send him news updates from Italy, information which otherwise might reach him late, or not at all. After a couple of pints, I found that I had assumed the totally unofficial title of 'Italian correspondent', and started looking out for news items that might be of interest for the magazine.

One of the first pieces I picked up and sent to Ken was a report that in 1970 Cesare Maestri was on his way to Cerro Torre intending to climb the mountain in winter by the south-east ridge, a route which at the time had turned back a number of expeditions including in 1968 a British team comprising Mick Burke, Dougal Haston, Peter Crew, Martin Boysen and Peter Gillman of the *Sunday Times.*

I had vaguely heard of Cerro Torre and its ascent by Maestri and his Austrian companion Toni Egger in 1959. According to the accounts of Maestri and Cesarino Fava, who performed a back-up role and wrote about the expedition, Egger and Maestri had reached the summit in deteriorating weather but Egger was swept away by an avalanche during their descent and killed. The only camera the couple had was lost with Egger. Like most people who had read the accounts from 1959 I took the claim at face value, because I had no reason not to. So why was he going back, and why in winter? Later it came to light that he had taken with him a petrol-driven compressor, which was intended to speed up the process of drilling holes to insert expansion bolts in the rock.

Maestri and his team did not complete the route in the southern hemi-sphere winter of 1970, and returned in the summer 1970-71 to finish the task with a new compressor motor and a winch to pull it up. The summer expedition was reported on a daily basis by news outlets in the Trento area. They reached the level plinth on which the snow mushroom at the summit rests but did not climb the mushroom itself.

There was clearly a story here, and accordingly I wrote to Maestri asking if he could let me have an account of the expedition and particularly some photos for reproduction in *Mountain*. The reply came back quickly and was combative in tone. The full text of his reply was reproduced in *Mountain* 23 for anyone who is interested, but my enquiry about photos was brushed aside:

> *I refuse to give photographic evidence, which I have in plenty, because if the doubters themselves are not capable of reaching the summit I don't see why I should be the one to give them the satisfaction of seeing it. This sort of satisfaction can only be obtained as we obtained it – by dint of technique, willpower, hunger, cold, sacrifices, resistance and frostbite. Let these gentlemen reach the summit and bring me down a piece of our compressor, because it is their job to provide to me the proofs which they expect of me.*

This was a reference to the fact that there was no photographic evidence of the success of the 1959 climb that resulted in the death of Egger.

The next thing to happen was that I received a telegram from Pete Gill-man, saying he would like to interview Maestri for the *Sunday Times* and would I act as interpreter? Clearly the story was spreading beyond the confines of the mountaineering world. Before I had plucked up courage to phone Maestri I received a further message that Ken Wilson would be coming as well. In the end there were four of us, Ken, Pete, myself and Leo Dickinson, who came to get footage for a BBC film he was working on.

The interview took place in July 1972, and happened to fit in with my journey back to the UK at the end of my posting in Rome. The four of us met Maestri at his shop in Madonna di Campiglio, but he invited us to his home nearby, where we talked in his study for a good part of the day. The whole interview was also reproduced in *Mountain* 23. Given the tone of the letter Maestri sent me I was somewhat apprehensive at the prospect of meeting him but our welcome was cordial, and one of the first things he said to me was that we two could address each other using the friendly form of the second person (like most European languages except English, Italian has formal and informal ways of addressing others; the informal is reserved for family and close friends such as climbing mates). The interview finally came to an end because the other three had to get to the airport for their return flight to England. Maestri drew a map to show them the way. I was concerned that we had outstayed our welcome.

I am not intending here to discuss Maestri's claim to have reached the summit of Cerro Torre on the 31 January 1959. A great deal has been written about this, and no doubt after his death there will be more. I am aware some people still believe the ascent took place in the way described but that the majority do not. All I will say to people who do not believe the claim is that there are four main issues they need to address:

If they were not climbing Cerro Torre, what were Maestri and Egger doing between 28 January and 3 February 1959?

Whatever they were doing it resulted in the death of Egger. How and where did this happen? ('Where' has been partially resolved by the discovery of his body in 1975 a couple of kilometres from the base of Cerro Torre.)

Whatever actually happened, it left Maestri severely traumatised and I believe he never totally recovered from this for the rest of his long life.

Above all, the great, unanswered question to be addressed is *why*? If we say the mountain was not climbed in 1959, why did Maestri claim that it was rather than reporting what they had actually done?

Evidence of what might have happened during the key period between 28 January and the 3 February has recently come to light but that is outside the scope of this article.[1] My purpose here is to examine the effect the 1959 expedition had on Cesare but to understand the context we need to consider his life before Cerro Torre, as well as the events of the previous 1957-58 expedition to Patagonia.

A good deal of what follows has been taken from books written by Cesare himself. It's not well appreciated outside Italy but Cesare was a writer as well as a mountaineer and his own words (translated here but kept as close to the original as possible) reveal a good deal about his background and character.

He was born on 2 October 1929 to parents who ran an itinerant theatre company so that he was rarely in the same place for long. This gave him an unsettled childhood, which was not helped by the death of his mother when he was eight years old. It also placed him in Italy during the 1930s, when fascism was rampant. Initially Italy and Germany were on the same side but after the death of Mussolini, Hitler took over Italy and ran it in the same way as other occupied countries. The Alto Adige region, where Maestri's father was born at the time when it was part of Austria, came in for some heavy bombing, perhaps as a punishment for siding with Italy at the end of the First World War. In his teens Cesare joined the Italian resistance, as well as the communist party, and saw at first hand the worst excesses that war can bring.

> *The only thing I knew how to do after the war ended was steal from the Germans anything that had commercial value ... My father was so worried about me that in 1947 he sent me to Rome to stay with my elder sister Anna, in the hope that she at least would help me to find a way forward ...*

1. For analysis of Maestri's claims, see R Garibotti, 'A Mountain Unveiled', *American Alpine Journal*, Golden, 2004, 46 (78) pp138–155, and K Cordes, *The Tower*, Patagonia Books, 2014, although a new edition is imminent, and R Garibotti with K Cordes, 'Completing the Puzzle: New Facts About the Claimed Ascent of Cerro Torre in 1959', Alpinist.com, posted 3 Feb 2015.

Maestri and Fava relaxing on the slabs below the Mocho, at the foot of the south-east ridge of Cerro Torre.

I was a young man on whom the war had left deep traces of sadness, hatred, death and misery...

In 1949 Cesare had his first experience of rock climbing, when Gino Pisoni led him up the Paganella, reached by bike and on foot from Trento. As so often happens with people who cannot see a clear way forward in their lives, he was thrilled by the mountains and took the decision to work towards becoming an alpine guide. He started by taking a job carrying supplies every morning from Molveno up to the Pedrotti hut, on the Bocca di Brenta, a height gain of 1,600m. The loads were between 30 and 40kg and the pay was calculated according to the weight. Rather than coming down immediately he would find some easy climbing to do, normally solo because he couldn't find any one to climb with. He comments that in his early climbing days he had difficulty in finding partners:

Other climbers regarded me with some diffidence. Therefore I went alone.

Of his initiation into climbing he wrote:

My problem was that I was born in a family which had no climbing tradition, and I did not discover the mountains until I was 20. Even then climbing for me was not an end in itself, but a means of establishing myself in society.

In spring 1952 Cesare completed his national service and it was after this that many of his solo ascents took place. He discovered that unusually he found it easier to climb down rock faces than up. Later in the 1950s, as more climbing partners became available, he became more interested in aid climbing, including bolting if placements for standard pitons were not available. Increasingly, climbing became a vehicle for expressing his anarchic views.

He was considered for the Italian expedition to K2 in 1954 and was interviewed by the expedition leader Ardito Desio. It seems to have been a case of dislike at first sight: the requirement to sign a document pledging obedience to the CAI commission set up for administration purposes may not have helped. He was not the only one. Riccardo Cassin also fell by the wayside at this point.

Maestri with Tenzing Norgay in October 1957 on what was, according to Tenzing, the Everest climber's first pure rock climb, the Paganella.

In spring 1955 Maestri attended a course for aspirant ski instructors at Cervinia, which he failed. To make up for it, he decided while he was there to make an ascent of the Matterhorn, still in winter conditions, by the Italian ridge. He reached the summit in bad weather and descended safely but was surprised to hear that his claim to have done the route under the prevailing conditions was queried by Jean Pellissier, a local guide, and his tracks had been followed to verify if his claim was true or not.

> *It was the first time I had experienced such an underhand blow from fellow climbers. It wasn't my ascent that they were querying, but the whole history of mountaineering, which until then I had assumed was based on trust and loyalty.*

On this occasion the affair was amicably resolved, and Maestri and Pellissier became firm friends.

In August 1955 Maestri set out alone to recce the north face of the Eiger, which he was thinking of attempting solo in one day. He reached the Hinterstoisser Traverse but disliked what he saw and came down again.

> *It was like a battlefield, with signs everywhere of forced retreats, shreds of clothing, a boot frozen into the snow, abandoned rucksacks, rope fragments waving in the breeze like ghosts.*

He retreated via the gallery window, writing that he had to break in from the outside and hitch a ride on a train. What the Swiss authorities thought about this is not recorded.

One of his more interesting guiding engagements took place in autumn 1957, when he took Tenzing Norgay up the ordinary route on the Paganella (grades III and IV). Tenzing was in Trento as a guest of the film festival and wanted to sample the rock climbing of the area. He admitted to being afraid during the climb because he had only ever 'walked' before and steep rock was new to him.

Maestri's relationship with Cerro Torre started as early as 1953, when he received a letter from Cesarino Fava, an Italian national living in Argentina, saying that in Patagonia there was a mountain that he could get his teeth into: '*Questo è pane per i tuoi dente,*' literally 'there is bread for your teeth.' The fact both Cesare and Cesarino came from the Trento region may explain why Fava chose Maestri to write to; there was an active Trento community in Buenos Aires at the time.

The idea lay dormant for a couple of years, then in 1955 the president of the CAI in Buenos Aires wrote officially to Cesare asking him to lead an expedition to Cerro Torre and promising financial support. Patagonia was virtually unknown at the time as a climbing destination; none of the peaks had been climbed with the exception of Fitzroy by the French in 1952. Unfortunately, later that year the CAI in Buenos Aires closed down due to internal disputes but the proposal was taken up a year later by the 'Circolo Trento'. Their offer was less generous than the CAI's and left Maestri to fund his own travel by sea to Argentina as well as providing his own equipment.

In spring 1957 Fava arrived in Italy and met Cesare for the first time. They happened to be discussing the forthcoming expedition in the presence of the Detassis brothers, Bruno and Catullo, who were immediately interested and asked if they might join the team. Not only was the request accepted but Bruno Detassis took over the leadership of the expedition from Maestri. Cesare himself seems to have suggested this because of Bruno's age and greater experience; having him in charge no doubt improved the prospect of attracting funding for the trip.

The project now became embroiled in Italian politics. With no funding available from the CAI in Buenos Aires, a request for funding was made to CAI headquarters in Italy. The request was turned down but while they were on their way to Argentina by ship, word reached them that funding had been granted to another expedition to Patagonia. This comprised Walter Bonatti and Carlo Mauri and they were already en route by air. In Argentina they were to be joined by Folco Doro Altan, who already knew the area from a previous reconnaissance.

So the 1957-58 expedition started badly and matters became worse when Bruno Detassis saw Cerro Torre for the first time and as expedition leader immediately banned any attempt to climb it. Instead they were to concentrate on some of the smaller unclimbed peaks in the area. Maestri was devastated, and it did not help when he met Bonatti and Mauri near the summit of Cerro Adela Nord: they were on their way down having beaten Maestri to the summit. Maestri's team accounted for the first ascents of Cerro Grande and Cerro Doblado among others, but they were poor rewards when compared to the original objective.

In the evening we arrived at our boulder camp. What sadness! It was a disaster. After the leader of the expedition left, the wind had carried everything into the water and sand. Rolls of loo paper were blowing here and there in the wind. They were like the tragic remains of a street carnival that finished in a fight. Our sleeping bags, pullovers and bivouac shoes were floating despondently in a pool of water.

Over a period of eight days in June 1960, Maestri and Claudio Baldessari put up a direttissima on the north west face of Roda di Vael in the Catinaccio group. Previous attempts had come to a halt below a large roof three pitches up the face. This tour de force came at the time when Cesare was reintroducing himself to climbing after the events of 1958-9, and received ample press coverage. The pair was accused of playing to the media by spending longer on the route than necessary, although their time was par for similar ventures around that time, such as the *Saxonweg* in January 1963. They hauled up from the base of the route what they needed by way of water, food, extra gear and even bivouac equipment, so there was no time constraint to the number of days they spent on the face.

We were cold, hungry and thirsty, and most of all needed to find someone who would make us feel part of a community, look after us. Nothing, only cold, desolation, and the wind howling through the boulders. We had no means of heating anything, but found some water from melting ice, and added a little Nescafé, and that was our only refreshment … It was a terrible night!

Later, while on the return journey, Cesare wrote:

We left with the feeling that we were leaving behind something unfinished. I must return, and I will!

Maestri's reaction to the events of the 1957-58 expedition is understandable but when he starts to make preparations to return in 1958-59, his rhetoric takes on a wholly new dimension. Here is a sample of it, describing the moment he was at one of his favourite viewpoints overlooking the Trento valley later in 1958:

There is the smell of autumn in the air … Amid the joy of the colours and scents of autumn, I feel heavy and sad. In a few days' time I will be on my way; I will be leaving Italy and returning down under, far away, to Cerro Torre. I will be continuing the work started by the first expedition.

I will die on Cerro Torre. Definitely I am going to die. The thought is fixed in my mind. Why am I going? Life should not be thrown away. I will leave for the Tower. I will grasp its walls with the strength of despair. I will climb to the summit, with or without a companion. But I won't be coming back. I am certain the Tower will take me, as it is holding me captive now.

What sadness there is in me, where has the overwhelming desire for life gone? If I know I am going to die, why am I going at all? It must be for reasons of pride. I am a man, and I am proud. I remember shouting this out at the top of my voice, causing a flock of chaffinches to flee in terror from a thicket.

But people don't kill themselves for reasons of pride. I tried to understand what were the forces that were pushing me inexorably towards the Tower. Was it my friends' money? The fact I had committed all my savings? That I had sold my car? That I had stated in public that the Tower was 'not impossible'? That I had promised myself that I would reach the summit?

Later we get:

Never before have I approached a mountain as if in a lottery; never before have I said: 'It's the summit or me,' but this time the stakes are high – so high that it can't be called climbing any more. This time the stakes are complicated by vanity, pride, sadness, mistrust, my rights and my conscience.

This was written retrospectively for public consumption but even so, it gives a remarkable insight into Maestri's state of mind when he left for Patagonia in 1958. It surely cannot all be explained by the disappointing outcome of the previous trip. Here is another quote from one of his books describing his feelings about failure:

It isn't the rain wetting the rock that makes me give up; it isn't the clouds rushing low through the fir trees that fill me with fear. There is no rational explanation.

The sense of defeat has gripped me and smothered me like an enveloping cloak.

It doesn't take much: the wind whistling less strongly, a sad thought or a happy memory, and something flips inside me. Then I am overcome by a sense of being repelled by the rock. Contact with it makes me shudder as if it was polluted. Everything is gyrating around me. The etriers, rope, hammer and pitons are the only things that tie me to the world.

> *The pitch above is easy. It wouldn't be hard even for beginners, yet my feet and hands don't want to part company with the holds where they are resting. The void becomes even deeper, and the silence more silent. With rapid, tense movements I get ready to descend.*

> *Now it is raining more heavily, and the clouds are filling the valleys. I would have a perfect excuse to explain my retreat but that's not what I want. Something new has occurred within me. It will take several days of soul-searching to understand the reason for this, and to restore my feeling of joy in victory.*

When he decided to return to Cerro Torre, Maestri had very little money. He scraped, begged and saved, and also sold anything he thought he could manage without, including his car, a Lancia Aurelia, a classy ride. In his quest for funding Cesare got backing from his mate Claudio Baldessari, who was to have come to Patagonia with him. They had hoped for a grant from the CAI, but in the event this was promised to another expedition bound for Patagonia, which again included Bonatti and Mauri. These two then cancelled their trip, and Maestri argued for the money to come to him but despite the intervention of a senior figure in the CAI this was again refused. Finally Maestri managed to persuade an industrialist in Milan to pay the cost of a one-way airfare to Buenos Aires. Since he was apparently not expecting to come back, this presumably resolved the money problem.

The next blow was that Baldessari was refused leave by the military authorities (for whom he worked) to go with Maestri.

Then, when all seemed hopeless, a letter arrived out of the blue from Toni Egger, whom Maestri had met previously at the Locatelli hut under the Tre Cime di Lavaredo, offering to come to Patagonia. The rest is history.

I'm going to jump now to the period after the end of the expedition and Egger's death. Whether this occurred in the way described or not, the fact remained that a man had died on an expedition led by Maestri, and the matter had to be reported to the Argentinian police. This is very much underplayed in Maestri's books but must have been traumatic at the time. He was a young man of 29, in a foreign country almost at the end of the known world and riven by political chaos. He must have been terrified of what might happen. Could he be arrested, even charged with being responsible for the death? In the event this did not happen and he managed to make his way penniless back to Italy, where his friends rallied round to help him return to a normal way of life.

One of the tasks that Maestri had to undertake on his return to Italy was to visit Egger's family in Lienz. When he did this he inexplicably failed to return to them Toni's possessions, particularly his diaries. This made it impossible for the family, especially Toni's sister Stephanie, to bring closure to

Maestri with his adopted son Gianluigi
from a *Paris Match* article hailing
Maestri for the second ascent of
the *Via dei Colibrì* (the Saxonweg)
on Cima Grande di Lavaredo with
Claudio Baldessari in March 1963. A
much later father and son shot taken
at a restaurant, not a ski lift,
in Madonna di Campiglio.

the questions surrounding Toni's death, questions that continue to haunt her.
All Maestri says is:

> *I had been back in Italy for a month, but neither the extended stay in Arg-entina nor finding myself in my own city and among my friends raised my morale, which was at rock bottom. Sometimes it seemed to me that I had cheat-ed death unfairly. For example, when I spoke to Toni's mum, I felt as if I had usurped a life and should not have been there. Toni had such a desire for life.*

> *During that night when I was alone on the Tower I thought I would have reached the peak of my grief, but I discovered that the real tragedy began now, with dark periods of silence, unexpected bouts of sadness and the need to go on repeating and reliving the accident time after time during the public lectures I had to give as a means of keeping myself financially solvent.*

It seems he was suffering from what we know now as post-traumatic stress disorder, though this was barely recognised as an illness in the 1950s.

In April 1959 Cesare suffered a skiing accident resulting in three months in plaster, bedridden. During this period he reached a decision to give up climbing and try motor racing, encouraged by some of his friends in Bolzano who gave him a car with a racing engine. Within a week of having his plaster removed he was at the wheel. Unfortunately this did not provide a livelihood; he had to accept that only the mountains could give him that. With great reluctance he agreed to take part as technical adviser on a course for mountain guides and porters, and a gradual return to climbing followed.

It was also after his return to Italy that Cesare's family life began to blos-som. It is time to introduce Fernanda, his future wife, and the boy who was to become Cesare's adopted son, Gianluigi.

A friend of Cesare's cousin, Fernanda had made an unsuccessful marriage

Maestri leading on the headwall of Cerro Torre in 1970, with the snow mushroom visible above to his right. The snow mushroom, which represents the true summit, was not climbed. Bolts were used on the headwall because, the team claimed, they had left their normal pegging gear lower down.

at a young age. Cesare courted her, initially in vain, but when he was in hospital following his accident, she began to come with his cousin to visit him and a bond developed. They started to live together, renting a house in Canazei, away from the gossip of Trento. Cesare started work on his book, *Arrampicare è il mio Mestiere* ('Climbing is my Trade'). Fernanda helped with the typing.

In summer 1959, an old friend of Cesare, Giulio Gabrielli, died in an accident on the *Soldà* route on the Marmolada. Cesare was involved in the rescue and helped to carry down the body. 'In some uncanny way I felt that the two tragedies might be connected.'

The accident seemed to bring Cesare and Fernanda closer together and after a year in Canazei they moved to Andalo, where Cesare began climbing again and Fernanda ran a small bistro. Cesare also took on the role of father to Gianluigi. His paternal instinct showed itself in March 1963 over the affair of the *Saxonweg,* on the north face of Cima Grande di Lavaredo. This route, which the Italians refer to more poetically as the *Via dei Colibrì* (literally 'Route of the Hummingbirds'), was put up over a period of 17 days in January of that year by a German party. Cesare and his climbing friend Claudio Baldessari decided to attempt the second ascent the same winter, having heard on the grapevine that the route was largely pegged up. Unfortunately the grapevine proved to be incorrect, and they had to abandon the attempt, having insufficient gear with them to replace the aid points that had been removed and finding those left in situ too insecure to use.

Word went round the village that Cesare had found the route too difficult and dangerous, and Gianluigi was teased at school because his father was a coward. Keen to support his adopted son, Cesare went back on the route with Baldessari and enough gear, and they climbed it in a fast time. They found that the rumour about gear being left in situ was true of the second half of the route, and amazingly discarded what they thought would be surplus food and equipment by throwing it off the face. But the route had a sting in the tail in the form of a badly iced-up section: it took another two days, for which they had almost no food, but in due course they emerged at the top and Gianluigi's reputation at school was restored.

Pietro Vidi in action on the *Compressor* route. One of the aid pieces placed with the help of the compressor is visible on the extreme right hand side of the photo.

Everything was now in place for Cesare's life to settle down. He had a wife and a son to whom he was devoted and they were financially secure. Towards the end of 1963 they moved to Madonna di Campiglio and opened a shop, which is still run by the family today. The stage was set for a happy future.

This was not to be. As the 1960s wore on, dark clouds again began to form in Cesare's mind. His PTSD returned but now it affected Fernanda as well.

What set this off were reports he received about the 1960s attempts to climb Cerro Torre, mostly by the south-east ridge. These all failed, but what incensed him most was that other Italians, especially Carlo Mauri, were referring to the mountain as 'impossible'. No one came out openly to say that Maestri and Egger had not reached the summit in 1959, but this was the clear implication.

This whole period is well described in another book titled *Duemila Metri della Nostra Vita* ('Two Thousand Metres of Our Life'), written jointly by Cesare and Fernanda. Again it was written for public consumption, and makes for dramatic reading. Here is a sample:

Fernanda: *Since he had been living with me, Cesare had not climbed anymore. The Tower had rendered him apathetic, indifferent and insensitive to what had previously been his greatest passion. He never spoke about the Tower by day. By night he cried out in his sleep, and while the nightmare lasted he sweated, trembled and cursed that mountain.*

Cesare: *Cerro Torre. The Argentinians call it the cursed mountain, the scream in stone: a stupendous creation. It fascinates you and terrifies you. 2,000 metres of ice covered rock, 2,000 metres of death, a trap ready to spring at any moment. And the wind! That bestial wind that howls by day and night through the valleys, and carries blocks of ice through the ravines with the sound of 100 reactors. On the summit there is a huge overhang that hangs over your head like death hangs over life. The Tower killed my companion, and morally it killed me as well. I would never return to that mountain.*

Fernanda: *Well then, it's not only the death of your companion. There is something that you are holding inside yourself. I want to know what it is that you have not told me yet.*

Cesare: *I have inside me the memory of days of hunger, thirst, exhaustion and fear, but above all of that obsessive wind. The memory of the huge icy crown of the summit collapsing, tearing Toni from the rock and hurling him into space like a rag doll. I have inside me the memory of when I remained alone, more so than I had ever been before, and of the sense of pity that I felt not for my companion but for myself because the avalanche had spared me. Fernanda, no mountain is worth a life … Now you know what I am holding inside, now you know what the Tower has done to me.*

Fernanda: *So it was that Cerro Torre entered my life. And immediately I hated it.*

There is a good deal more in this vein.

Against this background the 1970 expeditions were born and to cut a long story short, it was eventually decided that Fernanda and Gianluigi would go to Argentina with Cesare and his team and help with the preparations. The team would take radios with them and keep in touch if possible on a daily basis.

Again, I will not describe in detail the events of the southern hemisphere winter of 1970 and the summer of 1970-71. The team battled for 54 days during the winter and eventually had to give up due to frostbite, lack of food and the means of providing hot drinks. They left most of the gear in place and returned the following summer to complete the route, if reaching the top of the rock structure of the mountain (but not the summit mushroom) can count as completion.

The reasons for returning to the mountain in 1970 have been discussed at length: the *Mountain* interview of 1972 covers them to some extent. Certainly the wish to cock a snook at the people who doubted the outcome of the 1959 expedition came into it. But I believe the main reason for going back was that Cesare was still psychologically traumatised by the events of 1958 and 1959 and by his 'survivor's guilt'; he embarked on this project in a desperate attempt to relieve his mind of the blackness of PTSD and the turmoil afflicting it that had never entirely left him.

Having taken the decision to return to the Tower made me a free man again. I felt like someone condemned to death whose hands were unexpectedly untied when he was on the scaffold.

It is important, I think, to put the compressor used by the expedition, and mentioned earlier, into perspective. This understandably drew condemnation from most mountaineers but I don't believe it was an attempt to stoke up controversy. As has been explained previously, Maestri regarded it as normal to use expansion bolts to climb hold-less rock. He concluded rightly or wrongly, following the failure of several attempts on the southeast ridge, that the route must not be possible by conventional means and

Maestri on descent from Mount Kenya during his visit to Africa in 1973.

bolting would be needed. The rock of Cerro Torre was tough granite and hand drilling the holes to insert the bolts would be a lengthy task. He saw the compressor as the answer to this problem, and needless to say the manufacturers Atlas Copco were happy to oblige. In fact the team found it hugely time-consuming and exhausting to haul the compressor up the rock and frustrating to start it up each morning in sub-zero temperatures. Maestri stated in many places, including the *Mountain* interview, that he would have preferred to manage without it.

In 1982 he went further, claiming in an article that using the compressor as often as possible was part of the sponsorship deal and that the manufacturer's name be displayed on film. Does this explain why at one stance bolts are scattered around like shrapnel? Or why on some pitches bolts were placed alongside cracks that would have been possible with normal pitons? (Maestri claimed this was because they left their pitons behind.) Is the *Compressor* route a valid means of ascending Cerro Torre (or what remains of it after the 2012 de-bolting)? Opinions will vary, but for the record the route has 25 pitches, of which slightly under half were done with the use of bolts.

The south-east ridge, including parts of the *Compressor* route, was climbed entirely free in January 2012 by Austrian David Lama, supported by Peter Ortner. This fine achievement involved less commitment than it might at first appear; the pair had support from a film team with a helicopter. The film crew added more bolts to those already in place, though the climbing team had nothing to do with this new affront.

A few days earlier, Canadian Jason Kruk and American Hayden Kennedy had chopped over 100 bolts from the *Compressor* during what they described as a 'fair means' ascent; this too proved controversial. The young climbers were highly praised by some and criticised by others, not least Maestri himself. (They were also arrested briefly on their return to El Chaltén.)

It is important also to recall that the first undisputed ascent of Cerro Torre took place in 1974 via the west face, the work of Casimiro Ferrari, Mario Conti, Pino Negri and Daniele Chiappa. This was an outstanding achievement, which, due to the events of 1958-9 and 1970-1, often doesn't get the credit it deserves.

After the *Compressor* route, Cesare's life took a new direction. The family were still living in Madonna di Campiglio and running the shop, now accompanied by a second one. But in 1973 Cesare went on an extended trip to east Africa with a film director from Trento, Giorgio Moser, who was making a feature-length film for Italian television. Over four months they visited Kenya, Tanzania, Uganda, Rwanda, Burundi and Zaire, and Cesare climbed Kilimanjaro three times, Mount Kenya twice and Rwenzori once. The film was called 'Le Montagne delle Luce', the account of a climber (Cesare) searching for a fellow mountaineer lost somewhere in the mountains of Africa. The only evidence of where he went was a series of letters describing the places he visited, the people he met and the mountains he climbed. In the role of actor, Cesare had to follow where the clues led, eventually ending up at a 'heart of darkness', where he discovered that what he was following was a ghost: the phantom of an Africa that no longer existed.

In 1974 Cesare paid his first visit to Britain. This started off as a PR exercise on the part of JCB, the British partners of Atlas Copco. The visit included the first showing in Britain of the film that was made during the 1970 expeditions. Ken Wilson happened to find out about the visit, noticed that the dates coincided with the first National Mountaineering Conference in Buxton and asked me to find out if Cesare would be willing to attend as a special guest. He was, on condition that the Cerro Torre film would not be shown. I drove Cesare up from London to Buxton and we arrived at the conference hall to find Dennis Gray having his ear roundly bent by the PR officer of JCB, who was mortified that he had not been told in advance about the plan to invite Cesare to the conference. I'm doubtful whether Dennis knew any more about it than he did.

There was some anxiety about whether it was wise to allow Cesare to address the conference, since the story of the *Compressor* route would have been well known to many in the audience. Ian McNaught-Davis, the conference chairman, decided to risk it, and fortunately Cesare hit the right note by talking about the freedom of individuals to do what they wanted in the mountains without interference by official bodies, including (in Italy) the church. It went down well.

Memories from that visit include showing Cesare some of the climbing grounds of the Peak District. I took him to Stoney Middleton and tried to point him towards the rock in the hope that he might show off his soloing ability on Peak District limestone, but he politely declined saying that he hadn't got the right gear. He did however solo some routes on Froggatt the following day. I also recall introducing Cesare to Don Whillans and trying to get them into conversation: the two had clearly heard of each other and were standing together eyeing each other up, uncertain how to break the ice. They never did really, and perhaps that was for the best.

In 1974 I also got to know Fernanda. She had come over to London with Cesare but had to get back to Italy when he and I headed north to Buxton.

Maestri on the summit of Campanile Basso between Carlo Claus and Ezio Alimonta on an anniversary climb to celebrate the centenary of the first ascent in August 1899.

Accompanying the Maestris was a young lady called Bianca, whose role I think was to act as interpreter, though I never heard her speak English. Fernanda and Bianca formed a stunningly attractive couple. I spent two or three days showing them round London and joined them sometimes for dinner. I invited them to visit my wife and me for an evening, but in the event only Cesare made it. I arranged for Cesare to talk to a meeting of the North London Mountaineering Club, of which I was a member, and we were able to view the Cerro Torre film that had been a bone of contention at Buxton, but proved to be nothing special. This happened after the JCB showing, so all was okay on that front.

After 1974 Cesare's life became that of a family man with a business to run. He finally became a ski instructor as well as a mountain guide and became respected as an authority on mountaineering matters. During family holidays enjoyed at their holiday cottage in Sardinia, Cesare and Gianluigi went fishing and deep sea diving. During one such outing Cesare came to the surface too quickly and spent six hours in a decompression chamber to recover. In 1978 a fishing accident resulted in an injury to the index finger of his left hand which turned out to be irreversible and affected his ability to climb at a high standard, eventually prompting the decision to give up rock climbing entirely.

On 11 September 2001 the attack on the Twin Towers took place, and as many of us will remember the whole world shook with fear about what would happen next. As a member of the peace movement and a respected figure in Italy, Cesare felt that he was in a position to support that cause, and decided at the age of 73 to attempt something he had never done before, to climb an 8,000m peak. On the summit he would unfurl a banner in the name of peace. He chose Shishapangma as the objective, and through a trekking agency made arrangements for a trip there in 2002 with two younger climbers, Sergio Martini and Fausto de Stefani, both of whom had reached the summits of all 14 8,000m peaks. A Trento guide Giorgio Nicolodi also joined them.

Cesare chose to describe what happened in the form of a long letter to his much-loved granddaughter Carlotta, perhaps because she was the member of the family who most actively supported him.

> At the Chinese base camp situated at around 5,000m I felt fine, and couldn't wait to start the walk in. On 17 September we left for the climbers' base camp at 5,900m. In front of us was Shisha Pangma, called by the Tibetans 'the Ridge of the Meadows of Heaven'. At first everything went well, but at about 5,700m I began to gasp for breath and felt an overwhelming sense of tiredness. It took hours, and much assistance from my team, and others nearby, to get up the final 200m to the camp. There I was examined by a doctor who was with a Spanish team; he checked the oxygen level in my blood which showed as 25%, a level which would normally be fatal! My attempt ended there, but in fact the weather then changed and none of the other teams camped there made it to the summit. It was not until October 2003 that Sergio planted on the summit the flag I had brought for that purpose.

On his return to Italy Cesare wrote a letter to George W Bush pleading with him to moderate his response to the 9/11 massacre. He did not receive a reply.

So Cesare's last venture in the mountains resulted in failure. It would be fitting to be able to say that he spent the rest of his life in comfortable retirement, but sadly this was not the case. In November 2005 an Italian team finally succeeded in climbing Cerro Torre by the route he claimed to have done with Toni Egger. *El Arca de los Vientos,* as it was called, involved extremely difficult rock and snow-ice climbing and showed no sign whatever of a previous ascent. Pressure mounted again on Cesare to reveal what happened between the 28 January and 3 February 1959, causing his mental turmoil to return, if it had ever left him. Some who knew the circumstances thought that it might help his mental state if he could be persuaded to reveal the true events of that period in 1959, but he remained stubborn to the last.

He suffered a series of strokes, which gradually reduced his ability to move around, forcing him to use a walking frame. In 2018 he gave a final interview to French reporter Charlie Buffet, who had been following the Cerro Torre narrative throughout. As with so much of Cesare's life, this again roused controversy. Some saw it as a last-ditch effort to persuade him finally to help Toni Egger's sister seek the closure she needed, others as a callous attempt to extract information from a sick old man barely aware of what he was saying. During the interview Cesare changed his story somewhat but the true circumstances of Egger's death were not revealed.

The full story of Cerro Torre died with Cesare on 19 January 2021.

Acknowledgements

In researching this article I have received help from a number of others and would like to thank them: Leo Dickinson, Rolo Garibotti, Marcello Costa and especially Gianluigi Maestri, Cesare's son, who has been an invaluable source of information about his father, and has provided many of the original photos used.

LEO DICKINSON

Everest Unmasked

Messner, the Unions, and Humphrey the Dog

Recently, someone suggested to me that it must have been great making films in the 1970s because I was always surrounded by a strong support team.

Well, yes and no. This was after all the era of the all-powerful unions.

Take *Everest Unmasked* as an example. On Boxing Day 1976, my canoeing film *Dudh Kosi: Relentless River of Everest* garnered an audience on ITV of 18.5 million, a number unimaginably large in these days of myriad channels and pretty damned good for 1976. So I had the ear of the ITV network. Obviously.

But my suggestion we make yet another film on Everest went down like a lead balloon. The BBC and Thames TV had made several Everest films between them, including *Everest the Hard Way* and *Surrender to Everest.* None did very well in the ratings so my suggestion was not well received.

'But this is without oxygen,' I argued.

It was clearly going to be an uphill struggle, so to speak, and my first role on *Everest Unmasked* was as salesman. I had to sell the idea to the ITV network. Only Aled Vaughan, executive producer of Harlech Television (HTV), helped me. I was asked to make the case to the ITV network committee comprising Granada, Thames, Associated Television and Yorkshire Television. (The 'smaller' regions like Southern, Scottish, Grampian, West Country, Ulster and even HTV did not get to vote on my proposals.) The committee met every three months. Daunting. There was a lot riding on my persuasiveness and my belief in Reinhold.

Charles Denton, CEO of ATV, which later became Central Television, was a fan of my work, so I had his backing. (Charles later poached me from HTV. Ironically, my second film for him was *Eiger Solo*, featuring the Welshman Eric Jones. It was made with no outside interference from executives. Exactly how I liked it.)

Despite Charles's backing the committee had reservations.

Why would we want to make a film about an Italian we have never heard of, doing something [climbing without oxygen] in which we have no interest on a mountain we have already climbed, and for the first time, and one that we even named?

Reinhold Messner was flown over from Italy to try and add weight to the pitch and the head of the HTV PR machine weighed in by putting out

Reinhold Messner talks with Eric Jones at 9,000m above the summit of Everest in 1977, aboard a Pilatus Porter piloted by the legendary Emil Wick.
(Leo Dickinson)

a press release: 'Everest as we all know is in Switzerland.' This demonstrated how seriously they were all taking it.

When I pointed out the Switzerland gaffe to Aled he said, 'don't worry Leo. He only went to Cambridge.' Reinhold couldn't help laughing.

To assess the project's viability, I decided to fly over the summit of Everest with Reinhold and not allow him to breath any bottled oxygen. Eric Jones came too because he always looked after me in interesting situations. At the controls was the famous Emil Wick, pilot extraordinaire who, despite crash-landing one of their aircraft on Dhaulagiri in 1960, was in 1977 a sales agent for the Pilatus Porter we were flying in. I swear he was smoking through his oxygen mask.

At 9,000m Reinhold was definitely not behaving normally. He struggled to reload his Rollliflex camera, tricky at sea level, and asked me to do it but on the other hand he couldn't stop talking. This I took to be a good sign. He might have been speaking gobbledygook but at least he was compos mentis.

The flight cost $9,500, which I paid, not ITV, thus giving me another role: producer. They did reimburse me later, but I took the gamble to convince myself we weren't all mad.

Realising the enormity of the task ahead, I went to Canon's European headquarters in Amsterdam and asked their engineers if they would make me seven Super 8mm cameras that would run at 25 frames per second rather than 18, the normal speed for this format. To my surprise they took the problem to head office in Tokyo and manufactured exactly what I wanted. Canon never realised how their contribution changed the history of labour relations.

Expedition doctor Oswald 'Bulle' Oelz being interviewed at base camp by Leo Dickinson for the documentary *Everest Unmasked*. *(Leo Dickinson)*

The use of the Super 8mm presented me with yet another role: union negotiator. The Association of Cinematograph, Television and Allied Technicians (ACTT) announced they couldn't regard 'amateur formats' as acceptable to their members in case they undermined their professional operating standards. This was, of course, nothing to do with technical standards. They simply didn't want non-union amateurs being permitted to send in film to ITV stations. (I wonder how mobile phones would have gone down.)

To smooth things over, I attended various ACTT meetings and presented my case. It was, as you might have guessed, incredibly boring since most of what was said was bullshit, but it became clear that because 'amateurs' could not operate an Arriflex, since the camera was hugely expensive and no climber in their right mind would consider carrying this eight-kilo monster, the Super 8mm format would be acceptable. But believe it or not, ITV still had to pay the unions to allow me to give Reinhold a Canon camera to shoot footage on the summit. The main thing was the interests of the proletariat were satisfied.

We needed more money though, since I would now have to teach Reinhold how to use the new camera. (Film tutor: another hat I wore. I thought it best not to tell the union that three of these Super 8mm cameras also recorded sound, since that was two people's jobs.) Persuading Reinhold to bother at all carrying this very lightweight camera when he went to the top was the real challenge. But eventually he was persuaded and to his great credit said in a recent film that, 'without Leo's film camera, proving we reached the summit, we would not have been believed. The stills were not proof enough.' Even Tenzing Norgay wanted an enquiry and didn't believe

Peter Habeler, Messner's partner on the first ascent of Everest without bottled oxygen. *(Leo Dickinson)*

Messner and Habeler until he saw Reinhold's footage.

So far I'd been program originator, salesman, union negotiator and teacher as well as fulfilling my original roll as cameraman.

Then, horror of horrors, I discovered that I would have to take a union crew with me on the expedition, albeit a 'cut-down one'. The union convener told me it would be inappropriate to take a woman and since all personal assistants were female (welcome to the 1970s) the lack of toilet facilities would be a problem. Having a union crew involved me finding things for them to do such as filming an interview at base camp. This was almost useful despite HTV's most senior cameraman framing Everest without its summit on several shots. He did let me use his heavy wooden tripod to hold my 1,200mm Canon Super Telephoto lens.

Another of my roles on the film was 'researcher'. I contacted Capt John Noel to negotiate a fee for his material from the 1924 expedition. For some reason this slipped through the union's net as it was classed as archive material. As long as we didn't use more than four per cent in the final film it was acceptable. Let's just say no one ever timed this section.

Where I did come unstuck was 'researching' Prof Noel Odell, someone at Cambridge who as a geologist actually did know Everest wasn't in Switzerland, at least not yet. I took the Everest crew along: cameraman, an assistant cameraman, a sound recordist, an assistant sound recordist (to change the tape), an electrical lighting engineer, his assistant and *The Times* journalist Ronnie Faux to help with the questions. Ron was in the National Union of Journalists and therefore acceptable to the ACTT Union with which there was they had reciprocal agreements.

'We were redeemed and liberated, freed at last from the inhuman compulsion to climb on.' Peter Habeler photographs Reinhold Messner on the summit.

You may have spotted that the one person I hadn't brought was a PA to write down what everyone was doing. Yet there were, it seems, no shortage of toilet facilities in Cambridge and because of my omission the interview I did with Odell, the last man to see Mallory and Irvine alive was not allowed to be included in my film. Having been 'blacked', I had to explain the situation to the 86-year-old professor, who in his day spent longer than any other person above 26,000ft. It was the very last detailed interview he ever gave and when I remade the film four years ago I included this interview.

Terry Elgar was my editor at HTV and I worked with him almost every day for 12 weeks, shaping my narrative of how the Everest story unfolded, culminating with Reinhold's ascent. This does sound like a director's role but I wasn't allowed to have that title because it meant I would get two union jobs: cameraman and director. Once we had a picture that ran okay, I brought in my favourite commentator: Ian McNaught-Davis.

We had already collaborated on several projects, including the Dudh Kosi film, which was nominated for an Emmy. Our modus operandi was well established. We had found an expensive French restaurant in Cardiff and would park ourselves there. I would tell Mac the story and any amusing anecdotes over a bottle of wine or two, and we'd reconvene in the editing suite next morning.

Here we would play the film to him, minus all the effects, and make suggestions. Mac would make suggestions. On a project about the Matterhorn we had archive photos of Whymper and his team in the wrong order for Mac's narrative so we undid the Sellotape holding the film together and switched the Steenbeck editing machine back on. After a couple of days of this, Mac would go back to London in his Jag, write his version of the script based around my picture story, come back and record it. I would oversee the recording of the narration and suggest a different emphasis at certain points and sign it off. Job done.

At that point we'd retire to the boardroom to meet up with Aled and Wynford Vaughan-Thomas, one of the founders of Harlech and a former BBC journalist who had flown over Berlin during a bombing raid and covered the Anzio beach landings. (His experiences in the war had taught him the value of 'pointless optimism'.) We'd then open a bottle of whisky. I once brought Humphrey, our six-month Old English sheepdog, to one of these post-production parties. He peed on the carpet. 'Ooh, look at that,' announced Wynford in his muscial Welsh voice. 'Humphrey has weed on the boardroom carpet.'

And that's how 'Team Leo' made films.

After *Everest Unmasked* aired in April 1979, Clive James wrote a review for *The Observer,* focussing on Reinhold's motivation:

> *'It is inneresting to try zis climb whizzout oxychen … what is important to explore is myself.' Reinhold forgot to add that exploring Reinhold's self was important mainly to Reinhold. For the rest of us exploring Reinhold's self was bound to rank fairly low on any conceivable scale of priorities…*

> *Reinhold made it to the top. But the peril was not over. There was still the danger of brain damage – or, in Reinhold's case, further brain damage. The chances are that this would first manifest itself in the form of blood bursting blood-vessels in the eyeball, loss of memory, impaired speech functions and the sudden, irrational urge to participate in stupid television programs.*

> *Most of these symptoms duly appeared. Nevertheless, Reinhold's achievement could not be gainsaid. He and his friends had proved that it is not enough to risk your neck. It is in the nature of man to risk his brains as well.*

Reinhold loved every word.

THOMAS VENNIN

The Birth of Mountaineering

A Piquant Stroll through the History of Alpinism

The illustrations for this selection of Thomas Vennin's *brèves* are the work
of American artist Sheridan Anderson (1936-84), who captured the rebellious
mood of climbing in the 1960s and 1970s.

In 2019, the French writer and blogger Thomas Vennin published **La dent du
piment,** *a less than reverent or indeed accurate date-by-date take on the serious
business of mountaineering history. 'The Spice Tower' is a lot of fun with more
truth than you might expect. Vennin is a self-confessed armchair mountaineer
who lives in Bordeaux and learned very quickly not to take things too seriously,
as these excerpts illustrate. Translation by Eric Vola.*

Mountaineers have a problem with the last great problem. Each time
the last great problem is solved, a new one arises from nowhere. What
will they invent now they have made the famous first winter ascent of K2?
The pirouette that concludes this book[1] suggests going to Mars and having
a look there, but forecasts from eminent scientists studying the future of our

1. T Vennin, *La dent du piment: Balade épicée dans l'histoire de l'alpinisme,* Guérin, Chamonix, 2019.

planet suggest we may wish to consider a post-apocalypse ascent of Everest. We shall see.

Whether it is on Mars or a restyled Earth, the future of alpinism necessarily exists. Man, that innocent, cannot restrain himself from setting out to see what is going on up there. And so, perhaps one day someone will have the privilege to write a new story. And as far as this show is concerned, to do better than what has gone before will require some serious stuff. The little compendium that follows attests to that: our glorious predecessors did put the bar quite high, the scamps!

40 million years ago

After a monsoon evening and a bit too much wine, the Eurasian Plate wakes up with a severe hangover and the vague memory of a tectonic dance with the Indian Plate. Several months later, she gives birth to a charming baby 3,000km long and 8,848m high. The Heavenly Father is hopping mad but quickly falls under the spell of little Himalaya: 'Here is one who will make heads turn,' he (most likely) whispered, with a touch of concern in his voice.

Biblical Times

With no sponsor or logistics, Moses arrives at the foot of Mount Sinai simply equipped with a Gore-Tex tunic and his famous sandals. After the first rope lengths climbed at a headlong pace, despite the flood, the prophet sets the tone: he is going for an all-time record. At the crux move of the Burning Bush, the elements rage in a storm and lightning falls a few centimetres from his *piolet*. But Moses is touched with the grace of the Divine, nothing can stop him, and he literally flies up the mountain. On the summit, he is astounded to find God himself who gives him a severe tongue-lashing: 'Commandment number one? You don't climb mountains!' Mad with rage, Moses smashes the tablets of the Law on a rock and starts his descent. At base camp he falls into the arms of Aaron, his brother, mad with anxiety. To this day, Moses didn't get a Piolet d'Or for his contribution.

Year 1280

The Italian monk Fra Salimbene, pioneer of Alpine chronicles, relates that Peter III, king of Aragon, ascended the awesome Pic Canigou (2784m) in the Pyrenees. From his account, the king was soon abandoned by his two rope-mates, terrified by the storm, decides to carry on, solo, up to the summit where he finds a lake from which he sees a gigantic dragon emerging. Problem: the only known lake is the Estanyols, 500m below the summit and, as far as the specialists are concerned, you'll find more marmots than dragons. The tradition of taking an alpinist at his word is already in a bad way.

27 April 1336

Petrarch, the poet, climbs Mont Ventoux (1912m) with his brother Gherardo. To have his name inserted in the chronicles of alpinism for climbing a mountain easily accessible today by bicycle is the real achievement of

Petrarch, who was as much an alpinist as the Queen of England. This categorical point of view will have to be revisited eventually when a Tour de France stage concludes on the summit of the Grandes Jorasses.

26 June 1492
King Charles VIII is fed up with Christopher Columbus banging on about his proposed voyage across the sea. So for a change of topic, he orders Antoine de Ville to go into the mountains and climb to the summit of Mont Aiguille (2087m). This time, there's no 'has perhaps climbed', no dragons and above all, no cycle-able mountain pastures. Mont Aiguille is actually steep! Twenty seriously equipped guys are required to get to the top. A military organisation: the route is located, a siege starts, similar to the siege of a fortified castle, ladders and fixed ropes are used … In short, 461 years before the conquest of Everest, it is in the Dauphiné that the heavy Himalayan expedition is invented.

'Antoine! What do you see from up there?' yells the king who stayed at the bottom. 'The sea, your majesty!'

19 June 1741
The English show up in Chamonix. Disguised as though going off to mass and armed to the teeth to deter natives who are rumoured to be wild savages, eight subjects of His Majesty led by the young student William Windham and the adventurer Richard Pococke get up to Montenvers and discover, dumbfounded, the Mer de Glace, the Chamonix Aiguilles and Mont Blanc. The Chamoniard is discovered to be a non-violent primate, though a little too insistent with his traditional Alpine occupation: hawking key fobs and snow globes.

1760
Horace-Bénédict de Saussure, aristocrat from Geneva and no less marvellously dressed, finds an aim to his life during a journey to Chamonix that brings him to the foot of Mont Blanc. From that moment, the summit will not cease to haunt his nights. But the young Horace-Bénédict is particularly smart and knows that iron willpower and an unpronounceable surname are not enough to turn oneself into an alpinist. He knows as well that alone, he will get nowhere. So, he has the idea to entice the natives in proposing some reward in hard cash to those who would dare to take a risk up there and find a route to the summit. He even promises the jackpot to the one who reaches the summit. Along with being backward, the Chamoniard now becomes greedy … but the idea of HBDS is not so ludicrous for as well encouraging the first attempts on Mont Blanc, he also lays down the first steps in the valley's mountain guide trade.

22 December 1857
Today is the birthday, in Great Britain, of the first alpine club. Even though they were spending all their summers conquering the highest summits, British alpinists spent the winter moping around their Victorian living rooms with that fundamental and unresolvable question: how, *my dear,* to put a peg in with a cup of tea? Given the complexity of the question, Her Majesty's subjects decide to group together and create the elitist Alpine Club, electing John Ball as their first president. To keep honking at it they create the periodical *Peaks, Passes and Glaciers* which will be replaced from 2 March 1863 with *the very famous Alpine Journal* the reading of which allows one to understand how, during this period modestly labelled 'the Golden Age of alpinism', the activity of scrambling up peaks became, thanks to the English, a *gentleman's* sport.

23 July 1860

Edward Whymper, a young English engraver, blows his mind discovering the Matterhorn during a journey to Zermatt, where his father has sent him to fulfil an order from the Alpine Club to illustrate the book being published for its third anniversary. Edward Whymper is the one holding the pencil, but it is the mountain that will engrave itself in his head. Back in London, our young friend will have but one aim in life, to return to Switzerland and be the first to climb the Matterhorn.

1865

And lo, Chomolungma became Everest. At the beginning of the 1800s, the British undertake to endow India with cartography worthy of the name and launch the *Great Trigonometrical Survey.* From 1823, a certain George Everest takes things in hand and sends teams to explore the farthest regions to triangulate everything that does not move. Reaching the foot of the mountains of Himalaya, their theodolites go batso with one of them displaying the extravagant altitude of 8,840 metres. After checking and rechecking the square on the hypotenuse, Andrew Waugh, who took over from George Everest, decrees that this is the highest mountain in the world and proposes to name it Everest to honour the tremendous work of his predecessor. Using the excuse that it couldn't find a local name, which was the custom to keep, the Royal Geographical Society ratifies Waugh's proposal in 1865. Yet Chomolungma, as the Tibetans have always called the mountain, did appear on much older maps. Meantime, the Nepalis, of whom nothing was asked, decide that for them, they will use Sagarmatha. Some historians report that the affair was finally settled during a legendary game of rock-paper-scissor between Queen Victoria and the Dalai Lama during their historic and not at all fictitious meeting. The sheet feverishly held out by his holiness having been massacred by the Queen's scissors, we all say Everest and that's that.

29 June 1865

The flamboyant first ascent of the Aiguille Verte by Edward Whymper and his guides Christian Almer and Franz Biener. Four years after engraving it, Whymper has still not climbed the Matterhorn. Fed up with his repeated failed attempts and persuaded that the Matterhorn will end by killing them, his guides said 'Stop!' The flags are red, the weather is grey and the idea's black ... So, Whymper chooses the Verte (geddit?), which he climbs in two kicks. With their noses out of joint that an Englishman climbed their totem before they could, the most vociferous Chamoniards propose duffing Whymper up if he can't prove his success. Luckily for Whymper, Michel Croz comes through, calming them down in taking his side. The following week, Croz will even avenge the insult by putting up a new route on the Verte with Ambroise Ducroz, himself a Chamoniard. The story could have ended there, if that devil Whymper had not already gone again to the Matterhorn ...

14 July 1865

Matterhorn first ascent. After 8 July 1786 and the first ascent of Mont Blanc, 14 July 1865 marks the second greatest date in the history of alpinism. Several days after his success on the Verte, Whymper is back in Zermatt for a new attempt on the Matterhorn, now persuaded that the key is the Hörnli ridge on the Swiss side. Jean-Antoine Carrel, an Italian guide from Valtournenche who had participated in the previous attempts, gives his agreement to Whymper to go with him before finally, without telling him, making a new commitment with the Italian government for another attempt from the other side.

"Croz! Croz! come here!"

Raging mad, Whymper recruits the first guides closest to hand. No matter their skills, he must be ahead of the Italian attempt and Jean-Antoine Carrel, the traitor. It is then that he crosses the path of another Englishman, Lord Francis Douglas who is hanging around with his two guides: Peter Taugwalder and his son who bears the same name. The three agree to follow him. Several hours later, the party bump into Michel Croz. The famous guide has been recruited by the Rev Charles Hudson and the young Douglas Robert Hadow whose lack of experience makes Whymper hesitate. But he has no choice. If he takes Croz, he must take all of them.

If the choice of men is doubtful, the choice of route is good and by 1.40pm Whymper at last grasps his victory. While in a bit of a pickle way down on the Italian side, the poor Carrel suddenly notices some pebbles sadistically thrown down from the summit informing him of his defeat. Succumbing to his euphoria, Whymper envisages for one moment letting the Italian know about the rumours he's heard of an acquaintance between Carrel's progenitor and some bawdy *bersagliere* but the distance between the two men fortunately saves decorum and Carrel, dismayed, goes back down.

Too busy savouring his moment of grace, Whymper does not realise that the young and far too tender Hadow had been for quite a while on the brink of apoplexy and that their descent will start under worrying auspices. Croz takes things in hand and the lead, placing Hadow just behind him. And then, the drama … Some 80 metres below the summit, Hadow slides down both feet first and hits Croz with full force. In their fall, both men pull down Douglas and Hudson who topple over in the void with them. The Taugwalders and Whymper, spared by destiny, are the only survivors of this mythical ascent which marks the terrible end of the Golden Age of alpinism.

30 June 1868

Guided by Melchior Anderegg, Johan Jaun and Julien Grange, the Englishman Horace Walker gives his name to the highest point of the Grandes Jorasses and consequently, when climbed by the tremendous north side, to one of the greatest climbs in the Alps: the Walker Spur. Edward Whymper had already been in the neighbourhood to observe the Aiguille Verte, but because it was socked in with mist did not judge it useful to go up to the highest peak, contenting himself with the lower summit today named La Pointe Whymper. In some ways Edward was quite lazy...

2 April 1874

Birth of the Club Alpin Français, a French equivalent to the very distinguished British Alpine Club. While they were spending their summers observing the British conquer the highest summits of the Alps, the French alpinists spent winters moping about in the Parisian bistros with this haunting and fundamental question: how, my good lady, do the English manage to put in those blasted pegs with their cup of tea? Considering the complexity of the question, the founder members of the CAF decide to orientate their activity towards a more noble cause: spreading knowledge about mountains and encouraging participation. So, the mountains are fitted out with the first refuges, national parks are created, like the one for the Écrins, the first school trips are organised to enable French schoolchildren to discover the mountains – and one contemplates La Meije ...

16 August 1877

First ascent of La Meije by Emmanuel Boileau de Castelnau, member of the newly born Club Alpin Français (CAF), with guides Pierre Gaspard and son. After the conquest of the Matterhorn, the British decreed that all the great summits of the Alps had been climbed and that ended the Golden Age of alpinism. No argument. *Excuse me, Sir* [in English in the original], but that summit, just over there, a little to one side, what's wrong with that one? La Meije not classy enough to grace your Victorian living rooms? It smells gassy? That's the problem? *Le gaz?*[2] Maybe you were a little scared and put it to one side, hoping everyone would forget this small summit that doesn't even top 4,000m. It's true; some pitches are a bit spooky ... But ask the elder Gaspard. He didn't have the jitters getting up the famous pyramid blocking access to the summit on the south face. You can speak also with his client, the young Boileau de Castelnau, eminent *Cafiste*[3], just 19 years old but with guts to have Whymper quavering. And young Gaspard? Sent as a scout, as cannon

2. From the climber's expression: *il ya du gaz* meaning 'it is airy' as for example in: 'this traverse is bloody airy!'
3. Meaning, someone associated with the CAF.

fodder, up the most perilous pitches! There is the first great and splendid success of French alpinism stamped 'CAF': La Meije, *last but not least.*

1880

The British climber Albert Frederick Mummery and his Swiss guide Alexander Burgener attempt the south-west face of the Dent du Géant but rapidly give up faced with the technical difficulties. Before turning back, Mummery takes out a calling card on which he scrawls the following information: 'Absolutely inaccessible by fair means.' He slides the card in a bottle and gets home without knowing that the expression 'by fair means' will become as legendary as himself in Alpine circles, and even in Himalayan ones, where today one uses it to evoke an ascent without Sherpas, without fixed ropes and above all without supplementary oxygen. On the normal route of Everest, it is not rare to find calling cards with the variant 'By filthy means' inside oxygen bottles abandoned between a turd and a tibia.

5 August 1881

First ascent of the Aiguille du Grépon by Albert Frederick Mummery, Alexandre Burgener and Benedikt Venetz. Every pivotal period is symbolised by an alpinist and the mountain their name is attached to. After Saussure and

Mont Blanc, after Whymper and the Matterhorn, here is Mummery and the Grépon. But conversely, compared to the first two, who were completely obsessed by the mountain they had decided to climb, Mummery did not give a hoot about the Grépon. What matters to him is not the mountain as such, but the difficulty of its ascent. The nuance, subtle but fundamental, will bury definitively the Golden Age and allow climbers to enter a new era, 'acrobatic alpinism', which is practised on rocky walls where calves and forearms are severely tested, as for example in the Mummery crack on the Grépon. A true symbol. And if the Chamoniard was not sufficiently un-hinged after that, a few years later Mummery decides that he does not need anyone anymore to climb mountains and that the English toff who follows his guide like a little dog is a dead loss. A few deeds on the Grand Charmoz, the Dent du Requin or the Brenva, and here comes a new revolutionary concept signed Al-Fred: 'alpinism without a guide'.

What a man! What a time!

24 August 1895

Albert Frederick Mummery disappears on Nanga Parbat. Having invented acrobatic alpinism, explored the Caucasus and invented alpinism without a guide, Mummery is bored to tears. For him, time does not fly fast enough. But in June 1895, he crosses by chance the path of Marty McFly who, overwhelmed by this man so in advance of his time, agrees to lend him his DeLorean. Mummery adjusts the temporal convector to 2.21 gigawatts and flies away to Rawalpindi with the presumptuous intention of climbing Nanga Parbat, 20 years before his adventurers' colleagues will start envis-aging the question. Norman Collie and Geoffrey Hastings, the two friends whom he has taken with him, have so much difficulty to follow him on the vertiginous and iced slopes that on 24 August, our adventurer of modern times decides to go without them to the summit. He was never seen again. He was probably blown away by an avalanche, unless he exploded in flight after taking off from the summit in a spaceship of his own invention.

12 June 1907

Tom Longstaff, Karbir Burkhoti and the brothers Alexis and Henri Bro-chard offer themselves to the Trisul (7120m), first 7,000er to be climbed, and breaking the altitude record established 20 years before by the Swiss Zurbriggen on Aconcagua, who later fell into depression. There being no suicide to lament in the ranks of that superb team, scientists will not be able to establish a link between exposure to high altitude and neurasthenia. Some experiments will prove later that in case of a forced turnaround 50m from the summit, one must beware.

17 July 1909

New altitude record on Chogolisa. Disappointed not to have reached the summit of K2, the Duke of Abruzzi and his henchmen fall back on its neighbour Chogolisa, where they reach 7,500 metres, breaking the Trisul record. Bad weather forces them back 150m from the summit, but they come back to Italy with important information: from 7,500 metres onwards, men stop showing off.

28 July 1911
The Austrian Paul Preuss climbs the east face of the Campanile Basso in the Dolomites solo, without a rope and pegs. Preuss had a theory: 'a pitch must not be climbed if it cannot be climbed down without any aid.' In other words, abseiling is cheating. That gives a strong impression of his vision of climbing. If he had lived in the days of Himalayan conquests, Preuss would probably have been against wearing gloves. All the same, the east face of the Campanile Basso is grade V and at the time the event made quite some noise in Alpine circles. 'You are mad!' he was told by his rival and friend Tita Piaz, who himself did not hesitate to use a rope. 'Pegging is evil,' responded the Austrian, who managed to survive until October 1913 and a fall of 300m from the north face of Mandlkogel. As for Tita Piaz, he died 35 years later falling off his bicycle.

22 December 1919
First general meeting of the Groupe de Haute Montagne created at the initiative of Jacques de Lepiney and Paul Chevalier, two members of the Parisian climber's tribe who in winter use the Fontainebleau boulders to train and invade the Alps in the summer months. At the end of the Great War, two notions still create conflict among French alpinists. The old school lauds the grandeur of conquest in alpinism or a scientific aim, while the new one, flabbergasted by the deeds of Zsigmondy and Mummery, has but one yearning: climb like mad up the wildest walls. The GHM, wishing 'to gather the upholders of an alpinism of excellence' declares independence and rapidly gathers the world elite of alpinism. Besides its mythical magazine, *Les Annales de Alpinisme,* the GHM initiate the first guidebooks such as the *Guide Vallot* and also and above all the first French Himalayan expeditions. Now be worried, *messieurs les Anglais,* the French rooster has put his crampons on!

24 September 1921
During the first reconnaissance expedition to Everest organised and financed by the brand-new Mount Everest Committee, the British reach the north col and are officially the first to put a foot on the highest mountain in the world. In that familiar 'I-will-not-be-at-peace-with-myself-until-I-have-climbed-this-bloody-mountain' sequence, please welcome George Mallory.

Art & Literature

'Dom, Saas Fee', Hilda Hechle, c1920, watercolour, 55cm x 39cm. Täschhorn, Dom, Lenzspitze, Nadelhorn from slopes of the Trifthorn east of Saas Fee.
(Courtesy of Tony Astill/www.mountainpaintings.org)

DONALD M ORR

John Singer Sargent

His Mountain Sketchbooks

'Val d'Aosta'. *(Alamy)*

Any review of mountain art prompts this question: what do mountain paintings reflect? They can express a truth unobtainable in text. They can also deconstruct notions of reality. The message of mountain paintings may be philosophical, making us consider the nature and effect of existence, or of nature, of creation itself and humanity's role in it. Paint may conceal but also recreates; it covers but in doing so changes.

Inevitably, mountain art speaks to the nature of mountaineering. The way we see and approach mountains is reflected in the way we record them. These images are not simply illustrative. They magnify the nature and purpose of our involvement with the mountains, how we engage our imaginations in our perception of their landscape. In contemplating mountain images, we can experience, perhaps only briefly, a liberation, from business or professional cares, but most deeply from ourselves.

Whatever it is that calls us to the mountain environment, and it can be an invitation, a challenge, a demand, that impulse must be recognised and considered. It may be a call to witness, to experience, a summons to a privileged position, or even to the discomfort of doubt, but that inherent aspect of desire has to be acknowledged. Desire has the capacity to alter attitudes and conceal realities, to create a restlessness that is almost beyond understanding. Mountain art provokes memory in the mountaineer, revisiting intense experiences, the emptying of self and the process of refilling, or refuelling.

Text can be noisy and too often attempts to deal in absolutes. But in the space between the viewer and the canvas there is a silence or stillness; in that stillness we find the process of interpretation. We're looking not only at an impression, at the painting's structure or meaning, but also at the artist's state of mind. And in that understanding we may recognise that we're dealing with an examination of our own selves, our own fears and inadequacies. If this is the case for us as viewers with a passion for mountain landscapes, what of the artist whose speciality and income was derived from non-mountain painting? If mountain canvases can stimulate our desire, what were the motivations for a society portrait painter?

John Singer Sargent (1856-1925) was an American expatriate artist who became famous as the leading portrait painter of his day, rendering outstanding pictures of Edwardian era luxury and style. He was also devoted to mountain scenery and travelled extensively through the Alps and visited mountain settings across the world. Never a mountaineer, though he did walk significantly through Alpine areas, he recorded rocky mountain locations and environments throughout his life. Born in Florence to American parents he trained in Paris before moving to London. He lived most of his life in Europe, enjoying international acclaim and an extraordinarily successful career as a society portrait artist. While many of his studies reveal an awareness of Impressionism, his commissioned portraits were rooted in what was termed the Grand Manner, an aesthetic style derived from Classicism and the art of the High Renaissance. Yet Sargent's colour choice and paint handling established a style immediately recognisable as his own.

Over his long career Sargent travelled widely all over Europe, the Middle East and north Africa, made several trips to America, visiting, among other states, Maine, Montana and Florida. Each destination offered creative opportunities and we have more than 2,000 watercolours from his travel sketchbooks. His drawing from the outset was 'rarely less than dazzling in its fluency'.[1] In his watercolours there is a freshness and energy expressed with a fluidity often lacking in his more formal portrait studies. Similarly, his large-scale mountain pictures retained a freshness and vivacity that many of his studio portraits lost.

Despite his popularity, or perhaps because of it, Sargent had his critics,

---

1. R Hughes, *Nothing If Not Critical*, Collins Harvill, London, 1990, p101

some of whom saw him as a mere illustrator who relied on superficial dashing effects for his success. His expatriate lifestyle also clashed with emerging artistic trends in America, particularly the Ashcan School which was
centred on New York and dealing with urban realism often depicting life
in the poorer communities. Sargent's portraits of what the contemporary
American art world would have deemed 'high society' did not find a strong
audience in the States. While Sargent's drawing and compositions were
highly impressive and his paint handling techniques second to none he did,
it seems, occasionally lack tact, as in the case of the murals he produced in
the Boston area. 'The Church' was revealed as a beautiful young woman
while 'The Synagogue' appeared as a blind, unattractive old woman resulting in accusations of antisemitism. Sargent failed to understand how his
representations might offend and was both astonished and upset when he
was criticised. When the press fanned the controversy, Sargent abandoned
the mural project.

Boyhood and family life changed in 1870 when they moved, for the first
time, to Switzerland for the summer, to avoid the hot, unhealthy atmosphere in Florence where cholera and malaria were often prevalent in the
summer months. In addition, Mrs Sargent had just given birth to her second
daughter and was anxious about her infant's health. This seeking refuge in
the mountains was to become an annual event as Sargent's sister Emily was
an invalid who regained strength in the mountain air while John undertook
long, challenging hikes to nearby peaks, recording what he saw.

'When they reached Thun,' wrote Stephen Rubin. 'Sargent and his father
began a walking tour.'[2] By the time they reached Mürren, Sargent, then 14
years old, was using two sketchbooks and separate sheets for larger works.
'Sargent dated many of the pages and identified a number of sites, making
it appear that the sketchbooks were a chronological, pictorial record of the
journey through Switzerland.'[3] This peripatetic style continued. Successive
summer trips never remained in one place for long as the family enjoyed
a nomadic existence on holiday. Family letters reveal that while based at
Mürren they travelled extensively across the Alps and even visited spas in
the Pyrenees.

John Sargent's education had been largely private until 1869 when he
was enrolled at a day school in Florence where literature and languages
were foremost. His artistic abilities went beyond drawing and painting;
at this point, he was a highly accomplished pianist playing the works of
Mendelssohn, Beethoven and Schubert. Music remained a serious interest
especially in later life when it became one of his chief pleasures. In 1871,
the year after their first Swiss holiday, Sargent, accompanied by a drawing
tutor, made a sketching tour of the Tyrol. Much of the work contained in
these early sketchbooks can be viewed online, indeed downloaded, from the
Metropolitan Museum of Art. It is work of a very mature nature for one
still in his teens. The quality of line drawing, water-colouring and choice

2. S Rubin, *John Singer Sargent's Alpine Sketchbooks,* Metropolitan Museum of Art, New York, 1991, p7.
3. Ibid p7.

of subject matter disclose an adult capacity and an established technique in both drawing and painting where 'the ease and accuracy of judgement … would be hard to beat.'[4]

The few paintings examined here give the briefest introduction to a lifetime's interest. They range from the initial teenage expedition to those of middle years and Sargent's maturity. They reflect not only his awareness of differing mountain regions but also reveal his changing attitudes to mountain ranges and his varying treatments of the subject as each study was considered as unique. It may well be that this aspect was at the core of his creativity whereas his society portraits, while never simply a repeated process, did have to conform to the tastes of the culture that they represented.

While the stark Alpine summit at the head of a glacier made an obvious choice for a large canvas, his studies and sketchbooks reveal a noticeable delight in the whole mountain environment, a love of high places that never left him, and as du Montcel commented, 'adventure is not in things but in ourselves.' His society portraits created worldwide fame and engendered a large and comfortable income but his continued investigation of mountain ranges and his journeys to the rugged settings of high mountains from his teenage years to old age displays a love of that specific environment that was largely a private interest.

If 'a love of mountains, in a man, is more than anything the child in him which refuses to die'[5] then Sargent's first boyhood excursion to the Alps in 1870 may well reflect Mauriac's comment. What this love generated was a body of work based on the study of the mountain environment that was not rooted in commercialism or the desire to promote an interest or passion in others but simply because of the stimulation he found in these areas. One of the unifying aspects of his mountain paintings is the quality of light which he rendered in these studies which, apart from the structure of the mountains, is an overarching feature in his compositions. It may well be that Macfarlane's remark: 'it is the light of the mountains which has always attracted more comment than any other aspect of their beauty'[6] is particularly relevant to Sargent's collection.

Several large sketchbooks containing hundreds of drawings and watercolour studies were left to relatives on his death. They were never seen by the public; they were never exhibited during his lifetime. The Alpine Sketchbooks of his teenage years are still complete and record the awe and wonder he sensed in the high mountains, a form of eternity that we, through his continued work in this field, may share in.

'Schreckhorn, Eismeer'[7]

This large watercolour was produced during that first summer in the Alps in 1870. The view of the glacier and central peak was obviously created from

4. Hughes, *op cit* p102-3.
5. F Mauriac, foreword to *High Heaven* (J Boell & P Elek), London, 1947, p7.
6. R Macfarlane, *Mountains of the Mind,* Granta, London, 2004, p213.
7. 'Schreckhorn, Eismeer', watercolour and graphite on off-white woven paper, 27.6cm x 40.6cm, Metropolitan Museum of Art, New York, 1870.

'Schreckhorn, Eismeer'. *(Alamy)*

the north, from the Grindelwald end of the valley and features the dramatic crest of the Schreckhorn (4078m), first climbed by Leslie Stephen only nine years previously in 1861, with the summit of the Lauteraarhorn (4042m) in the background. This then was an area few would have witnessed and the spires of the Schreckhorn must have had an immediate appeal to the teenager.

His handling of the rugged, rocky ridge leading to the Nässilhorn (3750m) is part of a series of jagged diagonal lines receding to the towering Schreckhorn adding to the illusion of distance and the dominance of the summit. The aiguilles of the ridge are echoed in the icefall where the Obers Ischmeer drops to the Unders Ischmeer, close to the point where the Schreckhornhütte, built in 1877, now stands. The glacier forms a counter diagonal that supports the mountain while the white of the snowfields links to the colouring of the icefall allowing a framing effect of the rocky aspects of the mountain and enhancing the piercing perpendicularity of the scene. This concentration on spiked verticality is re-echoed in the left foreground where a soaring arête will lead to the Obere Buggel (2831m) and hence to the Pfaffestecki (3114m). Even allowing for a little dramatisation this is a remarkable painting for a 14-year-old boy, retaining as it does the freshness and stirring vividness that was captured the day it was painted.

'Val d'Aosta'[8]

Exhibited as 'Mont Blanc' (the highest peak in the central distance) this canvas has been referred to as 'Val d'Aosta' since 1935. This region is the

---

8. 'Val d'Aosta', oil on canvas, 92.1cm x 97.8cm, Tate Gallery, London, c1908-10.

'Cliffs at Deir el Bahri, Egypt'. *(Alamy)*

highest in Italy bound by Mont Blanc, Monte Rosa, Gran Paradiso and the Matterhorn. Given this vast mountain area, Sargent's painting is not one of isolated drama reflecting wonder and majesty; here is a huge mountain hinterland rolling off into untold distances: a barren, rocky landscape, a remote glacier, a far-flung peak and the suggestion that anyone entering this trackless waste must be aware of the consequences.

Painted in his maturity (in his mid fifties) there is sunshine and blue sky in the distance but a long way to go to achieve the final summit. It offers an open road but the gates to this route are hard and barren. Sun may reflect off the glacier, but deep shadows frame the view and clouds are brewing. It's a stark mountain environment, open and approachable but only for those who are fit, capable and determined. An honest, bold and impressive scene offering more to the viewer than merely a prospect of distant mountains, perhaps it was an indication of how he felt at that age: still capable, but aware of the wastes ahead.

'Cliffs at Deir el Bahri, Egypt'[9]

Painted near Thebes, this canvas reveals a vertical panorama in the desert. The bleaching effect of the strong sunlight causes the sky and sandy desert to be practically the same tone allowing shadow alone to delineate the structure of the cliffs. This is Sargent at his most Impressionistic. A painting that deals with the effects of light upon colour and structure based on his personal favourite subject matter.

Ostensibly a quite simple scene, it is Sargent's mastery of composition that creates a painting of two halves where the solidity of the cliff formation is balanced by a long diagonal ridge leading the eye off into the distance away from the dust and aridity to the lushness of the Nile waterway. Yet that device that enhances the illusion of depth does not hold our eye. It is

9. 'Cliffs at Deir el Bahri, Egypt', oil on canvas, 34.9cm x 62.9cm, Metropolitan Museum of Art, New York, 1890-91.

'Simplon Pass'. *(Corcoran Collection, National Art Gallery)*

instead drawn back to the towering cliff configuration, to the sandstone walls and columns we now more readily associate with the American south-west, although the increasing popularity of Wadi Rum and other desert climbing areas are perhaps reclaiming Sargent's vision. What is central here in this seemingly 'empty' painting is the beauty and subtlety of the desert environment, the open challenge to climbers to explore these sandstone cliffs beyond the, for Sargent, recognised mountaineering centres, and the overall invitation to enter this world of subtle colour and wonder.

'Simplon Pass'[10]

This canvas demonstrates Sargent's fondness for all aspects of mountain topography. This is not a simple view of a mountain pass from a distance whereby all details may be included but produced in the heart of the pass and including many of the mountain features he obviously enjoyed: the boulders and rock falls, the screes and moraines, the small patches of vegetation splashing colour across the rocks and the movement of water down the stony surface.

If it is true that 'the paintings of a period contain all its enthusiasm and illusions'[11] then nothing in the mountains escaped Sargent's eye. His expression of mountain landscape was determined partly by his reaction to it and partly by the structures, colour combinations and the light he experienced. He was unfailingly in close touch with the intricacies of mountain configuration to the extent that 'Sargent embraces difficulties one after another.'[12] Nothing was too complex. What arrested his vision in the mountains he recorded for all to see and contemplate.

10. 'Simplon Pass', 1911, oil on canvas, 71.8cm x 92.6cm, Corcoran Collection, National Gallery of Art, Washington DC.
11. T Martin Wood, Sargent, ed M Gioffredi, 2019 reprint of 1909 first edition by Jack, London & Stokes, New York, p7.
12. Ibid, p22.

MARTIN HOOD

The Family Gos

A Mountain of Heritage

The Gos family, from left to right, Charles, Émile,
Camille, Albert, Juliette and François.

Included in the Alpine Club's collection is an oil painting of a moonlit Matterhorn. A century ago, members would have instantly recognised the artist's name, a doyen of Alpine painting. His sons too were busy making names for themselves in the mountain arts, respectively as a painter, a writer and a photographer.

An exhibition in Switzerland recently celebrated the oeuvre of this talented dynasty. 'Les Gos: une montagne en héritage' opened at the Médiathèque Valais at Martigny in June 2020 and ran until the following January.

On a rainy August afternoon last year, we were welcomed into the exhibition by larger-than-life portraits of a remarkable family. These were the artist Albert Gos (1852-1942), and his three sons, François Gos (1880-1975), the eldest and likewise a painter, Charles Gos (1885-1949), the writer, and Émile Gos (1888-1969), the photographer who made the very portraits we were looking at. There were also two daughters, who like their brothers enjoyed all aspects of mountain life, but left behind no artistic legacy.

All four men loomed large over the Alpine culture of their time. Albert learned his craft between 1870 and 1872 at the Geneva School of Art under Barthélemy Menn (1815-1893), who introduced the principles of plein air

'Le Cervin', by Albert Gos.[1]

Albert Gos (1852-1942) at his atelier in Clarens, outside Martigny. (*Émile Gos*)

painting into Swiss art. After absorbing that teaching, Albert Gos ran with it. Preferring to paint in the open air, he left the school before graduating. He concentrated on painting mountains, particularly in the Bernese Oberland and the Valais Alps.

Importantly, he could make a decent living with these works. This mattered even more from 1878, when he married Jeanne Monnerat. François, the first of five children, arrived two years later. The couple settled first in Geneva before moving to Clarens, a village near Montreux.

During his most productive decade, the last of the 19th century, Albert was justifiably known as the 'Matterhorn artist'. Indeed, one of these paintings appears in Charles Gos's story 'Gladys', which portrays an aristocratic English lady climber who comes to grief on the Matterhorn.

In the Martigny exhibition, a painting by François Gos was placed close to his father's work. Modest in scale, its style is a touch more modern than Albert's, as if the artist had imbibed at the same sources as, say, Félix Vallotton (1865-1925), who also made an artistic pilgrimage from Canton Vaud to the French capital. François studied for five years at the Geneva School of Arts and Crafts and at the city's art academy before moving to Paris. Unlike Vallotton, however, Emil had to work for his living in a factory as a decorative artist.

On returning to Switzerland, he gave drawing lessons in Clarens. In 1910, he settled in Munich, and later spent three years in Holland before returning

1. 'Le Cervin', A Gos, 91cm x 74cm, oil on canvas, undated, Club Alpin Suisse.

A family en plein air. Albert Gos, the 'Matterhorn artist', on the Riffelalp, Émile Gos (1888-1969) filming *La Croix du Cervin*, and François Gos at Zermatt in c1920. *(Émile Gos/ famille Gos/Émile Gos)*

to Geneva, making a living with illustration, sculpture and writing, as well as painting. Travel posters were a forte. In 1913, he helped to start up an art school in Lausanne. Like his father, he showed a predilection for the mountain world, both as a climber and a painter.

Charles Gos, after studying in Lausanne and Paris, established himself as an author and journalist, focusing on military affairs and alpinism – mostly the latter in his short stories and novels: *Pres des névès et des glaciers* (1912), *La Croix du Cervin* (1919), *Propos d'un alpiniste* (1922), *Alpinisme anecdotique* (1934), and *Solitude montagnarde* (1943). Several of his books were translated into English, including *Song of the High Hills*, a novel that uses the mountains above Zermatt as the backdrop for a love triangle. Again, the plot is resolved by a fatal accident. In 1918, Gos married Edmée de Coulon, who died in 1930. In 1934, he took over the management of the mountain books department at the Victor Attinger publishing house in Neuchâtel. He remarried in 1947, and a son was born two years later.

Left: Charles Gos (1885-1949), alpinist and author.
(*Émile Gos*)
Above: 'La cabane du Mountet', by Albert Gos.[2]

Left: The photographer Émile Gos
was Albert's youngest son. His film
La Croix du Cervin was from a
script written by his brother Charles.
His interest in dance, theatre and
portraiture shows in the energy he
brought to his climbing photography.
Above: 'Mont Cervin avec la Riffelsee',
by Albert Gos.[3]

The Gos brothers climbed at a high standard, often without guides. Indeed, Charles Gos led the first guideless ascent of the Matterhorn's Zmutt ridge. He knew everybody in the world of alpinism, from the local guides to the prominent climbers who visited the Alps from abroad. He was elected a member of the Alpine Club in 1935, and once secured a half-hour audience with the 'climbing pope', Pius XI, this without the benefit of a Catholic upbringing – the Gos family came from a sternly Protestant background.

2. 'La cabane du Mountet', A Gos, 1876, Club Alpine Suisse.
3. 'Mont Cervin avec la Riffelsee', A Gos, 35.9cm x 47.4cm, oil on canvas, 1875, Musée d'art du Valais, Sion.

Charles Gos at his desk. An Anglophile and honorary member of the Alpine Club, he was between the wars a crucial source of information for the *Alpine Journal.* After his premature death, Geoffrey Winthrop Young wrote: 'I don't know anyone in the world of whom it can be said more truthfully that the mountains are his refuge, his hope, his inspiration and even the breath of his everyday life.'

For his part, the youngest son, Emile Gos, completed an apprenticeship as a photographer in Montreux, in the workshop of Rodolphe Schlemmer (1878-1972). He continued his training in German-speaking Switzerland, in Paris, Munich and London before moving back to Clarens and later starting his own studio in Lausanne. In 1939, he married Claire André, who gave him two children. Making a living with studio portraits and newspaper photography, he left a more durable legacy in landscape and mountain photography, sampled in the exhibition by a compelling slide show of his masterly medium-format images.

In 1922, he filmed his brother Charles's short story about the Matterhorn cross *(La Croix du Cervin).* This was one of the first films to be shot in the high mountains, predating Arnold Fanck and G W Pabst's *The White Hell of Piz Palü* by more than half a decade. Alas, only fragments of the original footage have survived.

Writing in the exhibition brochure, the art historian Maéva Besse points out that, in their day, the Gos family was by no means unique in passing the torch of mountain culture from father to son. On their own doorstep, there were the Töpffers and the van Muydens of Geneva, whose artistic productions spanned two generations. And, over in Chamonix, the Tairraz and Gay-Couttet clans presided for even longer in the world of mountain photo-

'Sommets dans le Brouillard', by François Gos (1880-1975).[4]

graphy. Even so, the golden age of the mountain artist may have ended with
the First World War. From the biographical sketches given in the exhibition
brochure, one surmises that François and Emile Gos had to scrabble harder
than their father to eke out a living from mountain art.

As for Charles, his fiction dwells frequently on human fallibility and the
dark side of mountaineering, even while recreating the glittering social and
alpinistic scenes of the Belle Époque. And one non-fiction work concerns
itself entirely with mountain accidents. This might signify no more than a
saturnine streak in the author's personality, burdened as he was by a long
and ultimately fatal illness. Or was he oppressed by a sense that the civilisation he grew up in, and its genial ways of living, were sliding into the abyss,
never to be retrieved?

References
'Les Gos: une montagne en héritage', Médiathèque Valais, Martigny.
'La famille Gos: une famille d'artistes', the website of the Gos family, is at
famille-gos.ch.

---

4. 'Sommets dans le Brouillard', F Gos, 78.5cm x 117cm, oil on canvas, before 1914, Musée cantonal des
Beaux-arts de Lausanne.

ALF BONNEVIE BRYN

George Finch and the
Leaning Tower of Pisa

Street-fighting man. George Finch on Everest in 1922.

In 1909, two young students headed for Corsica with dreams of becoming exploratory mountaineers. One of them was a pugnacious Australian, the future Everest climber George Finch. The other was Alf Bryn, a Norwegian who would make first ascents back home, help form the Norsk Tindeklub, become an engineer and write crime fiction. More than 30 years after their trip, he also published a much-loved account of his adventure with Finch, now published in English for the first time as **Peaks and Bandits***. Even before they set foot in Corsica, George Finch was on dangerous ground, as he scrapped in Genoa and went climbing on the Leaning Tower of Pisa.*

The only annoying thing that happened at the pub, where we ate macaroni and drank wine, was that the waiter refused to accept our counterfeit money. It did not help to insist that we had had it exchanged at the railroad station – we had to pay with real money.

The main street was still lit up when we came out of the pub. It was a little past midnight and George now had to study the nightlife in the port area to find where he thought there was the best chance of some entertainment.

Personally I have always been against throwing myself unnecessarily into warlike involvments. Mostly my attitude toward war is the same as that of Johan Herman Wessel, who so beautifully expressed his sentiment in his poem about Saint Sebastian:

I love Peace
And think War is always Wretched
Perhaps I would think War more lovely
Were I as brave as I am honest.

After wandering around a little we found a cellar pub just above the main street that separated the port area from the rest of the town. There we joined the company of some quite shabby persons of dubious nationality who were playing billiards for money.

We did not succeed in finding a common language. The billiard players gave the impression of knowing four or five different ones from the eastern Mediterranean, but it was not possible to reach any closer contact than Italian. George and I were relegated to a small phrasebook, published by Baedeker, in which it was never possible to find anything resembling what we really wanted to say.

When you play billiards for money and want to know what the wager is, it won't do to ask, *'Wie viel kostet das Zimmer? Qanto costa questa camera?* (How much is the room?)' We wouldn't understand the response anyway and could hardly answer according to the book: *'E troppo cara; mostramo una meno camera.* (That is too expensive, show me a smaller room.)'

It was somewhat of a miracle that we nevertheless solved the situation and managed to start some sort of gamble involving billiards.

The game was played with a large number of balls and a dish of money in the middle of the billiard table. Every time a player turned the dish over, the others shared the money. Here, George thought, was an opportunity to use the fake silver coins we had brought with us. He figured that even if we lost about twice as much as we won, this would still be a winning proposition. There was not much light in the cellar and his speculation seemed therefore to be of sound foundation.

We did well for a while. True, we did lose some of the large silver coins

Alf Bonnevie Bryn, engineer, writer and martial artist.

we had brought, but on the other hand got quite a few others back and saw to it that we got smaller coins that we knew were more valuable. Apparently no one took particular notice of the kind of money they were winning from us but it was clear that in the long run, this could not continue. I finally succeeded in convincing George to end the game while the going was still good. We quietly snuck out of the place while our rivals were busy in an animated discussion about some technical detail of the play.

It was a little past two when we came into the street again and the town seemed deserted. I suggested that we go back to the station and wait for our train and George was at first inclined to agree to this reasonable suggestion, although he was very disappointed in what Genoa nightlife had to offer in terms of excitement.

He was wrong about the nightlife. When we were about 300ft away from the pub, three of our earlier friends from the billiards game came into the street, very agitated and gesticulating. There was no mistaking their wish to join us again.

Under these circumstances I found it even more natural to get back to the station by the shortest possible route. It was probably related to my guilty conscience about the distribution of counterfeit money. But George was of the opposite opinion: here he finally saw an opportunity to experience something.

From the main street where we now found ourselves, a number of small, narrow alleys went down toward the port area. Most of them started with a few steps down from the street's southern pavement. George thought this was the right terrain.

I was in a difficult situation. It wasn't easy to know what was the riskiest – to separate from George or to follow him. I chose the latter and we went down one of the stairs toward the port alleys.

Not far behind us came the three billiard players. Two were big, one was small.

'It is clear,' I said to George, 'that they have not come to bid us a fond farewell.'

George was also aware of this. He looked brightly to the future.

'Well,' he said, 'if we're going to have a fight with three people down here – people who are well known in the area and probably use knives –

it is just as well that we start things. The element of surprise is not to be underestimated.'

We went to the right at the nearest street corner and waited. Right by the corner stood a dirty gaslight that barely illuminated the closest few feet around it. Our battle plan, according to my suggestion, was that George would take on the two big ones and I the small one. George thought this was fine.

As far as the element of surprise was concerned, I am sure it was present. When the three of them showed up around the corner, the first one (one of the big ones) received, without a trace of prior debate, a solid uppercut from George, while I, who lately had tried to specialise in jiu-jitsu, started in on the small one.

Someone who is completely unprepared and who has no idea of jiu-jitsu does not have a chance against a sudden attack when it is executed with sufficient brutality, and my opponent (if one could call him that, for he made no opposition) was lying in the street within a few seconds, where I too found myself due to my clumsiness, as I stumbled over him when he fell. Unlike him, I had not hit the back of my head on the cobblestones, and I got back on my feet quite quickly. My opponent – or rather my victim – was lying completely still.

When I looked to see what George was up to, I saw that he had grabbed the gaslight with his left hand and the second of the billiard players by the hair with his right hand. At short intervals he was banging the back of the man's head against the gas light.

After each bang, the billiard player sank down a little and gradually went to a sitting and then to a prone position.

The first one that George had become acquainted with had by then regained his feet. For a moment he looked at the remains of his two friends and then quickly resorted to flight-like retreat. The two remaining ones stayed completely still. It was what one might characterise as an annihilating battle.

'Now,' I said to George, 'I think it would be best if we follow my original suggestion and find the station as quickly as possible. First of all, we can count on the third guy soon being back with reinforcements, and second, I think it looks bad for those who are lying here. God only knows if they'll revive!'

For once George agreed, and after stumbling around a little in the now-empty port area, we finally found our way back to the main street and reached the station half an hour before our train was to leave.

I think it was a relief even for George when we finally had put Genoa behind us and were being jostled toward Pisa, where we once again would change trains to reach the port of Livorno.

Just before we reached Pisa, George, who was sitting opposite me, woke up. 'Bryn,' he said, 'it was noble of you to let me have the two big ones. I'll never forget that.'

'My dear,' I said, 'don't mention it.'

*

Pisa, which we reached in the morning, is generally known for its leaning tower, and among people who pretend to have a classical or scientific education, the tower is also known for Galileo Galilei's dealings with it. As we know, Galilei allegedly used the leaning tower to construct one of his many heretical theories, the one about bodies of different masses falling at equal speed in a vacuum.

We had a few hours to wait for our train to Livorno and set out in full gear into town and the big Piazza del Duomo, where the Campanile and other points of interest reside. The plan was basically to go straight up into the tower in a normal way and look at the view but the tower was closed; the guard who demanded one lira from tourists to let them in did not arrive until ten o'clock.

This was, in reality, a stroke of luck. Already at this point in time, the horrible practice had been instituted of gathering up a suitable group of innocent tourists and hauling them around through such historical monuments with a so-called guide, who in a hectoring manner rattles off a memorised lecture that has something to do with the monument, but never about something one has an interest in currently. I have on various later occasions been exposed to this curse on the travelling public, this curse for which even the Inquisition's most crafty torture would be altogether too mild a punishment.

It is obvious that these tour guides are driven by a malignant form of sadism. Not even promises of an increased honorarium can make them keep quiet about the chair which seated such and such a king or queen on some long-forgotten, insignificant occasion.

Only once have I seen a guide of this kind got rid of. It was a wonderful experience. With some French friends I was visiting a French castle, known for its old tapestries. We had successfully escaped from the flock of guided sheep and were having a nice, quiet time. But then we were discovered and the guide, who probably thought we had escaped too lightly, threw himself on us with a recitation about the history of the tapestry factory.

My French host, a distinguished, older gentleman, looked seriously at the guide and said: '*Désistez, cher monsieur, je vous en supplie, je suis sourd et en outre je ne comprends pas un mot de votre langue.* (Desist, dear sir, I am deaf and furthermore I do not understand a word of your language.)'

The guide shook his head and thereafter followed us at a polite distance. His conviction that we were dangerous and strange was not diminished by the fact that he was given an extra tip when we parted ways.

However, this was not what preoccupied me and George – George especially. George thought this was an opportune moment to climb the north face of the leaning tower, the least steep side.

I was doubtful about this enterprise, mostly because I thought it might disturb the local Pisans' patriotic sentiments and bring us into unwanted conflict with enforcers of the law. But George is not the kind who lets such petty concerns put a brake on his desire to act. He organised a camp on the north end of Piazza del Duomo, took off his hobnail boots, put on tennis shoes and attacked the leaning tower. He brought with him only an ice axe, which the study of the tower's façade had shown to be necessary.

I stayed in camp. I told George it was in order to guard our equipment, but my thought was also toward the expedition's future, and how it would be beneficial for both its members not to be arrested at the same time.

Scaling the leaning tower is fundamentally different from scaling a normal house wall. The tower is constructed of a number of circular balconies with richly sculpted railing and thick, smooth marble columns, which, along with the railing, form the outer

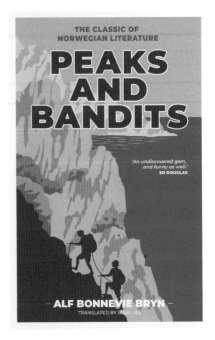

facade. The columns are too thick to be used as climbing poles, and the distance from the upper edge of the railing to the frieze on the underside of the next one is too great to be within the reach of the hands of even a tall man.

This was where the ice axe was useful.

When George stood on a railing close to a column he could get the tip of the ice axe into an opening in the railing of the balcony above. Squeezing his legs around the column and getting a hold on the ice axe with his right hand, he managed to scoot up until he had a hold with both hands and could lift himself up. It was quite a nice accomplishment.

So thought many members of Pisa's young male population who, far from being angry over the assault on the cultural monument, encouraged George with increasingly fiery shouts.

That's how it went all the way to the fourth floor. But then came what I had feared – the enforcers of the law. At first they also took it nicely and were satisfied to be part of the interested audience. But then some citizen or other must have alerted them to the fact that something was happening that ran counter to morals and the public order. They walked over to the foot of the tower and started to holler in an unmistakable fashion.

George also must have heard the false note that had mingled with the encouraging shouts, for he turned and looked down before he was about to start on the next landing. The two constables shouted many things at him, probably a reasonable choice of abusive words that constables in Italy employ toward miscreants caught red-handed, but this did not help in the case of George, whose knowledge of the Italian language was severely limited.

George did understand that he needed tools to help him out, so he pulled a phrasebook out of his pocket as he straddled the railing. After a short period of study he found something he obviously thought would suit the situation and addressed the officers of the law: *'Sono per la prima volta in Italia.* (This is my first time in Italy.)' And then: *'Viaggio per ristabilirmi.* (I am travelling for my health.)'

That clearly must have convinced the officers of the law, as well as the public, that he was crazy, something that from their point of view was not so difficult to explain, and the discussion died down. Satisfied with the results of his linguistic exercise, George started up to the fifth level, which he reached accompanied by an almost admiring public mumble.

There is every reason to believe that he would have reached the top and thereby have accomplished the ascent of the leaning tower from the north, had not the tower guard shown up in the meantime.

His view of George's endeavour was strictly mathematical. He regarded it as a cowardly attempt to avoid the entry fee, and along with the two constables he reached the fifth floor just as George was about to continue. The trip came to an end and George had to pay one lira, as if he were just an ordinary visitor.

Another 12 to 15 years would go by before the climbing of walls and tower facades became not just a very popular but also highly paid sport.

• *Peaks and Bandits* by Alf Bonnevie Bryn, translated by Bibbi Lee, is published by Vertebrate.

NICHOLAS HURNDALL SMITH
Sir Leslie and Me

Leslie Stephen (1832-1904), right, with his Swiss mountain guide and lifelong friend Melchior Anderegg (1828-1912), in c1870. (Alpine Club Photo Library)

Fleetest of foot of the whole Alpine brotherhood.[1]

I have just walked 25 miles to visit a simple grave, tucked away on the edge of Highgate Cemetery. I hope Sir Leslie Stephen is pleased. For him, 'even in London, walking has a peculiar fascination.'[2] He would, at a steady pace of four miles per hour, have polished off that sort of distance with ease and delight, most likely, as his daughter Virginia Woolf put it, 'without speaking more than a word or two to his companion.'[3] Between long walks, the Covid-19 pandemic has found me immersed in the writings and doings

---

1. E Whymper, *Scrambles amongst the Alps.*
2. L Stephen, 'In Praise of Walking', *Studies of a Biographer,* vol 3, 1902.
3. *The Times,* 28 Nov 1932

View towards Liskamm from the summit of the Rimpfischhorn (4199m).
(Nigel Bassam)

of 'L Stephen', a name I first saw in 2003 in Lindsay Griffin's Alpine Club guidebook *Bernina and Bregaglia.* Since then, it seems, Sir Leslie has followed me around. Or rather, it is I who has been following him.

I was introduced to alpinism in my early thirties by a fellow tenor, whom I met whilst studying singing at London's Guildhall School of Music and Drama. Christoph Wittmann had been in the elite Alpine section of the German army for his national service, and was the perfect person to open the door to steep terrain that I had always avoided until then, despite numerous trips into the mountains. After a concert in Lucerne in late summer 2002, we drove to the Bernese Oberland, and took *that* train up to the Jungfraujoch. On my first two days in a harness and crampons, holding an axe I did not know how to use, we climbed the Mönch and Jungfrau in fresh snow. Terrified by the exposure, especially in descent, I was also exhilarated, and on my return to London, attended a beginners' course at the Castle Climbing Centre.

Soon I found it difficult to slake my thirst for this new adventure. I decided to climb with a guide next, an Italian, Nadia Tiraboschi, another formative climbing relationship. Nadia was on the Italian expedition to K2 celebrating the fiftieth anniversary of the first ascent, achieving national fame by rescuing a snow-blind team member in trouble high on that notorious mountain. The year before, in 2003, we climbed the Biancograt, the most famous and beautiful snow ridge in the Alps. Standing on the Piz Bernina, I spied to the

Nick Hurndall Smith, Jean-Baptiste Chavanne and Bertrand Donninger enjoy a victory rösti at the Hörnli hut. *(Dave Dixon)*

south-west the towering bulk of Monte Disgrazia, first climbed in 1862 by Sir Leslie Stephen. And that's how I became hooked.

Sir Leslie Stephen: pioneering alpinist of the Golden Age and great literary figure, first editor of the *Dictionary of National Biography* and father to Virginia Woolf and Vanessa Bell. In 1865 he became the fourth president of the Alpine Club, a difficult year for the mountaineering world. I was quick to notice that his beard, at its fullest, matched his taste for mountains. His most significant ascents are all magnificent beasts:

1858	**Wildstrubel**
1859	**Bietschhorn**
	Rimpfischhorn
1860	**Alphubel**
	Blümlisalphorn
	Oberaarhorn
1861	**Schreckhorn**
1862	**Monte Disgrazia**
1864	**Zinalrothorn**
	Liskamm West
1871	**Mont Mallet**

Of his ten or so notable first ascents in the Alps, I have now climbed four, and attempted two more. So this is a story of unfinished business.

Left: Melchior Anderegg, Leslie Stephen and Douglas William Freshfield. Stephen's stance echoes the contemporary view of him walking 'from peak to peak like a pair of one-inch compasses over a large-sized map'. *(Alpine Club Photo Library)*

Below: Nick Hurndall Smith and Bertrand Donninger at the summit of the Zinalrothorn, the Dent Blanche behind.

In 2004, while Nadia was on K2, I went back to the Bregaglia, alone, and hatched a plan to attempt Monte Disgrazia with her the following year. But the 2005 weather was against us and we did not even leave the hut. Instead, we drove down towards Bergamo, and went climbing on the Pizzo della Presolana. Struggling to follow Nadia on its steep limestone, I realised that my climbing was not up to much. An eager guide, close beneath me on the Biancograt the year before, had been keen to point out more than once what beautiful boots I had. I got the message: they needed more wear and tear, and the *Corda Molla,* Disgrazia's north ridge would have to wait.

By 2011, I had widened my climbing experience and acquaintance, to which I had added a crack group of French friends. An ascent of the Old

Leslie Stephen with his
wife Julia at Grindelwald.
(Alpine Club Photo Library)

Man of Hoy with Bertrand Donninger cemented this new *entente cordiale,* and we met up with a larger group in Verdon later in the year. Staying at a climbers' *gîte,* we met a group of British climbers, some from the Alpine Club. 'You *must* join the Alpine Club,' Richard Nadin, the Alpine Club's membership secretary said to me, as we parted after a pleasant few days.

My French team decided to go climbing in Tafraout the following January, where we climbed the 800m *Great Ridge* of Assagour, the Lion's Face. Plans after that slowly began to focus back on the Alps, and first on the list of objectives was Monte Disgrazia, this time with Bertrand. In June 2012, I had a concert in Florence, before which I practised my rope work, hauling my colleague Chris up the staircase of the monastery we were staying in. I then took the train to Como and Bertrand drove over from Lausanne. In a portent of things to come, he announced he had a slight problem and wanted my help. Before we could go climbing, I was tasked with removing the remains of a tick, which he had partially scratched off, lodged beside one of his testicles. I forget which one. Then we drove to Chiareggio, and set off uphill feeling fit and ready. And tick-less.

At the Rifugio Porro, the guardian warned us of heavy snow on the ridge but we were not to be deterred. As we walked up, plaques periodically recorded how much the glacier had receded since Sir Leslie's day. Progress came to a welcome halt when we met three physiotherapists from Pavia who invited us to join their charming picnic. We took our leave reluctantly, and roped up on the Ventina glacier. Plodding steadily on, we eventually spotted the Taveggia bivouac high above and, after a short rock climb, reached the tiny hut at 2,850m. Bertrand promptly banged his head badly on the doorframe but we agreed this was the perfect place to rest our heads and we gathered snow to melt. Then our lighter failed. We took it apart and put it back together, trying everything to coax a flame out of it. I decided I would continue to trigger it for an hour. After 40 minutes, it finally lit. We rejoiced, prepared dinner, and lay there admiring views of the Bernina before bed.

Sunday dawned and setting off we saw 21 people in a number of parties snaking up the glacier below, heading for different routes. After a steep

The author enjoying the airy east ridge of Liskamm (4527m). *(Paul Winder)*

traverse, which showed signs of a recent avalanche, we headed further up the glacier in deepening snow. We passed the Oggioni bivouac at 3,151m, heading towards the north ridge, with the snow now waist-deep. We could now see just one other party of two, who had slept at the Oggioni approaching the bergschrund below Disgrazia's north face. Lindsay's guidebook describes our target, the *Corda Molla*, as 'a brilliant mixed route of a quality equal to any other of its standard in the Alps', and grades it at AD+. With this amount of unstable snow however, the approach alone was a challenge. We could not help wondering if the north face would have been a better option, had we had two axes with us. Matters did not improve even when we reached the ridge, as we swam on through the wet snow, finding it difficult to stay on the heavily laden crest.

We stopped 300m short of the summit. I later read, in the very first article in the first volume of the *Alpine Journal* of 1863, that Sir Leslie also did not reach the summit on his first attempt, with his 'trusty Oberland guide', Melchior Anderegg, Edward Shirley Kennedy and Thomas Cox, 'an English servant'. In an attempt to by-pass a buttress, I made a belay and Bertrand traversed around a corner. To regain the ridge, out of sight, he started up an easy crack and was struck by a falling rock. He fell and flipped upside down, with his boot jammed in the crack. Hanging from this, he levered himself upright and climbed back to the crest, unaware of how heavily he was bleeding from his calf. I followed on the unstable snow traverse and

In the centre is the Zinalrothorn (4221m), seen from the Rotgrat on Alphubel, with climbers Nigel Buckley and Nick Simons. *(Nicholas Hurndall Smith)*

retrieved his axe, where it had come to rest perched above an abyss after falling from his shoulder. Only then did I see the blood on the rocks, and realised that all was not well. I reached Bertrand, and his blood-soaked socks and pale expression confirmed my fears. Thankful for a telephone signal, I called for rescue since we were 'approaching the congealed and uncomfortable state of human icicles', just as Sir Leslie's party had during their aborted attempt.[4]

After an hour, a helicopter appeared through the swirling cloud and dropped a guide onto the ridge. Bertrand was assessed, whisked away and the deep cut successfully sewn up again in hospital. As I waited for the helicopter to return, glum and alone on the inescapable ridge, with clouds threatening to descend further, the party of two, who had climbed the north face, passed below on the upper Ventina glacier, no doubt wondering what drama was unfolding above them.

From kneeling in front of an embedded tick and coping with the faulty lighter and snowy conditions, to our eventual rescue, the tide seemed always against us, and with the guardian's words of warning in my mind, I tried my best to learn from this experience. In 1862, Sir Leslie, having turned back from the summit, must have watched in horror as the president of the Alpine Club, E S Kennedy,

---

4. E Kennedy, 'The Ascent of Monte della Disgrazia', *Alpine Journal*, March 1863, p7.

... dashed down the smooth and slippery course that the two others had formed. Stephen and Cox averted their gaze as a fellow creature rushed wildly past, but, unable to check him in his headlong plunge, they were almost instantly carried off their legs and hurled into the depths below. Entangled with the rope, and twisted, and tossed, and rolled over in every conceivable way, we were carried ... about 90 feet down the ice-slope, shooting in our course the bergschrund, across and over which we fell vertically some 20 feet through the air. A short distance below this bergschrund the human avalanche was arrested in the soft snow-bed that we had descried from above. Spectacles, and veils, and hats are scattered in every direction: cigars are destroyed, and pipes broken, and pockets, and shirts, and clothes, and ears, and noses, and mouths are filled with snow.[5]

In fact, the party was undeterred by this mishap, and regarded it as 'a most fortunate occurrence, for it was the means of saving much valuable time, and was not destitute of enjoyment, inasmuch, as it afforded us a new sensation ... Picking up ourselves and our property, we went on our way rejoicing.'

They successfully made the first ascent a few days later and 'a shout of exultation burst from all.' I felt more hesitant. Disgrazia, which translates as 'misfortune' or 'disgrace', would have to wait for our next attempt. Bertrand went out climbing the following weekend, but this was one of three small accidents he had in the run up to our attempt on the Matterhorn. Each one he shrugged off with charming Gallic nonchalance. But, reminiscent of Sir Leslie's tribute to his great friend the French artist Gabriel Loppé, the episode 'confirmed both our friendship and our common worship of the mountains.'[6]

Our Matterhorn attempt that year had a special significance. On the return from our trip to Tafraout, Jean-Baptiste Chavanne had learned that in our absence his mother had died of a form of blood cancer. I made the decision to climb for the charity Lymphoma and Leukaemia Research in her memory.[7] Fresh from a big performance in the BBC Proms at the Albert Hall, I arrived in Chamonix hoping for a few easy days of acclimatisation, but we spied a weather window and decided to go for it immediately. The result was that we had perfect conditions but it was a gruelling physical challenge. The generous donations, which kept coming in the lead up to the climb, added extra pressure, but made the taste of success all the sweeter. Having climbed the Lion ridge in Italy and down the Hörnli into Switzerland, we celebrated with a delicious rösti at the hut. From there, we walked back over the col into Italy, which allowed us to marvel at the pointed silhouette of the Toblerone mountain. It was a proud achievement to raise £10,000 to tackle blood cancer.

The 1865 disaster during the first descent of the Matterhorn, with four

5. Ibid, p3.
6. G Loppé was the first French member of the AC. L Stephen, *The Playground of Europe*, 1894.
7. Now called Blood Cancer UK.

members of Whymper's party falling to their deaths, had a huge impact on Leslie Stephen. This was the year he became president of the Alpine Club. He climbed less, and devoted himself more to his work. Alpine climbing went through a rocky patch. *The Times* called it 'wrong'. He helped, to some extent, to ease its recovery. Geoffrey Winthrop Young mentions this in his introduction to the re-issue of *The Playground of Europe,* and relates how, whilst he was an undergraduate, the young climber shared his enthusiasm with the older mountaineer.

> *For some five enthralling minutes I was listening to a memorable recall of incident and sensation on the glaciers before dawn, on the occasion of the famous first ascent of the Rothhorn.*

I would love to have had a similar chance to talk to Sir Leslie. On our descent from the Hörnli hut, as the angle and the headache eased, we spotted the Zinalrothorn, which looks improbable from this angle. Its leaning knife-edge arête seemed to call to me, and we immediately chose it as a future project. I was beginning to like this form of mountaineering, where you climb a mountain, spot another one, and then go for that. In the summer of 2013, I waited for Bertrand, who arrived in Zinal a day later than expected. Sir Leslie and his companions, like true Brits abroad, played cricket in the High Street as they waited for the weather to oblige before their first ascent,

> *... with a rail for a bat and a small granite boulder for a ball. My first performance was a brilliant hit to leg (the only one I ever made in my life) off Macdonald's bowling. To my horror, I sent the ball clean through the western window of the chapel, which looks upon the grande place of the village, the scene of our match. As no-one ever could be found to receive damages, I doubt much whether there are any permanent inhabitants.*

Bertrand and I made a 15-hour traverse, climbing the Rothorngrat and then down the airy north ridge, with its famous fin of rock known as the *rasoir.* This was the route Sir Leslie had first climbed almost 149 years ago to the day. We incurred the wrath of the Grand Mountet hut's grumpy guardian by arriving back late for dinner, slowed by rotten snow, but content. Sir Leslie wrote,

> *Here we stretched ourselves luxuriously on the soft green moss in the afternoon sun. We emptied the last drops of the wine bag, lighted the pipe of peace – the first that day – and enjoyed the well-earned climbers' reward. I have seldom known a happier half hour than that in which I busked on the mossy turf in the shadow of the conquered Rothorn – all my internal sensations of present comfort, of hard-won victory, and of lovely scenery, delicately harmonised by the hallowing influence of tobacco.[8]*

8. L Stephen, 'The Rothorn', *The Playground of Europe,* Longmans, 1871.

He and his companions, like me, were busy spotting more peaks to climb, contemplating a first ascent of the Grand Cornier.

In 2014 I finally became an aspirant member of the Alpine Club, and it was only then that I really began to appreciate the legacy of Leslie Stephen. And it seemed by chance that I kept revisiting, or attempting to revisit 'his' peaks. The Bietschhorn is another that caught my eye, from the Saas valley. Paul Winder and I set off that July to attempt a traverse, which was becoming my preferred method of climbing mountains. The walk-in to the Baltschiederklause from the Rhône valley is spectacular, and follows a series of watercourses flowing along overhanging terraces. From there we planned to attempt the north ridge and descend the west ridge to the Lötschental.

We spent a day acclimatising at the hut and brushing up on our rescue skills for the glacier. Conditions felt warm and unsettled. We set off next morning, and found that other parties were headed for less demanding objectives. All was going well, until the snow on the shoulder leading to Point 3706m became increasingly unstable, with no apparent desire to stay attached to the mountain. Snow started to slough downhill in small waves in spite of our careful steps. We sat down on the ridge for a rest, admitted defeat and contemplated our descent. Sir Leslie, on the Bietschhorn, wrote:

> *The descent was only varied by one incident. My legs having developed more decidedly erratic propensities ended by deserting their proper sphere of duty altogether, during a race down the rocks. I consequently found myself sliding at railway pace, on my back, over a mixture of ice and stones, and was much gratified on being stopped by an unusually long and pointed rock which ran through my trousers in to my thigh, and brought me up with a jerk.[9]*

On our return to the hut, the guardian shouted at me, unhappy that we had taken so long and put ourselves in danger by having a breather in the warm conditions. But no tumbles thankfully.

Next day we decided to traverse all the way around the mountain to the Bietschhorn hut and attempt instead the west ridge, which is predominantly rock. The route from hut to hut crosses steep ground, a fine expedition in itself, and once I did slide down a snow gully, glad that my ice axe was poised to arrest my fall. At the hut a friendlier guardian welcomed us in and we ate with her and her partner. After a few hours sleep, we left the hut at 2am and scrambled up steep icy rock leading to the Bietschjoch and the glacier beyond. Here it became clear that our ridge was plastered in fresh snow and we decided to call a halt there and then. Paul displayed his well-known skills and curled up on a rock for a catnap. As the sun rose, melting the verglas nicely for our retreat, the pinks, reds and blues of the Alpine sunrise intensified above the Valais peaks, a special moment for every alpinist.

After a restorative beer in the hut, we descended to a hostelry in Ried. In the visitors' book we found Sir Leslie's handwritten entry from the 1850s.

---

9. L Stephen, 'The First Ascent of the Bietschhorn', *The Playground of Europe*, Longmans, 1871.

Awaiting rescue, Bertrand Donninger
nursing his wounds high on Monte
Disgrazia's *Corda Molla*.
(Nicholas Hurndall Smith)

In seven days, we had enjoyed ourselves enormously, but not reached
a single summit. We curbed our dis-
appointment with a memorable traverse of Skye's Cuillin Ridge a couple
of months later.

In April 2015, I was diagnosed
with type-1 diabetes. My life would
change, according to most health
care professionals I met. Every day I
performed a new experiment on my
body, to learn how to combine exer-
cise and insulin. Two months later, I ran my fastest half marathon (aided
by the weight I had lost prior to diagnosis) and I headed back to the Alps
that summer, to attend the Alpine Club aspirant meet in Saas Grund. But
I felt like a beginner again, with the new challenges of managing my blood
sugar to overcome. On my first outing, I ate all the sweets I had with me
even before arriving at the hut. The guardian kindly supplied me with a bag
of sugar lumps. After a few more warm-up routes, which went well, my
partner Tim Pearson and I climbed the Hohlaubgrat on the Allalinhorn,
descending via the normal route, which is Sir Leslie's. We then decided to
attempt the Täschhorn.

The logical way to approach this from Saas was via the Alphubel, another
of Sir Leslie's first ascents. On the south-east ridge, there is an ice nose, and
there I suffered a severe moment of hypoglycaemia. I placed an ice screw,
let Tim take over the lead, and gingerly followed him to the summit, feeling
shaky and out of sorts. The descent down the north ridge felt like a nightmare, my confidence in tatters. Safely down at the Mischabeljoch bivouac
hut, I cried. It seemed climbing as a type-1 diabetic, reliant on multiple daily
injections of insulin, would indeed be different. Next day, having decided
to abandon our Täschhorn attempt, I argued with Tim and our partnership
broke on the route down.

Now a full member of the Alpine Club, I was determined not to be swayed
by these setbacks. In 2016 I headed out to Monte Rosa with Paul. We had
a plan to work our way across all the main peaks, staying in the well-placed
huts straddling the Swiss Italian border. I quickly realised why the tradition
al direction of travel for this is west to east, as the Breithorn (4164m) makes
a sensible first peak rather than the Dufourspitze, which is almost 500m
higher. After a day acclimatising at the Swiss Monte Rosa hut, we turned
back due to the affects of altitude and decided to miss out our first two
objectives, and head straight up the Grenzgletscher to the Signalkuppe on

Monte Disgrazia from the north-east. *Corda Molla* is the ridge on the left. Two climbers are approaching the bergschrund below the north face. (*Nicholas Hurndall Smith*)

the following day. The highest building in Europe sits on its summit at 4,554m. With pounding heads, we ate what we could from the superb Italian menu and with some relief continued down to the Gnifetti hut. Good early season snow conditions meant that I could take in the classic traverse of the tops, whereas Paul, nursing a migraine, chose to descend next day down a nearby cable car for a day in town, to return refreshed in the evening.

I made a lazy start and climbed the Piramide Vincent again, this time via its south-west ridge, and headed to the foot of Liskamm, which was very much at the top of our list of goals. Conditions on the glacier were excellent, and feeling confident I decided to recce the east ridge. I made my way slowly along the snow arête, being careful to avoid its notorious cornices, and before I knew it I was on the summit. Soloing this felt like a new chapter in my alpine career.

Back in the hut, Paul and I made plans to traverse the same peak from east to west the next day. A rope did not seem much use on the climb, and I was brimming with confidence again, on one of the most attractive mountains in the Alps, which has an almost Himalayan feel. On the descent of the south-west ridge, first climbed by Sir Leslie in 1864, there was a steep icy section where a rope and an ice screw might have eased the nerves, but soloing with a friend is one of my favourite activities and this turned out to be one of the best days out I have had: one to remember. Dodging some mixed weather over the next two days, we then tackled Castor and Pollux from the Quintino Sella hut and returned to London, content and full of pasta and genepi.

I climbed three more 4,000m peaks that summer, with my diabetes becoming easier to manage. I learned more about how to monitor and control my blood-sugar levels on a trip with another type-1 diabetic mountaineer with an insulin pump, which I now have too. In 2017 I took over the organisation of Alpine Club's aspirant meet, giving me the opportunity to focus on the peaks in the Saas area. The next of Sir Leslie's peaks, the Rimpfisch-horn, beckoned.

The glacial terrain on the traverse to and from this peak is magnificent, and required careful navigation after recent fresh snow. Nigel Bassam was now becoming my most regular climbing companion, and this trip cement-ed our partnership. E S Kennedy once described Sir Leslie as 'as a man more ready to assist than to impede in any difficulty'.[10] The same can be said of Nigel, who on that final ascent, when I felt intimidated by the exposure, confidently took over, leading us above the cloud to the chilly summit cross at 4,199m. In 1859, from this point, Sir Leslie would surely have looked across to Liskamm, and resolved to be the first to traverse its four-kilometre snow crest, which he did five years later.

What a pleasure it is to tread the boards of Sir Leslie Stephen's Alpine stage. We still have plenty to tackle. Unfinished business will doubtless lead me back to Disgrazia. The Schreckhorn, another mountain whose name and aspect inspires awe, also beckons, hopefully with a bivouac and traverse of the Lauteraarhorn, if fitness allows. Perhaps we will plan on 'taking a drop of brandy all round' as Sir Leslie did, to help pass the tricky step en-countered on the ridge between the two summits.

Once, he is reputed to have walked the 50 miles from Cambridge to Lon-don in 12 hours for an Alpine Club dinner. A fit man he most certainly was, at least in his prime, and one with an impeccable eye for awe-inspiring mountains demanding to be climbed. He once described the Weisshorn's pyramid as 'one of the most exquisitely beautiful objects in the Alps'[11], albeit one that took Paul and I nearly 20 lonely hours to traverse in 2018.[12] We had the entire mountain to ourselves as we battled deep snow, condi-tions that were far from ideal. But it is this cocktail of beauty, adrenaline and solitude that more than anything draws us back again and again, mind-ful of and inspired by our predecessors, to enjoy the greatest of Alpine pleasures. Leslie Stephen made the second ascent of the Weisshorn. For him it was not just about being the first to the top, it was the aesthetic pleas-ure and physical challenge that he loved.

Virginia Woolf wrote, on the centenary of her father's birth, of his im-mense charm[13], and it shines through in Leslie Stephen's writing as well:

It is pleasant to lie on one's back in a bed of rhododendrons, and look up to a mountain top peering at one from above a bank of cloud; but it is pleasantest when one has qualified oneself for repose by climbing the peak the day before and becoming familiar with its terrors and its beauties.[14]

---

10. *Alpine Journal*, vol 1, p7.
11. *Alpine Journal*, vol 1, p40.
12. 'A Weisshorn Traverse', www.alpine-club.org.uk.
13. *The Times*, 28 Nov 1932.
14. L Stephen, 'The Regrets of a Mountaineer', *The Playground of Europe*, Longmans, 1871.

Nature & Environment

'Nocturne des Alpes', Hilda Hechle, 1935?, oil on canvas, 92cm x 138 cm.
The Blumisalp group from the Oeschinensee. *(Courtesy of the Maas Gallery)*

ALTON C BYERS

The Greening of Khumbu

Past, Present and Future in the Himalayan Environment

Imja valley, Khumbu as seen from the upper slopes of Kongde Ri (6187 m).
(L N Sherpa)

Perhaps the time is not so far distant when travel agencies will include tours to the highest mountain in the world in their itineraries.

Erwin Schneider, 1963

During the 1970s and early 1980s, it was commonly assumed by the development community that the Himalaya were approaching catastrophic levels of environmental degradation, linked primarily to growing contemporary human and livestock populations. Landscapes throughout the mountain world were said to be experiencing unprecedented increases in deforestation, overgrazing, and the terracing of marginal land. In turn, these phenomena were claimed to be responsible for promoting near crisis levels of fuel wood shortages, soil erosion, slope instability, geomorphic hazards, and major watercourse siltation. Catastrophic consequences were predicted within 20 years, including the loss of all forest cover in Nepal by the year 2000.

Although the origins of the 'Himalayan crisis' models are obscure, the writer Erik Eckholm is usually credited with synthesizing the popular and

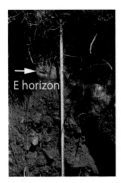

Far left: Podzolic palaeosol, or old, buried forest soil, found above the Khumjung monastery in what is now a shrub-grassland of cotoneaster, dwarf rhododendron, and juniper shrub. Note the pale-colored east horizon, indicating former moist forest conditions. *(Alton Byers)*

Left: Podzol, or actively developing moist forest soil, within a fir-birch-rhododendron forest on the trail to Debouche, below the Tengboche monastery. *(Alton Byers)*

growing concerns of the day in his seminal 1976 book, *Losing Ground.* In a chapter aptly titled 'Refugees from Shangri La', Eckholm describes the conclusions of a 1974 International Workshop on the Development of Mountain Environment' conference in Munich that warned of ' … the irretrievable loss to human use of the developing world's mountain resources – in some cases within one or two decades [i.e., the 1980s or 1990s] – unless the present rate of deforestation and land mismanagement can be halted … '.

Although supported by little quantitative or long-term data, a widely accepted paradigm for the international development community was established that became the foundation for dozens of multi-million dollar conservation projects throughout the Himalaya-Hindu Kush region. Especially during the 1980s, these well-meaning projects were typically designed to 'reverse the trends of environmental degradation' through tree planting, the introduction of simple but 'appropriate' technologies such as improved cook stoves, and improved land management techniques.

However, challenges to the 'Himalayan crisis' scenarios began to emerge by the mid 1980s, primarily from the academic community. Largely initiated by publication of the paper 'Uncertainty on a Himalayan Scale', authors Michael Thompson and Michael Warburton questioned the lack of quantitative data and case studies in illustration of the negative trends, as well as the reliability of popular figures and statistics being used to illustrate the problem.

By the early 1990s, however, the 'Himalayan crisis' debates began losing steam. The programmatic focus of most donors began to shift from government-led natural resource management initiatives, to those emphasising locally led community forestry, biodiversity conservation and new protected area programs. (Climate change would not surface as an issue for another decade.)

However, it should be added that a wide range of new mountain-oriented organisations and programs emerged as a result of the 'mountain crisis' debates, publicity and impact. They included: the establishment of the International Centre for Integrated Mountain Development (ICIMOD) in 1984;

The Imja Khola valley seen from the lower slopes of Thamserku (6608m). Results of soils and pollen analysis suggest these predominantly south-facing hill slopes were covered by cloud forests of fir-birch-rhododendron until about 2,000 years ago. Tree cutting and burning in the interests of converting the forests to pasture land began 2,000 and 5,000 years ago, most likely by non-Sherpa ethnic groups from the south. Between 400 to 800 years ago, about the time of Sherpa arrival, the open woodlands were converted to shrub-grasslands on the south-facing slopes seen today. *(L N Sherpa)*

the inclusion of mountains within the UN's 1992 Rio Earth Summit action plan for the 21st century (known as *The Mountain Agenda,* or *Chapter 13* of *Agenda 21)*; creation of the Mountain Forum in 1995; and establishment of FAO's Mountain Partnership in 2002. In a recent paper on geographical scholarship in Nepal, geographers Elsie Lewiston and Galen Murton also point out that critiques of the 'Theory of Himalayan Degradation' in the 1980s may have also paved the way for policies in support of community forestry programs that emerged in the early 1990s, in addition to a new focus on the value of traditional and indigenous knowledge.

So what about the 'crisis in the mountains' scenarios of the 1950s through the 1980s? Were they really based upon 'myths, misunderstandings, and misinformation', as forester Larry Hamilton of the East-West Center maintained? Or could they have been based upon actual fact, or at least triggered by certain social and biophysical conditions that may have existed at the time, over 70 years ago?

In retrospect, I think that the answer is, yes, the early development practitioners probably had good reason to be concerned. Although the linkages between farming marginal land and increased monsoon river siltation levels were a bit of a stretch, it's hard to believe that the early foreign and Nepali experts couldn't recognise a potential problem when they saw one. The more I view Toni Hagen's films of his journeys through Nepal in the 1950s and 1960s, re-read Harka Gurung's *Landscape Change in the Nepal Hills,* or flip through Facebook's 'Old Photos of Nepal' page, the more I see hill slopes that look vastly different from the ones seen today. There were fewer trees, more land was under terraced cultivation, there was much less infrastructure, and overall the landscapes look more stressed and less resilient.

In fact, a 2019 study by the East-West Center showed that forest cover in Nepal between 1992 and 2016 increased from 26 percent to 45 percent,

View of Tashinga, Phortse, and the Tengboche hill from the trail to Namche in 1956. *(F Müller)*

based upon the use of comparative Landsat satellite images. According to a recent article by Kathmandu-based journalist Peter Gill, this has primarily been the result of the success of Nepal's community forestry programs, coupled with the massive outmigration of predominantly young men to the Middle East since the early 2000s.

That is, with the change to community-based forestry management in the late 1990s, and the growing role of remittances as a source of family income, Nepal's forests became not only more sustainably managed, but there were also fewer demands upon their resources (e.g. the collection of fodder and fuel wood, which had exerted such strong pressures in the past). Land that was formerly farmed or grazed was now allowed to return to second-growth forest.

However, many scientists believe that Nepal's commendable increase in tree cover has not been accompanied by an equivalent restoration of biodiversity and forest function. Cardamom plantations have proliferated throughout the country since the early 2000s, bringing in much-needed income but at the expense of the removal of much of the sub-tropical forest understory and, as a consequence, wildlife and native plant habitat.

View of the Tengboche hill in 2010. Note the considerable expansion of forest and woodland coverage (letters a to f) upon both the north and south-facing slopes of the Imja Khola. *(L N Sherpa)*

The proliferation of new roads throughout Nepal is now being linked to an unprecedented over-exploitation of rare and medicinal plants because of the easier access provided to formerly remote sites, as well as to increases in landslide frequency, slope instability and river siltation. Lewiston and Murton point out while 'outmigration and land abandonment [have] contributed to absolute forest coverage, it has also contributed to declines in soil fertility and increases in invasive species' that in turn impact biodiversity.

Paralleling the development of the 'Theory of Himalayan Degradation', the Sagarmatha (Mount Everest) National Park was frequently cited as a representative case study of historical landscape stability, followed by contemporary landscape change and degradation, in the high Himalaya. Historically, this interpretation maintained that major landscape transformations (i.e. the large-scale conversion from the virgin forests and wilderness that the first Sherpa found, to the shrub-grasslands found on most south-facing slopes today) were the result of 500 years of settlement, population growth and pasture expansion by the ancestors of the Sherpa people. Despite this, ran the argument, ecological stability predominated because of the effectiveness of indigenous management systems.

Namche Bazaar, Kunde and Khumjung villages as seen from the slopes of Thamserku (6608m) in 1956. Note the bare, treeless hillslopes above Namche Bazaar *(photograph by E Schneider).*

The same scene in 1984. Note that in the interim period the Syangboche airstrip (b) had been constructed, as well as the first rock-walled exclosure above Namche that had recently been planted with seedlings. Forests in the vicinity of Kunde (c) appear to have changed little *(Alton Byers).*

Contemporary issues such as increasing forest loss, uncontrolled grazing and accelerated soil erosion were encountered or exacerbated only since the late 1950s. Factors of influence, according to most studies, included the imposition of nationalised forest policies in 1957, the consequential breakdown of traditional indigenous management systems, impacts caused by Tibetan refugee who arrived in the early 1960s, misunderstandings associated with the park's establishment in the 1970s, the rapid growth of tourism and various other factors.

In 1984, I spent 10 months in Khumbu as a PhD candidate in geography from the University of Colorado at Boulder, in part to test the credibility of these widely accepted scenarios of degradation. Based in the village of Khumjung, I and my botanist-geologist wife, Elizabeth, had ample opportunity to examine each of the various claims of landscape change and disturbance in some detail. It also gave us the opportunity to talk to people, take detailed measurements and photographs, and sometimes just to stare at the forests and mountains in front of us for hours, thinking about change. Several of our conclusions regarding the popular historic and contemporary landscape change and degradation scenarios are described below.

Historical Landscape Change

Were the Sherpas really the first people to inhabit the Imja valley, crossing the Nangpa La (5806m) from Tibet some 500 years ago? Did they really find a thickly forested wilderness before them, stretching from today's Thame village to Namche Bazaar, to Tengboche, to the treeline at Pangboche? And were they really the ones who cleared the south-facing slopes from Thame to Pangboche of their original forest cover?

According to the region's soils, which are capable of telling their own story the short answer is probably not. Trail cuts, cattle wallows and slumps along the trail from Thame to Pangboche do indeed reveal old, buried soil formations that were formed under moist cloud forest conditions and not the dry shrub-grasslands found today. Such 'podzols' are characterised by a distinctive 'E' or grey horizon (Figure 3) that has been leached of its iron and other mineral content from the constant seepage of water. Podzolic soils are still common today within the thick, fir-birch-rhododendron forests surrounding the Tengboche monastery, and can be seen at trail cuts from Tengboche to Debouche.

By identifying the pollen species found in the different soil horizons, collecting and dating the lumps of charcoal found at various depths and identifying the tree species represented by each piece of charcoal, we were able to re-construct the vegetation history of the Khumbu valley over the past several thousand years. And the results were surprising.

In brief, the pollen, charcoal and soil records suggest that moist and closed forest conditions did indeed exist some 2,000 years ago on today's south-facing shrub-grasslands. These forests became more and more open as the centuries went by, as indicated by increasing abundances of disturbance-loving bracken ferns. An abundance of charcoal throughout all soil horizons attests to the frequent use of fire as a forest-clearing tool.

The final conversion from open woodland to shrub-grassland took place between 400 to 800 years ago, meaning that while most books still maintain that the Sherpa were the valley's first inhabitants, beginning with their immigration from Tibet some 500 years ago, our data suggested that people had been visiting and burning the forests on the south-facing slopes of the region for at least 2,000 years, and perhaps as much as 5,000 years ago. Thus, what the original Sherpa settlers saw when they first entered the Bhote Kosi and Imja valleys was probably *not* a continuous cover of fir-birch-rhododendron forest throughout the valley, upon both its north- and south-facing slopes.

Namche Bazaar, Kunde, and Khumjung in 1995. An additional exclosure above Namche Bazaar (a) has been built in the interim. Mendaphu hill (b), site of the national park and army base, is beginning to darken with tree growth, although all trees were cut down in the following year because of security concerns related to the Maoist insurgency. *(Alton Byers)*

Rather, what they found was even better: more forest cover than seen today, for sure, but also ample pasture land as a result of a thousand or more years of cutting, burning and grassland expansion by people living in the valleys directly to the south, quite possibly from the area of Rai settlements such as Bung. Sherpa oral traditions speak of certain ruins in the Khumbu alpine zone as belonging to ancient Rai livestock herders, and Rai *dami* (healers) still travel to Khumbu to find certain medicinal and ritual plants. Over the next several centuries, the Sherpa would make their own modifications to landscapes throughout the entire region to produce the prospects seen today.

Contemporary Landscape Change

So what about the claims of widespread deforestation of the Khumbu's remaining forests since the 1950s?

In addition to the quantitative methods used in our study, such as erosion plot monitoring or groundcover sampling, repeat photography provided a valuable qualitative method for better understanding changes in the physical and cultural landscape over time.

The technique itself is simple: find an older photograph, or series of

By 2018, all of the exclosures above Namche (a through e), as well as those located in Kunde and Khumjung (f through h), were covered with trees. *(L N Sherpa)*

photographs taken over a period of time of a landscape, glacier or village. Find the precise photo-point used by the original photographer and replicate the historic photograph as accurately as possible in terms of season, time of day, weather and camera equipment. (Using identical lenses as the original photographer is hardly ever possible, but good substitutes can be made with modern digital cameras.) If changes between the photo pairs are apparent, for example changes in forest or ground cover, then ground truth verification is critical to the most accurate understanding of events or processes leading up to that change, usually by establishing sampling plots in the area of question. Oral testimony from local residents can add tremendous insights to when, why and how the changes occurred. Literature reviews, especially of older books written by early scholars, climbers and scientists in a region, can be extremely valuable as well as a source of additional historic photographs. Time-lapse satellite imagery and aerial photography can provide additional insights to more recent changes that have occurred, particularly with phenomena such as receding glaciers, growing glacial lakes, large-scale deforestation and other major features.

In brief, replication of photographs taken of Khumbu landscapes by the early climber-scientists of the 1950s suggested that, in contrast to catastrophic levels of land degradation reported in the literature, much of the Khumbu was still well forested, resilient and rebounding. Landscapes that appear to be 'degraded', such as the shrub-grasslands of concern to researchers of the 1970s and 1980s, were in fact highly modified as a result of centuries of grazing and pasture expansion. However, although heavily modified they were also quite stable in a geomorphic sense, thanks to the 'geomorphic glue' provided by dwarf rhododendron, cotoneaster and shrub juniper species which bound the soils to the slopes.

Additionally, in at least a dozen repeat photography expeditions to Khumbu between 1984 and 2018, I was able to document a steady return of forest cover throughout much of Khumbu. For example, Figure 5 shows a view of Phortse, Tashinga and the Tengboche hill from the Namche trail in 1956, taken by the Swiss-Canadian glaciologist Dr Fritz Müller while on his way to the Khumbu glacier. Figure 6 shows the same scene again in 2018, where considerable growth of colonising *Pinus wallichiana* upon the south-facing slopes to the left, and fir-birch-rhododendron upon the more northerly facing slopes to the right, is clearly visible.

What have been the reasons for such a dramatic re-growth in trees, both here and elsewhere in Khumbu? Paralleling Nepal's experience in general with outmigration and changing lifestyles, Khumbu's economy today has shifted nearly completely from the agro-pastoralism and trade of the pre-1950s to one based today almost entirely upon tourism. Climbers and scientists were the primary visitors to the region throughout the 1950s, with adventure tourists trickling in from the early 1960s. Tourism to the region grew steadily in the decades that followed, from 20 visitors in 1964, 5,000 per year in 1980, to 20,000 per year in 2000. Annual numbers ebbed and flowed through the decades depending upon national and international events, dropping dramatically during the Maoist insurgency (1996-2006), after the Palace Massacre (2001) and following the 2015 earthquake, but rebounding within a year or two afterwards. Tourist numbers reached a remarkable 60,000 per year in 2019 (not including support staff, which easily doubles the total), dropping to nearly zero as a result of the Covid-19 pandemic and cessation of all tourism in March 2020. As my book went to press (2021), most lodge owners in Khumbu were waiting out the pandemic, making repairs and buying supplies, in anticipation of a post-vaccine return of tourism at some point in 2021 or 2022.

Diets and lifestyles have also changed considerably in the past two decades as the result of easily available imported foods. Likewise, the use of dairy and other products from yak and yak-cattle crossbreed herds is decreasing as more convenient imported milk, cheese and synthetic materials become readily available. While yaks and crossbreeds continue to be used as pack animals from Namche to Everest Base Camp, their numbers are far fewer than they were a generation ago and, as a result, their pressures upon the landscape have decreased as well.

The Sherpa have long practiced an effective system of communal natural resource management characterized by the designation of *shingo nawa,* or forest guards, within each community. Geographer Stan Stevens, author of *Claiming the High Ground,* believes that these indigenous and historic conservation ethics were not as negatively impacted by the nationalisation of forests in 1957 as some scholars would believe, which could explain another reason why forests have rebounded in Khumbu. At the same time, forest management regulations imposed by the national park, starting with the park's creation in 1976, have likely had beneficial impacts as well. Forester Nick Ledgard, who supervised the Himalayan Trust nursery and plantation projects in Khumbu for over 30 years, believes that fire suppression, as a result of decreased livestock populations and annual pasture burning, may also have contributed to the rapid rebound of forests.

Since 1981, active forest regeneration programs have been conducted by the national park, the government of New Zealand and local communities, leading to a significant increase in forest coverage. Hundreds of thousands of fir, juniper, pine and other native species have been raised in nurseries located throughout the park and then planted in ex-closures in the vicinity of major villages. Forty-five plantations totalling some 165 hectares have been planted since 1981. Figures 10 to 13 trace the establishment and growth of tree plantations in the vicinity of Namche Bazaar.

Finally, climate change, especially warmer temperatures and increasing rainfall in Khumbu, may have facilitated more rapid tree growth in combination with the decreasing pressures of pack animals and fuel wood collection. In fact, recent studies in the Everest region are demonstrating how with increased temperatures and ascending snowlines, alpine vegetation is expanding upward to higher altitudes. Treelines, the interface between sub-alpine forest and alpine ecosystems, are also ascending to higher altitudes as a result of warming temperatures and decrease in cattle pressures. And glacial deposits newly exposed by melting ice are now being colonised by alpine wildflowers.

So once again, what about the c1970s statements of an environmental crisis in Khumbu? Were they wrong? Several of the claims made at the time were clearly overstated; von Fürer-Haimendorf's observation, that 'whole hillsides [above Namche Bazaar] which were densely forested in 1957 are now [1975] bare of tree growth,' is simply not supported by the photographic evidence. One glance at Figure 7 shows that there were no 'forested hillsides above Namche Bazaar' in 1956. As mentioned, my own soil erosion research found that while many hill slopes may look 'degraded' and 'erodible', they are in fact quite stable in a geomorphic since thanks to the soil binding quality of the local shrubs and vegetation.

But in general, the physical and social scientists visitoing Khumbu from the 1950s to the 1970s were there at a time when things were far different than they are today. Local people were much more dependent upon forest resources then than they are now; livestock and grazing pressures were much higher. Villagers were still recovering from the impacts of forest nationalisation that were enforced in the late 1950s. And an influx of Tibetan refugees resulted in additional pressures upon local resources and resource use for years. All of this translated into landscapes that at the time were under much more stress than they are today, where tourism has steadily replaced much of the previously agro-pastoral pressures upon the landscapes.

How the Sherpas of Khumbu deal with the relatively new and rapidly expanding problems of solid and human waste management, freshwater contamination and overcrowding, all directly linked to the growth in tourism, remains to be seen.

But, after 500 years of regularly adapting to changing political, economic and environmental trends, I'm sure that they'll figure it out.

• Adapted from the second edition of *Khumbu Since 1950,* by Alton C Byers and Lhakpa Sonam Sherpa, ECS Press, Kathmandu, 2021.

JULIAN FREEMAN-ATTWOOD

Restoring the Mountains of Wales

Death by sheep. The term sheep-wrecked might be hyperbolic but the clearance of temperate rainforest to feed sheep on mountainsides and has driven limited biodiversity in Wales to crisis point. This one is exploring the cemetery in Mwnt, Pembrokeshire. *(Ray Wood)*

I have always called my land here in the Berwyns of Snowdonia an estate. It is actually far too grand a title for what are essentially two hill farms put together with their respective blanket bog and heather moorland. The word estate refers only to how I remember the more sustainably managed land where I was brought up in Shropshire some 25 miles away, and the extensive, as opposed to intensive farming practices and tree planting still undertaken at that time. I have adopted these practices successfully here in Wales.

Boffins use the term 'shifting baseline syndrome' for how each generation takes as their baseline the state of the world's environment as they first experience it. Then the baseline shifts so that the next generation believes that what they have, or see, is not a point on the timeline but their norm. Of course, it is by then already a degraded environment: they just don't know it. I am sadly old enough to remember a time before 'industrial', 'chemical' or 'factory' farming, whatever you want to call it. The baseline isn't shifting very far now. We are so far down the road to destruction that there is not much further to go, not very much more to lose. So we must raise the bar again.

This has nothing to do with a rosy view of a halcyon past, although I really do remember that every ditch on the farm in Shropshire, now dead and stagnant, was clear potable water. I remember the myriad of insects and the noise of crickets on the parkland in summer, the frogs in ponds out of number, the butterflies and bees. The smeared insects on the car windscreen. We can get this back but most governments haven't got a clue how to, and many well-meaning people drafting new legislation have little practical experience. I am the opposite: absolutely no paperwork to my name but lots of first-hand experience.

When I took over the farms, there was a river polluted from sheep dipping, plastic silage bags blowing around in the wind and hanging on the thorny spikes of hedgerows, not a tree planted for several generations, no more hay meadows, grossly overgrazed fields and sheep dip, or nowadays 'pour-on' having killed all the dung beetles because it poisoned sheep faeces. By any standard a degraded land. Whatever happened to the love of land that indigenous, nomadic people of the world hold so dear? How can we talk of Wales being the 'land of our fathers' when it most certainly is no longer that? How can we bear to treat it this way?

The answer is that we are no longer the caretakers of land, revering Mother Nature. We're just factory owners. The trouble is, the roof is about to blow off the factory. So, when I set about reversing the fate of this bit of land, I found it hugely rewarding and still do every day. Other farmers need to realise there is so much that is positive for them in being nature's caretaker. How lucky is that? Happiness lies therein for all of us. Nature requires the long-term view. Planting trees is very long term but once a tree is over the first decade of establishing itself, even the mighty oak will give the planter a reward, much sooner than he might have thought. And it's a reward that endures. Although this is quite the antithesis to the quick-fix world we live in.

Fixing Wales' environment at all may prove very hard indeed. That's not just my opinion, but of very many learned environmentalists. If you had created a committee in the mid 1950s whose only remit was to ensure that the UK reduces its insect life, reduces animal and plant biodiversity, increases chemical use, grubs up hedges, removes indigenous trees, plants monoculture conifers, pollutes ditches with silage effluent and nitrates, then such a committee could say they did a splendid job. Because that is precisely where we are. We may just as well have had such a committee, so blind are we to our beloved nature. And increasingly we're more interested in the Internet and the world on a screen, while the real world suffers so appallingly.

There is now in Wales a consultation for the Agriculture Wales Bill. This process is the last-chance saloon, post Brexit, to do something radical but pragmatic. I don't mind saying I did not vote for Brexit but having said that, let's not pretend that Europe has been a beacon of good environmental practices or great defenders of biodiversity on farmland. Far from it. They have, though, been considerably better in the forestry sector, which we will come to in due course.

Environmentalist Iolo Williams, writing for *Wales Online* recently, described his beloved Welsh countryside as a 'green desert'. It is the same in the Lake District and much of the Yorkshire Dales. Most of Britain in fact. For those who bother to look, or care, this is plainly and unfortunately true. The media is full of hand-wringing reports about loss of tropical rainforest reverting to desert and meanwhile here we are doing just the same in Britain and what's more actually paying farmers to do it, ostensibly for the purpose of offering cheap food. Cheap food means a cheap environment which is why as a nation we will have to keep supporting agriculture but in quite a different way. That should save the worst of damage to the environment but keep food prices at a fair level in the shops for those on low incomes.

Having said that, back in 1957 33% of the gross income of the average family was spent on food. By 2017 that figure was down to 16% and by 2020 it was nearer 10%. You could describe this fall as progress but we are in this position now because of how little we care about the land from which our cheap food comes. In the food debate we always talk about food safety, which is of course important. But we don't talk about the health, and therefore safety, of the land. We talk about organic production not necessarily being more nutritious than what we call 'traditional production', but we forget that the biodiversity on the land of the organic farm is hugely greater. The taxpayer needs to support the organic farmer so that he can still sell his produce at the same price as the traditional production. If it was near to the same price you would go for the organic, wouldn't you? Farmers now refer to modern farming as 'traditional' as if farming organically is something nobody ever did in times past, or is just some old fuddy-duddy way of doing things. But it's not a matter of reverting to something, it's about sustainability and everyone knows what that means. It is true that right now we couldn't meet demand through a solely organic system but you could easily insist on a percentage of land on all farms were run that way.

Some say why support agriculture and not support, for instance, the steel industry. Quite simply agriculture is the only industry that so completely affects all our land: its long-term wellbeing and consequently our own. To expect less than 2.5% of the population of the UK to look after all the countryside alone is a fallacy. Unless, that is, you don't care what the land ends up like. We know that payments have been directed badly for many decades. Now is the time to direct payments to sustainable practices. Those farmers who think it's all a waste of time and merely part of some hippy green movement should expect no assistance from the taxpayer.

The UK is now one of the most nature-depleted countries in the world, in 189th place out of 218. One in seven native species are at risk of extinction. So where does our parlous lack of biodiversity come from? Much of the responsibility lies with agriculture and farming, which covers 70% of the UK. There are certain practices introduced over the last 50 years which have been the most responsible for damage. I will start with the practice of silage harvesting instead of haymaking from traditional hay meadows. And while it is easy to say what is wrong I will try to show the positive things that can be done to effect changes.

Silage and Hay

Silage is essentially pickled grass. It's a much more efficient method of feeding livestock in winter than hay and hugely destructive of nature. Silage fields have been described as having about the same biodiversity as a billiard table. Cutting grass in April and May destroys ground-nesting birds, which is where all our curlews and plovers have gone. They are fertilised with artificial nitrogen that leaches into watercourses and rivers, not to mention silage effluent from silage clamps. There are no wild flowers and therefore no insect life. By and large such fields are periodically ploughed up and re-sown with a monoculture grass for greater volume, where decades earlier there was a huge variety of plants within the grassland sward of most Welsh farms.

This and ploughing high on hillsides, where heather and scrub would normally grow, is an appalling practice producing excess carbon dioxide, severe runoff and compaction.

We know that the soil is in better condition in organic systems. Some also say, with the continued use of chemicals, we are down to the last decade or two of soil fertility. Pouring more chemicals on the land is no more the answer than pouring petrol on a fire. The film *Kiss the Ground*[1] is a real eye-opener. In the USA there are farmers adopting continuous cover cropping, not ploughing but direct drilling crops, who are making more money than those buying ever more expensive artificial fertilisers and sprays. Direct drilling keeps carbon locked in the soil. We should be thinking seriously of not ploughing land any longer. The technology is there for direct drilling. I recommend anyone interested in land to see the film.

Feeding livestock brings us to the thorny subject of overgrazing and animal agriculture in general, which is linked to human beings eating such large quantities of meat. Nobody wants farmers to go out of business and food production is their business but not at any cost. Their business model must now include being genuine stewards of the land and not just producers of meat. Lucky them I would say. That's a much more interesting and diverse life. It used to be said that you should leave your farm better than you found it. That has now become leaving your land in a state of higher production than you found it. Going forward it should be to leave your land in a state of greater biodiversity than you found it.

Payments should be made to encourage hay over silage. Even if 25% of silage ground on each farm were turned over to hay that would make a colossal difference in Wales as a whole. You don't get the same quantity with hay. What you do get is an almost instantaneous increase in insect life. And it is always the small creatures at the base of the food chain that matter most, whether we are talking insects in Wales or krill in the Southern Ocean.

---

1. *Kiss the Ground*, dir J and R Tickell, Big Picture Ranch, 2020, 1h 24m.

A landscape made by sheep. The view from the summit of Aran Fawddwy (905m), just 31ft short of the magical 3,000ft mark and the highest mountain in Britain south of Snowdon. *(Ed Douglas)*

I put down to hay meadow some 50 acres of ground below the house here in Wales some 15 years ago. It has been an unmitigated success. Dame Miriam Rothschild, the noted environmentalist, told me never to cut before the third week of July. If you do so before then you tend to take away the wild flower seed with the hay. After that, the seed is loose on the stalk and tends to drop off back onto the field during tedding and haymaking. This is next year's seed. As a result of these hay meadows and the subsequent increase in insects, the population of house martins, swallows and swifts has gone up tenfold. We used to have two or three swallow nests and four or five house martin nests. Now there are 40 nests between the two species taking advantage of our large roof overlaps, something we need, incidentally, to build into any new housing: simple to do at almost zero cost. After harvest we leave the meadows to recover for a month before then grazing quite heavily and closing again in late November.

Roads to perdition. The recently reconstructed bridleway in Maesgwm linking Llanberis to the Snowdon Ranger path. *(Ray Wood)*

Wild Areas
Each farm should be paid to set aside permanently 15% of their land, either for hay or to be 'wilded'. By that I mean areas of hawthorn and blackthorn scrub and 'open', rather than 'closed' canopy woodland. That should be a possibility within the new stewardship schemes. And farms need wildlife corridors so they don't simply become islands of good practice. Animals and birds need to move through the landscape. The more these areas join up with the next farm the better. With wildlife, unlike with building, ribbon development is good. For wilded areas you could do no better than to read author Isabella Tree's book *Wilding*. She and her husband turned over their whole estate to wilding and it is miraculous what they have achieved. (Ironically, it is now under threat from a huge housing development.) For the Wales white paper, I am not suggesting that. But I do suggest 15% of wilding on all holdings is realistic. That would be a start. Giving that much back to the natural world is not so very altruistic having stolen it all from nature since the last war. These open wild areas are good for a huge range of animals and insects.

Hedges and Hedgerow Trees
It is a misconception that simply planting hedges can alleviate all the ills of modern farming. That is not the case. Hedges are of course wonderful and very beneficial. If planted to make a wide hedge (three rows instead of two)

with a variety of plants, they are a good habitat and aesthetically pleasing. But they are only thin lines in the green desert. They alone will not reverse the destruction without the scrub areas mentioned above and without very large margins either side of those hedges that are also left to 'wild'. These large margins, and I am talking here 10m or 20m either side of the hedge, become part of the 'ribbon development' and the farmer should be paid for taking that percentage out of production permanently. There is no point in making any area bio-diverse only to plough it up and spray it a few years later. That's why the set-aside system was a failure.

Farmers are not good at tree planting. So I have long wanted to start up a Hedgerow Tree Society to encourage standard broadleaf trees to be planted in our hedgerows or to make sure that mechanical hedge cutters do not cut out natural tree regeneration. These hedge trees would take up no farmland at all. If you made it standard practice to have a hardwood tree every 25m in every hedgerow in Britain the figures are astounding. There are about 800,000km of hedgerow in total and at 25m spacing you could have about 40 trees per kilometre. That makes room in our hedges for some 32 million trees. This would transform our landscape at no loss of farmland *at all*. This plan in any agriculture bill would be a 'no brainer' and should form part of Wales' nature recovery. Even so, this will only go halfway to replacing the estimated 80 million ash trees that are thought will be lost over the next decade from ash dieback.

Tree Planting and Closed Canopy Woodland
I have been involved with forestry and landscape planting for the last 50 years. We need to understand a great deal more about how to plant trees, instead of simply getting confused with all the figures bandied around by various political parties vying to plant more millions of trees than their rivals. The number of trees is not in itself the issue. The question is how much land area are you going to cover with closed or open canopy woodland. You could create far more biodiversity with the right planting at wide-open canopy spacing with scrub, than twice the number of trees that are badly planned and planted. The Forestry Commission urgently needs to adapt its planting grant criteria.

On the continent they mostly adhere to continuous cover forestry. This is the best way to manage woodland, taking out groups of trees and replanting rather than the hideous clear felling practised in the UK. This is the fault of the Forestry Commission, which allows such destructive practices through felling licences. With clear felling you get a wood that's up to 50 years old and then that's it: no more old trees. And we really need those old trees.

The standard practice now is that the Forestry Commission want you to plant something like 1,600 stems per hectare, which means 2.5m spacing, for your planting grant. The point of this is so the trees compete for height. If it were an oak crop, you would thin the wood two or three times in the first 100 years to obtain final crop spacings. In reality, in modern times, without fulltime foresters as there were on the old estates years ago that would do this thinning properly, you just get long poles at 50 years: not thinned and subject to wind blow.

So, assuming that best forestry practices are simply never going to be present on the average farm, you are better to start planting in a completely different way where little thinning is required further down the line. We need to provide grants to plant at much wider spacings, with far fewer trees per hectare, or groups of trees with wide spaces between them. Hawthorn and blackthorn and holly make up an understorey that is good for wildlife.

On gorse and bracken hillsides in the Berwyns of north Wales, I have planted oak very cheaply in tubes 1.2m high at very wide spacings with the intention that it will look like natural regeneration. This works where you are only trying to protect the trees from sheep, not cattle or deer. I have just taken the tubes away on 15-year-old trees that are at least 12ft high. These will never be thinned and will be there for hundreds of years.

Such hillside planting of indigenous broadleaf prevents excessive runoff normally exacerbated by the puddling effect of the feet of too many sheep. This is another major problem, creating runoff that results in flooding down on the plains. The cost of a thousand oaks including labour and grow tubes, double staked against the wind, was only £5 per tree because we had no fencing to put up at all. Areas that are not much good even for grazing, or areas that should not be grazed, run to hundreds of thousands of acres in Wales and elsewhere. I find it almost comical when people agonise about where to plant the trees we need. Look out of your car window anywhere in rural Wales and the possibilities are endless.

As thorn is the mother of the oak, protecting the young oak sapling from browsing animals, so gorse and bracken offer the same function. Wide-spaced planting in gaps within gorse areas should be grant aided by the Forestry Commission. The burning of gorse must be stopped. This releases more carbon dioxide but also makes lots of potash. The farmer thinks that's good for grass. Actually, it just makes the gorse grow again but more vigorously. As for bracken, this denotes the most fertile of farmland. You will have little problem growing trees on bracken ground and there is plenty of that in Wales.

Since I am only protecting trees against sheep, I have also planted groups in the middle of fields. This goes against every sinew of the average farmer but if you think about it why should our landscape be merely made up of fenced off squares devoid of trees, especially on permanent pasture land? Even on the endless ploughed land in Cambridgeshire some groups of trees might be a part of this wilding process without greatly affecting production.

Another important reform is that we must now plant trees from our own UK native seed stock. Imported trees are not so well adapted to our environment and also bring in pathogens like Dutch elm and ash dieback. The importance of seed was well known in the great era of landscape planting in the 18th century.

The sad thing is that even a dark and uninviting conifer wood could become something quite special with a proper regime of thinning. That would

Snowdon from Moel Siabod. All British national parks have failed to offer sufficient protection and space for an improvement in biodiversity. *(Ed Douglas)*

let light onto the forest floor and then, even a conifer wood takes on the
attributes of a broadleaf wood with flora thriving on a lightened forest floor.
In the UK we are very bad at thinning. We never take out enough trees at the
right time to encourage the remainder to grow to maturity. Grants are more
necessary to help with the labour of thinning at 30 and 50 years of age than
for the actual planting itself. We cannot solve any of this without long-term
views. Nature requires it of us.

Grazing

Farming's carbon dioxide footprint is calculated at 9% of the UK's total, and in Wales at 14%. This is not just from use of diesel and the manufacture of chemicals and fertiliser or indeed methane from animals, all of which are significant. It is also from ploughing the ground, which releases considerable amounts of carbon. This has been measured, more easily done these days by satellites (again, see the film 'Kiss the Ground'), revealing that the CO_2 released in the northern hemisphere goes up hugely in March to May when the soil is bare. Once crops grow and cover the soil, like a mini-forest canopy, then the CO_2 reduces from June onwards. It is simply unnecessary to emit this seasonal CO_2 which can be alleviated by direct drilling. This keeps the soil in much better condition and contains moisture. Compaction is reduced as well.

It makes sense to graze sheep and cattle on the uplands where there is permanent pasture but only in the right numbers. And the numbers are currently far more than the land can bear and have been for decades. Farmers need to be supported to reduce numbers of sheep and perhaps add a few more cattle, which graze in a different, less harmful way. Such reduction will be resisted as ever by the National Farmers Union but there will be no chance of meeting climate change targets or increasing biodiversity in permanent pasture without doing this. The industry can bury its head in the sand but the problem will not go away.

What's more, by reducing grazing in the uplands and planting trees on hillsides, huge amounts of money will be saved from reduced flooding costs. We must also allow land to flood within historic flood plains and support farmers who are prepared to let this happen, rather than simply relying on more ditch widening and flood defences.

As for land use, Wales produces only 5% of the vegetables it consumes. It can't be right for a country to produce so much meat and dairy but so few vegetables.

Moorland and Blanket Bog

If there's an underrated environment anywhere in the UK, it's blanket bog. The world's peat lands hold twice the carbon as the world's forests and the UK holds 13% of the world's blanket bogs, the biggest carbon store in the country equivalent to 20 years of emissions. On top of that 70% of the UK's drinking water comes from peat lands. Yet 80% of the UK's peat bogs are in a poor condition. Welsh moorland is in a better state than the heavily polluted peat bogs of northern England, where restoration efforts are underway to cut carbon losses and reduce flooding. But burning heather in Wales should no longer be permitted on moorland and certainly not on blanket bog. Nor for that matter should heather be mechanically cut, which is done by Natural Resources Wales here in Wales. This is a waste of energy, uses fossil fuels and a tractor for the supposed gain of some black or red grouse, wonderful as they always are to see. This does not anyway work here in the Berwyns. There are far too many corvids and mammal predators for that. We all have much else to think about. Best leave the moors alone with minimal grazing.

Commercial Bird Shoots

In the early 1970s around four million pheasants and partridges were released into the British countryside. By the end of the last decade that number had risen to 60 million. The weight of game birds released into our countryside is now greater than the weight of all the wild bird population put together. The vast majority are pheasants and these chicken-sized birds do nothing but eat. Where the rearing numbers are huge – say 40,000 or 50,000 birds – the effect on local biodiversity is immense. The birds consume, when released, huge numbers of insects, beetles and worms. Hay meadows are also depleted of seed for next year. These sources are then no longer available to wild birds and the ground is much depleted.

Shoots close to Special Protection Areas (SPA), Special Areas of Conservation (SAC) and Sites of Special Scientific Interest (SSSI) have been a particular problem. From 2021 the Department for Environment, Farming and Rural Affairs (Defra) will require shoots in England to seek a licence to release the captive-bred birds within 500 metres of protected areas. Wales will need to follow.

This is not a moral statement about shooting. I shoot myself. This is a matter of numbers on a scale never seen before. Shoots hide behind the fact that in the past, if you released a pheasant, it instantly became, in the eyes of the law, a wild bird. That was when shoots were quite small by today's standards. It is plainly absurd to release 50,000 pheasants and pretend they are wild. There will soon be cases to clarify this but meanwhile the various conservation agencies need to take action. Even Natural Resources Wales acknowledges that with so many dead carcasses and road kill from these shoots, there is now an unnatural number of buzzards and red kites in certain areas, and a surge in mammal scavengers, particularly foxes, which eat rare native species. This is clearly upsetting the balance.

Furthermore, on big shoot days where 500 or more birds are shot, the cartridge count comes to 2,000 or 2,500. This has historically been a large concentration of lead going into the environment and ultimately watercourses, although this issue is now finally being addressed. It's true the shooting industry employs a number of people. But whether it's the rainforest of Brazil or in Wales, environmental destruction can never be justified on the basis of jobs alone. If that were the case we would applaud the chopping down of rainforest on the basis that the man with the chainsaw needs a job.

The Future

This is the last chance for the Welsh countryside. Our once great landscape, lauded the world over in poetry, music and art, can be saved but it needs a concerted effort over time and radical thinking now. All biodiversity is important. Our land here is no less relevant than a rain forest in central

Africa. And if we don't look at it like that, then there is little hope that we will consider it important enough to do something about.

David Attenborough said in January 2021, 'if we continue our current path, we will face the collapse of everything that gives us our security: food production, access to fresh water, habitable ambient temperature and ocean food chains.' He is absolutely right.

I will add one thing. Those who have chosen the path of politics have assumed the greatest responsibility of all. They need to move very quickly on this or be the ones pilloried by history and the ones subjecting future generations to a degraded world that must inevitably lead, in time, to great upheaval. Make no mistake about it; this is a threat to all of us.

ROB COLLISTER

A Flower with Latitude

Encounters with Purple Saxifrage

Purple saxifrage in Cwm Idwal. *(Rob Collister)*

One April, in an era not so long ago when we could go where we liked, I made my way up to a favourite cwm on Snowdon. It was during a prolonged dry spell: long-dead bracken stalks crackled underfoot, mosses were brown and desiccated, and I was able to amble dry shod where normally angels would fear to tread without wellies. At the mountain wall two shaggy long-horned feral goats were waiting to usher me into the cwm before drifting away out of sight. I headed up grass and scree aiming for the bottom end of a band of crags that slants steeply up the hillside all the way to the ridge crest far above. Damp, vegetated and unattractive from a climbing point of view, they looked, instead, as though they might be home to some interesting plants. Geologically, they are probably formed of a basic tuff, volcanic ash from an eruption in Ordovician times that filtered down through a shallow sea to mingle with calcium from the skeletons of countless marine creatures on its bed.

Sure enough, almost immediately, my eye was caught by a bright splash of colour, which at this time of year could only be one thing – a clump of

163

purple saxifrage. This always flowers early (I found it once in the Devil's Kitchen, Twll Du, on 8 February) but it was still a delightful surprise since I had not been consciously looking for it. The sight induced the same sort of excitement as hearing the first cuckoo of the year, a reassuringly familiar yet significant milestone in the annual cycle.

The excellent new book by Jim Langley and Paul Gannon[1] tells me that the purple saxifrage *(saxifraga oppositifolia)* holds the record for the highest flowering plant in the Alps, having been recorded at 4,450m on the Dom, in Switzerland. It also grows further north than any other flower so it is truly an arctic-alpine and almost at the southern limit of its range in Snowdonia. As the climate warms it will become increasingly uncommon here.

If I had to name a favourite alpine plant it would probably be this one. In the startling boldness of its colour and its ability to thrive in the most inhospitable places it has rivals, of course: king-of-the-Alps *(eritichium nanum)* springs to mind, or moss campion *(silene acaulis),* perhaps. But, for me, purple saxifrage has more memorable associations with mountains around the world than any other plant.

There was the occasion in Alaska when five of us were descending Mount Deborah after making the first ascent of the east ridge. I was climbing with John Barry and Roger Mear but as the ridge had achieved the status of 'last great problem' two locals, Carl Tobin and John Cheesemond, had dashed up to join in. At a time when nearly 500 people were thronging Denali, we were the only climbers in the entire eastern sector of the Alaska range.

We had been on the mountain the best part of a fortnight, initially sleeping in snow caves and latterly bivouacking in some alarming situations on the crest of a hugely corniced ridge. I was coming down last, climbing slowly and carefully under the weight of a 300ft rope on top of everything else. We were only a few feet from the glacier on some rather suspect rock and I was feeling tired and a bit sorry for myself when, suddenly, I noticed a little dab of purple by the toe of my boot. Totally unexpected, at first I was puzzled but as soon as I realised what it was my spirits lifted, instantly. It was like being welcomed back into the land of the living. It was quite an emotional moment for me though none of the others had noticed the tiny blooms and no one seemed interested when I mentioned them. No matter, there was a renewed spring in my step as we set off up the glacier.

Another occasion was in the wilds of Kyrgyzstan. John Cousins and I had crossed a high ridge into the otherwise inaccessible Terekty valley to attempt Pik Kirov, an unclimbed 6,000m peak in a remote corner of the Tien Shan. Lacking today's obligatory props of satellite phone or emergency beacon, we were far from any possible help should things go wrong. Finding the solitary dash of purple in a sea of moraine as we set off on the final push felt like a message of encouragement, as if we were being wished good luck. In the event, we did not reach the summit, retreating in a storm from high on the mountain, but given an extremely close call with a collapsing cornice,

1. J Langley & P Gannon, *The Alps, A Natural Companion,* Oxford Alpine Club, 2019. See Andy Tickle's review in *AJ* 2020.

Purple saxifrage in spring sunshine, south Spitsbergen, near Hornsund fjord.

Last chance to see? Saxifraga oppositifolia likes altitude or latitude and climate change is squeezing it out of British mountains.

I have always felt the flowers were indeed a good omen.

Then there was the campsite at 5,600m on the lower slopes of Makalu, in Nepal, a stony carpet adorned with purple rosettes, once we had cleared away the trash left behind by a recent trekking party. In fact, I seem to have found this lovely plant everywhere; everywhere that the rocks contain some calcium and can be described as base-rich, that is: at sea-level in the Lyngen Alps, Norway, having been dropped by boat to ski up Riekkavarri, one May; in profusion on bare shale around the Dix hut above Arolla; on the sun-drenched limestone walls of the Tenailles de Mont Brison in the Écrins; nearer home, on the basalt escarpment of the Quirang on Skye and where basalt has been intruded into the gabbro of the Cuillin.

Here in Wales it grows in many places on Snowdon and in Idwal, where the geology is right. I found it once on Moel Siabod, inspired to look there by the story of Evan Roberts, a quarryman from Capel Curig. Shooed out of the house by his wife on a day off, he came upon it purely by chance in the cwm above Llyn y Foel. He was so enthralled by the sight that he took to searching for it elsewhere and was soon discovering other unusual plants. He went on to become the leading authority on the arctic-alpine plants of north Wales, with an honorary degree from Bangor University to prove it. I met Evan just the once, after he had gone blind, when he was still able to describe in detail how to find the colony of mountain avens (*dryas octopetala*) that flourishes in a most unlikely spot in the Carneddau. Curiously, though, I have never been able to find the purple saxifrage again on Moel Siabod, despite several searches.

This time, on Snowdon, here it was, growing in profusion, not just on the crag but in the grass at its foot as well. In some places the blooms were etiolated and washed out; in others, an unusually deep vibrant shade, the difference presumably linked to varying mineral content in the soil. Kneeling to examine the flowers more closely, I noticed specks of calcium that had been extruded from the tips of tiny leaves. On limestone the whole leaf becomes encrusted with calcium, an adaptation believed to provide extra protection against wind and sun. For a few seconds my absorption was complete and when I re-awakened it was with an inkling of what Jim Perrin meant when he wrote of, 'those acts of attention that are the profoundest prayer': prayer in the sense of stillness and loss of self, anyway. Continuing upward, I found nothing else yet in flower but purple saxifrage was everywhere. Finally, I emerged from the shaded, ice-carved north face onto sunlit grassland, grateful and glad at heart, happy to leave the summit to the multitude toiling up the Llanberis path even at this time of year.

History

'The Khylas Mountains and village of Pangi 3 miles above Chiné on the Sutledge', Constance Gordon-Cumming, 19 June 1869, watercolour and body-colour, 48.2cm x 72.5cm. *(Christie's via Bridgeman Images)*

Charles F Meade

Charles Meade, left, with Pierre Blanc and two porters, en route for Kamet.
(Courtesy of Jasper Meade)

In 1898 Himalayan mountaineering was in its opening phase and there can have been few schoolboys at the time pondering the problems of climbing at high altitude but 17-year-old Charles Meade was one. He had been reading Conway's account of his pioneering expedition to the Karakoram six years earlier, and Professor Mosso's recently published treatise on the physiological effects of altitude, *Life of Man in the High Alps,* of which he wrote enthusiastically to his grandmother:

> *I am delighted with it. It agrees with all my theories of ascending Mt Everest, and goes one better. He says it is possible.*

171

Fifteen years later, Meade's series of attempts to climb Kamet (7756m) in the Garhwal Himal would prove to be a significant milestone in the story of climbing in the Himalaya. Elected to membership of the Alpine Club in 1904, vice-president in 1934 and honorary member in 1965, he died in 1975, aged 93. His brief obituary in the *Alpine Journal* provides scant detail of his long life and achievements; this biographical sketch fills that gap.

Charles Francis Meade was born in 1881. His father, the Hon Sir Richard Meade, was the second son of the third Earl of Clanwilliam. The Meades were a long-established family of Irish landowners but the first Earl (1744-1800) had 'dissipated to the last guinea' a 'noble fortune' on 'stableboys [i.e. the turf] and mistresses'[1] and Charles's grandfather had been obliged to forge his own career. A friend and political associate of Lord Castlereagh and the Duke of Wellington, he was appointed ambassador at Berlin (1823-27) and his son, Charles's father, followed him into the diplomatic service, attaining the position of permanent under-secretary of state at the Colonial Office. Tragically, Charles's mother Caroline, née Grenfell, died just a week after his birth.

Meade was schooled at Eton. A boy's experience of late Victorian Eton was formed largely by his house, the community of 30 or 40 boys in which he lived day to day, and the character of the master in whose charge he had been placed. Meade's housemaster was Arthur C Benson who combined school mastering with prolific writing[a] and would subsequently become a fellow and then master of Magdalene College, Cambridge. Benson was popular with parents and pupils; kindly and humane, rarely resorting to corporal punishment, he was held in great affection by the boys. A critic of the prevailing dominance of Latin and Greek in the school's curriculum and abhorring the passion for organised games and the glorification of athletic success, he gained a reputation as a radical. He was also homosexual but guarded against abusing his position of trust and pursuing physical relationships. Instead, he formed romantic attachments to older boys and young men, 'wooing his students to the very edge of propriety.'[2] His crushes included Meade's cousin, Julian Grenfell, future war poet, and later at Cambridge, George Mallory.

Given his interest in his charges it seems likely that Benson would have learned of Meade's enthusiasm for mountaineering and would have talked of mountains with him, for he was a member of the Alpine Club. He had been elected in 1895[b]; his application mentions ascents of the Matterhorn and Eiger, and 'all Skye mountains except Inac[cessible] Pinnacle'. But he gave up serious mountaineering in the following year after surviving a near-death experience when, having fallen into a crevasse, he was almost strangled by the rope:

a. His prodigious output included essays, poetry, novels, ghost stories, a two-volume biography of his father, the Archbishop of Canterbury and, incidentally, the words to Elgar's Pomp and Circumstance March No1 – 'Land of Hope and Glory'.
b. He remained a member of the Club until his death in 1925; curiously the death of this distinguished man passed unnoticed in the pages of the *Alpine Journal*.

Meade's housemaster at Eton,
A C Benson, c1899. *(A H Fry)*

Suddenly it dawned on me that I was doomed ... The strange thing was that I had no sense of fear ... I had no edifying thoughts. I did not review my past life or my many failings ...

But he spared a thought for his house at Eton, wondering 'how my pupils would be arranged for.'[3] According to Geoffrey Winthrop Young, Benson's guide, Clemenz Ruppen, faced with the prospect of being dragged into the crevasse by his client had been on the brink of cutting the rope: 'Benson never knew the whole story! Clemenz told it me during our long talks in night bivouacs.'[4]

From Eton, Meade went up to Balliol in 1899 when the college was enjoying considerable prestige and success. H H Asquith, prime minister and Balliol man, famously observed that graduates of his college were distinguished from lesser souls by their 'tranquil consciousness of effortless superiority'. But this atmosphere of self-confidence and entitlement was tempered by an enthusiasm for Fabian socialism, and Meade's tutor, A L Smith, historian and future master of Balliol, was the movement's most 'energetic prophet' within the college.

Meade approached undergraduate life by 'working steadily' though he was 'careful not to overdo the quantity [because] brain fever would be a terrible illness to get,' and faced with choosing a future career, he dreamt of mountains.

I think I have settled as far as I'm concerned to go in for diplomacy. You see I might get Lima or some nice out of the way place as secretary or something near some range of high mountains where I could spend part of my holidays exploring.

But a diplomatic career proved disappointing and was short-lived; he served for eighteen months as honorary attaché at Tangier:

I can't say that I dislike it more than like it at present. If one is up to one's neck in the European Colony one can scarcely be immersed in the East. There is an awful lot of work at present ...

On the outbreak of the First World War, Meade, aged 33, volunteered immediately, obtaining a commission in the Surrey Yeomanry, a Territorial

Guglia di Brenta from the south-west. The variation climbed by Blanc and Meade starts from the right hand end of the ledge beneath the summit on the sunlit south-west face and follows the line between sunlight and shadow.

cavalry regiment whose honorary colonel was his father-in-law, St John Brodrick, Viscount Midleton and former secretary of state for war, but an early entry in the diary, which he kept intermittently throughout the war, reveals his ambivalence:

> *I have no curiosity (which some people have) to know how great a coward I can be. I've been to the Alps and Himalayas and I know. The idea of perishing as a pawn in the game of the lunatic Warlords is humiliating. I prefer pestilence to modern war. The latter does not do its work so neatly. I must say I never thought that military glory would have come my way ...* [c]

After two years in training camps in the south of England, Meade joined his regiment on the Struma front in Macedonia, 'a sideshow within a sideshow', where he led mounted patrols – a last hurrah for the cavalry – into disputed territory which occasionally resulted in an exchange of gunfire, which he likened to ski jumping, combining 'the maximum of fear with the minimum of risk'. Of combat generally, he wrote with a twist of irony:

> *I can't imagine that fighting can frighten me any more than I have been frightened by climbing. Of course when in a desperate fix climbing you must pull yourself together if you can and climb better than you ever have before, and so save your life. Perhaps under similarly desperate conditions of fighting one might instinctively apply the same principle and run better and further that you've ever run before and so get court-martialled.*

As the war progressed his contempt for the army and its generals grew:

c. These sentiments could not have been in starker contrast to those of his Grenfell cousin, Julian, who in October 1914 wrote to his mother: 'I adore war. It is like a big picnic ... I've never been so well or so happy.' Julian was killed a year later.

Kamet, left, and Abi Gamin with Meade's col between them. *(C F Meade)*

The army is a miserable affair ... It is the worst infliction perpetrated on us by the Germans ... The danger for the high command is that one day a subordinate (probably a regular soldier) may do exactly what he is told. In that case it is all up with everybody concerned.

His antipathy to formal regimentation of thought or conduct ensured he remained a subaltern for the duration.

A few years after returning from the war, Meade acquired the Montgomeryshire estate of Pen-y-Lan and its management would be his principal occupation. 'For those who knew him at Pen-y-Lan,' wrote a friend of his later years, 'he comes most easily to mind in his 18th Century library, standing in front of a great wood fire. He bore an astonishing resemblance to portraits of his distinguished ancestors on the library walls, and when he spoke of mountains and mountain dwellers, one caught the tempo and flavour of an earlier age.'[5]

Meade's first Alpine climb had taken place in 1897 when, aged 16, he was on a family holiday in the South Tirol 'Papa has actually agreed to let me go to the top of some easy mountain, probably the Cinque Torri,' he wrote excitedly to his Grenfell grandmother, and continued:

The colours of the peak are wonderful. One big one looks as if a bottle of claret had been upset over it and the wine was tracking down. Other parts of

Officers of 21st Surrey Yeomanry in 1914. Meade is in middle row,
second from left.

*it look as if they were made of gold. … It has one great advantage: it looks
absolutely inaccessible.*

Three years later, following a walking tour through the Vanoise and
ascents of Aiguille de la Grande Sassière, Mont Pourri and the Aiguilles
Rousses, he had been hooked by the Alps ('I am craving fearfully for next
year to see them again.') and alpinism: 'Climbing for me must soon begin
in earnest.'

Meade spent the next three summers enthusiastically climbing across the
Alps and in 1904, aged 23, was elected to the Alpine Club. He was proposed
by his uncle Willy, W H Grenfell, public servant, exceptional sportsman[d],
created first Baron Desborough. Amongst Meade's supporters was his Eton
housemaster, Benson. His application lists more than 70 expeditions, prin-
cipally in the Graians, Dauphiné and Dolomites. After an absence of two
years while he was in Morocco, Meade resumed his frenetic pace and by the
end of the 1909 season his assiduously compiled personal record lists 119
expeditions. Most of his climbs had been by established routes[e] but in 1909
he was inadvertently involved in making a new and desperate variation up
the final section to the summit of the Guglia di Brenta, also known as Campanile Basso, the spectacular 300m spire in the Dolomites.

d. Amongst his more extraordinary feats, he had stroked an eight across the Channel and swam across the
pool beneath the Niagara Falls, twice, the second occasion in order to prove the first to disbelievers.
e. In 1903 he made the first descent of the NE arête of the Jungfrau. The first ascent was made by a Swiss
party in 1911.

The first ascent had been made in 1899 but during the succeeding 10 years there had been few further ascents. Meade and his guide, Pierre Blanc, had made good progress to within 50 vertical metres of the summit when they missed the way, lured, like so many since, onto difficult ground by the sight of two ring pegs. To reach the first peg from the terrace on which they had arrived, required combined tactics at the start. From his position standing on Meade's head, Blanc launched himself onto the steep wall above and inched his way towards the first peg where he untied the rope from his waist and threaded it through the ring, repeating the procedure at the second, and eventually found a belay directly below the summit. Meade was now faced with the second's nightmare, an exposed traverse beneath an overhang: 'I was obsessed by anxiety lest the rope ... swing me off sideways across the precipice to dangle to and fro like a pendulum over the revolting abyss into which I had so long been gazing.'[6] And worse, the rope had jammed above him. As he ascended, the slack 'dropped in a great coil' and should he have fallen the resulting violent jerk would have pulled Blanc from his stance and both of them 'would inevitably fly off into space.' The passage (now graded V/A0) was negotiated safely and the summit reached with enormous relief. The extremity of the situation just overcome was emphasised by their later discovery that the climber who had placed the two pegs only a few weeks earlier had slipped from a point above the second, the rope had snapped and he had fallen 300m through the air to his death.

Meade paid three visits to the Himalaya in 1910, 1912 and 1913 to explore the approaches to Kamet and attempt to climb it. On each he was accompanied by Blanc, of whom Meade wrote: 'the ideal companion for Himalayan mountaineering is a friend like Pierre with whom one can quarrel furiously without causing disastrous results.'[7] Meade and Blanc had first climbed together in 1901 and over the succeeding years forged a friendship that surpassed the usual relationship between client and favourite guide and lasted a lifetime. When their serious climbing days were over, Blanc was often invited to stay at Meade's Welsh home and together they walked over the local hills.

But on 12 April 12 1913 they had just arrived in Bombay, as Meade recalled:

> ... at three o'clock in the morning I suddenly awoke with the sensation of lying in a warm bath. The darkness was profound, but, just outside the cabin, a deafening clamour of Hindu mail-sorters throwing mail-bags about the deck signified that the P&O liner in which my guide Pierre Blanc and myself had been travelling, was at the end of its journey ...[8]

And he was glad to be back in India en route for the Himalaya, for he had been enchanted by 'the double spell of those two most potent magics, the snow-mountains and the East'. After two days sweltering across the Indian plains by rail they reached the cool of the foothills, and on 1 May set off on foot for Kamet. Meade's pleasure in the trek is apparent from his account, so sharply observed and vividly described:

> *... in the early morning, the pine-trees were dark against a white sunrise; already we heard the staccato shouts of the ploughmen urging on their little oxen; below us among the tree-tops there still lingered streaks of cool night-mist, almost as blue as wood-smoke. The air was fresh as water ... [and] in a clearing of the jungle, there glimmered ... an apparition so dazzling that it took us some moments to realize that what we saw was a pink rhododendron tree in full bloom, lit up by the first rays of the rising sun, so that all its thousands of flowers shone like jewels.*[9]

They arrived at their base camp at about 4,850m on the Kamet glacier on 7 June and were immediately weather-bound for two weeks.

At one o'clock in the morning of 21 June they launched their summit bid:

> *There was a crystal clear quality in the moonlight, and the snow was sparkling like diamonds in its rays. The Bhotias were bubbling with energy and high spirits; like us they were relieved that the long period of waiting was over.*[10]

Their intention was to 'rush' the mountain – there would be no establishment and stockpiling of intermediate camps – and by 10 o'clock they had reached 6,100m where they pitched two tents: one for Meade and Blanc; seven porters occupied the other. But Meade had developed acute mountain sickness, which, together with fresh snowfall and the cold, halted them for 48 hours. On 24 June they pressed on again over more difficult ground, snow-covered rocks and a steep snow and ice slope which necessitated a prolonged bout of step cutting by Blanc, to reach an easy-angled glacier-plateau up which they laboured:

> *The endless monotony of toiling up the bleak slopes of this ghastly plateau through an increasing depth of powdery snow, and under a burning sun became a torment.*[11]

A second camp was made at about 7,000m, one hundred metres below the col, which now bears Meade's name, between Kamet and its neighbouring peak, Abi Gamin[f], and from which a steep but straightforward snow slope leads to the summit 600m above. Next day, Meade, Blanc and three Bhotias set out for the top but Meade, still struggling with the effects of altitude, soon gave up; Blanc and the porters pushed on to the saddle before turning back, exhausted. Although unsuccessful in reaching the summit, Meade had solved the question of the correct route, the answer having eluded Longstaff, Slingsby and Kellas, all of whom had made prior exploratory visits. His 'dashing raid' contrasted with the ponderous tactics employed

---

f. Meade identified this peak as Eastern Ibi Gamin in his article on the Kamet group's nomenclature for the *Alpine Journal* 1920 (vol 33, p70). Smythe, in his account of the first ascent of Kamet, followed Meade, but the most common modern name is Abi Gamin.

Meade and Pierre Blanc at Zermatt station. *(Courtesy of Jasper Meade)*

by Frank Smythe's 1931 expedition which made the first ascent following Meade's route: six climbers, 41 porters and five intermediate camps established over a fortnight.

Meade's experience of climbing in the Alps and Himalaya made him eminently qualified to be invited to join the Mount Everest Committee, convened in January 1921 to organise the first expeditions to reconnoitre and attempt the mountain, and yet it seems he was not considered automatically for membership of the expedition. He was just 40 years old, five years older than Mallory but 15 years younger than Harold Raeburn, who was appointed climbing leader. It's possible he had simply counted himself out. With three young daughters, family responsibilities may have weighed with him. Or in the light of his difficulty acclimatising on Kamet, perhaps he saw no prospect of going high.

With Percy Farrar, Meade shared the responsibility for equipping the expeditions – a thankless task. Whilst he was grappling with the problems of the quality and quantity of essentials such as clothing and tents, Meade was interrupted by more trivial matters: Raeburn wanted an alarm clock. His request was forwarded by the committee's secretary, Arthur Hinks, who added a characteristically sarcastic aside:

Raeburn asks for an Alarm Watch to wake himself up in the morning ...
This comes into your side of the equipment. The President [Younghusband]
suggests that something to rock him to sleep is more likely to be necessary.[12]

And inevitably there would be criticism of what was provided. Mallory's complaints resulted in an improved two-man tent, lighter and easy to erect in high winds, which was christened the Meade. It was essentially a modified version of the Whymper tent with a flysheet and was still in use on Everest in 1953. As Mike Parsons noted in *Invisible on Everest*, Meade's 'perceptions on equipment ... are frustratingly absent from his own writings.'[g] Following the return of the 1922 expedition Meade, who had now settled in Wales, resigned from the MEC but continued to take an active interest in the conduct of subsequent expeditions. He was a protagonist in the wrangle between the Alpine Club and the MEC sparked by the controversy around the choice of leader of the 1936 expedition (see *AJ* 124, p129), and a vocal advocate of the merits of small expeditions.

Throughout the 1930s Meade was a keen observer of developments in climbing in the Alps and Himalaya and contributed a number of essays on mountaineering to non-specialist periodicals such as *Cornhill Magazine* and *Blackwood's Magazine,* several of which were included in his first book, *Approach to the Hills,* published in 1940. Meade disapproved of the 'recklessness of life', 'predilection for mechanization' and the spirit of 'bitter nationalism' and competition displayed by the 'new adventurers' but unlike Col Strutt, who castigated them in the pages of the *Alpine Journal*, he allowed: 'it is possible that those who have a more conventional outlook on life than the new adventurers might find there is something to be learnt from them.'[13] But he believed: 'mountaineering is a pursuit in which the sporting instinct may enter at times, but the deepest motives behind it are a longing for adventure, a love of nature, and a sentiment that can only be called mystical.'[14] The last of these, 'the longing for perfection', Meade considered 'the strongest of the motives that can lure us into the hills.' He explored and developed this view through the writings of philosophers, poets and mountaineers in his book, *High Mountains,* and it is clear that mountains provided him with a special 'happiness' which even in its most dilute form had 'more significance in it than the mere satisfaction produced by spending an agreeable holiday.'[15]

In the early evening of 1 June 1953, the telephone rang at Meade's home in Wales. The caller was Sir Alan 'Tommy' Lascelles, a good friend and distant relation, who was also the Queen's private secretary. The news of the first ascent of Everest had just been received at Buckingham Palace and Lascelles, knowing of his 'cousin's' lifelong interest and involvement with Everest affairs, had telephoned to pass it on before the public announcement. 'Charlie, they've gone and done it, Everest has been climbed,' he said. To which Meade replied simply, 'What a pity.'[16]

---

g. Eric Shipton had no luck trying to elicit information. 'The "Meade" tent is really a smaller edition of the "Whymper",' he wrote in *Upon That Mountain,* 'and is named after the well-known mountaineer C F Meade – I have asked him why, but he could not enlighten me.'

Acknowledgement

I wish to thank Jasper Meade for his help and hospitality and for his permission to reproduce quotations from CFM's unpublished letters and diaries.

Endnotes
All unreferenced quotations are from CFM's letters and diaries.
1. 'Introduction to Clanwilliam/Meade papers', Public Record Office of Northern Ireland, 2007, p5.
2. P & L Gillman, *The Wildest Dream*, London, 2000, p28.
3. A C Benson, *Along the Road*, London, 1926, p87.
4. A Hankinson, *Geoffrey Winthrop Young: Poet, Mountaineer, Educator*, London, 1995, p55.
5. R Fedden, *Alpine Journal* 81, p270.
6. C Meade, *Approach to the Hills*, London, 1940, p36.
7. Ibid p214.
8. Ibid p189.
9. Ibid p205 & p212.
10. Ibid p245.
11. Ibid p251.
12. Hinks to Meade, 18 Mar 1921, RGS EE 38/1.
13. C Meade, op cit, p102.
14. Ibid p100.
15. C Meade, *High Mountains*, London, 1954, p9.
16. J Meade, personal communication.

ERIC VOLA

Summer's Winter

Pierre Mazeaud and the 1961 Frêney Tragedy

At the Fourche bivouac hut Pierre Mazeaud takes a photo of himself and his three companions on the eve of their fateful departure to the central pillar of Frêney. From top to bottom: Pierre Kohlmann, Antoine Vieille, Robert Guillaume and Mazeaud. *(Mazeaud Collection)*

Many British climbers came to believe that Pierre Mazeaud – alpinist, jurist and French government minister – didn't like the 'Rosbifs'. This was true even of Doug Scott. When I told Doug I had asked Pierre to write the foreword of his book *The Ogre*, which I had translated (*Les Éditions du Mont-Blanc 2018*) he was quite astonished. Then I explained that this belief was erroneous, resulting solely from the clash that occurred on the 1971 international Everest expedition. On one side was Norman Dyhrenfurth's deputy Jimmy Roberts and Don Whillans, and on the other Pierre and other European stars: Yvette and Michel Vaucher, Carlo Mauri and Wolfgang Axt. Both sides had separate and conflicting objectives without the resources to do both. Don and Pierre had the strongest voices though, and so we heard more from them than the others.

But Pierre, born in 1929, was and is a true mountaineer; his best friends are or were mountaineers, such as Walter Bonatti. He never confused politicians with climbers. (Only one family with whom he grew up remained important as non-climbing friends: the Debré, a family like his own made up of eminent lawyers of whom one – Jean-Louis Debré – was president of our constitutional court just after Pierre.) Race, colour, rank, social class or nationality never had any importance to Pierre, particularly where climbing was concerned. Only the talent, daring and honesty of the climber mattered to him. This is what he said about Doug having read his book:

> *It is of course through those lines* [concerning Doug's dramatic descent] *told with brevity that one understands who Scott is. Indeed, an outstanding alpinist but a man cultivating simplicity as a philosophy, mixing a deep humanism with a rich culture.*

> *For me a very great man.*

> *So, thank you, dear Doug, thank you for those two hundred odd pages studded with brilliant photos, thank you for allowing us to share this passion for summits, shared with human beings who believe in nothing less than the strength of friendship.*

Pierre Mazeaud understood what that meant: the strength of friendship. On 11 July 1961, soon after Doug turned 20, seven alpinists were caught in a huge storm on the central pillar of Frêney, near the top of Mont Blanc. Five days later, a helicopter brought the three survivors to Courmayeur. Pierre Mazeaud was one of them. A new book has been published in France by the author Virginie Troussier, *Au milieu de l'été un invincible hiver* ('In the middle of summer an indomitable winter'[1]), which Pierre Mazeaud considers the best-written version of this drama. Revisiting his epic battle reminds us of the bonds that can be forged from such overwhelming tragedy.

Prelude
The central pillar of Frêney, an 800m spike of beautiful red granite just below the summit of Mont Blanc on its Italian side, was in 1961 one of

1. V Troussier, *Au milieu de l'été, un invincible hiver*, Guerin, 2021.

Mont Blanc's flying buttress, the central pillar of Frêney in the centre of the frame, and the vision of Walter Bonatti. *(Bonatti Collection)*

the 'last great problems' of the Alps. Today it remains one of the great classic routes in the Mont Blanc range. In 1973, it was the hundredth route in Gaston Rébuffat's famous book *The Mont Blanc Massif: The 100 Finest Routes*, chosen because he considered it the greatest route for any alpinist and so the first of them all. Far away from anywhere, a snow and ice route in itself just to get to its foot, the greatest rock difficulties are concentrated at the top at over 4,500m and the risk of bad weather making retreat difficult made it then and make it now a route demanding deep mountaineering expertise and total commitment. As Rébuffat wrote in his book:

Other routes present greater and more sustained difficulties, but none demands such powers of decision [making] and such exact mountaineering judgment, this because of the remoteness and the difficulty of retreat in case of bad weather. The Frêney Pillar is the most striking example of how the difficulty of a route is made up of several factors besides the difficulty of the climbing itself.

In July 1961, I was enjoying my first year in Chamonix, the year I started climbing serious routes. I vividly remember a scene soon after the Frêney drama when I saw Mazeaud, his hands and feet covered with bandages, being carried on the shoulders of one of his pals on his way to the post office. He was fulminating, shouting abuse at civil service 'assholes' who because of their regulations had refused to bring him an important official letter to his hospital bed. The fact I was 19 years old and that the victims died in the order of their age, the youngest being just 22, put an indelible mark on me which is still there today. Another personal link with that drama is Robert Guillaume's girlfriend, Muriel, whom I met then. Later, I climbed with her and her future husband, Mike Gravina, youngest son of the Countess Gravina, better known perhaps to Club members as Briggsy. We had met at Jesus College for an annual Cambridge Alpine dinner after which we did some

Roberto Gallieni and his guide, Walter Bonatti, who with Andrea Oggioni, joined forces with the French team. *(Bonatti Collection)*.

night climbing on the walls of his college in dinner jackets and EBs. Muriel has remained a friend, despite not seeing her often as she moved long ago to Los Angeles. But each time I think of her, I remember Robert Guillaume as he was, a strikingly good-looking 25-year-old rock climber, and of his pals that died with him, and the three who survived.

After Walter Bonatti, Jean Couzy and René Desmaison in 1957 were probably the first to think of doing the first ascent of the Frêney pillar. However, Jean Couzy was killed in 1958 by a stone fall in the Devoluy. In August 1959, Bonatti with Andrea Oggioni and Roberto Gallieni managed to climb the lower part of the pillar but without enough equipment had to come down. In 1960 there were several attempts by Bonatti, Michel Vaucher, Desmaison with Mazeaud, Julien, Lagesse, George Payot, Audibert and Laffont, and probably a few others.

At the beginning of July 1961, Mazeaud and his best friend, Pierre Kohlmann, with Antoine Vieille and Robert Guillaume decided to have a go at the central pillar under the noses of the Chamonix guides. Pierre 'Le Maz' Mazeaud was 32 years old and already a *magistrat;* Kohlmann, known as 'Pierrot', was 26, a chemist living like Pierre in Paris where he taught climbing to blind people. The pair had made their most important ascents together, including a few firsts, the most recent being the winter ascent of Piz Cengalo's north couloir in February 1961. Robert Guillaume was 25, a superb rock climber nicknamed 'Le Patissier' for the work he was doing at night to be free to climb during the day. Already selected for the Jannu expedition in 1962, Terray thought highly of his climbing capabilities. Antoine 'Tonio' Vieille was a 22-year-old colossus, the son of an admiral who had a few months before made the first winter ascent of the Bonatti pillar. They were all at their physical best.

Meeting Bonatti

Saturday 8 July. The French team of four reached La Fourche bivouac hut and at midnight started down to the Brenva glacier. But the weather was too warm, so they returned to the little hut to await colder conditions. As night fell on Sunday 9 July, they were woken by the arrival of three Italians. They recognise Walter Bonatti with his usual climbing partner Andrea Oggioni and his friend and client Roberto Gallieni. Walter and Andrea are back from Peru to try something new on 'his' mountain, the Italian side of Mont Blanc which he knows inside out and where he has already added some beautiful lines, the Grand Pilier d'Angle and the Pilier Rouge du Brouillard with Andrea. All three are 31 years old. Andrea, a worker living near Milan, established the Pel e Oss (skin and bones) climbing group when he was just 18 and was the first to introduce Walter, then a fine gymnast, to climbing. Andrea had become his best friend and climbing partner. Roberto, *l'ingeniere* (the engineer), had a tie factory in Milan. He started mountaineering aged 12 and climbing at a high level had become a close friend of Andrea and Walter. By the time of the Frêney he was much more a friend than a client.

Bonatti was at the top of his fame after his first ascent, solo, of the southeast pillar of the Petit Dru in 1955, a year after being abandoned on K2 to survive a harrowing bivouac above 8,000m with his Pakistani porter, Mahdi, who despite Walter's care was left badly frostbitten and crippled. Walter's method of revenge was his incredibly risky solo and numerous major first ascents in the Mont Blanc range. Walter was never interested in risking his life for a handful of banknotes, so Gallieni was there because Walter considered him fully capable of the last major unclimbed line on Mont Blanc and the most beautiful too. After his first attempt two years earlier, this time Walter has a well-prepared plan.

Bonatti told the French team, 'You were first. Go to the pillar, we will do another route.' But Guillaume and Mazeaud, both great admirers of Walter, immediately replied: 'No way! You were the first to think of it, we know that. Let's go together.' The decision was taken to form one party. As Walter wrote in the bivouac notebook:

We decide to collaborate in a true sense of comradeship and mountaineering. We will start at midnight. Weather good. Target: The Frêney central pillar.

The following day, after getting to the col de Peuterey (4000m) at 6am and resting, the Italians headed to the Rochers Gruber to fetch equipment Walter had left there two years before, while Pierre Mazeaud's team moved up the first section of the pillar. The stage was set.

Day One

Monday 10 July. At 8 am Pierre starts climbing the pillar. Late that afternoon the Italians, having fetched the equipment left at the Rochers Gruber, catch up with the French who have climbed the first 300m section of mixed ice

The first day on the pillar. *(Mazeaud Collection)*

and rock. They prepare their first bivouac slightly above the point Walter reached in 1959. The Italians have a small bivouac tent, the French only a plastic sheet to cover their sleeping bags. The first night is freezing cold, but good. Kohlmann reminds Mazeaud that this is their 30th bivouac together. They still have 500m to go. They hope tomorrow to reach the base of the Chandelle where the greatest difficulties are concentrated. If everything goes well, they should be on the summit of Mont Blanc on Wednesday. The night passes peacefully.

Day Two

Tuesday July 11th. At 3.30am they wake up to a clear sky. They drink hot tea and wait in their duvets for the sun to rise. Walter leads up on the second section of the pillar, climbing fast. At noon they reach the foot of the last section of 80m, the Chandelle. Mazeaud and Kohlmann take the lead and equip the first very difficult pitch. They reach a good platform and are quickly joined by Robert Guillaume and Antoine Vieille. At 2pm, Pierre Mazeaud starts up the second difficult pitch on magnificent rock. Out of the blue, while banging in a peg and standing in an etrier, he hears a long ringing sound, like a phone. Then, as Mazeaud later describes in his book *Naked Before the Mountain,* 'his fingers feel like they're starting to burn and flying

With the climbers close to success, at the end of the second day Mont Blanc was engulfed in storm. Here Kohlmann and Mazeaud stand shivering, trapped high on the pillar. *(Bonatti Collection)*

sparks are running up the hammer.' The storm starts with extreme violence. The air is saturated with electricity. Mazeaud shouts to be lowered down, leaving his hardware sparking on a peg. Just as Mazeaud reaches the ledge, where the others are preparing a bivouac, there's a huge flash and a deafening bang. A hundred million volts of lightning hits them. Kohlmann suffers from permanent hearing problems and wears a hearing aid. As the lightning strikes, a blue spark comes flying out of Kohlmann's bad ear and he collapses in Mazeaud's arms. A Coramine stimulant injection revives him. Now practically deaf, this amateur Mozart performer starts to disconnect from his companions. Later he will lose contact with reality.

The storm rages violently all night. Lightning strikes them several times. Mazeaud later writes:

> *The anguish of death seizes us, and we cannot do anything, no movement, no word, only thinking – yes, of death – and waiting for its arrival … It is midnight but the light is as strong as the glare of a blast furnace. At times, we jump, one after the other. One particularly violent strike shoves our faces against the wall, the same one that makes the Italians jump in the air. Afterwards I will have marks on my ankles, small black stars. Sparks come flying out of our hands and feet.*

Walter Bonatti describes the same sensation of horror and dread. Mont Blanc's highest pillar has transformed itself into a lightning conductor. The lightning strikes last all night. He writes in *The Mountains of My Life*:

> *Sometimes they go away, and we are relieved; sometimes they seem to concentrate around us and anguish clutches at us. We are there, full of life, but absolutely helpless in front of this furious outburst of nature's power. Near us, attached to the pegs that hold us above the abyss, all our climbing equipment*

After a nightmarish bivouac, the climbers attempt to escape upwards but were driven back as the storm dug in. *(Bonatti Collection)*

is suspended: pegs, crampons, ice axes. One could not imagine better bait for lightning. We would like to get rid of them, but if we do, how would we get up or go down? … We feel a force pulling at our legs as though wanting to tear them out. Lightning just skimmed past. We howl savagely. We are alive, but we know that any moment the storm can reduce us to ashes …I have the strong feeling that we are lost, and it is I believe the feeling of all of us.

Lightning hits Kohlmann a second time. Unconscious, he slumps down on his rope. Mazeaud stops his fall and revives him again with another Co-ramine shot. Now he is completely deaf. But both men can still understand each other.

He cries slowly looking at me; I have never loved him more and I embrace him. What is stronger than friendship?

Day Three and Four

Wednesday July 12 and Thursday 13. 7am. The storm has relented but snow now falls continuously, thickening the silence. It's 80m of climbing to the top of the pillar at 4,500m, then a nice snow ridge to the summit of Mont Blanc and an easy descent to Chamonix. But progress will be difficult, the wall is shrouded in ice, the cracks are full of snow. Just when they're ready to start the wind strengthens to gale force and thunder booms again around them. Climbing up is impossible. What should they do? 'Wait,' Bonatti says. They believe bad summer weather like this can't last much longer. What they don't know is that from the Channel to the Alps, the whole of France is being swept by an exceptional storm. Gales blow at 140kph. Ships are being blown ashore. Sixty-four Spanish sailors are lost at sea. In Chamonix and Courmayeur, friends and family start to worry.

For two more days, they wait for the weather to clear. Despite the cold, the wind and the snow they continue to hope they will get out by climbing to the top. Some people, particularly in Italy, will criticize this decision, but if all of them chose that solution it was neither pride nor ambition to climb the pillar at all costs. They only have 80m to climb and then it will be much easier, quicker and far less dangerous to come down from the top of Mont Blanc by the normal route than retreat down on the Italian side. Being seven in such awful conditions, sorting the ropes takes a long time and demands much effort. In the freezing blast of the storm, putting a peg in and a sling on takes a lot of time and effort. With the overhangs and difficulties of the route below, they all know that going down will be extremely hazardous. Mazeaud recalls later, 'We all knew the danger of descent and all of us had in mind the tragedy of the Eiger.'

At the end of the third day, again at midnight, the sky clears, stars shine and their hopes revive. At last, they can light up their stoves, which the gale has prevented them from doing for the last two days. But in the morning the storm is on them again. Forty hours have passed since it started and they realise now that going up will be impossible. These two days of waiting have sealed their fate. When asked much later why the youngest die first, Mazeaud replies bluntly: 'The older are more resilient.'

Day Five

Friday July 14th. Bonatti's note at La Fourche has been found by his close friend and climbing partner Gigi Panei who has gone looking for him, skiing up in the night despite the storm. Four hours later he is back to Courmayeur and a rescue party of five guides quickly forms, reaching the Gamba refuge that same afternoon.

At 3.30 am Bonatti's watch wakes him up. He has no more doubt: 'we must get down at all costs. If we wait, our strength will go, and it will be too late … ' Everything is stiff and frozen. It is now impossible either to go up or wait. Bonatti and Mazeaud take the decision to go down. The drastic weather conditions, with little or usually no visibility, make it an overly complex venture: 600m of abseils to the foot of the pillar, a large plateau with deep

On the fifth day, the climbers decided to retreat down the south side of the mountain. *(Bonatti Collection)*

snow to cross, finding the abseils off the Rochers Gruber, descending the Fréney glacier, getting up to the Innominata col to get down to the Gamba refuge. Bonatti knows the area and the way to Gamba; he has led a rescue party up most of that route.

At 6am, they start the descent. Bonatti takes the lead. Mazeaud follows suit, Oggioni comes last, pulling the abseils and securing each man as he descends, an arduous role which will finally take its toll on him. Sorting the ropes takes an age. The wall is plastered with snow, their clothes are stiff with ice, their ropes are like wires, whirlpools of snow and mist blind them and muffle their voices and their shouts of: 'Abseil free!' Several times the rope gets stuck in precarious positions. They abandon one of them. After 12 hours of exhausting efforts, they finally reach the bottom of the pillar, where powder snow reaches their bellies. They head for the col de Peuterey. Before night falls, they find a crevasse to shelter in for their fifth bivouac.

This fifth night will be the worst. The cold is insane. The weather station at Helbronner records -18°C, so it must be -22°C or lower at their bivouac 400m higher. With the wind chill they're facing temperatures of around -50°C. Their clothes are frozen hard; the French have lost their canvas sheet, torn away by the gale the previous day. The wind howls, unrelenting. They are all exhausted. Mazeaud's feet are frozen but Kohlmann's state is the worst. They share their last food, some prunes and bits of chocolate, some sugar and dried meat. Kohlmann's hands are frozen black. Bonatti hands him a small bottle of methylated spirit to rub his hands with. Pierre Kohlmann thinks he is being offered a drink and puts it to his mouth and takes two swigs before Walter can snatch it from his grasp. While Kohlmann goes to sleep, Bonatti worries: 'Have we lost our minds?' A last cup of tea and then they have no more gas for their burners, so they suck snowballs, burning their mouths without giving them the water their bodies crave.

Mazeaud remembers talking endlessly with Antoine Vieille, even joking about women:

> *He told me: we won't be in Chamonix tomorrow, too bad, we won't know who will win the Tour de France[2] … and I will not be able to make love to Anny!'*

They spent the night smoking their last cigarettes.

Day Six
Saturday 15 July. They wake at 3.30am. During the night another 60cm of snow has fallen. They know that none of them will survive a fifth bivouac. They must reach the Gamba refuge before nightfall. Bonatti writes later: 'if not, it will, most certainly, be the end of us all.' The seven men start down, Bonatti leading. They reach the Gruber rocks, but the slope is steep and in danger of avalanching with so much snow. Bonatti decides to belay each of them on the rope, one at a time. Around 9am Antoine Vieille slows down, falls, gets up. Mazeaud gets his rucksack off, pulls his rope, but Vieille collapses again. Mazeaud and Guillaume try to revive him but after half an hour or so, at 10am, the youngest of them has ceased to fight and slowly dies. Bonatti comes back up. They put Antoine's body in the Italian tent canvas. Pierre Mazeaud bangs in a piton and clips in his friend's corpse. Bonatti will recall 24 years later:

> *When Vieille died, I was beside Kohlmann. I told myself: you must show yourself strong. So, I spoke harshly. All six of us were roped. I told them: if we do not want to end like Vieille, we must not lose one minute. It was a whiplash that I had to deliver … That day, coming down the Pillar, I was the one who knew the way. If I let go, we all die. This is what kept me alive.*

They all follow Bonatti. The fog lifts, helping them find the long and dangerous abseils down the Gruber rocks covered in snow. Around 1pm, Bonatti hears voices: the rescuers, but where are they? Then the voices stop. They will learn later that the rescue party[3] of five Courmayeur guides, having reached the Gamba the afternoon before, have continued during the night up the Brouillard glacier in deep snow, stopping because of the dangerous snow conditions near the Frêney pass, way off to the right, thinking that Bonatti and Mazeaud's parties have headed for the Eccles bivouac[4]

2. On Sunday 16 July 1961, Jacques Anquetil won the second of his five victories in the Tour de France with two commanding time trials and a shrewd ride through the mountains after leading, as he predicted, the race from the first day.

3. They went down to Gamba where more rescuers joined them. The leader of the rescue team decided to wait until daylight to go back up, this time by the Frêney route, rejecting Gary Hemming and John Harlin's proposal to go right away in the night to the Innominata col. Gary and John had gone to rescue two pals, a Swiss and a German, who retreated from the Peuterey ridge down to the Craveri bivouac (Dames Anglaises). They had left a rope on the Gamba side of the col de l'Innominata that helped their pals get down to Gamba and also the following day helped Bonatti, Gallieni and Kohlmann.

4. Also known as the Giuseppe Lampugnani bivouac from one of the founders of the CAI.

MONT BLANC

Mt BLANC
COURMAYEUR

1

POINT EXTRÊME

BIVOUAC
DE LA « CHANDELLE »

COL ÉCCLES

COL
PEUTEREY

POINT EXTRÊME
DES SAUVETEURS

2

ANTOINE
VIEILLE

3

ROBERT
GUILLAUME

4

POINT OU FUT
RETROUVÉ
KOHLMAN

OGGIONI
BIVOUAC MAZEAUD

KOHLMAN

5

REFUGE GAMBA

The illustration in Paris-Match that detailed the team's high point, the route
taken by the rescue party and where each of the four victims met their end.

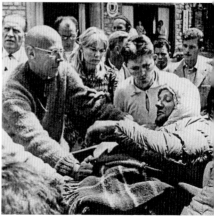

After a dreadful seventh bivouac, Pierre Mazeaud is brought down by the Italian rescue part. Evacuated by helicopter to Courmayeur, welcomed by his father and his girlfriend Dany.

250m higher. Bonatti believes that option is too avalanche prone which is why with Mazeaud and Oggioni's approval they are choosing to descend the Gruber rocks and the Frêney glacier, the classic way down.

At 5pm, after the last of many abseils, they are down the Rochers Gruber. Through deep snow, they traverse, so very slowly, the heavily crevassed Frêney glacier. Exhausted, Oggioni has given his rucksack to Gallieni but falls every four paces. They are in sight of the col de l'Innominata. Behind the pass is the Gamba refuge and safety. They know that rescuers will be waiting there for them. They abandon most of their equipment except for a few pegs and karabiners. Bonatti and Gallieni go ahead to equip the steep slope up to the pass, the last difficulty. Mazeaud follows but then hears Oggioni shouting. He explains with gestures that Robert Guillaume has disappeared. The storm blinds them; their searches and calls are in vain. Next morning, the rescuers will find his body in the snow.

Bonatti, unaware of the drama that has just occurred, has climbed up the steep 90m slope to reach the col in total darkness. In the deep snow it has taken him three hours and it's now 9pm. Mazeaud, Kohlmann and Oggioni reach the 50m rope held by Bonatti and tie in. It is Oggioni's turn but he cannot get up nor untie the iced knot blocking his rope in a peg. Even with Gallieni's help, Bonatti cannot pull him up. Death has started its work on Oggioni. Hours go by. At midnight Bonatti asks Mazeaud to stay with Oggioni. They will spend their sixth night out roped to a peg on a wall, while Bonatti heads to the Gamba refuge to send them the rescue party.

Without warning, Kohlmann unties himself and pulling on Bonatti's rope reaches the col de l'Innominata, raving mad. Gallieni manages to catch him and attach him with a karabiner to his rope. Pierre Mazeaud will explain later to Paris-Match's journalists that Kohlmann thought his two companions wanted to abandon him.

The Paris-Match coverage was extensive, illustrating how the tragedy caught the imagination of the French public. Bonatti was honoured in France but was met with distrust in Italy.

Day Seven

Sunday 16 July. Around 1am, Oggioni starts becoming delirious. Mazeaud remembers looking at his watch when Oggioni, the partner with whom Bonatti has done so many new routes, gives up the struggle. It's 2.15am. Mazeaud will write:

Andrea, I saw you fall asleep. I saw you die and you made me understand that death is nothing.

Kohlmann has been behaving erratically during the descent of the col de l'Innominata and nearing the Gamba refuge, he now believes his companions want to kill him. He goes berserk and jumps on them. They keep him off by tightening the rope on both sides of him but now can't move. Finally, they manage to untie themselves from their iced rope by rolling their pants down and running away from their deranged companion. As a consequence, it takes Bonatti and Gallieni three hours to reach Gamba instead of one. In total darkness, Bonatti pulls ahead, acting on instinct, with Gallieni still on his rope. At 3am, they reach the hut where 30 rescuers are sleeping. They immediately go out to help the others while Bonatti falls into a deep sleep. They find Kohlmann who has the strength to ask them if they have found Pierre Mazeaud before dying in their arms following a final bout of delirium at around 4am.

At 6am the rescuers bring Mazeaud to the Gamba refuge[5], where he tells Bonatti his best friend and partner Oggioni is dead. Mazeaud himself is told of the death of his own best friend Pierrot Kohlmann: 'as close to me as a brother'. Pierre Mazeaud is on the verge of coma when the rescuers reach him. In hospital a protein blood test shows that instead of a normal value of 95, his has fallen to 28. The death threshold stands at 25; he probably had an hour or so left when he was found. At around the same time, a doctor performs an azotemia test on Bonatti's blood as he rests on a sofa at a friend's house to check his kidney function. When the results come back they are off the scale. Physiologically he should be dead. His friend tells him

5. Under difficult flying conditions (low ceiling, strong wind, snow fall) a French gendarmerie Alouette dropped Gaston Rébuffat at Gamba (16 July before 6am) to organise the transportation of the survivors and rescuers to Courmayeur as well as the bodies of Kohlmann and Guillaume. Nine rotations were necessary, the last with the body of Guillaume at 11am. A last flight at 2pm crossing the Petit Saint Bernard pass, 50 feet above the ground due to the low ceiling, brought Mazeaud down to the Saint Luc Hospital in Lyon.

later that his body's heat has left his impression on the sofa's fabric, like the Turin shroud.

The Aftermath

In several Italian newspapers, Bonatti was criticised for his role, accused of having run for the refuge after abandoning his companions. ('They can't forgive me for coming back alive,' he told the well-known Italian journalist Dino Buzzati, a quote that became the headline on Buzzati's piece for *Corriere della Sera*.) In Monza, Oggioni's hometown, some of his dead partner's friends and kin whom Bonatti went to see showed him some sullen hostility. This grieved him deeply. Dino Buzzati, who had become a close friend of Bonatti and later a friend also of Mazeaud, took his defence in his *Corriere della Sera* article, published on 21 July. Having responded to the main complaints against Bonatti, he concluded:

> *If one really wants to criticise what occurred (something always too easy to do when one is quietly sitting at home in one's armchair and not suspended above dreadful abysses, with -30°C, whipped by a merciless storm, hands torn by frost) the question that one should ask is not: what more Bonatti should have done? But: how could he have done so much? ... Unfortunately, when such a tragedy occurs, the survivors, who knows why, are always looked at askance, almost as if one is disappointed to see them back. As if having come back alive constituted some sort of abuse on their part. Let us forget the expedition or party leaders; as absurd it may be, they are made scapegoats ... To eliminate the slightest shadow, the merest doubt about Bonatti's behaviour, we have, luckily, Pierre Mazeaud's declarations, loyal, enthusiastic, and crystal clear. Not counting what the famous guide Gaston Rébuffat who participated in the rescue wrote in Le Monde...*

As Bonatti wrote in *The Mountains of my Life*:

> *I survived, that is all. Maybe because more than the others I did not want or could not let myself die.*

Pierre Mazeaud gave complete public support to Bonatti and the French government awarded the Italian the *Mérite sportif*. In his book *Naked Before the Mountain* he wrote without ambiguity that he owed his life to Bonatti and that without him he would also be dead. As a government minister he lobbied for France to award Bonatti the *Legion d'honneur*, the country's highest award, for 'his courageous conduct and the fraternity shown during this dramatic enterprise.' Their close friendship lasted until the death of Walter Bonatti in September 2011.

I need also to remind the reader of the controversy René Desmaison created by pretending to have done the first ascent of the pillar alongside the Anglo-Polish team of Bonington, Whillans, Clough and Djuglosz, some weeks after the drama. Desmaison also accused the French journalist

Philippe Gaussot who had covered the event of being biased towards the British. Pierre Mazeaud had been a climbing partner of Desmaison, on the Cima Ovest for the first ascent of the *Couzy* route in 1959, along with Pierre Kohlmann and Bernard Lagesse. But despite their friendship, Mazeaud, exasperated by René's lies, wrote to Lucien Devies, editor of *La Montagne et Alpinisme,* stating that Devies would soon be forced to retract Desmaison's claim that his ascent of the central pillar should be counted alongside the Anglo-Polish team as the first.

I cannot see how better to finish than by quoting Virginie Troussier, the inspired author of *Au milieu de l'été un invincible hiver* ('In the middle of summer an indomitable winter'), who concludes her book as follows:

> *I met Pierre Mazeaud at his home, to get the grist of what matters, what remains beyond the facts. A thoughtful handshake and a slight movement of the head already tell me much, our interactions and conversation make us feel and appreciate more than understand. They are things we cannot define; one just knows when it is there, the intelligence, the uprightness. Sharing a silence with Mazeaud, at the start of our talk, settles on us very naturally. From his being radiates a strength that seems to open a path to the sky. On his desk, I see all the photos of mountains, notably one in black and white with Bonatti, another one (a large format), the famous one of the La Fourche refuge with his three friends, Vieille, Guillaume, Kohlmann. But in the course of our discussion, I understand that memories exist in Mazeaud through a gesture, a smile, a look: they are not separate from him; they are part of him.*

> *From that tragedy, Mazeaud emerged shattered. One year after, he made a first ascent with Bonatti on the Petites Jorasses east face and they decided afterwards to go to the Rochers Gruber. The beauty of the site imposed itself once again. Mazeaud told me: 'it is like the Himalaya.' Together they become aware of all this shared passion. They understand that they must accept the mystery, give up this exhausting search of a why that does not exist, get out of this night. To know that the soul of their companions will remain in the hollows of the summits brings them comfort. The skin of their friends forms one with the world. The ultimate place is not the tomb but the mountain. In the end only places remain, at the end of it all, they continue, they persevere with the souls of the ones who crossed them, those who stayed in them ... Living and being dead can coincide. The two conditions can denote a point that is common to them, beyond any logic, not traceable, which cannot be proved, but a point where relations become clearer. Kohlmann, Guillaume, Vieille and Oggioni are invisible but they are not gone...*

> *'But this tragedy, is far away now,' Mazeaud says.*

> *'For you, it's far away?' I ask.*

> *'No, for me it is not from today, it is from yesterday, but it is from a past that*

still hits me. Obviously when one has lived through such a drama, it is difficult to get out of it. I think often about it, and with age, even more so.'

Of that ascent he remembers clearly flames of joy, flaring up, sparks of brilliance. The deepness of the memory grows. The more time takes you away from loss, the more you have the need to rally, or collect it … It is possible to recall an intense happiness, which later was transformed into tragedy, and still feel this joy despite the devastating grief that followed. This feeling is happiness brought back for a few seconds, like lightning. There are areas that remain intact in our memory, insensitive to the passing of time, allowing us to bring back to life the precise intensity. Whatever happens, this time will always seem happy. The hours spent staring at the truth, of a human being, a scenery, are always rewarding. The truth is never given without risks or after-effects. The friendship that those alpinists shared is a human success, a rarity in itself. Friendship is an event in the life of a human being, an indelible event, which will follow you everywhere. The faces of Pierre Kohlmann, Antoine Vieille, Robert Guillaume, Andrea Oggioni will always remain young, they will live amongst them, in them. We live with our missing ones, and this relation is one of deepest things that is given us to live.

Pierre Mazeaud wrote another foreword for a book I translated: Andy Cave's *Learning to Breathe* (*L'ombre et la lumière*, Nevicata, 2013). In fact, he agreed immediately, without thinking about it.

I liked [Cave's book] because in his text I could see my own beginnings on the Fontainebleau boulders and the Saussois cliffs, where we were climbing with the boys from the Club Olympique de Boulogne-Billancourt [made up of Renault factory workers such as Lucien Berardini], all boilermakers or coach-builders, who were the elite of mountaineering in the period 1960-70. Some comparisons moved me more than others: the death of his friend Brendan, a brother to him, and that of my friends on the Frêney pillar in 1961 … Friends, he has many: how much I have liked to read him speak of Dougal Haston, John Harlin, Doug Scott – I have known them so well … Now I would like to know the author. I have shared some of his passions and as he I believe that without passion life is not worth living. Meet him to tell him my admiration, and also my respect, respect to the underground miners, to the alpinist with an exceptional record, respect quite simply to the man.

This meeting took place a year or so later at the Fontainebleau boulder of *La dame Jeanne*, a remarkable and enjoyable moment for those two great mountaineers.

This told, I hope now Alpine Club members will accept that the 1971 Everest controversy was simply a clash between two groups of climbers with two different objectives that could not both be satisfied given the means gathered by the expedition leader. And that they will see Pierre as one of us: a true climber and mountaineer.

Sources

W Bonatti, *À mes montagnes,* Arthaud, 1964. In English, *The Mountains of My Life*, Penguin, 2010.
O Guillaumont, *Pierre Mazeaud l'Insoumis,* Editions Guerin, 2012.
P Mazeaud, *Montagne pour un homme nu,* Arthaud, 1971. In English, *Naked Before the Mountain,* Victor Gollancz, 1974.
V Troussier, *Au milieu de l'été un invincible hiver,* Editions Guerin, 2021.
E Vola, *L'affaire Frêney, Alpine Journal,* 2012, p257.

JOHN MCMAHON MOORE

The Tre Cime and the Great War

Military Vie Ferrate and War Walks in the Drei Zinnen

An Austrian 80mm field gun supporting the frontline
north of the Toblinger Knoten.

The Tre Cime or Drei Zinnen massif north of Cortina is a popular rock
climbing, mountain walking and *vie ferrate (Klettersteige)* area. Remnants
of First World War military engineering are widespread. Those involved in
the conflict are commemorated in chapels near the CAI Auronzo and Drei
Zinnen (Locatelli) huts. Some military installations have been re-instated as
walks, scrambles and vie ferrate.

On 23 May 1915 the Italian government, induced by Franco-British territorial promises, abandoned neutrality and declared war on the Austro-Hungarian Empire, already embroiled in campaigns against Russia and Serbia. The Austrians' strategic objective against Italy was to hold the border and prevent the loss of South Tyrol, Trieste and parts of what are now Slovenia and Croatia. With very few regular troops available, the defence of the Dolomites was left mainly to reserve depot troops and volunteer militia, including members of local shooting associations *(Schiessstände)*. The pre-war national border, now the Bozen-Belluno Province boundary, ran along the ridge east and westward from the Tre Cime/Drei Zinnen peaks.

In the weeks before the war, the Italians occupied positions on the border ridge from Croda d'Arghena to the Paternsattel, Gamsjoch and Büllelejoch. While last efforts to negotiate non-intervention were still taking place, the Austrians stationed a few hundred *Landschützen* (yeomanry) in the Drei Zinnen hut and at points on the Schwabenalpenkopf-Innichriedel Knotcn ridge north of the Zinnen plateau (Langenalp). News of Italy's declaration of war did not reach the Italian troops until the following day when shots from Austrian field guns hit the Paternsattel and destroyed an Italian barracks. In retaliation, the Italians bombarded the Drei Zinnen hut, which burned down.

Offensive activity in the early days of the conflict, from May to July 1915, comprised sorties by small groups of Austrians who assaulted three points: the Paternsattel, the Croda d'Arghena ridge west of the Drei Zinnen and the Paterno/Paternkofel summit. In the first two cases, despite having gained their objectives, they were forced to withdraw for lack of support. Italian defenders on the Paternkofel summit beat off a rock-climbing patrol assault. Attempts to scale the steep scree and snow-filled northern gullies between the Zinnen summits were easily repulsed. In August, the Italians made a mass attack and captured the ruins of the Drei Zinnen hut and Sextenstein summit, creating a salient that came within 300m of the Austrian positions on the flanks of the Torre di Toblin/Toblinger Knoten. Subsequently, the Sextenstein summit changed hands briefly several times but despite the various attempts to recapture it, the Italians held the position until the end of October 1917.

The winters of 1915-16 and particularly 1916-17 were extreme and apart from underground excavations and maintenance of positions, military action and defence work were confined to four-month periods between June and October when snow had melted enough to permit mobility. An exception was the attempted recapture of the Sextenstein in April 1916, using a snow tunnel to approach the Italian position. Avalanches and blizzards cost many lives and regularly disrupted supplies. During the mountain campaign, avalanches, hypothermia and frostbite are estimated to have killed 10,000 Austrian and Italian troops. Aerial ropeways were built to sustain supply lines, particularly for those positions frequently isolated by deep snow.

In the course of the war, both sides occupied key summits on both ridges as defence lines and observation posts for artillery spotting. The Italians installed searchlights on the summit of the Cima Grande/Grosse Zinne and Paternkofel. The Austrians did similar things on various summits along the Schwabenkopf-Innichriedel ridge, notably on the summit of the Toblinger Knoten tower.

The Dolomites front was a 'side show' to the main fighting between Italy and Austria-Hungary, which was concentrated eastward, along the Isonzo valley where the Italians wasted many lives in numerous futile large-scale offensives. In the last week of October 1917, following a surprise attack at Caporetto on what is now the Slovenian border, the Italian armies collapsed and retreated headlong for more than 150km to the banks of the River Piave north of Venice. The rout, vividly described in Ernest Hemingway's novel *Farewell to Arms*, left the Italian situation in the eastern Dolomites untenable. Positions were abandoned and troops and civilians flooded down the valleys towards Venice. The last Italians left the Tre Cime/Drei Zinnen area on 5 November 1917, a year before the collapse of Austria-Hungary and the armistice. It was during the hasty retreat southward down these valleys that Erwin Rommel established his reputation by capturing large numbers of prisoners.

A curious and touching footnote to these sad events is that among the Austrian troops in the Zinnen sector was a 16-year-old girl, Viktoria Savs. Posing as a boy, she joined the Austrian forces with her father and served as a mule driver and messenger from June 1915 to 1916. She was then in the firing line until January 1917, when she lost a leg below the knee from rock fall caused by a shell explosion as she climbed to an exposed position to deliver a message. Her extraordinary story was the subject of a recent biography by Frank Gerbert, *Die Kriege der Viktoria Savs: von der Frontsoldatin 1917 zu Hitlers Gehilfin*.

Access to the Italian positions was from Misurina and Auronzo. The Austrians were supported from Innichen (San Cándido), Sexten (Sestó) and Höhlensteintal (Val di landro) south of Toblach (Dobbiaco). Since most of the action was in German-speaking South Tyrol, I have used traditional German place names in the following account of some key localities and events from the conflict. Routes described in Cicerone's *Via Ferratas of the Italian Dolomites,* Vol 1, (Italian names) are cross-referenced by the guidebook route numbers (MISUR2-5). The tourist map 'Dolomiten Front' (Kompass, 1:50,000) shows the front lines in the eastern Dolomites sector from 1915 until 1917. The Tabacco 1:25,000 topographical map (Dolomiti di Sesto/Sextener Dolomiten, Sheet 010) is useful for navigation and place names.

Paternsattel/Forcella di Lavaredo

The Patternsattel pass (2454m) between the Kleine Zinne and Passaportenkopf, on the walk from the Rifugio Auronzo to the Drei Zinnen hut was a key section of the Italian line. Apart from a few hours on 26 May 1915, it was in Italian hands throughout.

There are remains of Italian trenches, artillery emplacements and the

Temporary grave of Austrian guide Sepp Innerkofler, dug by Italian garrison on the summit of the Paternkofel. The body was exhumed after the Italian withdrawal and reburied at Sexten/Sesto church. Innerkofler's sacrifice was memorialised in this portrait by Tyrolean artist Franz Defregger (1835-1921).

sites of barracks on the south flank of the pass near the modern Rifugio Lavaredo and the lower slopes of the Passaportenkopf at the start of via ferrata (MISUR 5). This was the access point for the supply tunnel route to the Sextenstein positions and was completed in October 1917 only weeks before abandonment of the Italian positions.

Paternkofel Summit

For several days in the first week of the war in late May 1915, Sepp Innerkofler, the famous guide and warden of the Drei Zinnen hut, led rock-climbing patrols up the north side of the Paternkofel (2744m) to the unoccupied summit, from which to provide artillery observation and fire support for the attack on the Paternsattel. Each night the patrol returned to the Austrian lines. Bad weather on 27 May made ascent of the north side of the Paternkofel impractical. The Italians took advantage and used the easier south flank to occupy the summit.

An impractical decision was made to try to re-capture the Paternkofel summit by a rock-climbing assault. The attack began in darkness on 4 July and culminated in Innerkofler attempting to take the summit alone after climbing a chimney and throwing hand grenades, several of which failed to detonate. He was shot or hit by stones thrown by the defenders and fell backward. His body became entangled in the rocks and was later recovered

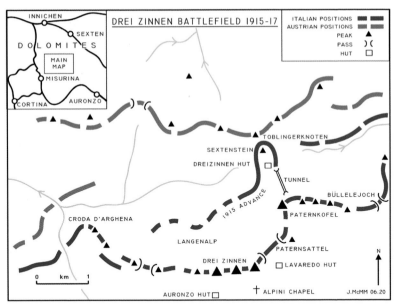

Simpified map showing Italian and Austrian positions in the Zinnen sector between August 1915 and October 1917.

by the Italians and buried on the summit in a grave marked by a wooden cross and plaque made from flattened tin cans with the words 'Sepp Innerkofler, Guida'. His body was subsequently exhumed and buried in Sexten, his home village. There has been controversy about whether Innerkofler was killed by the Alpini summit garrison or covering fire from an Austrian machine gun.

The Paternkofel summit area was subsequently much modified by blasting and became the site of a permanent artillery observation post with shelters and strong points on ledges and a large searchlight mounted on tracks. The route of Innerkofler's patrol assault is still identifiable (MISUR4-5) and a ledge where the party paused is marked by a cross.

Paternkofel Tunnel

In September 1916, the Italian command authorised construction of a 400m tunnel as a secure access route safe from enemy fire and avalanche risk from the Paternsattel to the exposed forward positions in the Sextenstein salient. It was also to provide loopholes for infantry and artillery and act as an assembly and sally port for renewed attacks on the Austrian lines. The original exit, now the start of the underground via ferrata (Sentiero De Luca-Innerkofler, MISUR 4) named after the leaders of the 1915 defenders and attackers, is near the Frankfurter Würstel pinnacle south of the Drei Zinnen hut.

To the south the upper tunnel portal gives access to a traverse of the east face of the Paternkofel to the Gamsscharte (Forcella del Camoscio) where it crosses the Innerkofler assault route. From the col a cable protected section

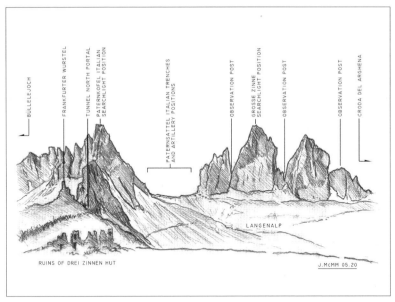

BULLELEJOCH
FRANKFURTER WURSTEL
TUNNEL NORTH PORTAL
PATERNKOFEL ITALIAN SEARCHLIGHT POSITION
PATERNSATTEL ITALIAN TRENCHES AND ARTILLERY POSITIONS
OBSERVATION POST
GROSSE ZINNE SEARCHLIGHT POSITION
OBSERVATION POST
OBSERVATION POST
CRODA DEL ARGHENA

LANGENALP

RUINS OF DREI ZINNEN HUT

J.McMM 05.20

A sketch view south from the ruins of the Drei Zinnen hut at the foot of the
Sextenstein north flank towards the Italian Paternsattel positions in 1917.
John Moore's sketches are drawn from contemporary photographs in the
style of military sketch-artist Richard Heuberger.

leads east along the Italian front line (MISUR5) over the Bödenknoten to
the Büllelejoch. Beyond the modern south exit, the tunnel was destroyed by
the Italians in October 1917. Ironically, it had been completed only weeks
before the Italians abandoned their positions.

From the Gamsjoch a scramble leads to the summit up the Italian access
route. Southward, the trail follows the Italian supply line partly in tunnels,
across the Passaportenscharte col and emerges on the Paternsattel near
some support trenches.

Sextenstein/Sasso di Sesto

Italian troops took Sextenstein (2539m) and the ruins of the Drei Zinnen
hut in August 1915 in their only mass attack, following a preliminary bom-
bardment. This was in preparation for an attempted breakthrough northward to the Puster valley. The rounded Sextenstein summit became the tip
of a salient extending more than a kilometre north of the main Italian positions. The front lines here were less than 300m apart. The summit position,
heavily sandbagged and protected with barbed wire, is easily accessible by
footpath. It was overlooked and threatened from Austrian posts on the summit of the Toblinger Knoten a few hundred metres to the north. From summer 1915 to autumn 1917 a warren of tunnels and caverns was excavated for
stores and accommodation of the garrison. Although not of great strategic
importance, the Sextenstein had a view of access routes to Austrian ridge

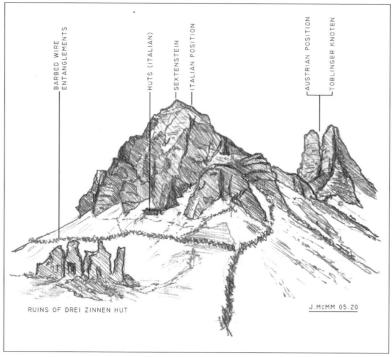

Sketch view northward from the ruins of the Drei Zinnen hut towards the Sextenstein and the Italian forward post and Toblinger Knoten tower with its Austrian observation position, 1917.

positions and was a useful artillery observation post and potential jumping-off point for future attacks.

Despite several attempts to re-capture it, including the snow tunnel assault in spring 1916 and a night attack along the ridge, the Austrians took the summit post. They were unable to mop up defenders in the tunnels and caverns beneath and were eventually forced to withdraw yet again for lack of support. Another attempt made shortly afterwards with the objective of blowing up the Italian positions failed when the explosives did not detonate. The Italians retained the hill until their withdrawal.

From the summit there are excellent views of the the Zinnen plateau (Langenalp) battlefield: beware of unexploded munitions scattered about the hillsides. The tunnels and caverns, some of which were excavated in relatively soft shale and limestone, are unstable and dangerous.

Toblinger Knoten

The Toblinger Knoten (2617m) is a 300m rock tower in the centre of the Austrian defence line. It dominates the rounded summit of the Sextenstein (2539m) to which it is linked by a smooth whaleback ridge a few hundred

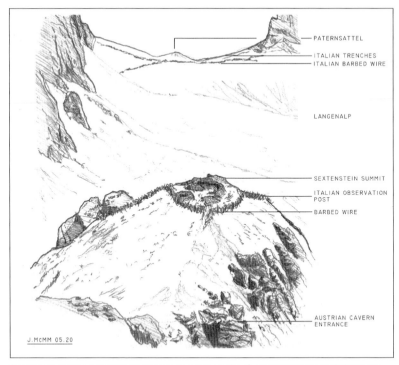

PATERNSATTEL

ITALIAN TRENCHES
ITALIAN BARBED WIRE

LANGENALP

SEXTENSTEIN SUMMIT

ITALIAN OBSERVATION
POST

BARBED WIRE

AUSTRIAN CAVERN
ENTRANCE

J.McMM 05.20

Sketch of Italian forward observation post on the Sextenstein summit from the Toblingor Knoten (from 1010 telephoto). Underground tunnels and caverns were accessed from the Italian position. The Austrian April 1916 snow tunnel ran along the crest to beyond the Italian wire.

metres long. After Austrian withdrawal in August 1915 from the Drei Zinnen hut and Frankfurter Würstel area, and the Sextenstein summit, the Toblinger Knoten became a key point in the Austrian line.

Initially, positions were established on shoulders of the towers and numerous caverns and galleries excavated. After an exploratory night ascent of the normal climbing route, visible in daytime from Italian positions, by Field Padre Hosp in November 1916, it was decided to occupy the summit. This was done by constructing platform and ladder access up the steep north chimney, sheltered from enemy observation and fire. The risk of lightning strikes on such an exposed summit led to installation of a copper cable earth and subsequently a Faraday cage to protect the garrison during electric storms.

Observation posts and firing positions were built on the summits and caverns with loopholes excavated. The initial work was carried out at night wearing white sheet camouflage in full view of the Italians on the Büllelejoch who could hear the hammering and repeatedly swept the summit with searchlights. The sappers' only protection was to stand absolutely still against a snow background. When completed, the Austrian positions were

Left: View from the Paternsattel northward towards the Drei Zinnen hut and Sextenstein and Toblinger Knoten front line positions from August 1915 to October 1917.

Right: Viktoria Savs, who fought for the Austrian-Hungarian army on the Drei Zinnen frontline disguised as a man. Having lost a leg during the fighting, her true identity was discovered. Born in Merano, which was ceded to Italy after the war, she subsequently lived in Hall, Salzburg and Belgrade.

inaccessible but the Italian posts on the Sextenstein summit beneath were within easy rifle and machine gun range.

The snow tunnel and other attempts to recapture the Sextenstein were launched from points flanking the Toblinger Knoten. In late 1916, following detonation of large Italian mines beneath their positions elsewhere in the Dolomites, the Austrians became concerned that a mining project might be underway from the Sextenstein to beneath the Toblinger Knoten. Countermining proposals were made but fighting in the area ended before excavation could begin.

There are two via ferrata access routes to the Toblinger Knoten summit. The gunfire-sheltered military access up the north chimney has been restored with cables and steel ladders (MISUR2). Some of the original platforms and wooden ladders are still in place. Feldkurat Hosp's November 1916 night route on the south side (MISUR3) has also been re-instated with some protection and is now generally used for descent.

Wildgrabenjoch-Innichriedelknoten Ridge

The Wildgrabenjoch-Innichriedel ridge, with the Toblinger Knoten a few hundred metres north of the Drei Zinnen hut at its centre, was the main Austrian defence line. The ridge retains numerous defence works including observation posts, trenches and caverns together with artillery, machine gun and searchlight positions. Permanently manned posts were established on summits and passes. In addition to sandbags, wire mesh crates filled with stones and rock fragments were widely used to consolidate trenches on unstable scree slopes. In places, barrack huts were secured with rock bolts and cables. Supplies came by pack train up valleys from the north, supplemented from the second year of the war by ropeways. Foundations of barracks, headquarters and medical facilities can still be seen, sheltered under north-facing rock bluffs.

The ridge is an excellent walk with impressive views across no man's land towards the Zinnen north faces and Italian lines.

Other Localities

Besides mountain locations, the Monte Piana military cemetery next to the Toblach-Cortina road (SS51) a few kilometres south of Toblach and the 1880s Austrian 'blockhouse fort' (Landro Sperre), whose guns and mortars were removed for use at the front, are both interesting. There is an excellent open-air museum with preserved trenches on the summit plateau of Monte Piana.

Events in the Drei Zinnen area illustrate aspects of the First World War in the eastern Alps, including the curious and inexplicable high-command obsession that advance in valleys could only progress after capture of the heights. Consequently, Italian attempts to reach Pustertal did not include any significant attempt to break through down the main valleys or along the road to Sexten over the Kreuzbergsattel pass, some of which were almost undefended in the first days of the war.

The Italian Austro-Hungarian conflict cost many lives. Other than acquisition of Friuli, Trieste, the Trentino and German-speaking South Tyrol to the Brenner pass, Italy achieved relatively little from a war declared mainly for mercenary reasons, and one that had disastrous political consequences.

Restoration and maintenance of vie ferrate and walks in this area is due in great part to the Friends of the Dolomites Association (Verein der Dolomitenfreunde). I am grateful for the enthusiasm of Italian and South Tyrolese friends for local history and also the following sources. My thanks go to Jim Harvey for his help and endless patience and help in preparing my drawings for publication.

References

'Dolomitenfront 1915/17 Carta Turistica', 1:50,000, Kompass Map.
'Dolomiti di Sesto/Sextener Dolomiten', 1:25,000, Tabacco Carta. (010)
G Fletcher and J Smith, *Via Ferratas of the Italian Dolomites: North, Central and East Dolomites vol 1,* 2009, Cicerone Guides.
P Kübler and H Reider, *Kampf um die Drei Zinnen,* Athesia, Bozen, 1997, 189pp.
H Von Lichem, *La Guerra in Montagna 1915-18, vol 2: Il Fronte Dolomitico,* Athesia, Bolzano, 337pp.
M Thompson, *The White War,* Faber and Faber, London, 2008, 454pp.

C A RUSSELL

One Hundred Years Ago

Members of the 1921 Everest Expedition at camp. Back row, left to right:
A F R Wollaston, C Howard-Bury, A M Heron, H Raeburn. Front row, left to
right: G L Mallory, E O Wheeler, G H Bullock, H T Morshead.

*We are having a most extraordinary winter up here. Men of seventy-five and
eighty tell me they have never seen so long a period of drought. We have not had
any rain worth mentioning since last October, and very little snow.*[1]

The exceptionally dry spell experienced in many Alpine regions during
the early months of 1921 continued into March when favourable conditions enabled Hans Fritsch with his guides Othmar Supersaxo and Gustav
Imsenge to make the first winter ascents of the Dürrenhorn, Hohberghorn
and Stecknadelhorn. Starting from the Mischabel hut the party crossed the
Ried glacier from the Windjoch to reach the Hohbergjoch and the short
south-east ridge of the Dürrenhorn. After traversing the Hohberghorn and
Stecknadelhorn Fritsch and the guides continued to the Nadelhorn before
returning to the Windjoch and descending to the hut.

The fine and settled conditions continued for much of the climbing season
and several notable expeditions were completed. In the Mont Blanc range

1. Written by the American-born bibliophile and archivist Henry Fairbanks Montagnier (1877-1933) from his
home, the Chalet Beau Réveil at Champéry. Montagnier was instrumental in uncovering the true story of the
first ascent of Mont Blanc.

George Finch joined forces with S L Courtauld and E G Oliver accompanied by their guides Adolf and Alfred Aufdenblatten to repeat the route to Mont Blanc de Courmayeur by way of the Frêney glacier and the upper section of the Peuterey ridge pioneered by James Eccles and his guides many years earlier. In the Bernese Alps the guideless party of Hans Lauper and Max Liniger completed an outstanding climb by forcing a route up the steep rib bordering the north-west face of the Mönch. After overcoming numerous exposed snow and rock pitches the party reached the north-east ridge a short distance from the summit.

In September a famous route on the Eiger was completed when the Japanese climber Yuko Maki with Fritz Amatter, Fritz Steuri and Samuel Brawand made the first ascent of the north-east, Mittellegi ridge. The main step on the ridge, which had been descended on two occasions and had defeated many attempts to ascend was finally overcome by the guides with the aid of iron stanchions and a long pole provided with hooks.

In May the Mount Everest reconnaissance expedition led by Lt Col Charles Howard-Bury left Darjeeling with a number of local men as porters, having received permission to enter Tibet and approach Everest (8848m) from the north. The organisation and arrangements for the expedition were overseen by a joint committee of the Royal Geographical Society and the Alpine Club chaired by Sir Francis Younghusband. Four members of the Club were selected to assess the prospects for an ascent. Alexander Kellas and Harold Raeburn both had recent Himalayan experience: Kellas on Kamet and Kabru and Raeburn in the Kangchenjunga region. George Mallory and, at short notice, Guy Bullock in place of Finch who withdrew owing to illness were experienced alpinists. A fifth member, Alexander Wollaston was included as doctor and naturalist. The party was completed by a detachment from the Survey of India led by Henry Morshead and Oliver Wheeler, the geologist Alexander Heron and baggage animals, all provided with the co-operation of the Indian government.

Despite early setbacks – Kellas died during the approach march and Raeburn was absent for a long period while recovering from dysentery – and frequent spells of bad weather the expedition achieved its main objectives. The northern, north-western and eastern approaches to the peak were reconnoitred in depth: ascents to the Lho La (6026m) at the head of the main Rongbuk glacier and a col to the west provided extensive views to Nepal and the Khumbu glacier; and a route was identified to the North Col (6985m), reached by Mallory, Bullock and Wheeler from a camp on the East Rongbuk glacier. In addition a large area in the region was surveyed for the first time and the geology and flora examined.

In South Africa exploration of Table Mountain (1087m) was continued by members of the Mountain Club. George Londt and other leading climbers completed several new ascents including *Panda Crag* and *Columnar Face,* both very severe routes for the period.

In the Canadian Rockies in August Henry Hall Jr and a companion with the guide Edward Feuz Jr made the first ascent of Mount French (3234m), one of the high peaks in the British Military group east of Palliser Pass. In the following month L S Crosby and J W A Hickson with Feuz reached the north, higher summit of the unclimbed Mount Fifi (2621m), one of the imposing rock towers in the Sawback range near Banff.

In the far north members of an expedition organised by Oxford University visited Spitsbergen to study the fauna, flora and geology and to explore the interior. In August a party including Tom Longstaff and Noel Odell traversed Mount Terrier (1211m) for reconnaissance and survey purposes during a journey for some distance inland. An expedition led by James Wordie explored the remote Arctic island of Jan Mayen where Wordie and two companions made the first ascent of Beerenberg (2277m), the volcano in the north of the island.

At home G S Bower, H M Kelly and other outstanding climbers continued their exploration in the Lake District. *Innominate Crack* on Kern Knotts led by Bower and other severe routes were completed during the year. A welcome event was the formation of the Pinnacle Club for ladies, founded by Kelly's wife Emily 'Pat' Kelly 'to foster the independent development of rock climbing amongst women.' Members were required to have mountaineering experience and 'the ability to lead and to direct rock ascents of a moderately difficult order.' Eleanor Winthrop Young was elected as president with Mrs Kelly as secretary.

In March the death occurred of Edward Theodore Compton, the distinguished Alpine artist and mountaineer whose work is admired for his outstanding ability to represent in form and colour mountain scenes throughout the Alps and in other parts of Europe. Edward Theodore Compton, who settled in Bavaria, completed a number of notable expeditions with Karl Blodig including the first complete descent of the east face of the Aiguille Blanche de Peuterey.

This account is concluded with an extract from a summary of the Mount Everest expedition by Norman Collie, president of the Alpine Club.

The 1921 expedition was, in the nature of things, merely a reconnaissance; and when all the difficulties and unforeseen mishaps that always occur in preliminary explorations are taken into account, one must congratulate Colonel Howard-Bury and all the other members of the expedition on having been so extraordinarily successful.

• The editor of the *Alpine Journal* would like to congratulate and thank Chris Russell who has been contributing his snapshot of the mountaineering world 'One Hundred Years Ago' for 50 years.

Area Notes

'Weisshorner', Hilda Hechle, 1927?, watercolour, 32cm x 54cm.
Monte Rosa, Lyskamm, Breithorn, Klein Matterhorn, possibly from Solvay hut.
(Courtesy of Tony Astill/www.mountainpaintings.org)

LINDSAY GRIFFIN

Alps & Dolomites 2020

The south-south-east face of the Grandes Jorasses. Not all routes are shown:
1. *Gogna-Machetto* (1972, 1400m, probably ED2). 2. *Phantom Direct* (1985,
1400m but much more actual climbing, ED2/3). 3. *Plein Sud* (2010, stopping two
pitches below the exit). 4. *Diamond Ridge* (2016, 1600m) leading to the upper
Tronchey ridge. 5. *Tronchey Ridge* (1936). *(Sergio de Leo/Marcello Sanguineti)*

A combination of superb winter conditions at the start of the year, followed
by Covid-19 restrictions keeping most European climbers' travels close to
home, produced many fine ascents throughout 2020 in both the Alps and
Dolomites. This report, whilst not definitive, documents a representative
selection of the year's major adventures on rock and ice, many carried out
in a suitably bold and committing style.

Major Repeats
Arguably the most notable ascent in the Mont Blanc range, and indeed
throughout the Western Alps, was not a new route at all but the second
ascent of the legendary *Phantom Direct* on the **Grandes Jorasses.**

The south-south-east face, or Tronchey Wall rises 1,400m from the Pra
Sec glacier to the summit of Pointe Walker (4208m), making it the tallest
in the range. The lower section is characterised by steep, compact granite,
while the upper sports a pronounced central pillar. Right of this pillar a huge

The Tronchey Wall of the Grandes Jorasses seen from the upper Pra Sec glacier. 1. *Original Route* (1972, Gogna-Machetto, 1400m, probably ED2 VI and A2). 2. *Phantom Direct* (1985, Grassi-Luzi-Rossi, 1400m but much more actual climbing, ED2/3, VI,5 or 6). 3. *Plein Sud* (2010, to two pitches below the exit, VI,5, M6+ R, repeated once). 4. Part of the *Diamond Ridge* (2016, Richardson-Rinn, 1600m, 5c A0) leading to the upper Tronchey ridge. *(Marcello Sanguineti)*

deep gully leads to a small gap above the third tower high on the Tronchey ridge Grandes Jorasses left lies a more open couloir-depression rising toward the top of the Pra Sec ridge.

In August 1972 Italians Alessandro Gogna and Guido Machetto became the first people ever to cross the Pra Sec glacier, when they climbed the wet, steep lower wall of the south-south-east face, experiencing Eiger-like stone fall. They then proceeded up the more enjoyable central pillar to the summit of Pointe Walker. Their route has likely never been seriously attempted since and is probably ED2 in today's currency. Later, visionary ice climber Gian Carlo Grassi saw another possibility: ephemeral ice smears leading to the huge gully. Over many years (during which time the line was also attempted by others, including a British party) Grassi made six 'reconnaissance' attempts. Then in June 1985, following the snowiest winter for years and in unseasonal low temperatures, he found the Pra Sec glacier well covered in avalanche debris and the ice smears beautifully formed. With Renzo Luzi and Mauro Rossi, Grassi reached the base of the gully to find no ice. What to do? Instead, the three made a delicate and irreversible 200m rising traverse over snow-covered slabs to reach the hanging couloir-depression left of the central pillar. Grassi's intuition had paid off. It was in excellent condition. With a storm closing, threatening to trap the climbers in a vast avalanche funnel, they unroped and climbed rapidly over technical ground to the summit. Since then, a repetition of the *Phantom Direct* (aka *Gianni Comino Memorial Route,* 1400m, ED3, VI/5 or 6) has been one of the most sought-after ascents, Grassi accurately predicting that his route, 'would not be repeated for a long time.'

In 2010 Grassi's projected line was almost climbed, when four Italians reached and then climbed the great gully to a highpoint a couple of pitches below the exit to the Tronchey ridge, where they met unclimbable blank rock. They descended, naming their almost completed route *Plein Sud* (VI/5, M6+R), repeated once.

In early 2020, ice routes in the Mont Blanc range were in splendid condition. On 21 January, Frenchman Yann Borgnet and Charles Dubouloz, after driving from their homes in Annecy, left the Val Ferret at 4am in a temperature of -12°C, and reached the start of *Phantom Direct* at 9.30am. High winds and poor visibility accompanied the difficult climbing in the upper section and they arrived on the summit 10 hours later, only two hours faster than the 1985 ascensionists. They had just repeated the longest ice climb in the Mont Blanc massif. The descent through the night was taxing and the Boccalatte hut only reached at 4am the following day.

One of the most impressive summer second ascents in the massif came on 18 July when Federica Mingolla, at 26 years old one of Italy's leading female alpinists, and Leonardo Gheza repeated *Incroyable* on the Red Pillar of Brouillard, **Mont Blanc.** By the end of the 1980s the smooth walls forming the crest of the Red Pillar, right of the classic *Bonatti-Oggioni,* had been crossed by three routes: *Via del Dilettanti* (1980), *Gabarrou-Long* (1983), and *Les Anneaux Magiques* (1989). Since that time most climbers assumed there could not be room for another; most that is bar Matteo Della Bordella. Over two days, 30 June and 1 July, and with new climbing partners, Francois Cazzanelli and Francesco Ratti, Bordella created *Incroyable* between *Anneaux Magiques* and the *Gabarrou-Long,* finishing the climb on the good ledges below the last top section of the pillar (also the finishing point of *Les Anneaux Magiques*). The eight pitches have one belay bolt each, and a total of 20 bolts for protection. However, the route was not climbed free; that had to wait until the 8 July when Bordella returned with Cazzanelli, Ratti, and Isaie Maquignaz, and led the crux at 8a. The others freed the remaining pitches before rappelling the *Gabarrou-Long.*

Given the location and altitude of the technical difficulties – the route has obligatory moves of 7b – one might have expected a healthy passage of time before the route was attempted again. Frederica Mingolla was working on the evenings of 16 and 17 July, a Thursday and Friday, serving dinner at the Monzino hut. However, she decided there was time on the Friday to climb the *Ratti-Vitali* route on the west face of the Aiguille Noire de Peuterey with Lorenzo Pernigotti, make the 22-rappel descent, and be back in time for work before leaving early next morning with Gheza, with whom she had not climbed before. The plan worked. After a short night at the Monzino,

The east face of the Grandes Jorasses and the lines of: 1. *Mad Max* (2020); 2. *Il Giovane Guerrerio* (2020); and 3. *Little Big Men* (2006). The approach from the right and a traverse down to the snow terraces is nowadays preferred to the original direct starts up the stone-swept rock walls below. *(Antonio Giani)*

the alarm rang at 3am on Saturday and the two reached the foot of the Red Pillar four and a half hours later. Mingolla led all the difficult pitches, the crux on her second attempt. By 4.30pm they were rappelling from the top of the route. It would be normal to climb on this pillar after a night at the Eccles bivouac hut, but both parties made their free ascents in a day from the Monzino.

The Mingolla-Gheza partnership was formed, and the pair followed *Incroyable* with another prestigious second ascent, also of a recent Della Bordella route: *Il Giovane Guerrerio* on the remote east face of the Grandes Jorasses. Della Bordella had wanted to climb a new route on this face for almost a decade but after an ascent of *Groucho Marx* in 2019 he spotted the various crack systems that could be linked to produce a logical line – up the steep walls between the 1942 *Gervasutti* route and 2006's *Little Big Men*.

On 6 and 7 August, Della Bordella, Luca Moroni and Matteo Pasquetto climbed 12 new pitches (350m) to reach easy terrain below the Tronchey ridge. Only three hand-placed bolts and a few pegs were left in-situ, and four pitches were 7a or above, with obligatory moves at this standard. The hardest moves, around a large roof on the 15m third pitch, are 7b+, but the crux is a thin slab pitch of 7a, which took three and a half hours to lead. The three bivouacked at the top of pitch nine and the following day gained the Tronchey ridge, which they followed to the summit. Tragically, during the descent of the Rocher de Reposoir to the Boccalatte hut, Pasquetto slipped and fell to his death.

Pasquetto – *il giovane guerrerio* [the young warrior] – was a talented young alpinist with great potential and the route was named for him. He had made a new route on Aguja Standhardt in Patagonia, repeated *Divine Providence* on the Grand Pilier d'Angle, *Groucho Marx* on the Jorasses east face, and made the first solo ascent of *Delta Minox* on the Bregaglia's Cavalcorto, one of the most run out and technically difficult slab climbs in that range.

Gheza and Mingolla completed the second ascent in a day during mid August, finding the climb technical and committing: you would lose all your gear if you had to retreat from high on the route. In the short time span between completing *Incroyable* and this line, the pair had also climbed *Manitua* on the north face of the Jorasses. Quite a season.

Widely reported as a first ascent, a line on the west face of the **Aiguille du Plan** was climbed on 21 and 22 February by Slovaks Ondrej Huserka and Evka Milovska, and named *Mystery* (600m, 15 pitches, M8, C1, 85°). They bivouacked at the top of pitch eight, and used aid on the final 20m: a loose, overhanging, vegetated crack. The route is in fact the unnamed shallow corner immediately right of *Grand West Couloir* (Gabarrou and Picard-Deyme, 1975, 700m, V/5 and aid), first climbed in summer 1977 by Gordon Smith (UK) and Tobin Sorenson (USA). This pair also found the crux to be the last pitch: an awkward slanting corner-crack choked with ice, followed by a large icicle-laden overhang turned on the left. They also made one bivouac, as they were 'training' for the Jorasses, but didn't start until midday, finishing the route in 13 hours climbing time.

In a remarkable 17 hours on 31 July, Filip Babicz made only the second known ascent of the *Complete Peuterey Ridge*. Climbed netween 11-13 July 1973 by Germans Gottlieb Braun-Ewert and Rudi Kirmeier, this involves starting in the Val Veni, traversing Monte Rouge de Peuterey via the 1,200m south-south-west and north ridges, then across the col des Chasseurs to reach the south ridge of the Aiguille Noire. From here it follows the *Peuterey Integral* to the summit of Mont Blanc. While the statistics are staggering – 4,000m of ascent, 8,000m of climbing and around 900m of rappels, making it the longest ridge in the massif – it is well to remember that Jean-Marc Boivin's solo of the *Peuterey Integral* in 1983 took just 10 and a half hours, and since then complete re-equipping of the long rappel descent from the Noire has made this section faster and less scary. The brothers Hugo and Oscar Schmitt noted this when they completed the Integral 10 days earlier in a little over 12 hours.

The south-east flanks of the Aiguille Blanche de Peuterey and Peuterey ridge seen across the tormented Brenva glacier. A. Punta Gugliermina. B. Aiguille Blanche de Peuterey. C. Mont Blanc de Courmayeur. D. Grand Pilier d'Angle. E. Brenva Face. The routes are: 1. *North-east Couloir of Brêche des Dames Anglaises* (1913, D-). 2. *Vols Uncertains* (2020). 3. *East Face of the Aiguille Blanche de Peuterey* (1893, 1300m, graded AD+ but likely harder today). *(Lindsay Griffin)*

Babicz, a Pole now residing in the Aosta valley, spends some of his time making speed ascents. Exactly a month later, he returned to the Aiguille Noire and set a record time for an ascent of the classic *South Ridge*. The 1,200m arête, which has a guidebook time of 10-12 hours for a roped party, was climbed in just 1h 30m: a fixed rope was in place for the obligatory 25m rappel from Pointe Welzenbach. The previous fastest time was probably Boivin's 2h 45m. Babicz set off at 4pm in running gear with just rock shoes, harness, chalk, one sling and a descender. He was in time to make a casual descent of the east ridge in evening light.

When it comes to mixed outings with ephemeral ice, changing conditions can annihilate former reputations. So it was for *Sagzahn Verschneidung*, the great corner system between the 3,227m **Sagwand** and the 3,410m **Schrammacher** in the Valsertal of the Austrian Zillertal Alps. The late David Lama made four attempts before succeeding on the first ascent of this 800m line in February 2018 with Peter Mühlburger. The difficulties – up to M6 – were concentrated into six pitches, and some aid (A2) was needed around a roof. Lama had developed this little-known area as a winter playground and rated this route as one of the hardest he had put up there. Several subsequent attempts to repeat it would fail, adding to its status.

In November 2020 a friend of David Bruder and Martin Feistl sent them a photo of the line, showing it was in excellent condition. On the 11 November this pair climbed detached ice with excellent rock protection to make the second ascent, free, at M6 WI4. They encountered none of the friable rock or outrageous technical climbing that Lama had experienced.

New Routes
In the Vanoise, west of Mont Blanc, the less well-known **Epéna** (3421m) was one of the last 'big peaks' in the Alps to be climbed (1900). The north face, almost 3km in length and a maximum of around 750m high, is revered by the French mountaineering community due to its relative isolation, tranquillity and being arguably the highest limestone wall in the French Alps (as opposed to their Pre-Alps). The descent, on the south side of the mountain, is long and complex, and the rock on the north face is compact yet often friable, with characteristically small downward-sloping holds and poor protection, even if using pegs. Making the first winter ascent of this face has been a coveted, if not nearly impossible project for decades, but in February 2019 it finally fell to a French team that succeeded on the classic northwest spur of the Pointe Orientale (765m, TD 5c, *Rod-Schneider,* 1966).

Manu Pellissier made his first foray onto this face almost three decades ago, and each winter for the last 20 years has watched out for viable ice-mixed conditions; on one attempt he was forced to bail just 130m below the top of the *Rod-Schneider.* But in 12 hours on 27 November, with Luc Mongellaz and Jessy Pivier, he completed the first ascent of *The Fridge* (900m, 5c, M5, WI5) on the north face of the Brèche Perdrieux, the col between the Pointe Orientale (3348m) and Pointe Centrale (3307m). The three started at the base of the 1966 *Rod-Schneider,* then worked up the depression to the right, arriving on the summit ridge with the feeling of having achieved something special. Three days previously, to create a descent on the north side, this team had climbed a west-facing 500m gully at M5 WI5, between Pointe Occidentale (3293m) and the 3,321m Petite Glière to the south-west, equipping it for an eight-rappel descent. From the top of *The Fridge* it took the trio three hours to traverse over the Centrale and Occidentale summits to reach the top of their equipped descent, crawling through the night along the sharp and difficult ridge. They regained their car 20 hours after leaving. The news of such remarkable conditions quickly became known and the route was repeated twice just three days later.

In February Sébastien Ibanez and Baptiste Obino made the first ascent of the east couloir of the **Brèche Punta Gugliermina** (the gap immediately north of the summit). Accessing this line requires a tortuous ascent of 1,800m from the Val Veni, or a traverse from the top of the Skyway téléphérique and complex navigation of the chaotic Brenva glacier. The two chose a third option, a double paraglider. With Ibanez in control during the flight, Obino held onto the equipment: two 15-litre bags full of gear in one hand and a 45-litre bag in the other. The first half of the route is steep ice smears followed by two hard mixed pitches, while the second half is much more straightforward. *Vol Uncertains* gives around 940m of climbing at a grade of V/5 or 5+ and M5. The name comes not only for the means of approach, but also from an intense moment during the c20-rappel descent: while trying to pull a jammed rope both climbers suddenly found themselves dangling from a single peg. The route got a repeat in the autumn from an Italian party that approached in a long day from the valley and bivouacked one hour below the climb.

Surprisingly, *Il Giovane Guerrerio* was not the only new line climbed on the east face of the **Grandes Jorasses**. A month before this route was opened, Jérémy Brauge, Victor Saucède, and Jérome Sullivan put up *Mad Max* (800m, 7a+, 7a obl, a tribute to the late Max Bonniot, and the film of the same name) to the right of the *Gervasutti* route. Much of the climb is on steep cracks and slabs of excellent granite, which are difficult to protect. At the top of pitch seven it shares a belay with the *Gervasutti*, immediately below the latter's A2 pitch. From here the three moved right and climbed a bold 7a+, the crux pitch. The pitch above was led at 6b and A1 but would be 7b free. The team bivouacked at the top of pitch nine, reached the Tronchey ridge next day – 9 July – at the end of pitch 11, and continued over the summit. Natural pro was used throughout, except for a single hand-placed bolt on the second belay. The route is better protected from rock fall than some of those further right.

Demonstrating that it is still possible to discover new lines in full view of Chamonix, over two days in January the Spanish Bru Busom, Martin Elias and Marc Toralles filled the gap between the classic *Cordier Pillar* and, to its left, the *Ghilini-Giacomo* route on the west face of the **Grands Charmoz**. Named *Le Grand Charme,* the 650m route has sustained climbing at M6+ with the last three pitches, where the three had to remove crampons and progress in boots, giving pure rock climbing to 6b. On the first day they took the téléphérique to the Plan de l'Aiguille and climbed the initial pitches up to the snow patch, where they bivouacked. Next day, they threw off the bivouac gear and spent from 9am to 11pm reaching the summit, from where they rappelled the *Cordier* through the night.

Two interesting new rock routes were climbed at lesser-known venues. High up at the head of the Piantonetto valley in the Gran Paradiso range the remote 3,692m **Torre del Gran San Pietro** was first climbed by Douglas Freshfield. The steeper and rocky south face has several established lines but toward the left side rises a slim but highly conspicuous pillar, vertical to overhanging in its 250m of height. Remarkably, for such an evident feature, an obvious line of cracks and corners up the front face remained unclimbed until 18 August, when Hervé Barmasse and Stefano Perrone, completely alone in this corner of the range during one of the busiest summers on record, climbed it to create *Dall'Inferno al Paradiso,* from hell to heaven, marking the transition from the hell of Covid-19 to the heaven of returning to the freedom of the mountains. To maintain a spirit of adventure in this

The west faces of Grands Charmoz and (right) Aiguille du Grépon with the new mixed line *Le Grand Charme* between the rock pillars of *Ghilini-Giacomo* (left) and *Cordier*. The first ascensionists bivouacked in the lower snowfield. *(Lindsay Griffin)*

relatively wild corner of the Alps, the pair have only released a photo of the line, and noted they climbed nothing harder than 7b, all on natural gear (though at least one bolt was placed during the rappel descent).

The mountains of Ticino, part of the Swiss Lepontine Alps, are relatively little known outside the local climbing and walking community. Within this range is the Poncione d'Alnasca (2301m), a sort of 'Matterhorn' of the area, an impressive summit pyramid with a vertical south face overlooking the deep Versaska valley that runs north from the tip of Lago Maggiore. This 500m granite face, perched high above the valley floor, has, over the decades, attracted the attentions of well-known 'local' climbers such as Emilio Comici, Walter Bonatti and Marco Pedrini. During forays with various partners in 2015 and 2016, the Italian Matteo Della Bordella, who grew up close to Lago Maggiore, completed a 16-pitch route up the left side of the wall but was unable to free it. In 2018 he managed on several occasions to free all but the eleventh pitch. Wondering whether this pitch was simply too hard for him, he asked Alessandro Zeni, a strong and extremely talented climber who has led 9b, to join him for another attempt. On the second visit to the wall at the end of November 2020, and working from a portaledge, Zeni, who had previous latched the huge dyno on the crux pitch 11 that gives the route its name, now solved the problem of the weird third-pitch dyno (7c) to complete the first free ascent of *Leap of Faith* (8a+ or 8b, 7b+ obl). Della Bordella then managed to free pitch 11 and celebrate the conclusion of a five-year odyssey.

Late in the year, a long route of high technical difficulty was completed in

Looking south along the Grandes Murailles ridge with the Valtournenche to the left and upper Grandes Murailles glacier on the right. A. Punta del Cors. B. Punta Ester. C. Punta Lioy. D and E. Les Jumeaux, Puntas Giordano and Sella. F. Becca di Guin. *(Francois Cazzanelli)*

the Glarner (also Glarus) Alps of Switzerland, the region to the north-east of Andermatt, best known for its highest summit, Tödi (3614m), a popular and coveted ski tour. The **Gross Ruchen** (3137m) lies a little to the west of Tödi and has a classic route on the north face (1200m, AD). To the right of this Dani Arnold and Roger Schaeli, climbing together on a big mountain route for the first time, completed *Egidius*, a 1,300m mixed line climbed on 24, 25 and 28 November at WI6+ M7. Arnold had first tried this line in 2009 with Stephan Ruoss, but at that stage in his career was unable to climb the first section of major difficulty, above half-height. Arnold and Schaeli spent two days preparing the route before their final attack. To above the crux sections the belays are equipped with one bolt, allowing for an easier retreat. Some bolts protect the cruxes, but natural protection is essential. The line got a quick repeat on 23 December from Germans Lukas Hinterberger, Walter Hungerbühler and Michi Wohlleben, who found it impressive in size and 'very scary' in the upper section due to dangerous conditions.

A few days after his ascent of *Sagzahn Verschneidung,* Feistl, climbing with Sven Brand, created his own partial new route on the **Sagwand** with the obvious 300m *Direct Start* to the original route on the face, *Rampenfuhre*, at M6 WI4 X. They continued to the top to record a total of 950m of climbing. To complete a fine hat trick, Feistl re-united with Bruder in the **Karwendal,** and in a very long day on 20 December climbed the massive 1,000m corner

The south face of Torre del Gran San Pietro and the line of *Dall'Inferno al Paradiso* up the obvious pillar.

system between the Grubenkarspitze and Plattenspitze to create the highly technical *Stalingrad* (WI7, M8, A1). Although the Karwendal is better known as a rock-climbing venue, this line has been attempted several times in the past, and as long ago as 1992, when the visionary Franz Prechtold fell, and was injured, from the crux pitch five.

Enchainments

Long ridge traverses, or *enchaînements* in the Alps can enable climbers to have a full, high-standard Himalayan experience without the altitude. There were several remarkable high-level journeys in 2020, but probably the most outstanding was a winter traverse around the northern rim of the Valtournenche completed by Cervinia guides François Cazzanelli and Francesco Ratti. The pair linked the **Furggen Chain**, the **Matterhorn**, and the **Grandes** and **Petites Murailles**, a total of 20 summits, 51km distance and 4,800m of ascent. They had attempted this project in the winter of 2019, only to fail near the end due to impossible cornices.

In 2020 the two Italians left the Theodul hut by the Theodul pass (3295m) at 7am on 20 January and had descended to the valley from the col des Dames, south-west of Mont Blanc du Creton (3406m) – the last peak of the Petites Murailles – by 1pm on 23 January. Their first night was spent in the Carrel hut having traversed the Matterhorn, and the second and third at the small Perelli and Paoluccio bivouac huts situated on the Murailles ridge. They climbed along the lengthy east ridge of the Dent d'Hérens but did not go to the summit, instead aiming directly for the col des Grandes Murailles and the Perelli. Minimum temperatures were -23°C.

The first continuous traverse of the sharp and technical rocky ridges of

Roger Schaeli heads towards steep ice pillars on *Egidius*, north face of Gross Ruchen. *(Courtesy of Roger Schaeli)*

Grandes and Petites Murailles was made over three days in the summer of 1940. Seven years later another Italian team linked the Matterhorn with a traverse of the Grandes Murailles, also with two bivouacs. In 1985 Cazzanelli's father, Valter, with Marco Barmasse (father of Hervé) made the first winter crossing of the Grandes and Petites. In August 2018 François Cazzanelli and Kilian Jornet traversed the Grandes and Petites Murailles in a fraction under 11 hours.

Cazzanelli would return in September 2020 and with Nadir Maguet traverse the Matterhorn via the Furggen and Italian ridges then continue to traverse the frontier ridge west over the Dent d'Hérens to the Valpelline: the whole c35km odyssey was completed in less than one day.

Another marathon effect took place in the Valais, where two Swiss, Nicolas Hojac and Adrian Zurbrügg, polished off all 20 peaks of the **Monte Rosa**

Dani Arnold squirms around a difficult chockstone on *Egidius,* north face of Gross Ruchen. *(Roger Schaeli)*

massif over 4,000m. They completed these in just over 13 and a half hours on 8 July. Conditions were excellent: their biggest fear had been daytime heat softening the snow, but this was not the case. By dawn they had already completed 10 of the summits. For those who fancy a repeat of this feat, the summits are: Nordend, Dufourspitze, Zumsteinspitze, Punta Gnifetti, Punta Parrot, Ludwigshorn, Corno Nero, Balmenhorn, Piramide Vincent, Punta Giordani, Lyskamm East, Lyskamm West, Felikhorn, Castor, Pollux, Roccia Nera, Breithorn Gendarme, Breithorn East, Breithorn Central, and Breithorn West. They reached the Klein Matterhorn cable car at 12.30pm, having covered 29km and made around 4,500m of altitude gain (starting from the Monte Rosa hut).

Covid-19 restrictions gave impetus to an idea proposed by Ines Papert to Caro North of a self-propelled journey from east to west across Switzerland, climbing routes that were new to both. The two women had no outside support, travelling by bike, pulling their equipment on trailers, and buying food locally. Eventual statistics were 18,000m of ascent, 600km travelled, and six routes up to 350m in height. Starting from the Austrian border on 10 August, the two climbed: *Intifada* (7a+) on the marvellous limestone of the **Rätikon**; *Peruvian Dust* (7a+) on the clean granite of the **Teufelstalschucht**

Silvan Schüpbach climbing the thinly iced *Linea Bianca* section of *Crossway of Friendship* on the Piz Badile. *(Matteo Della Bordella)*

above Andermatt; the ultra-classic *Excalibur* (6b) on the **Wendenstöcke**; *Deep Blue Sea* (7b+) on the right side of the **Eiger** north face; *La Fête des Pères* (7a) on the south face of the **Gastlosen**, and finally the traverse of the **Aiguilles Dorées**, Mont Blanc massif.

A far greater achievement, but in the same style, came from Belgians Sébastien Berthe and Nicolas Favresse. The idea came from Berthe, who wanted a summer project that would test his limits but would have much less environmental impact than an expedition involving many flights. His plan was to be the first to climb in a single summer season the so-called Alpine Trilogy, three now-legendary 8b+ multi-pitch climbs created in 1994 by three equally legendary climbers: Beat Kammerlander's *Silbergeier* on the **Rätikon**; Thomas Huber's *End of Silence* at **Berchtesgaden** and the Stefan Glowacz route *Des Kaisers Neue Kleider* at **Wilder Kaiser**), generally considered hardest of the three. At the time of their ascents, these routes represented the most difficult multi-pitch Alpine sport routes, and while not cutting edge by today's standards, will still prove a challenge to most of the world's top climbers. Berthe needed a partner, and at the last minute Favresse was forced to cancel his plans for Norway due to pandemic restrictions and was looking for an alternative. However, he had one condition: he had to bring his dog. This worked well for Berthe who has a dog of his own and from 2 to 28 August the two biked a distance of 650km with their trailers and two dogs to attempt the three routes, eventually redpointing each in a single day. With some reserves to spare they then headed over to the **Eiger** and made a one-day free ascent of *Odyssee* (1400m, 8a+).

The north-east face of the Piz Badile and (left) the Cengalo in excellent 'winter' conditions. 1. *Memento Mori* (1980). 2. Cassin (1937). 3. *Amore di Vetro* (2016). 4. Crossway of Friendship (2020) to junction with north ridge. Combining the first section of Amore di Vetro with the upper half of Momento Mori produces Amore Supercombo. *(Tom Bärfuss/David Hefti)*

The Ephemeral

Good winter climbing conditions on the Piz Badile are an extremely rare and highly transient occurrence. Being in the right place at the right time is crucial, along with local knowledge. Towards the end of November, Matteo Della Bordella and Silvan Schüpbach heard from Marcel Schenk, the preeminent connoisseur of the mountain in winter, that conditions appeared to be perfect. They set out from the Sasc Fura hut on 26 November with no set plan, ploughing through deep snow to reach the start of the north ridge. From here a vague ledge system leads left across the north-east face and they followed it for around 400m up thin, poorly protected ice over slabby rock to below *Linea Bianca*, the visionary 1978 rock route by Igor Koller and Stanislav Šilhán that was the first to breach the steep

Marcel Schenk moving left from the *Cassin* snowfield towards the upper section of *Memento Mori* during the November ascent of *Amore Supercombo. (David Hefti)*

Marcel Schenk leading largely unprotected ice-covered slabs on the upper section of *Memento Mori* during the ascent of *Amore Supercombo,* northeast face, Piz Badile. *(David Hefti)*

Marcel Schenk on the ephemeral ice runnels of *Amore Supercombo*, northeast face of Piz Badile. *(David Hefti)*

and poorly protected slabs right of the *Cassin* route. The pair followed this 'white line', front-pointing delicate thin ice and climbing mixed to M6 to the north ridge, where they continued to the summit and spent the night in the Redaelli bivouac hut. The line was named *Crossway of Friendship.* This was not the first time *Linea Bianca* had been climbed in winter, as M Clerici had soloed it over four days in December 1986, but it was the first ascent as an ice-mixed route.

The following day it was the turn of Schenk himself, who with fellow Swiss David Hefti combined two of his own 2016 routes: *Amore di Vetro* (800m, M5 R 80°, a little right of the *Cassin* to cross it at the snowfield, then a beautiful sliver of ice between it and *Memento Mori* to the left), and *Nordest Supercombo* (800m, M7 R, 80°, the *Cassin* to the snowfield followed by *Memento Mori* to the summit). The two Swiss found conditions on *Amore Supercombo* 'unbelievable' and even managed to place a few ice screws. They reached the summit with plenty of time to spare to make the descent in daylight. Even so, the route was a serious proposition, with very long run-outs. But the word was out, and this new combination only had to wait three days before receiving a second ascent.

Free Ascents

In the summer of 2006, Christophe Dumarest and Patrick Gabarrou added a second route to the Pilier Dérobé (Hidden pillar) of Frêney, high on the south face of **Mont Blanc**. The hard pitches of this line, situated to the right of the original route and named *Jean-Chri* after the renowned French alpinist Jean-Christophe Lafaille, who had died on Makalu earlier the same year, were led by Dumarest. He climbed free to 7a+ and used aid on everything harder, estimating it might all go free at 7c. He wasn't far wrong. Over a weekend during the summer of 2020, David Bacci and Matteo Della Bordella climbed the route at 7b+, finding excellent solid granite, sharp and

Alessandro Baù on pitch seven of *Space Vertigo*, Cima Ovest di Lavaredo. *(Giovanni Danieli)*

with an abundance of cracks for natural pro. The Hidden pillar was first climbed in August 1963 by Tom Frost and John Harlin at VI and A3, but later freed at 6b/c. It has arguably the longest approach to any route on Mont Blanc, and although short (the pillar itself is 300m) the difficulties occur above 4,400m.

The Torrone valley on the south side of the Bregaglia is home to a selection of highly impressive rock walls, not least the great barrel-shaped buttress forming the south face of **Punta Ferrario**. In 1959 the noted Italian activist Vasco Taldo (1932-2014), who made the second ascent of the Central Tower of Paine one day after Chris Bonington and Don Whillans, and a number of now classic new routes in the Bregaglia-Masino and Dolomites, pioneered the first route on the face (originally VI and A1 but around 7a free). In 1980 a very strong team of four Slovaks, Clernik, Hyzny, Marek and Piacek climbed a c450m direct route via the central diedre, finishing up the last four pitches of the Taldo at a somewhat undergraded VI and A2. In common with other routes on the face (there are around five in total), this *Slovak Direct* has only rarely been repeated and a free ascent has been very much a longstanding problem. The best effort came from Simone Pedeferri, who tried it in both summer and winter, but failed to complete the exit to the diedre, which is invariably wet. In August 2020 the stars aligned. There was a flurry of activity, which resulted in ascents of various routes on the face including the first free ascent of the *Slovak Direct*. Paulo Marazzi and Giacomo Regallo reached the dicdrc quickly via the easier lower section but found the first hard pitch freed by Pedeferri a bold and committing 7a layback. Higher, the exit over the capping roofs of the diedre was remarkably dry and Marazzi on-sighted it at 7b. The two reached the summit, and after an awkward rappel descent of the Taldo, were back at their bivouac the same day.

The north face of the Cima Ovest showing: 1. *Space Vertigo* and 2: *Pan Aroma. (Giovanni Danieli)*

The Dolomites

There were many fine achievements in the Dolomites, often at high standard with minimal or no use of bolts. Three of the most active pioneers in this region, Martin Dejori, Titus Prinoth and Alex Walpoth from the Val Gardena, managed to solve the 'last great problem' of the **Pala di San Lucano** when they forced a direct route up the great, c1,150m south face of the Terza Pala. *Guardian of Dreams* was climbed between 1 and 4 November, is 1,400m or 34 pitches in length and has a crux pitch of VIII+ A0, which Prinoth climbed with just three pegs and Walpoth, coming second, freed at IX. The whole route was protected with natural gear including around 35 pitons: no bolts were carried. The route, which has largely excellent rock and lies between the 1972 *Anghileri-Gogna-Lanfranchi-Rava* on the left, and the 2019 *Leduc-Vanhee,* was climbed ground up in a continuous push.

Other, highly active modern pioneers, particularly when it comes to creating big bold routes without recourse to bolts, are Alessandro Baù, and Nicola Tondini. Proving that independent exploration is still possible on the most famous rock faces in the world, in 2019, with Claudio Migliorini, they completed *Space Vertigo* up the wall right of the classic 1959 Desmaison-Mazeaud route, *Via Jean Couzy* (FFA Mauro Bolo, 1999, 8a+) on the north face of **Cima Ovest.** Rigorous in their approach of opening each pitch from below and not using aid, it took three years to finish their dream project, which requires 'strong arms, a very good head, and obligatory 7b climbing, often some distance above protection'. Due to the nature of the rock and portaledge camps, the belays were bolted, though no bolts were used on any of the pitches, resulting in run-out climbing and many long falls. However, the route was not completed free in a single push.

In September 2020 the three returned, hauled portaledges and provisions to a point at one-third height, and on 9 September began a free ascent. Due to slightly damp rock, they were only able to complete three pitches the first day, so returned to the ground for the night. Next day they jumared their ropes and spent the next two nights at the portaledge camp, freeing the remaining difficulties. On the fourth day they completed the 21-pitch route to the summit. The crux is 8a, five pitches are 7c or 7c+, and another eight are 7a+ to 7b+. Each pitch was freed on lead by at least one member of the team and the route was judged the most demanding the climbers have created, making it in turn one of the hardest in the Dolomites.

Also from the Cima Ovest comes the story of a remarkable lone ascent, with Lukasz Dudek (Poland) making an audacious roped solo of Alex Huber's 2007 route *Pan Aroma* (550m, 8c) on the north face. With Jacek Matuszek he had in the past made free ascents of *Bellavista* (8b+) and *Project Fear* (8c) on the same face, and the *Spanish* route (8b+) on the Cima Grande. Dudek prepared by working two days on the route in 2019 with a friend, and in 2020 several dozen roped-solo ascents of sport routes up to 8c in Poland. Then in July he made further inspection of the route alone. On 7 August he completed every pitch clean on his first attempt and reached the summit at night after 17 hours on the face. While the roof pitches are spectacular, Dudek says it is the long 60m rightward traverse, the original pitch six, that provides the technical crux.

He timed his ascent to arrive at the most difficult section of the route around midday, when the temperature on this shadowed wall would approach maximum. This would keep his fingers warm and stop him getting pumped too quickly.

Finally, the Dolomites continue to see increased development of mixed and thin-ice potential on the big faces. The **Rochetta Alta di Bosconero**, best known for its classic north-west pillar or *Spigolo Strobel* (1964, 650m, VI+ A1), was in splendid conditions for ice-mixed climbing in January and February. The large depression on the north-west face, partially taken by a 1920s Grade III rock route, was climbed on 30 January at M6+ AI5+ (14 pitches, 730m of climbing) by Santiago Padròs and Diego Toigo. A week previously this pair, together with two friends, had bailed on the line after climbing four demanding pitches, which included the route's cruxes. Long run outs and a couple of falls made the day too exciting to continue at that time. Named *Madre Tierra*, the new line was repeated just three days later by Matteo Furlan and Mirco Grasso, who confirmed the grade and quality of climbing. However, Grasso realized there was another system of gullies out to the right that led all the way to the summit and knew he had to check them out. He returned on 16 February, this time with Alvaro Lafuente. The latter had just arrived in the area and was recommended to Grasso as a potential partner. Grasso proposed that Lafuente climb a mountain he'd never seen before with a complete stranger: Lafuente accepted with enthusiasm. The two climbed the first five pitches of *Madre Tierra*, finding them in much better condition than a couple of weeks earlier, and therefore easier, before moving right and climbing a logical ice gully to the top. The route was named *Apus* and graded M6+, AI5, UIAA V. On the same day other parties climbed *Madre Tierra*, almost turning a two-week old route into a modern classic.

• Thanks to Rodolphe Popier and route authors for help in compiling this report.

SIMON RICHARDSON

Scottish Winter 2020-21

Greg Boswell watches carefully as Callum Johnson leads the first ascent of
New Age Raiders (IX,9) on Church Door Buttress in Glen Coe. The route forces
its way through exceptionally steep ground right of *The Ninety-Five Theses*,
another testing IX,9. (Hamish Frost)

Not surprisingly, Covid-19 dominated the 2021 Scottish winter season.
After a slow start, December proved to be an excellent month for mixed
climbing and the most technical ascents of the winter were climbed during
this period. But everything changed on 5 January when Scotland entered
lockdown. Those living in the city areas of Glasgow, Edinburgh, Dundee
and Aberdeen were unable to visit the mountains, but elsewhere climbers
were able to travel within their local authority area. For those based in Highland Region this meant almost unlimited access to the major climbing areas,

Callum Johnson on the run-out first pitch of *The Flying Fox* (VIII,8). This serious and sustained route climbs the right side of Hayfork Gully Wall on An Teallach. *(Marc Langley)*

although most elected to climb locally. To everyone's relief, travel restrictions finally eased (for most) on 19 April.

Despite the late start, it was a cold season extending well into May, but inevitably it was the Covid-19 restrictions that shaped the pattern of activity. The Cairn Gorm ski road was closed on 24 December, which limited climbing in the Cairngorms but instead there was considerable focus on the Southern Highlands, which were accessible to many climbers living in central Scotland.

The most significant trend was the emergence of a new guard. The first ascent reports are full of new routes by Tim Miller, Jamie Skelton, Callum Johnson and Will Rowland. These climbers are all talented, very motivated and move fast, which resulted in dozens of impressive ascents. Arguably the most outstanding achievement of the season took place in Glen Coe on 12 March when Jamie Skelton and Tim Miller climbed the three classic grade VIIs on each of Bidean nam Bian's big cliffs in a day: *Neanderthal, Un Poco Loco* and *Central Grooves*. They took 15h 30m car to car. As in the Alps, enchainments have been done before in Scotland, but this is the first time difficult mixed routes, rather than fast-flowing ice climbs, have been linked together.

Callum Johnson starting up the second pitch on the first ascent of *Never Never Land* (VIII,8) on Beinn Eighe. The wide crack can just be seen exiting the roof's left-hand side provided a strenuous crux. *(Tim Miller)*

Northern Highlands

The first significant new route of the season fell to Callum Johnson and Tim Miller on 3 December when they climbed the right side of the Hayfork Gully Wall on An Teallach. *The Flying Fox* (VIII,8) shares the same bold start as *Silver Fox* before taking impressive ground to the right. The following day, Johnson and Miller climbed another new route on the Eastern Ramparts of Beinn Eighe. *Never Never Land* was also graded VIII,8, making it two new VIIIs on consecutive days for the dynamic young duo.

Johnson visited Barrel Buttress on Quinag with Andy Mackinnon on 28 December and came away with the first winter ascent of the summer E2 *Beefheart*. This excellent VII,7 was described as 'well protected, steep with a real out-there feeling'. Further south that day, Tim Miller and Jamie Skelton

Dave MacLeod on the first pitch of *Nevermore* (VIII,8) on Ben Nevis. The route continues up the overhanging corner up and right. *(Iain Small)*

made the first winter ascent of *Groovin' High* (VII,8) on the Far East Wall on Beinn Eighe. Excellent cracks and good hooks meant the climbing was as enjoyable as it is in summer. On the Bonaidh Dhonn, Rob Giddy, Tim Miller and Callum Johnson climbed *South by South-East* (V,6), a winter-only line taking the obvious corner on the left side of the crag between *Netsky* and *North by North-West*.

Skye

Big news from Skye was the first winter ascent of *Mongoose Direct* (VIII,8) on Sgurr Mhicconich by Jamie Skelton and Tim Miller. Their ascent was based on the summer line and took advantage of useful ice that had formed in the right wall of the corner on the first pitch. On Blaven, Ian Hall and Katharina Lenz climbed *Vaccination* (IV,4), the good-looking corner in the buttress above *Escape from Colditz*.

Ben Nevis

Iain Small and Dave MacLeod succeeded on an outstanding new route on 7 December with the first ascent of *Nevermore* (VIII,8) on Number Five Gully Buttress. Several teams had eyed up the great, soaring, overhanging

Dave MacLeod on the first winter ascent of *Rose Innominate* (IX,9) on the west face of Aonach Dubh in Glen Coe. This pitch climbed more of a seam rather than a crack, with axes resting on dirt rather than hooks: a bold lead. *(Helen Rennard)*

corner on the right side of the buttress but its unrelenting steepness had deterred all attempts. The buttress faces south-east, meaning it is very much a mid-winter venue, best climbed before the sun rises too high in the sky.

Three days later, Tim Miller and Jamie Skelton notched up the first new grade IX of the season when they climbed *Metamorphosis* (IX,10). This summer E2 was first climbed in winter by Iain Small and Gareth Hughes in March 2009 and graded VIII,9. Small and Hughes took the natural winter start up the deep crack of *Cranium* (an E1 alternative start to *Heidbanger*) before moving right to join *Metamorphosis* for its third pitch, whilst Miller and Skelton followed the complete summer line.

Robin Clothier and Simon Richardson made several first ascents whilst checking routes for the new edition of the Ben Nevis guidebook. *Mavericks* (V,5) takes a varied line crossing *Raeburn's Arete*, and *Badlands* (VI,5) climbs the line of icy grooves between *Italian Right-Hand* and *Bydand*. They also found *That Untravelled World* (IV,4) right of *The Chute*, the icefall *Shangri La* (V,5) left of *Poseidon Groove*, and *The Last Ridge* (IV,4), the well-defined right edge of the gully of *La Petite*. Richardson also teamed up with Mark Robson for *Into The Wild* (V,5), a companion route to *That Untravelled World*, Richard Bentley for *Lost Horizon* (III,4) left of *Shangri La*, and Helen Rennard for *Midnight Blue* (V,5), a direct line up the front face of the steep buttress left of *Red Gully*. On the Douglas Boulder, Huw Scott and Nathan Adam added *The Final Fowl* (IV,6) on the cracked wall just right of West Gully.

Interestingly, there was considerable interest in some of the less-frequented corries on the mountain. Will Rowland continued his exploration of Coire Eoghainn with *Strike While the Iron Is Hot* (IV,4) with James Cooper. Helen Rennard and Simon Richardson also visited the corrie and added a fine IV,4 left of *The German Night Prowler*. Richardson and Robson also visited Coire Ghaimhnean, coming away with the excellent *Paradox Buttress* (III,4) to the right of *Five Finger Gully*. The same pair also added the first routes in Sloc nan Uan, the shallow corrie on the east flank of the mountain.

Glen Coe

In late December, Greg Boswell and Callum Johnson added *New Age Raiders* (IX,9) to Bidean Nam Bian in Glen Coe. This superb addition to Church Door Buttress climbs very steep ground to the right of *The Ninety-Five Theses*

Robin Clothier on the first ascent of *Shangri La* (V,5) on the Upper Tier of South Trident Buttress, Ben Nevis. *(Simon Richardson)*

before the angle of the crag eases to the right. A few days later, Boswell returned with Graham McGrath and Hamish Frost to add *False Penance* (IX,10). This route takes previously unclimbed terrain up the overhanging groove left of *Un Poco Loco*.

The following day, Dave Macleod and Helen Rennard visited Stob Coire Nam Beith and made the first winter ascent of *Tarbh Uisge* (IX,8). They also visited the west face of Aonach Dubh with Andy Nelson and made the first winter ascent of *Rose Innominate* which resulted in a bold and technical IX,9. Next door, Mike Mason and Huw Scott climbed *H5N8* (IV,5), the deep straight gully near the right side of No3 Gully Buttress. Also on Aonach Dubh, Will Rowland and Peter Staves found *Midnight Express* (VI,6), a direct version of *Midnight Cowboy*.

On Buachaille Etive Mor's Blackmount Wall, Alistair Docherty and Matt Rowbottom discovered the excellent *Froth Corner* (VI,7), which lies immediately right of the 'undercut cave' on *The Chasm* to *Crowberry Traverse*. They also added *Lockdown* X (IV,6), the gully just to the left. On Central Buttress, Jamie Skelton and Nicky Brierley made the first winter ascent of *Appalling* (VI,7). Unlike summer, the turfy nature of the climb made it a rather good winter route.

Western Highlands

Jamie Skelton and Matt Glenn continued last season's winter interest in Garbh Bheinn by making the first ascent of *Fathomless* (VII,7) on 3 December. The route starts up the summer HVS *Excalibur* before moving right. Fathomless is only the second winter route to be climbed on the upper tier of the South Wall and follows Neil Adams and Alasdair Fulton's winter ascent of *Sgian Dubh* back in January 2009. Skelton maintained his focus on the South Wall through January, making first winter ascents of *Bayonet* (V,6), *Sala* (VIII,9) *The Peeler* (VII,8), *Menghini* (VII,8) and *Chib* (VI,6) partnered variously by Nicky Brierley, Helen Rennard, Tim Miller and Morag Eagleson.

Also on Garbh Bheinn, Robin Clothier and Simon Richardson found the excellent *Dogs of War* (VI,7) on Pinnacle Buttress, and on North-East Buttress, Al Matthewson and A Veitch succeeded on *Open Secret* (III/IV), the right-bounding corner of the slabby section on the Second Tier. Further right, Steve Kennedy and Andy MacDonald added *Hidden Agenda* (IV,4) and *Troll Gate* (II). Nearby on Stob Coir a'Chearcaill, Will Rowland and Garry Campbell climbed *Twelve Pointer* (VI,6), a direct on Charcoal Buttress.

Heavy snow throughout January prompted development of the low-lying Mad Man's Crag in Coire nan Frithalt on Maol Odar. Robin Clothier and Simon Richardson climbed six 150m routes in the grade IV to VI range. Nearby, Steve Kennedy and Andy MacDonald continued their exploration of the Zeppelin face on Creach Bheinn with two good routes. *Good Times Bad Times* (IV,5) takes the slab left of *Bring it on Home*, and *Kashmir* (IV,5) follows the slim corner to the left.

Southern Highlands
Lockdown restrictions resulted in enthusiastic exploration of the Southern Highlands. In early January, Rosie Rothwell, Joe Barlow climbed *Frosty Peat* (I/II), the broad buttress 500m south of Arrow Buttress on Meall Nan Tarmachan. Two days later, the same pair added *Hexellent* (II) and *Ba Buttress* (III) to the left side of Coire Ban on Meall A' Choire Leith. On Ben Lomond, Sam Wainwright and Sebastian Wolfrum found *Break Dance* (IV,5) on the rightmost buttress in the corrie, and on the Upper Tier of The Brack, Ole Kemi, Stuart McFarlane made a fine discovery with *End of The Line* (V,7), which takes the wall right of Elephant Gully.

On Cruach Ardrain, Marco Limonci, Danny Church and Orazio Lo Tauro had a good find with *The Sicilian* (IV,4), an icefall on the southern edge of Meall Dhamh. Nearby on Ben Vorlich's south face, Sebastian Wolfrum and Douglas Fransson Lee discovered *End of The Rope* (III,4), which lies left of Central Rib. In Coire Cruinn on Meall Dubh, Duncan Helm and Alex Urquhart-Taylor found *First Ice* (III/IV), the prominent icefall on the short wall left of the previous routes.

Glen Lyon was popular. In Coire Laoghain on Meall Ghaordaidh, Willie Jeffrey and Anne Craig climbed *Yellow Peril* (II), the gully left of *The Lyons in Winter*. Jeffrey also teamed up with Paul Morris to add *WHO Han Whitewash* (II) left of *A Wee One*, and *Desmond's Dilemma* (III) on the buttress at the head of the corrie. Nearby on the north face of Creag an Tulabhain, Freddie Crawley ascended *V Gully East* (II) and *V Gully West* (II) in the company of Jamie Grant and Zoe Thornton. On Stuc an Lochan, Craig Gudmondsson and Jim MacGarlanc climbed the prominent left-leaning *Cat Gully* (I), and Duncan Helm and Alex Urquhart-Taylor found *Vaccinator* (IV,4), the icefall on the gully's right wall. The same pair also climbed *The Cat's Rake* (III) the icefall 40m to the right. Gudmondsson also added two new routes to Creag na Gaoth on Ben Chonzie with Stuart Mckeggie: *Lockdown Grooves* (III,4) and *Essential Fun* (III,4).

Late Season
The spring was unseasonably cold which gave plenty of opportunities for those limited by lockdown to enjoy some late season winter climbing. April was unusually dry which meant there were few opportunities for mixed climbing, but the gullies in the high north-facing cliffs were well filled with snow. The classic lines in the Northern Corries saw many ascents, but as usual, it was Ben Nevis that provided most of the late season sport. The winter has been consistently cold with no significant thaws, meaning little ice had formed on the high cliffs. The natural drainage lines formed beautiful plastic ice however and *Point Five* was climbed as late as mid May.

Towards the end of the month there was still ice high on the Ben in Comb and Green gullies with winter only starting to lose its grip. Despite the late start, it has been a six-month long season. A considerable number of excellent new routes had been climbed, but one can only wonder what might have been if Coronavirus had not intervened.

IAN WALL

Nepal 2020-21

A woman guards oxygen cylinders for a patient after refilling them at a factory during last spring's Covid-19 surge in Kathmandu. *(Alamy/Navesh Chitrakar)*

Just as the spring 2020 mountaineering season was about to get underway in Nepal the world was overwhelmed by Covid-19. It was poor timing, since the authorities were hoping to celebrate Visit Nepal 2020, a widely heralded tourism drive. Many countries were imposing lockdowns or restricting movement and Nepal was no different, closing its borders to international travellers on 22 March. Rumours also emerged that the government was about to restrict movement within the country, with domestic flights grounded and roads closed. Many Nepalis left the capital to return to their villages, many of them people employed in the travel and tourism industry, including the mountaineering service industry. A nationwide lockdown was announced for 24 March. Life came to a sudden standstill and for the time being everybody followed the government's order.

Tourists had been arriving from early March and many trekkers were already in the mountains. It took a while for information about the lockdown and travel restrictions to be disseminated in trekking regions but as news spread there were two reactions. One was an urgent need to get back to Kathmandu and on to home countries. The other was to carry on with the trek and deal with the fallout once back in Kathmandu.

With roads, domestic and international airports closed, many were trapped, unable to get clear information. The Trekking Agencies Association of Nepal in coordination with the ministry of tourism and the Nepal Tourism Board initiated a transport plan for the return of trekking groups to Kathmandu. Several embassies organised repatriation flights. These were organised by chartering specific carriers and so new tickets had to be purchased since existing tickets were not transferable. Those who chose to continue with their trek ignoring travel advice found themselves in difficult situations with visas expiring. There was a lack of hotel accommodation as hotels and restaurants were closed, as was the immigration department. In the lively tourist hub of Thamel, the shutters came down.

The Smith family from Aberdeen set off on their EBC trek in mid March from Salleri in lower Solu Khumbu just before Nepal imposed its lockdown. Julie, Chris and their young children trekked to Lukla, where they became stranded for three months before lockdown eased and they could continue. Their movements were restricted to their teahouse and they weren't allowed into Lukla. They occupied their time in the grounds where the children could play. Eventually they completed their trek visiting Gokyo with two Nepali friends who accompanied them most of the way and were able to reassure local people the family had not just flown up from Kathmandu but had, in fact, been in the region for months and had had PCR tests in Lukla.

Within a few weeks of lockdown, daily wage earners were feeling the strain. Street vendors, porters and small business owners were running out of money, meaning no food and in some cases no home as they were unable to pay rents. As always in Nepal there was little help from those elected to protect citizens and that lack of support was plugged by many voluntary organisations. Food kitchens were set up to feed the poor, not only for people but for street animals which no longer had the waste from hotels to rummage through.

Although resilient Nepalis have found ways to overcome hardship in the past, this time it was different: an estimated 200 businesses have permanently closed in Thamel. As usual in Nepal the population is divided between those who accept the situation and have the backup to weather the storm and those who don't. Many Indian migrant workers who returned home have not yet come back to lift their shutters and hotels have had to close, including, surprisingly, some of the biggest and best established businesses in town. However, Kathmandu and Nepal generally remain vibrant and optimistic and there is still a lot of renovation of old buildings going on with many new structures more in keeping with the architecture Kathmandu was once famous for.

Change of Government

Just before Christmas 2020, prime minister K P Sharma Oli dissolved parliament following splits in the ruling Nepal Communist Party and elections were announced in two stages for April and May. This decision had the

Ian Wall with the late Ang Rita, the 'Snow Leopard', still the only person to have climbed Everest in winter without oxygen. *(Ian Wall)*

endorsement of the president, an old ally of K P Oli, but in February Nepal's supreme court overturned the dissolution as unconstitutional. Oli was forced to form a caretaker government while the conflict played out on the streets: all this in the middle of a pandemic. Further legal action resulted in the NCP itself being divided into its old constituent parts and the Maoist faction led by Pushpa Kamal Dahal withdrew its support in the spring. By July K P Oli had run out of options and was forced to resign, to be replaced by the Nepali Congress veteran Sher Bahadur Deuba, the fifth time he has been prime minister. Oli's tenure was marked by an apparent swing towards China, which tried to mediate between the various communist factions. Deuba's return to office signals a cooling of that relationship.

The Death of Legends
One of Nepal's best-known climbers, Chhiji Nurbu Sherpa, passed away in August 2020. He was the managing director of Highlight Expeditions and recognised as one of the top Nepali climbers summiting 13 out of the 14 8,000m peaks. His first 8,000er was his home mountain of Makalu, climbed aged 27. He climbed K2 twice and Everest five times. He had recently been on Everest in winter with Alex Txikon, reaching 8,000m and suffering frostbite. The circumstances surrounding his death were not publicised. Chhiji Nurbu was 40 years old.

It was also with great sadness that the mountaineering world learned of the death of Ang Rita Sherpa, the Snow Leopard, in late September 2020. Ang Rita Sherpa scaled Everest 10 times without bottled oxygen. Born in 1948 in Yilajung, a small village in Khumbu, Ang Rita first worked as a porter in 1963. In total, he achieved 19 summit successes on 8,000m peaks by the end of his career in 1999: 10 times on Everest, four times on Cho Oyu, four times on Dhaulagiri and once on Kangchenjunga, all completely without bottled oxygen, with the one exception: during 1983 he slept at the South Col on oxygen. In 1984, he opened a new route variant via Everest's south buttress with the Slovaks Zoltán Demján and Jozef Psotka. On 22 December 1987, Ang Rita succeeded in making the first and so far, the only winter ascent of Everest without supplementary oxygen. In bad weather, with Korean Heo Young-ho, the two climbers were forced to bivouac at 8,600m. 'We spent the whole night just below the summit,' Ang Rita recalled later, 'doing aerobic exercises to keep our body active which is the only way to survive there.'

In October 2020 Ngawang Tenzin Jangpo Rinpoche, spiritual leader at Tengboche monastery died at the age of 85. He had been the abbot of the Buddhist monastery for 64 years, since 1956. Ngawang Tenzin was born in Namche Bazaar in 1935, reportedly on the same day as the Dalai Lama, 6 July. As a child he insisted that he owned a house in Tengboche. The monks of the monastery subjected him to a test. They presented him with a collection of objects. Ngawang seized those that had belonged to Lama Gulu, the builder of the monastery. Since then, he had recognized as a *tulku* and the reincarnation of Lama Gulu. The monastery burned down in January 1989 but the Sherpa community rebuilt it with financial support from several organisations including Sir Ed Hillary's Himalayan Trust. The monk was critical of the commercialisation of Mount Everest. 'Climbing Everest has become a fashion. All people want to do is reach the top,' wrote Ngawang Tenzin Jangpo Rinpoche. 'The Sherpas of Khumbu may not know everything, but they are suffering the consequences of the people's greed.'

Autumn 2020

While most tourists avoided Nepal during the spring season one or two groups managed a few successes during the second half of the year. From 1 September 2020, due to a sharp increase in Covid-19 infections, only Nepali returnees, diplomats and employees of UN aid organizations were allowed to fly into the country. Nepal also banned all UK residents from entering the country. According to the department of tourism, permission was granted for expeditions to Luja Peak (6726m), Cheungyari-2 (6506m), Ama Dablam (6814m), Surma Sarovar (6523m), Rokapi (5467m), Manaslu (8163m) and Thapa Peak (6012m) for the winter season 2020. Luja, Manaslu and Thapa Peak were Nepali expeditions; the others were foreign.

In the late summer of 2020 a government spokesperson announced that an 18-member expedition from Bahrain had received a permit for Manaslu and for the purpose of acclimatisation Lobuche East as well. The team of the Royal Guard of Bahrain arrived in mid September on a charter flight, entered a one-week quarantine programme and then headed immediately for Khumbu. An unfortunately timed press release in Bahrain back in April 2020 as to the ambitions of the expedition caught the Nepali government on the back foot and in an attempt to smooth the situation the commander of the Royal Guard, Sheikh Nasser bin Hamad Al Khalifa, had relief supplies sent to those Nepalis most seriously hit by the pandemic. The expedition went on to complete both objectives but not without controversy. A video clip emerged showing a backpack being unloaded from a helicopter while a mountaineer also disembarks. The video clearly showed this taking place at camp one on Manaslu. Seven Summit Treks, the expedition's agent, didn't respond to enquires as to whether the climber was part of the Bahraini team. They reached the summit – or at least the high point the fixed ropes reached just below the actual summit – on 15 October 2020. The expedition was preparation for an attempt on Everest in spring 2021.

Despite the pandemic, the Nepali government gave the go-ahead for the busiest Everest season on record, banning mention of the Covid-19 outbreak at Everest Base Camp. *(Lhakpa Sherpa)*

Not content with letting one high-profile team into Nepal, the government went on to grant permits for Ama Dablam to Sheikh Mohammed bin Abdullah Al Thani, a member of the Qatari royal family. Known as Moe Al Thani in the climbing world, the prince was the first Qatari to climb Everest in 2013.

As a result of pressure from mountaineering agents in the tourism sector the Nepal government opened the country for foreign tourists to go mountaineering and trekking on 17 October 2020 but strangely enough not for other tourism purposes. As a result, permits were also issued for teams to climb Baruntse, Gyalzen, Himlung and Manaslu.

Cho Oyu was first climbed via the north-west flank but when the Chinese increased the price Nepali guides proposed a new and technically straightforward route on the south side of the mountain for clients of commercial expeditions but to date this has not yet progressed.

Earthquakes can reduce the height of mountains in an instant. After the big earthquake hit Nepal in 2015, scientists suspected the height of Everest might have changed. Both China and Nepal decided to mount independent expeditions and using all available technology measured the true height of the world's highest mountain. Despite delays in releasing the results, for obscure political reasons, the new official altitude as of 2020 is 8,848.86m: an increase of 86cm from the 8,848m that was declared in 1954.

Winter 2020-21

Two young Nepali friends, Tenji Sherpa and Vinayak Jay Malla, have between the two of them summited Everest (once without oxygen), Lhotse, Manaslu, Ama Dablam, Cholatse's north face, Lhakpa Ri and Nuptse. Malla also has experience climbing in the European Alps as well as in India. They went unsupported to Manaslu although the winter veteran Simone Moro, from Italy, was also there, along with Iñaki Álvarez and Spanish climber Alex Txikon. Eventually both teams were forced to descend without success. Vinayak and Tenji gave the mountain a good shot but after several weeks trapped by bad conditions had to withdraw to base camp and eventually Kathmandu. Meanwhile, back in Khumbu, at least 14 climbers summitted Ama Dablam on 14 January 2021, including the Qatari prince Sheikh Mohammed bin Abdullah Al Thani and his team.

Although K2 is definitely not in Nepal, the success of the Nepali team in making the first winter ascent (see Pakistan notes, pp260-7) certainly had an impact there, where wild scenes of celebration greeted the returning heroes. The 10 Nepali climbers from three different expeditions chose to work together and in a remarkable show of solidarity the leaders waited 10m below the summit for everyone to catch up so they could take the final steps together to the summit singing Nepal's national anthem in unison. Nims Purja made the ascent without supplementary oxygen. This demonstration of unity was for ordinary Nepalis in obvious contrast to their political leaders, who have spent recent years paralysing the government.

Success on K2 undoubtedly put Nepali climbers on the mountaineering world map as a force in their own right. Nepali climbers have played a significant role in many major expeditions to the greater Himalayan peaks, from Everest in the 1920s, Nanga Parbat in the 1930s, and several first ascents of 8,000m peaks in the 1950s, including Everest. Despite their contribution to mountaineering, Nepali mountaineers have often been written out of its history. The attention they got for K2 was well deserved.

Spring 2021

As the winter season drew to a close all eyes were on what would happen in spring. Reports of a large number of permit requests were appearing in the press, people were optimistic but the pandemic continued and there was a political decision to be made, would the country open to mountaineering or remain closed?

Commercial expeditions and their clients have long laid siege on Everest. However, in recent years, a new business model has been fine-tuned that came to fruition on K2, the perfect platform to execute this new approach, which will generate huge profits for those companies who adopt it. It basically involves getting the most climbers to the summit as quickly and reliably as possible. The main agency, Seven Summit Treks also extended its two for one approach. Most agencies already provide the option of including Lhotse but spring 2021 saw Annapurna and Dhaulagiri included on the itinerary with helicopter transfer included in the price and on hand to ferry clients from base camp to Pokhara for a short rest before the Dhaulagiri element of the package. The success of this approach was proven on Annapurna, regarded as the deadliest 8,000m peak, when 67 clients reached the summit on the night of 16 April 2021. To ensure the 'quickly as possible' element, ropes were fixed for the entire route, including sections that are not normally equipped. This resulted in Seven Summit's rope fixers running out of rope at 7,400m, just above camp four. With progress halted, clients had to retreat back to camp four until the company helicopter came to the rescue with more rope and oxygen.

As with all service businesses, success relies on the provider being able to read and deliver consumer demands. In this case the lure was based on attractive opportunities, easy solutions to overcome technical difficulties, maximum safety and a high percentage chance of success at a very competitive price. It's an example of the old adage: 'Stack 'em high and sell 'em cheap.' In a bid to keep costs down all agencies running expeditions on Annapurna agreed to contribute to manpower and other resources required for fixing the route.

Yet no matter how good the infrastructure is, how well planned the itinerary and how skilled and strong the team, it still comes down to weather and mountain conditions on the day. Those few days around 16 April proved ideal in allowing such large-scale success. One client from Taiwan suffered superficial frostbite and decided he didn't want to commit to the effort of descending the dangerous section between camp three and camp two. So he hired the Seven Summit helicopter to take him to Kathmandu for a few days before returning to Dhaulagiri to join the other members of the Annapurna team. All clients were obviously pleased with their success; it seems these days, perhaps for the majority, that adventure is only meaningful if the adventure is illuminated. As for ethics, that will be a never-ending debate. In the end Dhaulagiri was not to be; there was a surge in Covid-19 cases and other issues so the expedition was abandoned just above camp two.

No doubt the huge profits agencies enjoyed blurred any anxiety about 'what if'. What if the weather broke while clients were high on the mountain? What if some of the avalanches clients witnessed had taken a slightly different fall line? What if helicopters were grounded and the ropes and oxygen supplies had not been delivered at the critical moment? There is still a high level of risk in this style of mountaineering. Mountaineering has no rules or regulations, and we like that, but this approach has raised ethical and safety questions within the guiding world.

Pandemic Everest

Nepal, like other countries with a high number of people employed in tourism, has found itself in a difficult situation over the last 12 months. Lockdown brought great hardship to millions of people who earn an income as daily wage earners. Nepal has no welfare and the loss of income for over a year meant great pressure was exerted on the government by the large trekking and expedition agencies and hotels to open the country for mountain tourism. Many of the owners of these organisations make large annual financial donations to political parties. With the combination of mountain tourists anxious to get into the mountains, the agents looking for financial rewards and the government considering the impact of another closed season on the national economy, the government backed down and Nepal opened for mountain tourism while, inexplicably, other forms of tourism remained closed.

The spring 2021 season saw the highest number of clients ever recorded on Everest expeditions with the ministry issuing 408 permits. This was despite several major international outfitters cancelling their operations due to concern over the pandemic. The north side of Everest remained closed to international expeditions although there was one Chinese team granted permission to attempt the mountain from Tibet. Due to concerns over the spread of the virus it was decided to send a party of Chinese guides to the summit to keep the southern mountaineering teams out of China for fear of infection. However, this expedition was abandoned before it left base camp.

Despite a quarantine regulation being imposed in Kathmandu for foreign arrivals, tourists were seen wandering the streets of Thamel before moving on to their mountain destinations. Early in the season Everest ER, the heath facility supported by the Himalayan Rescue Association and situated at Everest Base Camp, reported an unusually high number of people arriving and seeking medical attention for 'AMS issues'. Symptoms of the virus and AMS are very similar and those with severe symptoms were immediately evacuated to Kathmandu by helicopter. Although many expeditions were testing their own clients for the virus there was no government authorised testing facility at base camp and so from very early on in the season the government denied there was a health problem within the base camp communities, a position it maintained right through to the end of the season.

Base camp took on an unusual atmosphere this season with each expedition having its own individual patch of moraine with a strictly controlled

A wide shot of Baruntse, location of the major new route *Heavenly Trap*
from the Czech climbers Radoslav Groh and Márek Holeček. *(Márek Holeček)*

perimeter area cordoned off. Clients and staff were kept inside their area and
the usual inter-expedition partying did not, more or less, take place, although
there were reports that some compounds were a lot louder than others.

Yet while base camp covers a considerable area and physical distancing is
straightforward, at higher camps there are limitations on available space and
in many situations, especially if the weather deteriorates, expedition clients
mix and share tents and other facilities. As the season progressed more and
more people were evacuated with AMS or pneumonia-like symptoms only
to be tested for and diagnosed with Covid-19 once back in Kathmandu.
Many of those evacuated and other members still in base camp did not have
the recommend insurance and so they continued to be registered as AMS
sufferers, thus disguising the true number of positive cases coming from
Khumbu. Not only did the government refuse to accept what was becoming
obvious based on the numbers testing positive after leaving EBC, it reacted
to the situation by enforcing a news blackout. Clients, expedition operators,

hospitals, medical staff and the media were all under some sort of government warning not to publish any news connecting the virus and Everest.

Lukas Furtenbach, owner of Austrian agency Furtenbach Adventures, was the first to react to what his team regarded as a health threat higher up on the mountain. After a full expedition discussion his team withdrew. Staff members were paid their full wages and certain team members who wanted to stay on were accommodated on other expeditions. Some agency owners were far more insouciant, shrugging their shoulders at the fuss. Mingma Sherpa, owner of Seven Summit Treks and the biggest operator on Everest said: 'Even though the coronavirus has reached the Everest base camp, it has not made any huge effect like what is being believed outside of the mountain. No one has really fallen seriously sick because of COVID or died like the rumors that have been spreading.' In fact, a number of people had been seriously ill. Beyond Everest though, Khumbu reported fewer cases than other parts of Nepal, according to the *British Medical Journal.*

A topo of *UFO Line*, Holeček's companion piece in the Hunku valley on the north-west face of Chamlang (7321m) climbed in 2019 with Zdeněk Hák.

On 7 May, 12 Sherpas from Seven Summit Treks reached the summit, including Kami Rita, who got his record 25th summit. This opened the gates for the rest of the teams to start their summit bids. The first summit occurred during the good weather window around 12 May and all of that team and their infrastructure were back in base camp before the first impact of Cyclone Tauktae hit Nepal from the west of India a few days later. Another weather window opened around 20 May but at the same moment Cyclone Yaas was forecast to hit the eastern region of Nepal towards the end of May. This prompted a rush of activity: some teams decided to go for the summit during the short weather window while others were caught in their rotation programmes and weren't in the right place at the right time so hunkered down for the storm to pass. Others decided to call it a day. A large number of teams were rolling Lhotse onto the back of Everest and some of those expeditions decided to cut short that element while yet again other teams decided to take the risk of an ascent before the storm hit hard, as it was predicted to do.

Provisional reports suggest 534 people stood on Everest's summit from the Nepal side in 2021, none from the Tibet side. As the season ends, four deaths have been recorded, two foreign nationals and two Sherpas. On 2 June Sherpa climbers recovered the body of a Swiss climber who died above 8,000m on Everest while descending from the summit. This is not the first time that such a rescue has been carried out at that altitude. In 2017 Dawa Finjhok Sherpa and team recovered the body of an Indian police officer who died the year before from 8,400m.

It goes without saying that this season has created a huge amount of controversy both in the Nepali media and the wider world. On one side was the government and agencies keen to open Nepal and generate income, there were daily-wage-earning Nepali staff crying out for work, the clients wanting to come. Then there were those people who wanted to keep Nepal closed. More outspoken critics have accused the clients of being insensitive to Nepal's situation and the situation of the communities through which they passed, of being wealthy, arrogant and egoistic and adopting the attitude of former imperial nations. Less has been said about the government or the agents that facilitated the situation. It is estimated the government generated $4.2m dollars from Everest in spring 2021. Had they acknowledged the health situation at Everest Base Camp, they might well have been under more pressure to close the mountain but if they had then they would have likely been obliged to offer carry-over permits as they did after the earthquake in 2015.

On a more specific note, there were many questions and accusations focussed on the amount of oxygen used on Everest when the general population was being denied access to basic health care with hospitals running out of oxygen supplies. On the face of it this would seem to be a reasonable point. However, oxygen for altitude is provided via a regulator capable of delivering a maximum flow rate of four litres per minute. Covid-19 patients require a 10 to 15 litres per minute. The medical mask and cannula system doesn't fit on current high-altitude regulators, the medical masks need to be disposable or allow sterilisation but modern altitude masks are not able to be sterilised in the same way. And at a cost of $300 they would be prohibitively expensive for Nepali hospitals to consider.

Less than 14km away from Everest as the bearded vulture glides is Baruntse (7125m) in the Makalu Barun National Park. On 19 May, during the spell of fine weather, Márek Holeček and Radoslav Groh set off to climb a new route on the north-west face in pure alpine style. They reached the summit on 25 May (See 'Heaven's Trap' on page 3) but by then the weather system blowing in off the Bay of Bengal was creating violent winds, low temperatures and a serious amount of snowfall. Their situation became extreme as they spent their sixth night out just below the summit in these extreme elements. Next day they managed another 100m of descent but the ridge they were descending is technical and to attempt it in whiteout conditions would be to tempt fate as both sides were heavily corniced. By Saturday 29 May the weather had improved and the pair were able to complete their descent of 1100m through unstable snow conditions down to less technical ground from where they were evacuated by helicopter back to Kathmandu. They received medical examinations but apart from minor frostbite and a huge loss of weight the two were remarkably well after their ordeal and 11 nights spent in atrocious weather conditions. They called their route *Heavenly Trap* (1300m, ΛBO+, VI+, M6+, 80°).

The route on Baruntse is a sobering counterpoint to the route Holeček climbed in 2019 on the north-west face of nearby Chamlang (7321m) with Zdeněk 'Háček' Hák. A longstanding objective with multiple attempts, the north-west face rises for two kilometres above the Hunku valley with sustained mixed climbing and few spots for a bivouac. The two Czechs climbed

The glacial approach to the foot of Baruntse's north-west face. For images of the climb see pp3-14. *(Márek Holeček)*

loose rock, hard mixed and bullet-proof ice to reach the top of the face in four days and the summit on 21 May. Two days later they were back in base camp. They called their route *UFO Line*, to commemorate the ascents of Doug Scott and Reinhold Messner, who reported seeing a UFO. Both agreed it was the hardest climb they'd done in the high mountains and graded it initially ABO, before offering a more comprehensive grade of 2,500m, ABO, M6, WI5. It's worth pointing out that the new route on Baruntse was ABO+. What a contrast to Everest.

Doug Scott (1941-2020)

It would not be right to conclude these notes without mentioning Doug Scott. Doug will be remembered as one of the 'hard men' of modern mountaineering. His skill in difficult situations and tenacity on technical ground was at a level rarely seen. His list of first ascents in the Nepal Himalaya is extensive with the south-west face of Everest in 1975 being the best known. But there was another side to Doug: he was a caring and compassionate human being. In recognition of the support Nepali porters

Doug Scott, remembered in Nepal for his relentless efforts to support the nation's disadvantaged though Community Action Nepal. *(Ian Wall)*

and Nepali expedition colleagues gave Doug on his many expeditions, he founded Community Action Nepal (CAN) in 1989, initially to improve the working conditions for lads working in the mountain tourism sector. Later CAN developed a support mechanism for remote hill communities in which his friends and their families live. He strongly believed that if villages could provide good education, health care and some form of income-generating activity there was a good chance that seepage of local people into the cities of Nepal could be reversed. CAN still operates and those communities, the CAN staff and many of the Nepali people with whom Doug came into contact with will sadly miss his warmth, dry sense of humour and his contribution to helping to improve their daily lives.

On a personal note, I would like to add that without Doug I would never have moved to Nepal and been able to lead the life that I so enjoy today. I am forever indebted.

Alex Mathie & Ed Douglas

Pakistan 2020

On the first ascent of K6 Central. *(Jeff Wright)*

Against all odds, 2020 saw a number of significant ascents in the Pakistani Karakoram. While it is scant insult to the others to single out the first winter ascent of K2 as perhaps the most 'historic', teams elsewhere established significant new lines at a variety of elevations, to unclimbed summits or unclimbed aspects of rarely visited peaks.

In August, when Pakistan's borders reopened, an opportunistic expedition to the Shimshal paid off for Felix Berg, Patrick Münkel, Gabriel Stroe (Germany), and Mirza Ali Baig and Arshad Karim (Pakistan). The Germans, who had originally planned to visit the Tien Shan, along with the

Priti and Jeff Wright. *(Jeff Wright)*

Pakistani climbers, made two first ascents in three days. Berg, Münkel, Stroe, Baig and Karim made the first ascent of the 5,770m AM Peak (800m, AD-) on 20 August. Two days later, Berg, Münkel, Karim and Stroe made the first ascent of the 6,105m Koh e Dhg'hg (1100m, TD-, M4/5, 60°). Berg returned to the Shimshal in late autumn, climbing a possible new route to the summit of Ambarin Sar (6170m) in a one-day push on 28 November.

In October, Jeff and Priti Wright (USA) travelled to the Charakusa valley, along with Colin Haley (USA), who had solo climbing plans in the area. Haley's expedition was cut short due to illness, but after acclimatising up to 6,200m on nearby Pakura peak, the Wrights made plans for an attempt on unclimbed K6 Central (7155m). On 3 October, the pair left ABC and on 8 October made the third ascent of K6 West (7140m) via a line on the west face that Graham Zimmerman and Scott Bennett used to descend K6 West in 2015. A day later, on 9 October, the pair made the first ascent of K6 Central, rounding out both a new route of over 2,000m vertical gain, and an astonishing 'alpine sabbatical' during which the pair climbed all six classic north faces of the Alps as well as the *Ragni* route on Cerro Torre.

Also in October, Pierrick Fine and Symon Welfringer (France) travelled to the Toltar glacier, in Hunza, where they aimed to make the first ascent of the 2,500m south face of Sani Pakush (6951m). The pair spent two weeks acclimatising and then waited for a weather window. On October 16, they left camp and started up the south face, climbing the hardest pitches of the route (M4+/5) at approximately 5,600m. After two taxing bivouacs the pair were able to get a decent rest at a third bivouac a crevasse on the summit ridge at 6,400m. The following day (October 19) they made a lightweight summit bid, leaving most of their equipment at the bivouac and climbing the final 500m of variable snow to the summit. The following day they descended from their final bivouac to base camp, reversing their line of ascent on a combination of abalokovs and down climbing. Their route, *Revers Gagnant,* weighs in at 2,500m, ED1, 90°, M41, WI41 and is the second known ascent of Sani Pakush, which was first climbed via the north-west ridge by a German team in 1991.

Around the same time, Muchu Chhish (7452m) – the highest unclimbed peak in the world after off-limits Gangkhar Puensum – saw two attempts, both of which ended short of the summit. Czech climbers Pavel Kořínek,

Nirmal 'Nimsdai' Purja, on the summit of K2 after the first winter ascent.
(Nirmal Purja)

Pavel Bém and Jiří Janák reached an altitude of 6,400m before retreating in bad weather. Philipp Brugger (Austria) and Jordi Tosas (Spain) reached 7,000m but were repelled by dangerous avalanche conditions.

The ascent in Pakistan, *writes Ed Douglas*, that got the most attention was the historic first winter ascent of K2 by an all-Nepali team that reached the summit on 16 January in temperatures of -40°C but also, mercifully and un-usually, low wind. Of the 10 climbers, who paused just before the summit so they could reach it together, the best-known in Europe is Nirmal 'Nimsdai' Purja, the former special forces soldier who made short work of the 14 8,000m peaks in 2019, his so-called Project Possible. He was the only climber not to use bottled oxygen. While Purja is a Magar, the other nine were Sherpa, drawn from three teams: five climbing with Team Nimsdai, but with logistics from the commercial operator Seven Summit Treks, three led by Mingma Gyalje, more commonly known as Mingma G, and one Sherpa from Seven Summit.

Given the scale of the achievement – the last and hardest winter ascent of the 14 8,000ers with attempts stretching back more than 30 years from some of climbing's biggest names – the media coverage was unsurprisingly extensive. There was also a great deal of negative speculation, criticism and allegation around the ascent. As a fluent English speaker with strong connections in the UK and an effective PR team, much of the focus was on Purja in western media, although Nimsdai himself stressed the collaborative effort. In Nepal, the media was more generous, profiling the Sherpa 'stars' rather than simply repeating a list of names.

The charismatic Mingma Gyalje, or Mingma G, an IFMGA guide with three previous ascents of K2, once without oxygen, was particularly visible, as leader of the second team included in the summit party, along with partners Dawa Tenjin and Kili Pemba. While Purja's team, well stocked with formidable *domestiques*, could draw on significant resources, Mingma G's was more piratical, relying on crowdfunding to scrap together the necessary funding. One team member pulled out under pressure from his family, and as Mingma G told *Outdoor Journal*, 'For my remaining team members, I convinced their wives and we travelled to Pakistan before they could change their minds.' Both Dawa and Kili work in Norway in the summers, and their families didn't want that certain income jeopardised.

Arriving in Pakistan on 7 December, they completeted formalities and flew to Skardu on 10 December and left Askole on 13 December with what Mingma G descried as our 'invisible footmen', the team's Balti porters. 'They were very strong and always cheerful. Though my team had better food to eat, wore branded gear and carried lighter bags, the porters were happier and faster than us on the snow.' The ironies of the situation were not lost on Mingma G. He grew up in the Rolwaling valley, like many of the strongest modern Sherpas. 'My relatives would bring back chocolates from foreign climbers, and I used to think that if I became a porter, I would also get to eat lots of chocolates,' he told the *Nepali Times*. At age 19 he went to Manaslu and never looked back, with five ascents of Everest, 13 8,000ers under his belt and just Shishapangma to go. Though a professional guide, he climbs outside his work, with the first ascent of the west face of Chobutse under his belt, the mountain he looked up at as a boy.

His trio reached base camp on 18 December, three days before the official season began to find the well-known and popular guide Ali Sadpara and his son Sajid, with their client, Icelandic climber John Snorri, who had previously climbed K2 in summer. This must have been an awkward situation since Mingma G had been expedition organiser with Snorri on K2 the winter before. With a Chinese member anxious to quit because of Covid-19 at home and Mingma G suffering ill health, when a Sherpa was hit by ice he called it quits, much to the annoyance of Snorri and Slovenian member Tomas Rotar, who accused Mingma G of being more interested in the commercial side of things than he was in the actual climbing. The Sherpa denied that he gave up too easily, concluding: 'When there is success, people try to take the credit, when there is failure, people try to blame.' It is clear from interviews he gave that Mingma G felt he had something to prove.

On 21 December, the first official day of the winter season, the team went up to camp one, which the Sadparas and Snorri had already fixed, then next day continued to camp two, fixing rope as they went. After that the weather deteriorated and they descended to base camp during the Christmas period when scores more climbers and Sherpas arrived, including the large Seven Summit team: K2 was as busy last winter as it often is summer. On 27 December they went back up and on 29 December were fixing rope above camp two to the bottom of the Black Pyramid at 7,000m, where they spent the night.

They had planned next day to fix to camp three (7200m) but while they had 900m of rope, 600m of this was high-quality 6mm Mingma wanted to save for higher up the mountain. So Mingma G radioed Chhang Dawa, leader of the Seven Summit commercial team who was also managing logistics for Nimsdai Purja. Mingma G asked Dawa to ask Purja's team to bring up more rope. After fixing for much of 30 December using what line they had and scavanged rope, Chhang Dawa, part of Purja's team, arrived and they continued fixing to 7,300m where they stashed more gear. On the way down to their previous night's camp, Mingma G met Nims coming up. While they knew of each other, they had never met before.

'All by himself, he was carrying 200 metres of rope for the later part of the expedition,' Mingma G told *Online Khabar*, a Nepali news website. 'He did not complain that he was alone nor did he make a deal of it. That day, I had a lot of respect for him.' In fact, Mingma Tenzi was close by as well, one of the partners of Purja's company Elite Exped. Born in Yaphu village, in Sankuwasabha district close to Makalu, K2 would be Tenzi's ninth 8,000er and Purja had picked him out as someone particularly reliable as a rope-fixer who had worked on Broad Peak and Gasherbrum I. He and Nimsdai descended to camp two.

Back at their higher camp, Kili Pemba was showing signs of altitude sickness and so Mingma G's team returned to base camp where the weather deteriorated. Nimsdai had invited them to a party he was hosting for New Year's Eve and as they walked over from their base camp they met two of Purja's team who had been sent to collect them. Several bottles of whisky, vodka and rum later it was 3am and the teams were firm friends. 'We bonded over booze,' Mingma G said. Purja was anxious to get on with things and proposed starting the summit bid on 2 January. 'He was worried that the foreign climbers would acclimatise and follow us to the top,' said Mingma G. 'I was too. But we were in no shape or form ready for the summit push and with bad weather looming, he agreed.' (Ali Sadpara, of course, was no 'foreigner'.)

Strong winds swept through base camp from New Year's Day to 7 January and when he returned to camp two, Purja discovered that his tents had been destroyed and his paraglider gone. Mingma G, on the other hand,

The K2 in winter summit climbers. From top left: Dawa Tenji Sherpa, Mingma G, Dawa Temba and Pemchhiri. From bottom left: Mingma David, Mingma Tenzi, Nirmal Purja and Gelje. Not pictured: Kili Pemba Sherpa and Sona Sherpa. *(Sandro Gromen-Hayes/Nimsdai)*

had buried his team's gear at camp three and it was safe. 'It was a good decision. If we had lost that, our expedition was over.' Despite the obvious setback of a destroyed camp, Purja was soon planning a summit bid with Mingma G on 15 January. Nimsdai's team left on 12 January, since it would be carrying more gear, and Mingma G followed on 13 January.

Nimsdai below the Bottleneck. *(Nirmal Purja)*

Apart from Tenzi, Nimsdai could rely on another Sherpa superstar, Mingma Gyabu 'David' Sherpa, born in Faktalung in Taplejung district, far to the east of Nepal. Unlike other Sherpas on K2, there was little tradition in his family of climbing for a living and he started as a trekking porter, then a kitchen helper on Manaslu in 2009. That led to an NMA course and his first break, offered by his uncle and mentor Dorje Khatri, the trades union activist who would perish in the Everest avalanche of 2014. Mingma David gives great credit to his uncle's influence, whose death left him shattered. In his first two years he climbed Everest three times and is currently the youngest Nepali to have climbed the 14 8,000ers. As part of Purja's Project Possible he climbed eight in six months.

On 13 January Mingma G and his team climbed to their camp below the Black Pyramid where Purja's team had also stopped, albeit in a different

Gelje Sherpa proudly displaying the Liverpool FC shirt he took to the summit of K2 in winter. Both he and Dawa Temba are devoted Reds fans.

location. Over the radio they discussed their conflicting weather reports. This would be the crux of the whole attempt. Purja and the Seven Summit team were relying on forecasts from Europe. Mingma G, with a few thousands dollars sourced in Nepal, was using the weather forecaster Krishna Bhakta Manandhar, retired senior meteorologist at Nepal's Meteorological Forecasting Division. The western forecasts said the climbers should stay put on 14 January because the weather would be bad. Manandhar promised good weather. (It was Krishna Manandhar who accurately predicted the storm that killed at least 43 trekkers and porters in the Annapurna region in October 2014. His warnings went unheard in the mountains.)

The Sherpas weren't the only ones agonising over the weather. The Sadparas, father and son, were with John Snorri at camp two and using the same forecasts as Purja and Dawa. Winds at camp two on the morning of 14 January were stronger than at camp three and so the Pakistanis and Icelander descended. 'It was like the mountain gods telling us to have K2 all to ourselves,' Mingma G said. With fine weather that morning, both he and Nimsdai were eager to push on and the two teams met at the site of the summer camp three where tents were put up while Nims and two Sherpas fixed another 300m. Next morning, Kili and Dawa Tenjin descended to Mingma G's earlier stash to bring up equipment and then Mingma G, Mingma David and Mingma Tenzi, with Sona Sherpa assigned to help by Seven Summit in support of their own rope fixing, headed for the site of camp four.

Below the wall barring final access to camp four, the four Sherpas found a wide crevasse that took them precious time to work around, trying first right, then descending and going back up on the left. 'Again it was the same,' Mingma G reported, 'so we descended all the way back just above camp three and then branched out even farther. There we finally found a narrow crevasse covered by some fallen ice where it was possible to cross. At first, I feared that I might fall into the crevasse but I had Mingma Tenzi belaying me which gave me the courage to move forward and cross.'

Reaching camp four the Sherpas all believed their team would climb K2 but it was already 4pm and they now had to descend to camp three, which they reached at 6.30pm. The plan had been to leave for the summit at 11pm but more rest was needed so the climbers woke at midnight. Still feeling tired from the day before, Mingma G now gave up his plan of climbing without oxygen but borrowing a regulator cost him time and fitting it cooled his hands. Kili, Dawa Tenjin, Sona, Nimsdai and Mingma Tenzi were ready before the others and set off but since portions of the route still needed fixing there was no panic.

Mingma David, Pem Chhiri, Gelje, all from Nimsdai's team, together with Mingma G, now followed the others who were already just below camp four. When Mingma G got there he felt chilled in the wind and wondered about returning. But he warmed his feet kicking the ice, which was prevalent in the winter season, and by the time the climbers reunited at the end of the Bottleneck traverse at 6am, the sun was out and all the climbers were feeling warmer. Mingma Tenzi fixed the route to the summit with the others carrying gear in support. This took all day and they reached the top together just before 5pm. In around three weeks since arriving at base camp, and with only 11 days of climbing, the Sherpas and Nirmal Purja had climbed K2 in winter.

The speed of the Sherpas and Mingma G's confidence in his weather forecaster were two factors in their success. Several Sherpas spoke too of Nirmal Purja's encouragement, despite being the one without oxygen. But weather conditions were also more benign. In her recent book on the 8,000ers in winter, Bernadette McDonald considered the possibility of K2 being climbed in winter. The meteorologist Karl Gabl thought success unlikely in the next 10 years because of ferocious winds but the Polish filmmaker Dariusz Załuski thought otherwise. A veteran of nine winter 8,000m expeditions, he said: 'I think now it's much easier to climb than ten years ago. The weather is much better.' There's a certain irony that climate change may have given the Nepalis a leg up K2 even as it causes such chaos in their homeland.

The logistical support in general and the use of oxygen in particular drew complaints. The noted Russian alpinist Denis Urubko, who has his own history with K2 in winter, said: 'Oxygen is a powerful doping. I'm sorry to find out the really weird way people react. In the event that an athlete in boxing, running, skiing, cycling and other disciplines use doping – he gets total contempt, reactions of disgust. And punishment by the official authorities. But in mountaineering, people who use doping become heroes.' The Polish winter veteran Adam Bielecki took a similar line. 'Climbing eight-thousanders with oxygen is like participating in the Tour de France on an electric bike. The nature of such an achievement is completely different.' Nirmal Purja, of course, was not using oxygen on summit day.

Other winter climbers were not so dismissive. 'K2 in winter has been climbed and now come on!' the Italian Simone Moro said. 'In the future, those who think, want and know they can do better, both the K2 and other 8,000ers are waiting for them. Today the Sherpas have rightly received a well-deserved place in history.' It was that attitude that greeted the successful climbers first in Pakistan and then when they returned to Kathmandu. Almost lost in the celebrations was the tragic news that Catalan climber Sergi Mingote had died in a fall descending on 16 January from camp one, having been up to camp three to acclimatise. He was alone at the time but team-mates spotted a sudden massive change in his elevation on his GPS track. An experienced high-altitude climber, and one who carried his own gear, Mingote had been trying to complete the 14 8,000ers without supplementary oxygen inside a thousand days.

The occasionally melodramatic world of 8,000m climbing now comes with an iceberg of online commentators who were quick to question the integrity of the K2 ascent, fuelled by comments from others on the mountain. For example, Polish climber Magdalena Gorzkowska told Polish television that the Sherpas had threatened to cut the fixed lines if any western climbers tried to follow them. Later she said she had been reporting a joke made at base camp. Perhaps her comment was the source of a seemingly grief-stricken outburst from the well-respected climber Nazir Sabir in comments to Pakistani television about ropes being removed and the suggestion that this might have played a role in the death of the Pakistani hero Ali Sadpara and others in February.

It must have been galling for Sadpara to watch others arrive at base camp and then hurry past him to the summit, even more so when his weather forecast in mid January turned out to be wrong. Bad weather trapped those with ambitions to repeat the Sherpas' success at base camp but another weather window appeared in early February. More than 20 climbers converged on camp three at 7,300m on 4 February but with only a handful of tents available. Ali Sadpara was one of those who had made sure to have shelter available. What others were thinking is uncertain. With temperatures plummeting to -40°C and climbers arriving after dark, climbers were forced to cram into the few tents available, hardly ideal preparation. Chhang Dawa Sherpa of Seven Summit had reported on 1 February that an eight-strong team of Sherpas had gone back up to check the condition of camps and recover any buried or broken fixed ropes as well as depositing bottled oxygen. John Snorri's filmmaking partner Elia Saikaly said promised oxygen was not where it was supposed to be.

Given the terrible night they endured, it's surprising anyone continued to the summit but Ali Sadpara, his son Sajid, their client John Snorri and Chilean climber Juan Pablo Mohr were among a number who did. While the rest turned around, these four continued but Sajid's oxygen equipment malfunctioned at 8,200m and his father advised him to descend and wait at camp three. The wait proved in vain. The bodies of the three men were found during this year's summer season but the circumstances around their deaths had yet to be determined. One more death was recorded that day. The Bulgarian Atanas Skatov, a 42-year-old plant biologist and vegan activist, fell to his death descending from camp three. Seven Summit issued a statement saying he had made a mistake clipping between ropes but that version has been disputed with at least one report of a broken fixed rope. Given the number of ropes now on the Abruzzi and the number of commercial expeditions already offering K2 to clients, the problem of redundant fixed ropes will have to be monitored.

MARCELO SCANU & ED DOUGLAS

South America 2020-21

Although there have been restrictions because of Covid-19 in both countries, many climbs have been made in windows with freedom of movement. The Central Andes of both countries is now the zone with more first ascents and new routes; much is still to be explored and climbed in this savage and partially unknown region with high and interesting mountains.

Llullaillaco, Northern Andes, Salta, Argentina
Llullaillaco (6739m) is a volcano and the most sacred mountain for the Incas in the northern Argentine-Chilean Andes. A new route was done on this volcano that lies on the Argentine-Chilean border. An Argentine group comprising Christian Vitry (leader, archaeologist and climber), Adrián Gandino, Gerardo Casaldi and Federico Sánchez climbed its south face and then moving onto to the south-south-west for the last section. It's a mixed route with an 800m ice couloir up to 50° combined at the start and end with big blocks. The summit was reached on 1 February 2021 at 3.45pm. They called the route *Huamán,* Qechua for 'hawk'.

Veteran Sergio Ceruti, aged 72, soloed an unclimbed 5,200m volcano south of Llullaillaco on 30 January and christened it Chungara. Also on the expedition were Julio Altamirano, Martín Giraudo, Eduardo López Jordán and Emilio González Turu.

Cerro Pabellón, Northern Andes, Catamarca, Argentina
During March 2021, Argentines Carlos Appolonia, Andrés Zapata and Marcelo Scanu explored Earth's largest volcanic caldera, 45km from north to south and 24km from east to west, located in the province of Catamarca. On 22 March they climbed Cerro Pabellón (c5250) by its north face. This beautiful triangular shaped volcano had only one previous ascent from the south in 2015.

Cordillera de Ansilta, Central Andes, San Juan, Argentina
This nice range has seven principal peaks. Argentine Gabriel Fava ascended various new routes on the Agujas del Glaciar Frías due east of Pico No7 de Ansilta or Sarmiento (5780m). These needles can be approached by a two-day trek from Barreal. There are also many boulders nearby. There are now more than a dozen routes, many climbed in January 2021.

Cerro Mono Verde, Central Andes, Chile
This 4,524m mountain lies 70km north-east of Santiago. On 26 November 2020 Rodrigo Benavides and Bruce Swain climbed the north-east couloir

The volcano Llullaillaco (6739m), the most sacred mountain for Incans in the northern Argentine-Chilean Andes. *(Christian Vitry)*

(800m, 30°-50°) establishing most probably a new route and making the absolute second ascent of the mountain.

Cerro Alto Mardones and Cerro Punta Gallardo, Central Andes, Chile

A group from Santiago comprising Chileans Alvaro Zerené, Alejandra Morales, Yorly Batlle, Adrián Gambetta and Juan Pablo Cabbada drove to the Parque Andino Juncal entering by the Quebrada de Lagunillas and heading north to a camp at 3,400m in a zone with springs. Next day they departed at 5.30am and reaching the end of the Quebrada de Lagunillas climbed Cerro Cabeza del Inca Este (4105m) by its east face reaching its summit at 10am. It had only one previous ascent in 2019.

From there they decided to attempt a possible route to the nearby Alto Mardones (only one known attempt in 2019). They reached a col at the end of Quebrada de Lagunillas from the north, to reach a ridge with many spires. Because of these, they descended 50 meters to the Quebrada del Juncalillo

On the summit of Cerro Punta Gallardo. *(Paz Pillancari)*

and rounded the west face of the mountain across scree to turn the spires and access the upper section of the north-west ridge, climbing 30m of loose rock (III) gaining the summit at 12.45 on 1 November and not finding previous traces.

Another expedition ascended Cerro Punta Gallardo (20 to 22 November 2020). Chileans Alvaro Zerené, Paz Pillancari, Edison Sanhueza and Juan Pablo Cabbada left Santiago for the *termas* (hot water springs) of Colina in the Cajón del Maipo, entering by the Cajón del Estero Carreño and heading south-west to camp at 3,500m at the foot of their mountain. They departed at 8.30am after a cold night to head east, climbing a snowfield on the west side of the mountain with loose rock and an angle of 40° before reaching a zone of rock pinnacles. These were easy but exposed. They reached the north-west ridge and once more ascended scree and snowfields. Near the summit they climbed rock reaching the top at 3pm. The summit comprises two towers, east and west, with the same altitude. They reached the west one before down climbing with a rappel in the pinnacle zone. The mountain has an altitude of 4,271m on the Chilean IGM map and because they found no trace of a name, they christened it as Punta Gallardo for a climbing friend who died in an avalanche in 2019.

The route up Cerro Punta Gallardo. *(Alvaro Zerené/Juan Pablo Cabbada)*

Cerro Negro Pabellón, Central Andes, Mendoza, Argentina.
In late November 2020 Argentines Luciano Badino, Chicho Fraccia and Matias Hidalgo Nicosia made a three-day approach from Tupungato to the south-east face of Cerro Negro Pabellón, a massive mountain that is officially 6,157m although 6,068m has also been offered as its true altitude. The group climbed the face that suffered from bad ice and snow conditions. This route (1200m, D+, 70°) finished on a plateau after 12 hours' climbing. The group retreated without reaching the summit but having climbed an excellent line.

Cerro Moño, Central Andes, Mendoza, Argentina
Argentines Mauro Schmiedt and Sebastián Martino arrived at the Refugio Soler on 16 January. Next day they crossed the Atuel river and entered the Valle de las Lágrimas, near to the 1972 Uruguayan plane crash. They crossed the Río de las Lágrimas, passed El Barroso and after eight hours camped at 2,600m. On 18 January they climbed a gully to a ridge, reaching a valley where all Moños glaciers melt to camp at 3,800m. That night they heard heavy rock fall but couldn't judge its origin. Days later they discovered a 6.4 earthquake in nearby San Juan province had triggered this.

The Valle de las Lágrimas, famous for the location of the 1972 Uruguayan plane crash. *(Mauro Schmiedt)*

On 19 January they left at 6.30am, climbing some *penitentes* to the start of a gully, the only access to a plateau near the summit. At 10.30am the pair stood atop the beautiful unclimbed summit of Cerro Moño (4699) that lies on the Argentina-Chile border. They then ascended nearby Risco Plateado (4999m), possibly by a new route. There they found unusual cloth and a woolen doll, indicating a much earlier ascent. It should be added that at nearby Volcán Sosneado (5189m) there have been interesting pre-Columbian discoveries some months ago. It appears it was one of the many high-mountain sanctuaries being used until today, the southernmost one pushing the known Inca border far from its previous limit.

Cerro Ulises Vitale, Central Andes, Mendoza, Argentina
This 5,194m peak in the Portillo range had been attempted once before in 1955 by a group that included Argentine climber Ulises Vitale, getting to

The route on Cerro Moño. *(Mauro Schmiedt)*

The line of *¡Viva Perú Carajo!* up Nevado Huamashraju East (5434m).
(Iker Pou)

100m from the top by its south-east face. A group of Argentines (Heber Orona, Lito Sánchez, Adrián Miranda, Claudio Fredes, Ulises Corvalán, Gerardo Castillo and Pablo González) departed from Manzano Histórico in early December 2020 walking 10km through the Pircas Creek valley camping at 3,100m and the day after 11km to base camp at 4,200m. On 3 December they made a long traverse to reach the north-east face finding that the summit couloir had snow *penitentes*. They ascended it and a snow slope reaching the summit seven hours later. It was christened as Cerro Ulises Vitale, the route (550m, 40°-50°) was on a mountain very different to that attempted in 1955 with many glaciers having disappeared.

Picos del Barroso, Central Andes, Chile

Chileans José Vial and Roberto Mayor Brierley climbed Chile's southern-most 5,000m peak on 18-19 September 2020. After a nine-day trip they reached their 3,200m base camp. The pair climbed snow and ice ramps (steepest sections of 65°), spent a night at 4,800m below the summit ridge before climbing the Chilean summit (5135m) by this new route.

Cerro Las Peinetas and Volcán Quinquilil, Central Andes, Curarrehue, Chile

These volcanic massifs are located 15km of Curarrehue in Araucanía province and are better known for their skiing and winter climbing. Cerro Las Peinetas (2052m) has a central tower first climbed in the summer of 2002 via a five-pitch VS, climbed in winter in 2015 by Juan Señoret at 70°, M3.

In action on ¡*Viva Perú Carajo!,* judged objectively safe for the Andes and of high quality. *(Iker Pou)*

Right: Steep climbing on the first ascent of Cerveza, Pan y Ácido on Concha de Caracol (5640m). *(Anna Pfaff)*

During the winter of 2020, on 28 July, Señoret and his brother Cristobal climbed a new route up the south face of Cerro Las Peinetas (450m, AI5, M5) up steep ice and snow features of the face to the frozen summit ridge along which they reached the top.

Emilio Frey, founder of the first climbing club in the Argentina, Club Andino Bariloche, and a key player in the 1896 Argentina-Chile border commission, made the first ascent of Volcán Quinquilil in 1897. Climbers now approach from the south and there are a few winter routes put up by Juan Señoret and the Ecuadorian climber Gabriel Navarrete, including the peak's 400m south-east face in 2014. Señoret also made a ski descent of the normal route in 2019 with Christophe Henry, including sections of 70° and requiring rappels. In August 2020, the Chileans Víctor Astete and Uber Quirilao repeated the *Navarrete-Señoret* route, which is around 70° with some steeper sections.

The line of *Cerveza, Pan y Ácido* with the bivouac marked. *(Anna Pfaff)*

Peru

Good conditions during the southern hemisphere winter and a window of access despite the pandemic, which has been especially cruel in Peru, meant a number of talented climbers converged on the country's mountains in the middle of 2021. After their pioneering activities in the rocky mountains east of San Marcos in 2019, the Spanish brothers Iker and Eneko Pou were back in the **Cordillera Blanca** during July 2021, climbing a new mixed climb on the south face of **Nevado Huamashraju East** (5434m), Huamashraju translating as 'mountain of fear'. The 600m line follows 'thin slivers of ice that, sneaking between the rock, cross the entire wall like a spider's web'. Climbed in a 15-hour round-trip from base camp and graded M7, 80°, the Pou brothers were hugely positive about their creation, which they called *¡Viva Perú Carajo!*: 'The route is of immense quality and unlike most of the ice climbs in the Cordillera Blanca, which are quite dangerous due to looking seracs and falling ice from above, this is a very safe line, more typical of those found in the Pyrenees or the Alps. It's also worth noting that this mountain is relatively close to Huaraz and the approach is not particularly difficult.' They report that temperatures never got above -15°C during their climb.

Elsewhere in the Cordillera Blanca, Álex González and Jaume Peiró, two very young climbers from Spain, spent four days and three nights putting up a new route on the north spur of **Chaupi Huanca** (4850m) in the Rurec valley. The idea came when the two climbers, who are a couple and very active as LGBTQ+ campaigners, consulted the Pou brothers, who climbed the route *Zerain* in the valley two years ago. The north spur is an obvious and dramatic feature and had been attempted twice before, first by a team from Argentina and then by one from Ecuador. González and Peiró were critical of the unnecessary fixed gear, including bolts next to cracks that the second party had added. They offered the grade 8a?, 6c/A2. The pair had acclimatised climbing La Esfinge (5235m) in Parón via the classic 1985 route, freed in 1997 at 5.11c.

Colombians Andres Marin and Alex Torres and the American Anna Pfaff climbed what is likely a new route on the south face of Concha de Caracol (5640m), or 'snail's shell' in the Cordillera Vilcanota, taking a line to the right of the route put up in 2019 by the Pyrenean guide Oriol Baró and

The route had been tried before a decade ago by Nate Heald and party. Conditions were much more favourable in 2021. *(Anna Pfaff)*

harder too, at ED, 90°. The line had previously been attempted in 2011 by a team including the well-known American guide Nate Heald, which ended close to the summit ridge because of unconsolidated snow. (Heald provided ground support to the team.) Starting on 13 July, the three climbers climbed their 700m line and then had a cold bivouac on the ridge at 5,500m before descending next day via their route, which they called *Cerveza, Pan y Ácido,* 'beer, bread and acid', apparently the wish list of what they were missing during their bivouac.

Reviews

'Toby's Point, Arymer Cove, Devon', Hilda Hechle, c1920,
watercolour. 28cm x 39cm. Near Ringmore, south Devon.
(Courtesy of Tony Astill/www.mountainpaintings.org)

Reviews

Emilio Comici
Angel of the Dolomites
David Smart
RMB, 2020, pp248, £31

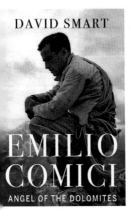

DAVID SMART

EMILIO COMICI

ANGEL OF THE DOLOMITES

On 7 August 1915, as the summer sun bleached the fields of northern Italy, the poet and proto-fascist Gabriele D'Annunzio arrived over the port of Trieste in a flimsy biplane piloted by his friend Giuseppe Miraglia. The white city, D'Annunzio noted, shone against the backdrop of the Carso, the limestone plateau that traditionally divided Italians from Slovenes and offered Triestino climbers a training ground for the challenges of the Dolomites.

From his cockpit, D'Annunzio, then in his early fifties, released bombs on Austrian submarines floating in the harbour and also threw packets of messages – garnished with green, white and red ribbons bought from a Venetian haberdashery – to the people below who were watching the air raid from Trieste's main piazza. Written in D'Annunzio's florid style, they promised that soon the Italian tricolour would fly over the castle of San Giusto, the city's heart. Irredentists, desperate to be free of Austrian rule and part of a reunified Italy, stood in the streets and cheered during later bombing raids, despite the risks.

There's no evidence that Emilio Comici watched this first air sortie over his city, but it's safe to say that if he didn't then he would have heard all about it, and would have revelled in its daring. In this fascinating biography, improbably the first for such a titan of 1930s climbing, David Smart makes it clear that news of Italian success left Comici exhilarated. How could it not? Italians in the city had chafed for centuries under rule from Vienna, whose brutality they blamed for the war. Plus, he was 14 years old and already vulnerable to the romance of adventure. Italian boys' clubs were shut down by the authorities so they had more time on their hands to dream of freedom. Always a bit of a *mammone*, a mummy's boy, he would strum the family's mandolin as she made his dinner and sing about their beloved city, and how it fretted under the Austrian heel.

Among the names that would have thrilled the teenage Comici was Napoleone Cozzi, a brilliant pre-war climber who made the Val Rosandra just outside Trieste a training ground, a *palestra,* where a young alpinist could perfect the skills required for the hard new climbs being put up in the Dolomites by such great names as Paul Preuss, Angelo Dibona and Tita Piaz, the so-called 'devil of the Dolomites'. And it was in the Val Rosandra that

Looking good. Left: Emilio Comici in his signature climbing jacket and basketball shoes at Val Rosandra outside Trieste. Right: With journalist and occasional benefactor Severino Casara and good friend Emmy Hartwich-Brioschi, who had been Paul Preuss' lover, at Lake Misurina in 1935.

Comici would start on his path to fame, if not fortune. But as Smart makes clear, Cozzi was also an irredentist, famous for his arrest in 1904 and subsequent trial in Vienna after Austrian secret police discovered what are now called IEDs hidden under the floorboards of the Trieste Gymnastics Society. Years later, during the war, when Comici walked those same floorboards, notions of climbing and adventure were inextricably fused in his mind with the nationalist, irredentist cause that so inspired him.

Politics, however, was moving on rapidly. The colourful, ludicrous extravagance of Gabriele D'Annunzio had morphed into something new and darker. In October 1922, while Comici was doing his national service, Mussolini's fascists levered their way to power. Already a member of the Associazione XXX Ottobre, the date news of Austria's defeat reached Trieste, Comici joined Mussolini's party and became one of the *squadristi,* a black shirt. Something in the fascist aesthetic appealed to Comici, a climber who would have understood very well how to use Instagram: it was modern, clean and seemingly progressive, and well dressed, like he was: so unlike the well-heeled romanticism of Mitteleuropan alpinists like Julius Klugy, long a mentor to successive generations of alpinists in Trieste, including Cozzi. For a working-class climber like Comici, the future seemed elsewhere. After he climbed his eponymous route on the Cima Grande, one of the most striking landmarks in the history of alpinism, he wrote in the hut book: 'By the same light that illuminates the value and tenacity of the Italians of Mussolini, we have opened the path to the north face of the Tre Cime di Lavaredo.'

There is a great deal to recommend this book, not least David Smart's ability to paint a broad canvas without exhausting the reader's attention. All this historical perspective is not only fascinating and rich with detail, but also necessary, because of the equivocal place Comici holds in the climbing firmament, the glamorous risk-taker adding sheen to Mussolini's project. At times, Smart strains a little too hard to excuse Comici's political allegiances, although I think mostly he gets it right. I would like to have heard more from Comici's near-contemporaries on this; Fosco Maraini famously tore up his fascist party membership card when his father enrolled him. Comici, on the other hand, averted his gaze. Towards the end of the book, Smart writes:

> *Even after the Trieste section of the CAI hung signs forbidding Jews in its huts, Emilio had fretted over the predicament of his Jewish friends, not as if racism was a core program of his beloved party (which, after 1938, it was), but as if it was some kind of unintended oversight by a regime he saw as benevolent.*

For much of this book, until its poignant and fatal conclusion, I wondered whether Smart's considerable talents would have been better deployed writing a history of the whole sixth-grade scene, which for English readers is woefully underexplored and yet forms the basis for the explosion of big-wall climbing in Yosemite and elsewhere after the war. Because Emilio Comici did seem to bob around on the surface of his own unusually interesting era, like a cork on a storm-tossed ocean. The portrayal of his childhood is, presumably through necessity, somewhat hurried. The poor leave little trace. But it's clear he had little meaningful education. That left him with a sense of inferiority, especially around some of his intellectual clients, and a lack of traction in the wider world.

Music was a comfort and a pleasure throughout his life and there is a wonderful scene towards the end of the book when, now living in the Dolomites, he takes up the piano under the instruction of one of his clients, Rita Palmquist, a Dane who had performed concerts all over Europe. Mussolini had tried to suppress folk songs and mandolin playing because they led to unmanly display of emotion. But Il Duce approved of the piano, which he could play himself. Comici had some natural talent and persevered, but learning the piano in his late thirties was understandably frustrating. After one lesson ended badly, Comici stood up and closed the lid, telling his teacher:

> *You have witnessed the most splendid symbol of my spiritual life. A closed door. You see, I have worked hard to develop my body, my muscles. I managed to do so, but at the detriment to my inner life. A few years ago, I thought I would be a writer, but it was an illusion. In the spiritual realm, there is a closed door for me.*

Palmquist, understandably, was deeply moved at this declaration, the austere man of the mountains revealing briefly the torment beneath the surface, a man 'who some accused of turning climbing into a mechanical thing, was, in fact, deeply sensitive.' And the rest. Smart paints a convincing portrait of a man who was if anything hypersensitive, particularly to criticism. Like his beloved home city Trieste, Smart writes, Comici had a certain *distacco*, an aloofness from the world, and a self-sufficiency, or *lontananza*, that added to the impression that he was somewhere on a higher plane. 'There have been few more haunted alpinists,' Smart writes at one point. He's speaking of ghosts, but it stands for his character too.

This self-absorption, from an Alpine outsider like Comici, must have come across as arrogance to some, and petulant arrogance when the Dimai brothers were rude about him after the Cima Grande climb. Comici appealed to the fascist authorities for resolution, but they just shrugged and suggested he stand up for himself. Even when he took the initiative and soloed the north face to counter the Dimais' sniping, he had to spoil the effect by having another sulk. You want to shout at him across the decades: you made your point, Emilio, let it go! Enamoured of press attention but reluctant to engage through a natural shyness, Comici certainly suffered for his art. He wanted to be taken seriously as a man but often ended up as a symbol of something, of a legend that became a trap that slowly compressed him.

Perhaps that was what the piano playing was all about. It was also to please his ageing mother, a kindness the fascists would have frowned on as effeminate. One of the most striking aspects of this book is the ubiquity of women. They're everywhere in this story, a reminder that women have more often been excluded from the story of climbing, not the actual climbing. There's the Slovenian Mira 'Marko' Pibernik, as Smart calls her, although she preferred her maiden name Debelak, since her first marriage was arranged and soon discarded. A woman familiar to students of Ben Nevis history, she was on the first ascent of *Slav Route*. She'd also swung leads on the first ascent of the 900m north face of Jôf di Montasio. There's Riccardo Cassin's climbing partner Mary Varale, who brought Comici to Lecco to teach them pegging and later quit the CAI because of its blatant misogyny. Comici would take her on another truly great Tre Cime climb, the *Spigolo Giallo*. Anna Escher, one of his richest and most regular clients. And Emmy Hartwich-Brioschi, Paul Preuss' lover at the time of his death, introduced to Comici by their mutual friend, the rather flaky journalist Severino Casara. Paula Wiesinger is there, the first woman to climb grade VI in the Dolomites. Trieste itself was home to more women climbing grade VI than anywhere else in the world, in particular Bruna Bernadini, who rarely followed. Finally there was the celebrated poet Antonia Pozzi, another of Comici's clients, a brilliant young woman who faced her own demons. She took a long cool look at Comici and saw him high on his lonely perch among the mountains where ' … you will only see/your rope/encased in ice/and your hard heart/among the pale spires.' She committed suicide aged 26 but Comici, the 'sullen, poor, uneducated kid from the docklands of Trieste', seems not to have noticed.

Towards the end of his short life, Emilio Comici began to grasp more fully his place in the world, how the populism of men like Gabriele D'Annunzio had twisted the urge of all Italians to be free. Comici had gone to the Dolomites so that an Italian might, in his own country, surpass the achievements of the Germans there. Naïve perhaps, even self-regarding, but not I think necessarily malign. The only new route he climbed in the war, during which he served as a minor fascist functionary, was dedicated to Italo Balbo, Mussolini's great rival who had opposed Italy's Nazi-style race laws. Smart offers this as an indication that Comici's fascist ardour was cooling. I'm not so sure. Either way, we shall never know whether Comici would have joined Cassin, who'd had his own flirtation with fascism, in fighting with the partisans against the Nazis. Because shortly after the Angel of the Dolomites was dead.

'They will only get me in the end,' Comici wrote of the mountains even as his passion for climbing waned. Ironically, it was the *palestra* he created in Vallunga that did for him, a place where he could teach but also perform for an audience, a banal accident caused by a rotten rope. Having fallen 30m and struck his head, he stood up again, blood streaming down his face, the broken ends still clutched in his fist, before dropping dead on the ground. David Smart has done the English-speaking climbing world an immense service with this book, capturing all the grandeur and vanity of our sport and the politics that informs it, all trapped in the amber of the 1930s, that turbulent era that looks so much like our own.

Ed Douglas

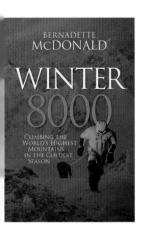

Winter 8000
Climbing the World's Highest Mountains in the Coldest Season
Bernadette McDonald
Vertebrate Publishing, 2020, pp272, £24

Winter 8000 is the latest book from the prolific keyboard of Bernadette McDonald. Her love affair with stories emerging from Eastern Europe in general and the Poles in particular is once again central to this book. They were the first to climb in the greater Asian ranges in winter but over the past 40 years they have been joined by climbers from other nations who have also mastered 'the art of suffering', the phrase coined by Voytek Kurtyka to describe what is needed to succeed in the Himalaya in winter. As new nationalities gained summits, the Polish dream of being the first nation on all the 8,000m summits in winter proved too much. To state the obvious, climbing 8,000m peaks in winter is likely the most dangerous form of mountaineering. The weather is violently unpredictable throughout and becomes increasingly worse in the later winter months. Even fixed ropes ascents of the *voie normales* can become death traps. As McDonald writes:

> *Winter climbing in the highest mountains is acknowledged as fundamentally dangerous, even by those who are most passionate about it. Like religion, it has saints and martyrs, sacred and forbidden places. Thirteen of those sacred 8000ers have now been climbed. Will the lure of this special genre of high-altitude climbing fade when K2 is finally climbed in winter? Will the saints retire to their sofas and the martyrs fade into the history books? Or will the quest for better lines, faster times, smaller teams drive alpinists to keep returning in winter. But for those who are smitten with the 8000ers but abhor the growing crowds, will they increasingly choose the quiet season?*

This rather loaded paragraph gives you a flavour of what to expect. McDonald makes it clear that it is difficult to distinguish between the saints and the martyrs. I recommend a pinch of salt be taken with some of the author's comments. She is shrewd not to take sides when the ramifications of tragedies lead to caustic breakdowns and the blame game, ramped up by an ill-informed press and the public. For the climbers themselves, the author does her best to find the human side of their stories, whether in success or failure and, all too often, tragedy. She reminds us that in the end all climbers are responsible for their own lives and families, as well as their comrades. But the choices become much more brutal in winter.

The book was published just a few months before K2 was climbed in January 2021. I'll come back to that later. What is clear is that there are an increasing number of climbers choosing the winter season to avoid the crowds experienced during pre and post monsoon on 8,000m peaks. Winter climbing is somewhat safer today than it was 40 years ago at the beginning of the winter story. Weather forecasts are pretty accurate. They alert climbers to windows of good weather almost down to the minute. Global warming means it is not as cold in the high mountains as in 1980 and helicopters mean rescue is possible even above base camp. All that said, the risks are still enormous.

The author openly admits she has written about fewer than half of all the winter expeditions on record. McDonald's skills as both a researcher and a writer are displayed in her ability to turn what might be a long list of mountain encounters into a series of enthralling stories from each of the 8,000m peaks, with each giant having a chapter dedicated to it, starting with Everest, the first 8,000er to be climbed in winter, with Leszek Cichy and Krzysztof Wielicki reaching the summit on 17 February 1980, the spearhead on a well planned and executed expedition led by the legendary Andrzej Zawada. Zawada is recognised internationally as the godfather of winter mountaineering. His vision begot and began the Polish quest to make first winter ascents of all the 8,000ers. He inspired a generation and beyond.

From the outset, there was controversy. For a start, what constitutes the

The price and prize of winter at 8,000m. Left: Cory Richards' self-portrait taken after surviving a massive avalanche on Gasherbrum II. Right: Simone Moro on the summit of Shishapangma in 2005. *(Cory Richards/Piotr Morawski)*

winter season? On Everest, the summit was reached outside the official Nepali definition of winter, that being the months of December and January only. But December often holds some of the best and benign climbing conditions, while February is most often and very much full-on winter. There have also been many first 'winter' ascents in March. And as knowledge about the winter months grew, some expeditions made use of November to place high camps and then complete ascents in December, avoiding worsening conditions after Christmas. Simone Moro and others claim that these ascents are cheating. Rules are rules, but what if none are agreed? And moral codes are wonderful until the primal drive for survival takes over.

McDonald recalls an encounter with Zawada in 1994 when she asked why he preferred winter mountaineering to summer. His response was, 'because the Himalaya in summer is for vimmen.' I can picture the twinkle in his eye as he said this. But Polish motives to climb in winter are much more complex. During the communist years, Polish climbers could expect better food on expeditions than they enjoyed at home. With each climbing success, the adulation of the public increased and also the opportunities to travel and break free from the drudgeries of work to go on state-sponsored trips.

Sadly, over the next three decades the dream turned sour. As the Wielicki generation grew older, less experienced climbers were drafted into the Polish 'mission' to be the first. Then, as other nationalities entered the game and enjoyed success, competition grew. The Poles took more chances and inevitably lives were lost, culminating on Broad Peak in 2013. One of Poland's national heroes, Maciej Berbeka, died high on the mountain and accusations of poor leadership, personal misjudgement and abandonment filled the national press. Similar stories followed, and not just for the Poles.

The author's intimate knowledge and friendship with many of the individuals in this book makes the story telling all the more powerful, and heartfelt. She remains unjudgmental in most instances, although one can detect distaste for some of the egotistic excesses of Simone Moro. To his credit, Moro has become one of the great winter mountaineers, with four winter firsts to his name: Shishapangma in 2005; Makalu in 2009; Gasherbrum II in 2011; and Nanga Parbat in 2016. McDonald also takes pains to describe the very different nature of the large well-financed expeditions compared to some of the small alpine-style trips of lesser-known climbers. These alpine style trips are more likely to end in failure and tragedy, best exemplified by the loss of Tom Ballard and Daniele Nardi on the Mummery Rib of Nanga Parbat in March 2019. Had they climbed the route, often described as 'suicidal' by experienced observers of Nanga Parbat, it would indeed have been a remarkable first. The route has never been climbed in summer or winter. Their loss is an example of pure alpinism leading to the most terrible conclusion.

In his review for the *Scottish Mountaineering Club Journal,* Sandy Allan points out that all the individual and personal stories in *Winter 8000* could and should have been told by the climbers themselves. I agree with this, but the reality is that a market for these stories exists only in certain countries and Britain is not one of them. To this reviewer, it seems that the topic of mountaineering is increasingly dealt with through third-hand commentaries rather than first-hand accounts. For this reason, alpine journals remain extremely important to mountaineers.

The publishers of *Winter 8000,* Vertebrate Publishing, recently reported a decline in interest even for well-known British climbers' books. Perhaps the romance of mountaineering is dying. Perhaps it being replaced by what Voytek Kurtyka describes as 'the tyranny of numbers', where records of first, fastest, longest, furthest become more important than storytelling. McDonald suggests this as a possible trend in the passage quoted at the beginning of this review. It may be that the market will dictate that only books by television personalities, celebrities and environmentalists with mountain themes will be successful in the future. Old-fashioned mountaineering literature may seem just that, old-fashioned, requiring a passion and understanding of risk and adventure. Harsh mountaineering experiences are outside the comfort zones of urban modernity. I believe that without Bernadette McDonald's commentaries, many stories from other nations would not be heard in the English-speaking world.

My criticisms of the book are these: it could do with maps or diagrams for each of the mountains showing the routes climbed to help distinguish between difficult climbs, first ascents and the *voie normales.* And a full list of all winter expeditions in an appendix would be fascinating for those wanting a complete record of success and failures, and the reasons for those failures.

The first winter ascent of K2 by the Nepalis earlier this year came too late to make the pages of this book. Despite the controversy surrounding this ascent, it was and will remain a remarkable ascent for many reasons.

It certainly put the skills and fortitude of Nepali climbers on show for the whole world. Yet it also reminded me of a point Reinhold Messner made a few years ago when he asked, 'when tourism reaches the summit of Everest, what hope for true alpinism?' The late Doug Scott had a chance meeting with Nims in Kathmandu a few years ago. He told him: 'I've heard of you. You're obviously a great climber, but when are you going to do something new?' Is a winter ascent of K2 by the Abruzzi something new?

We must accept and do our best to understand different viewpoints even if we do not agree. Climbers in different countries are at different stages of development of their climbers' psyches. I'll let Bernadette McDonald have the final word:

> *Their stories are neither perfect nor complete. There are unanswered questions, bad decisions, unnecessary risks and broken bonds. There are tales of loyalty and bravery, ambition, commitment and vision. There are friendships wrought under such harsh conditions they can never be destroyed. These imperfect tales are all that we have and, in sharing them, we can try to understand the souls of the Ice Warriors, those men and women who find the greatest fulfilment in the highest mountains in the coldest, shortest, darkest days: the cruel days of winter.*

John Porter

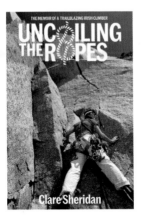

Uncoiling the Ropes
The Memoir of a Trailblazing Irish Climber
Clare Sheridan
Mweelrea Press, 2020, pp208, £18

The marriage at the heart of this outstanding memoir epitomises the loving and joyful coming together of a divided Ireland. Its author Clare Sheridan enjoyed a sheltered and religious upbringing in the Republic and the kindred climbing spirit she met in Chamonix and built her adult life with was a Northern Irishman who'd served in the British army and who liked to joke on drives from Dublin to Fairhead that they would soon leave 'the grey skies of the Irish Republic for the blue skies of a Free Ulster!'

The border they crossed back and forth then is now, in the grindingly inevitable consequences of our pig-headed politics in Westminster, a tinder-dry horizon over which there lies a not-so distant threat of a return to the days when Sheridan, hurrying on Friday nights from Dublin to Belfast, would step off the train to a 'chaos of sirens and diversions … it seemed that bombs were going off all over the place … Sometimes the blast and flash were just a street away as we drove north out of the city towards the silence and darkness of Fairhead.' As I write this there's news of some angry young men petrol bombing a bus on the Shankill Road and leaving it as burned out as the promise famously made on the side of another bus during the 2016 referendum campaign.

The long history of British involvement in and impact on the island of Ireland seems written in the landscape of Sheridan's childhood. Family hill walks traversed settings like Gougane Barra, an old hideout for rebels in conflict with the English crown where, as her father leads them down an intimidating ravine, they find themselves at a spot where on a dark night in 1921 IRA guerrilla leader Tom Barry and his flying column daringly evaded British troops. From the Beara Peninsula, where in 1602 an Elizabethan army defeated the Gaelic chief Donal O'Sullivan Beare, they look out across Bantry Bay where in 1796 a French fleet coming to the aid of the United Irishmen was thwarted by storms and the Royal Navy. The book sings with beautiful Irish place and mountain names: Coomhola, Borlin Valley, Knockboy, Glengarriff. Music to the reader's ears.

When she turns 16, Sheridan and her sister Bairbre set out on an impressively independent all-Ireland bicycle tour. Pedalling into Ulster, amid the red post and telephone boxes, the English place-names on the signposts had a 'flat and one-dimensional' look. Their school history and geography had told them the real names as they would expect to read them: Doire, Tír Eoghan, Fir Manach. (The same British appropriation of Irish toponyms is the backbone of Brian Friel's landmark 1980 play *Translations.*) Years later it turns out her soulmate Calvin Torrans had made the equivalent pilgrimage in the other direction at the even younger age of 13, and solo.

Sheridan writes very frankly about religion and the social conditions prevailing in Ireland because of it. A youthful faith that burgeons into a truly felt vocation as a nun gives way to Sartre and Marx and daring talk of atheism during teacher training at University College Dublin. Besides, at Dalkey Quarry and over in Glendalough and elsewhere there's a new religion rearing up in her life: climbing. But the old religion doesn't leave the stage and later in life when she's moved in with Torrans in Bray but neglected to marry him there's a chilling scene as a Franciscan pays an insistently nosy visit to their new home. An attempt to fob him off is briefly resisted by his sandaled foot jamming the threshold as she tries to close the door. As a teacher in a highly conservative National Schools culture the possible consequences of exposure for living in sin were chilling. Earlier, in 1972, her sister, also bitten by the climbing bug, is running the UCD Mountaineering Club stand at freshers' week when another officious cleric confronts her for putting her God-given body at risk through mountaineering. Sadly it's only after he's gone that, with classic *esprit de l'escalier,* Bairbre thinks of answering, 'What about that pope, Pope Pius XI? He climbed Mont Blanc and the Matterhorn!'

The greatest obstacle though between Sheridan and her mountains is not God but man. She is forgiving and subtle but forthright in her account of the undermining misogyny she experienced in the predominantly male climbing community. 'Girls don't climb,' she's told, just as she makes the step up from hillwalking as a very young woman. The magazines only feature women as absurdly sexualised objects in the ad pages and the guidebooks are full of route names with amusing double entendres alluding to damp cracks and so on. 'I didn't find them a bit amusing,' she tells us, simply. Even her true love Torrans is comfortable repeating an axiom he's learnt in the army: 'Women weaken legs.'

There's an extraordinary chapter about her all too short closeness with Alison Hargreaves ('all bouncing curls and spiky ambition') who comes to stay with them in Bray for an Irish lecture she gives in February 1995. By that August Hargreaves has lost her life descending from the summit of K2 and disapproving newspaper columnists (notably female, Sheridan observes) are condemning this young mother who 'acted like a man' for her 'reality-denying self-centredness'. Sheridan, who by 1995 was a mother of three boys herself, has this to say: 'She acted like a man? Yes. Because for too long the choice of being selfish like that has only been open to men.'

The thrilling accounts of her climbing are scattered with refreshingly honest references to the female experience of it, having to rule out having a pee when strangers climb too close, managing the onset of her period just as she commits to the Walker Spur, even having to consult about the pill being contraindicated at altitude before her first Himalayan expedition (no simple matter in the Ireland of the day). The intersection of motherhood and climbing has brought her both triumph and retreat. As Torrans' Himalayan career gathered speed she consciously took a back seat, watching from the sidelines as her purist husband got on the wrong side of elite Irish climbing politics and found himself uninvited from the siege-style expedition that put the first Irish climber on top of Everest. But closer to home a fair sharing of the childcare delivered opportunities that she converted into dazzling successes. For instance the Bonatti Pillar, now sadly for my generation a collapsed legend, which she'd dreamt of leading since the 1970s and succeeded on in 1996 (after tip-toeing past her children's tent before dawn and being stopped in her tracks by the youngest waking up to demand love and attention on her way to the life-and-death highpoint of her Alpine career). Satisfyingly, when she descended to the Flammes de Pierre bivy ledge afterwards, she was handed a strong, sweet coffee by a suitably impressed Ivano Ghirardini. And how many pregnant mums have done the Cuillin Ridge at 26 weeks? Sheridan is hard as nails.

She and Torrans will leave a colossal legacy in their development of Irish climbing and of Fairhead in particular, a famously serious venue completely beribboned with new routes they've put up over five decades. The book will convey to you the magic of the place and the commitment they've put into it. But above all I love it for its portrait of their Alpine endeavours in a now vanished Chamonix where you roughed it in Snell's Field, where the Bonatti Pillar still clung to the Dru and where you might spot Gaston Rébuffat on the téléphérique. To me, in this gripping but modestly told narrative full of dazzling achievements, Sheridan's most enviable boast is that 'for years my summer address was c/o Snell Sports, Chamonix.'

Nick Simons

Without Ever Reaching the Summit
Paolo Cognetti
Harvill Secker, 2020, pp 145, £10.99

This gentle little book pays homage to Peter Matthiessen's *The Snow Leopard.* Paolo Cognetti, born in
Milan in 1978, the year of publication of Matthiessen's classic, almost 40 years later followed in the
American author's footsteps on a trek through inner
Dolpo in northwest Nepal.
Matthiessen, an adherent of Zen Buddhism, famously didn't see a snow leopard. He wrote: 'Have you
seen the snow leopard? No! Isn't that wonderful?'
And in that non-seeing he is content. Cognetti ech-
oes that same non-attachment to goals in his *Without Ever Reaching the Summit* title.

He notes that Matthiessen had used a very specific word for his journey –
gnaskor, (pronounced *nekor;* a pilgrim is a *nekor-wa*) or 'going around a place'
– and contrasts this Tibetan idea of pilgrimage, where there is no point of
arrival, with pilgrimages to Jerusalem, Rome or Mecca.

'Without a destination, how do we know if we have been purified?'
Cognetti sees a connection between the need for a holy city at the end of
a journey and the mountaineering 'obsession' with gaining a summit.
'Christians plant crosses at the tops of mountains, Buddhists circle around
them,' he writes. 'I found violence in the first gesture, kindness in the second; a desire to conquer as opposed to embrace.'

Paolo Cognetti garnered literary prizes and massive sales with his loosely
autobiographical novel *The Eight Mountains* set in the foothills of the Italian
Alps. It's a story of deep friendship between a city boy and a child of the
alpeggio who remains heafed to his mountain homeland even as traditional
life there disintegrates. In this latest work Cognetti pretty well dismisses the
idea of a mountain people still existing in the Alps: all are now 'citizens of
the immense European megalopolis, or of its wooded periphery'. In the
most popular areas of Nepal too, modernity was bringing its mixed bless-
ings. How would it be in Dolpo?

The Eight Mountains had about it a captivating simplicity, redolent, perhaps, of its Alpine pasture setting. This quality, plus the fact that I too had
followed Matthiessen's trail past Phoksundo lake to remote Shey gompa
and the Crystal Mountain (leading a trek for Mountain Kingdoms in 2011)
had me looking forward to Cognetti's latest offering with keen anticipation.

Maybe I was expecting too much. *The Snow Leopard* is a work of hallu-
cinogenic beauty, much more a spiritual journey than a quest for the world's
most elusive big cat. Together with *The Tree Where Man Was Born* (1972)
it was written when Matthiessen was at the height of his literary powers,
at least as regards his non-fiction. Indeed he told the essayist and poet Mark
Tredinnick in 2000 that he could no longer find the place where the lyric

prose of *The Snow Leopard* came from.

Cognetti, by contrast, has written an engaging travelogue, peppered with quotes from Matthiessen and thoughtful insights. In a sense he is trying to *be* Matthiessen, keeping a journal (but who doesn't?), drawing maps, seeing signs in natural occurrences, imagining one of the porters to be some kind of shaman watching over him. It's a Sealed Knot performance: the props are good and the location spot on, but it lacks the blood and guts of the original.

Few westerners had visited Dolpo before the 1970s. Matthiessen accompanied the naturalist George Schaller who wanted to study blue sheep in the region of Shey gompa and the sacred Crystal Mountain that overlooks it, a place of pilgrimage for Buddhists. They and a small trail crew walked in all the way from Pokhara, crossing into Dolpo by way of the Jang La, west of Dhaulagiri, a trek of some 250 miles; they were away from Kathmandu for two and half months.

Inner Dolpo is often portrayed as a sort of sanctuary where the traditions of ancient Tibet live on, isolated from the cultural genocide perpetrated by China in Tibet itself. 'It had survived somehow thanks to history's forgetfulness,' writes Cognetti. Or so he was told. The reality is a good deal more nuanced. In Saldang, a settlement at 3900m and barely 20km from the border patrolled by China, he witnesses the timeless scene of women threshing barley with flails to a synced rhythm, but also satellite dishes and the litter of plastic packaging and cans of fake Red Bull. Sooner or later, Cognetti predicts, there will be a road direct to China, the Nagaon riverbed will be reduced to landfill, 'and the last vestiges of an ancient Tibetan culture will disappear amid garbage and cell phones.'

Cognetti does not see a snow leopard. Nor was he ever likely to. While Matthiessen spent two weeks at Shey, scouring the hills with his binoculars between bouts of meditation and deep introspection, Cognetti camped by the gompa for just two nights. He and two friends had joined a commercial trek along with seven other Europeans: in all a caravan of 25 mules and 22 men. Cognetti shades his fellow trekkers very much into the background, an intrusion, perhaps, into his reverie.

What is lacking in *Without Ever Reaching the Summit* is any serious analysis of Matthiessen as a writer, his character or *The Snow Leopard*'s abiding popularity. The *Leopard* is anything but an easy read if the many pages of spiritual self-interrogation are to be wholly understood, and certainly no Nepal primer for the 21st century visitor. Richard Mabey, in an introduction to a 2010 edition of *The Snow Leopard* confessed himself 'in need of some spiritual porters' as he tried to comprehend Matthiessen's reflections on Zen and the infinite. 'I understand the words, though not always their meaning,' wrote Mabey. 'I admire their implicit morality.'

Cognetti regrets he stumbled upon *The Snow Leopard* a little too late to know its author. Matthiessen had died in 2014, aged almost 90. Mark Tredinnick was more fortunate. In 2000 he visited Matthiessen at his home on Long Island and together they took a walk along the shoreline, discussing his work and 'nature writing' in general: a label Matthiessen abhorred but, given his eloquent advocacy for wildness and the dignity of all beings, one he could hardly shake off.

The 47 pages devoted to Matthiessen in Tredinnick's *The Land's Wild Music* – 'a roving study of the literature of place' – will tell you much more about the mind and literary artistry of the author of *The Snow Leopard* than Cognetti seemingly comprehends, though less about the route and contemporary Dolpo.

Although *The Snow Leopard* is Matthiessen's best known work, in the depth of its personal introspection and spiritual complexity it is somewhat atypical in an output of more than 30 novels and non-fiction, apart from his Zen journals (1969-82) published under the title *Nine-Headed Dragon River* in 1978. (In the preface, Matthiessen, with self-deprecating humour, warns the 'unwary reader' that this Zen book was composed against the best instincts of its author, 'who has no business writing upon a subject so incompletely understood.')

Matthiessen undertook his journey to Shey in a mood of prolonged anguish following the death, a year and half earlier, of his wife Deborah Love at the age of 44. He points out her grave to Tredinnick during their shoreline walk, doing so 'without fuss or sentiment'. Setting the background in *The Snow Leopard*, Matthiessen writes of an earlier trip to Nepal in 1961 and the buying of a small bronze in the Asan bazaar as a gift for his new wife. He continues:

'My wife and I were to become students of Zen Buddhism, and the green bronze Buddha from Kathmandu was the one I chose for a small altar in Deborah's room in the New York hospital where she died last year, in the winter.'

This quiet sentence lets us peer for a moment into Matthiessen's deep well of grief, writes Tredinnick:

… in the winter'. The first time I read that phrase, with the comma that precedes it like a sob – I wept.

Without Ever Reaching the Summit will not have you reaching for the tissues. Cognetti does not have the penetrative depth of Tredinnick or the ringing prose mastery of Matthiessen. However, if this modest offering draws you to a re-reading of the source of its inspiration or an exploration of Matthiessen's wider literary territory it will have performed a rewarding service.

Stephen Goodwin

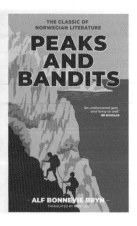

Peaks and Bandits
Alf Bonnevie Bryn
Translated from Norwegian by Bibi Lee
Vertebrate Publishing, 2021, pp128, £16

Norwegians are not renowned for an overwhelming sense of humour. A country that divides between winter darkness, heavy rain and 24-hour summer sunshine, with a population roughly one-third that of Greater London sprinkled across an empty but spectacular landscape and 13,000 miles of coastline resembling a page ripped from an atlas, Norway has much to feel serious about. Being the richest nation per capita on earth, thanks to North Sea oil, proba- bly lifts spirits but the best joke skilfully delivered may be met by a nod and a smile or a mere rumbling guffaw.

Welcome then a book that might brighten any dull day, possibly the first humorous Norwegian story to be translated into English. *Peaks and Ban- dits* by the Norwegian climber and author of detective novels Alf Bonnevie Bryn tells the story of an expedition to Corsica by Bryn and George Ingle Finch, the Australian mountaineer who became famous for his part in the 1922 Everest expedition. Finch designed oxygen equipment that enabled him to be among the first climbers ever to reach 28,000ft.

Peaks and Bandits became an admired classic of Norwegian literature for its eccentric verve. It describes how in 1909 the two mountaineers deter- mined to sharpen their hopes of a Himalayan expedition with a climbing holiday in Corsica. En route they paused at Pisa where, whilst the guardi- ans were at lunch, Finch, armed with his ice axe, attempted the less steep north face of the famous leaning tower. He reached the fifth floor before the guardians reappeared and ordered him to stop. He addressed them from a pocket phrase book: 'This is my first time in Italy,' he declared. 'I am travelling for my health.' When he did retreat he was accused of avoiding the entry fee and charged one lire, as if he was just an ordinary visitor, thus avoiding compromising paperwork.

Finch had a life-long addiction for climbing man-made structures; unable to resist any challenging facade he might possibly swarm up. Among many first ascents he counted the south-east corner of the white ballroom behind the palm gardens of Oslo's Grand Hotel which he climbed, though a pro- fessor of organic chemistry, having just delivered a lecture to the Norwegian Alpine Club about the first Mount Everest expedition. He was also expert on how to deal with snakes, having grown up on an Australian sheep farm. Confronted by a yard-long Corsican snake George regarded the reptile with almost sentimental interest. He approached close, grabbed it by the neck and in a fraction, removed two fangs from its upper jaw with a penknife. 'He belongs to us now and shall be our mascot,' George declared. They agreed to call the snake James and it remained with them for the rest of the holiday, an accessory in numerous practical jokes.

The bandits of the title came from the original Corsican *bandito*, meaning someone who had been banned or excommunicated; sharply distinct from someone classed as a *brigante* or robber. Bandito suggested lesser crimes and allowed a more comfortable place in Corsican society although certain family names nevertheless continued to reflect old levels of suspicion and some became famous enough 'to receive visits from tourists'.

The holiday happened in 1909, although the book did not appear until 1943. It is more a reflection of life on the island and its history at the turn of the century than an instruction of how to climb Capo al Dente, the Cinque Frati or any of the summits they attempted. There was little evidence that Corsica was crowded with climbers at the time. 'The difficulties concerning the ascent were first and foremost that we were too lazy to get up early enough in the morning,' Bryn confessed. On the Capo al Dente, where the group spent time on the summit sunning themselves, they left a pipe case with notes about their ascent. Bryn said the case was returned 16 years later after the summit had been climbed, possibly for a second time. An extraordinary account, that gives glimpses of a wider history and a few amusing moments.

Ronald Faux

Rock 'n' Roll on the Wall
Silvo Karo
Translated from Slovenian by Gorazd Pipenbaher
Silvo Karo, 2020, pp304, £26

In the first paragraph of his introduction, Silvo Karo declares himself not much of a writer, admitting that, when prodded by friends, he had wondered, 'What would I write about?'

Two hundred pages later, Karo leads us through overhanging rock high in the Himalaya that has the quality of a ploughed field. He refrains from superlatives. The situation itself is enough: his and Janez Jeglič's mind-bending alpine-style ascent of Bhagarathi III in 1990. 'Such things happen, you live through them if you're lucky, and then you keep your mouth shut,' he adds by way of emotion. Yes, of course. Fortunately, Karo doesn't keep his mouth entirely shut. And he has plenty to say.

Silvo Karo was born and raised in communist Yugoslavia, and worked on his family's farm from the day he could stand. Hard work forged him, and in describing his pre-climbing years he reflects upon working high on a church roof, untethered of course (free soloing for Jesus), and the joy of carrying large objects on swaying scaffolding, which helped hone his sense of balance. Which, naturally, led to games like finding harder way ways to 'play' on the high roofs while carrying planks of wood. Hey, we all find our fun. But then he casually mentions, as if it were an afterthought, that by the end of elementary school he'd started thinking of other occupations. *Wait.* That last scene was at elementary school?

As he progressed to working in factories, he made the most of it: 'Work or fun, the salary was always the same.' Something in that mindset predisposes everything. And when you're carrying around an invisible key, it's only a short step to finding the lock it fits. Once he discovered climbing, his drive, that irresistible force, led him and his partners from the scrappy climbs of the Julian Alps to some of the greatest alpine ascents in history. 'We were like dogs picking bones,' he writes. They had so little, and did so much; he recalls an early outing with his mentor, the great Franček Knez, a laconic man with an abiding love of mountains, and being astounded that Knez didn't lock the door to his apartment. 'He claimed that he had nothing worth stealing.'

Some of the most fascinating passages in Karo's book come not from the climbing – which is, in the truest sense of the word, awesome (and harrowing, incomprehensible, and superlative depleting) – but in his reflections on growing up, the time of change, the era and the culture in which he lived and learned, one often between two worlds, east and west. When Slovenia gained independence, there was much to celebrate. But is anything ever all good or all bad? 'The sense of collective identity was disappearing and being replaced by individualism. Egos started taking over and everyone kept to their own piece of land, so they wouldn't have to share their crops with anyone else.'

Karo's writing is straightforward: no theatrics and no forced drama. Boring? Hardly. His ascents and the seemingly endless, horrific storms through which he climbed need no fluffing. The closest he comes to self-celebration might be after his and Jeglic's legendary climb of Cerro Torre's south face in 1988, where he writes, 'I brought a large bottle of wine back to base camp, and in the evening we drank to our suffering and perseverance.' If you're looking to read someone's therapy session, this probably isn't your book. Thank god. But don't think of it as unreflective, either. Karo seems a hard man with a soft heart, and in the raw style of his writing, we come to know his uncomplicated nature.

At times Karo describes the immaculate landscapes with a level of feeling and eloquence that betrays his opening declaration, even if the writing gets slightly rough in spots, occasionally slipping into non sequiturs or with characters emerging without any introduction. But such examples are minor, and hardly diminished my enjoyment of the book. If you have even a shred of appreciation for the magnitude of his ascents, and for the historical significance of Slovenian alpinism – of which Karo played a major role – then his unpretentious storytelling might give something even greater: the space to ponder what it was like.

And yet for all the praise of Karo's climbs, and his ability to endure – the suffering and perseverance – even more impressive is his evolution. Karo never stayed static, avoiding the sad spiral of many climbers as the game passes them by. Rather, Karo's attitude led him to embrace the changing times, from nationalistic sieges to stealthy alpine-style ascents, always taking the best of his inherent athletic competitiveness and his mindset, blending skills learned from sport, aid and speed climbing, then applying them to new objectives with fresh eyes. If there is a formula to becoming our own versions of Silvo Karo, perhaps that is it: embrace positive change, discard the bullshit and keep going. Simple. Complicated. Life. Sure, this is a climber's book, giving us a glimpse into the workings of an icon, but it's also something more. While few of us can even begin to approach Karo's accomplishments, most could do worse than to emulate his outlook.

Kelly Cordes

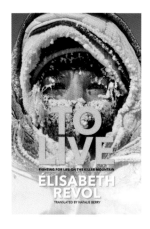

To Live
Fighting for Life on the Killer Mountain
Élisabeth Revol
Translated from French by Natalie Berry
Vertebrate Publishing, 2020, 154pp, £24

'The summit of Everest!' writes Élisabeth Revol at the start of her book about her ascent of Nanga Parbat (8125m) in 2018 with climbing partner Tomasz 'Tomek' Mackiewicz. Somewhat bemusing, but it soon becomes clear that this achievement, followed the next day by success on Lhotse, was the 'ray of light' that brought her back to life a year after the tragedy of the 2018 expedition in the course of which Mackiewicz died.

Nanga was his obsession: this was his seventh attempt at climbing the mountain in winter, Revol's fourth and their third together. On 28 January 2018 they left camp four at 7,300m and set off for the summit in pure alpine style, carrying the absolute minimum, intending to return the same day. They reached the summit late, at about 6.30pm, but as Mackiewicz had not worn his snow goggles during the climb he was rendered blind. What should have been a profound celebration – theirs was the second winter ascent of Nanga Parbat and the first by a woman – was now a life-threatening situation and Revol was faced with the enormous challenge of trying to get her sightless climbing partner down the mountain.

She drew on her many years of mountaineering experience and her unswerving determination to guide him but after descending for 900m he could no longer walk and blood was pouring from his mouth. Her immediate priority was to find shelter but the position of their last camp eluded her and a crevasse provided the only protection from strong, sub-zero winds. Tomek's comfort and safety were her priorities as she waited for the rescue which her friend Ludovic was attempting to co-ordinate from his base in France. As the long and punishingly cold night dragged its feet across the mountain Revol realised that she would have to respond to Ludovic's urging

Élisabeth Revol and Tomasz Mackiewicz on Nanga Parbat.

and try to get to a lower altitude, since a helicopter rescue of two people at 7,380m was not possible and Tomek could no longer move.

What follows is both tender and pragmatic: she anchors Tomek as safely as she can inside the crevasse, using the ice axes which were vital for her retreat down the mountain but feeling that they were better employed in keeping him safe. In addition, she leaves all her extra equipment to provide him with as much warmth as possible. Alone, equipped only with a pole and desperate to get help for him, she begins to descend the mountain. The photographs and topos included in the book give the reader some idea of the enormity of the challenge awaiting her, in particular the 'varnished wall' of the *Kinshofer* route for which she has no tools.

Facing another night in the open in extreme cold and having been without food or water for two nights and three days she knows she must find shelter or die. Her description of a second night in a crevasse plunges the reader into her world of sleep-deprived hallucination where she is offered hot tea in exchange for her boots, one of which she finds she has taken off and has to recover from the depths beneath her, too late to prevent her foot succumbing to severe frostbite.

The narrative combines courage and enormous resilience with the raw emotion of leaving Tomek alone. 'Guilt overwhelms me, drowns me.' The urgency and apparent hopelessness of her situation and her impassioned internal dialogue drive the reader inexorably forward. Revol takes command of the situation, focusing on staying alive in order to get help for Tomek. 'I no longer want to be that small vessel in the immensity of the ocean, tossed about by the waves and the wind, without a rudder, unable to control anything. I take over the helm.' She was in a race against time, exacerbated by a storm system approaching the mountain.

The arrival of elite mountaineers Denis Urubko and Adam Bielecki is signalled by 'the ballet of light beams' that Revol sees in the darkness at 5,950m. On being told of the desperate situation on Nanga Parbat they had selflessly abandoned their attempt to climb K2 and were flown by helicopter with Piotr Tomala and Jaroslaw Botor to base camp. Revol was saved but it was impossible to rescue Tomek. Physically and mentally vulnerable, she was unaware of the next ordeal she had to face: the media onslaught in Islamabad. 'What I had experienced on the mountain was nothing compared to the violence of my return.'

The extremes of press coverage painted her both as heroine and betrayer and attracted comment and judgement both positive and negative not just from the mountaineering community but from those who could have had no conception of what she had achieved and endured: 'Who knows the exact circumstances? Who was there?'

In the aftermath of this furore she found herself questioning her own unceasing desire for altitude, escape: the simplicity of life and focus she describes as her addiction. It illuminates her life but also drives her to seek out harder challenges and greater performance, often at the cost of other relationships. Her ascent of Everest was recuperative. It brought her back full circle to her childhood dream of climbing the mountain whose poster decorated her bedroom wall; to a realisation that to live fully is to be in the environment she loves but not to be its prisoner.

Val Johnson

Everest
From Reconnaissance to Summit, 1921 to 1953
Edited by Peter Gillman
Folio Society, 2021, boxed, vol 1 pp536, vol 2 pp208, £199

The centenary of the first Everest expeditions is upon us, unleashing, like a small avalanche, a number of projects, exhibitions, films, retrospectives, books and media extravaganzas, not least the Alpine Club's own exhibition and catalogue launched as this review was being written. With the obvious exception of the latter, how much of this will change or even refresh what we know about this eye-catching moment is open to question. So much of our understanding is captured in the fleeting glimpse Noel Odell had of George Mallory and Sandy Irvine being swallowed by the summit mists. Did they or didn't they? We do love a good mystery.

Yet while that is an understandably compelling moment, it tends, like the clouds that covered our intrepid heroes, to obscure a broader and no less human story, one that is considerably deeper too, and remains to be uncovered. If you thought there was nothing left to say, think again. That realisation dawned on me looking through this astonishing compendium, expertly

With 268 images, the Folio Society's collection is the most extensive visual record of the early Everest expeditions yet published.

edited by Peter Gillman, in two volumes, of photographs and writings from the more significant Everest expeditions between 1921 and 1953. While a collector's item, given the price, it is a magisterial undertaking, exhaustive but not exhausting, spreading, as it were, many more cards on the table and in doing so adding fresh perspectives.

Let me give you just one example from the 268 spellbinding photographs on offer. On page 51 of the album is an image familiar to me, of a head lama and a group of monks at a monastery. (As it happens, I have a copy on my wall at home.) I've sometimes glanced at this and assumed it was taken at Rongbuk, since that's the monastery most often in our minds when we think of the north side of Everest. But of course it isn't, it was taken at a monastery miles away in the Kharta valley on the day Charles Howard-Bury and Sandy Wollaston visited. Howard-Bury reports on the warm welcome they received and gives the name of the monastery as Ganden-chhöffel. Ganden, the first of the three major Geluk-school monasteries in the Lhasa area, was founded in 1409 by the great reformer Tsongkhapa. The first abbot of Ganden also founded Tashilhunpo at Shigatse, to which this little outlier was attached. 'Chöffel', these days written Chophel or sometimes Choephel, means something like 'spreader of the dharma'.

The abbot told Howard-Bury the monastery was around 500 years old and was founded by a saint called Jetsun Ngawang Choephel. Jetsun means 'reverend' and Ngawang Choephel is a common enough name; I know nothing about this one. The abbot also told his visitors a story about the monastery's foundation, which happened after a great, sudden flood, a feature of Himalayan life long before climate change. A frog was taken and buried under the temple's central pillar. Annoyingly, there had been subsequent floods. Howard-Bury then has a glance round the monastery, speaks of Tibetan antipathy towards Indians (not strictly true) and then mentions that he took the photograph now on my wall.

It's a slight encounter but the history behind it is rich and in a strange way adds a fresh perspective on the strange world of climbing mountains. The frog is the giveaway. As an animal it transforms itself, a useful teaching aid for Buddhists. The frog also appears in legend as a source of (witch-inspired) leprosy, a disease a famous 11th century female saint called Machig Zhama suffered from. Her father suggested she use her magical powers to drain the lake in the Kharta valley, allowing it to be settled and her to be cured. It didn't work. (The cure came later through methods that can only be described as 'for the broad-minded'.)

Machig Zhama was a *dakini,* a shifting, playful category of feminine divinity. The Tibetan word is *khandro,* meaning 'space dancer'. Many climbers will appreciate the appeal of space dancing: literally, psychologically, culturally and politically. In Machig Zhama's day, long before the Geluk school and the first of the Dalai Lamas, the tantric practice of *chöd* was transforming Buddhism in Tibet. Among the many translations of this mind-bending term is 'crazy wisdom'. Once again, climbers may empathise. The Everest climbers, judging from this wonderful collection, sometimes have the look of a cricket team invited to play out of season. But you sense from the space in these photographs that Everest changed them irrevocably.

In Machig Zhama's time, more than 900 years before George Mallory, the wider Everest region was known as Latö Lho, or south Latö. It was known as the interface between powerfully different cultures that shared a common spiritual practice. It was in spaces like this, the world's margins if you like, that the most interesting stuff happened. It's no coincidence that other favourite arenas for the more extreme practice of *chöd* were charnel grounds and cemeteries.

Forgive the diversion but one of the great strengths of such a large selection is that the indigenous societies and workforce these expeditions relied on, without which they would have achieved very little, are given a lot more space to be seen than is usually allowed. And that gives us so much more to consider in reviewing these landmark expeditions. Far from being a blank on the map, we can see in the Tibetan and Sherpa faces that Latö Lho was known and precious ground. It's no coincidence that the *beyul* of Tibet, the sacred valleys revealed in visions, are threaded through such high mountain regions. In that sense they hold the same appeal for ordinary Tibetans as they do for us, except their goal is more often spiritual practice than summits.

The other 267 images in this book were no less of a pleasure for me. The greatest tour de force is the foldout panorama made from images seamlessly brought together and taken by Howard-Bury from the Lhakpa La. It is a magnificent view of Everest that includes a plate camera in the foreground, a reminder of how the 1921 pushed photographic limits and to elegant effect. I adored Frank Smythe's shot of Jack Longland having his haircut. And the photo he took from his tent at 27,400ft, past his feet and the pack frame of one of the porters. In artistic terms a dud, but it speaks eloquently of bitter cold and extreme suffering; what a Buddhist might call austerities. Smythe took another of my favourites, a group of Tibetan children and an old man, known as Father William to the climbers, sitting around a gramophone in the village of Kharta Shika. Alf Gregory's work is also shown to great effect and it's instructive to compare both their styles and the worlds they were photographing. I came away sensing that the 1930s expeditions were more closely linked to 1953 than they were to the pioneers of the 1920s and why that might be.

Alongside the album, with its 268 images each carefully captioned by Gillman, is another 208pp volume of excerpts from the Everest climbers themselves, telling the story, with a short preface from Jan Morris and an introductory essay from Wade Davis setting it all in its historical context. There are two expertly drawn maps, although they include the international border that wasn't agreed until the 1960s. Like I said, Everest is more a space than a frontier. I was pleased to see the inclusion of Charles Bruce's encounter with Dzatrul Rinpoche, head lama at Rongbuk monastery, and of the Rinpoche's own view of the 1922 disaster in which seven porters died. Dzatrul Rinpoche was the great, evangelising Nyingma-tradition guru who founded nine new monasteries, including that at Tengpoche on the south side of Everest, re-establishing a tradition in the area dating back a thousand years just as the world discovered these hidden places for the first time.

Ed Douglas

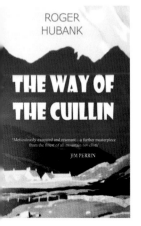

The Way of the Cuillin
Roger Hubank
Rymour Books, 2021, 234pp, £10

In his latest novel, Roger Hubank takes us to Skye. His first novel, *Hazard's Way*, which won the Boardman Tasker prize and the Grand Prix at Banff in 2001, was located in the Lakes. Subsequent locations include the Alps (*North Wall*), the major peaks (*Evening Light*) and the Peak District (*Taking Leave*). All his novels thus weave their personal narratives with a background that becomes more than a location but a character in itself – and in *The Way of the Cuillin* I found that character to be the most powerful and affecting of all.

As with *Hazard's Way*, Hubank has selected a telling moment of recent history. *Hazard's Way* took place on the eve of the First World War. Now we intersect with the Spanish civil war and the Sudeten crisis of 1938 that led to the illusory peace of Munich and presaged the Second World War. Appearing before us are the three generations of the Marlowe family, who include an archdeacon and a Conservative MP. They gather at Glen Brittle, intending to commemorate a route first climbed by Stephen Marlowe, the family patriarch. There are generational clashes and political disputes. Family tensions emerge, revelations are made, long-festering secrets surface.

The cast of characters is Hubank's longest, so much so that he has helpfully listed the most important 24 opposite the opening page, adding:

'Sundry others include mountaineers, fishermen, an innkeeper, an airline pilot and a passenger.' *Alpine Journal* readers are likely to delight in the cameo parts awarded to celebrated mountaineers. One is Norman Collie, 'a white-haired old man sitting by the window' at the Sligachan Inn, gazing out towards the Cuillin, a description that invokes a scene in the *The Last Enemy* by Richard Hillary. We also encounter Bill Murray, glimpsed at the bar on the same occasion.

Hubank takes us from the House of Commons to the battlefields of Spain, with further scenes set in artists' haunts in Fitzrovia and flashbacks to the Western Front. But always he draws us back to the Cuillin, sometimes for a respite from the personal and historical struggles that are being enacted; sometimes as a threatening accompaniment to conflicts that leave you wondering how they are to be resolved. Hubank delights in the adhesive gabbro, the sweeping scree, the striated clouds hanging over the corries, the rushing burns, the fairy pools, the enchanted places.

Each time he took us there I succumbed to pangs of nostalgia for the Cuillin, recalling magical days of struggle and reward, of solitude and friendship that I suspect are beyond me now. The denouement leaves you both stunned and reflective, wondering whether Hubank is telling us it was inevitable or avoidable, a question that haunts you as much as the scenery where it played out. This is an ambitious novel, audacious in its scope, delicate in the path it weaves through its complex relationships, enticing as it lures you on to its end. Its success in realising its ambitions provokes one further question: where will Hubank take us next?

Peter Gillman

Broken
2020: The Year Running Records Were Broken
Ally Beaven
Vertebrate Publishing, 2020, pp150, £13

I'm no fell runner. But I've rubbed shoulders with fell runners, among them the best of their day: friends such as A A Robertson, John Disley, Eric Beard and Joss Naylor. I've photographed them in action and I have the greatest respect for them for I've always enjoyed moving fast over the hills myself, though perhaps not quite so fast. But this book is not about mere fell running; it's about adventure running – indeed ultra running.

To be an ultra runner on the same wavelength as the denizens of this book, you must first be a mountaineer, a competent navigator and an imaginative yet meticulous planner. And you'll need to inhabit the right kind of body, which you'll endeavour to keep super-fit. A high pain-threshold is axiomatic.

Every year a series of international ultra-running events takes place,

Not only broken, but wet too.
Sub-optimal weather in the Lake
District on the Bob Graham Round.
(Steve Ashworth)

of which the best known are the
Saharan Marathon des Sables and
the Ultra-Trail du Mont Blanc. At
the domestic level are dozens of testing annual events such as the Welsh
1,000m Peaks Race, the Ben Nevis
Race, and the OMM (originally the two-day Karrimor Mountain Marathon), which besides considerable fell-running prowess demands a high level of orienteering skill.

Many of the characters featured in this book however, while often competing in such events, seem to get more satisfaction from competing, personally, against themselves. This I can understand, for I suspect that most
mountaineers find great satisfaction in pushing the boat out further than
usual over rugged and unfamiliar mountain country, not to beat anyone
else but just to see if it can be done. We fondly remember that 'one more
summit', that 20-hour day, that bivouac long after dark, exhausted but at
peace with our ego.

The advent of Covid-19 in the spring of 2020 caused the cancellation
of the season's competitive fell and ultra-running events, but for some of
the best runners in Britain, men and women, it provided an opportunity to
plot, plan and train for more interesting personal projects. Typically these
involved what are dubbed FKTs: fastest known times.

FKTs are a logical American innovation giving runners an opportunity
to race the clock in places where an actual race is not possible. There are
FKTs for most if not all existing routes and records. Otherwise you select,
or dream up a route of your own, time yourself and record it on the international FKT website. And then someone comes along and does it faster and
amends the website. Random examples of domestic FKTs include, at the
time of writing, local jollies such as the Colchester Orbital at 2h 18m 47s
and the Basingstoke Canal Towpath Trail at 7h 45m 1s to the rather more
serious Cuillin Ridge at 3h 14m 58s and the gruelling Pennine Way at 2d
10h 4m 53s.

Of course other appropriate details are recorded such as distance, altitude gain and so forth, besides certain verification requirements. But one
has only to enter FKT on Google and take it from there. There are some
records however for which the FKT website is not appropriate, for instance
Lakeland's Bob Graham Round or the 24-Hour Munro Record.

For those involved the style of any expedition is important. The ideal is:
person goes for run in the hills. An informal, enjoyable day out with perhaps
one mate, and which happens, surprise, surprise, to establish a new FKT.
However a major multi-day run, a serious attempt to smash a celebrated

record for such as the Continuous Complete Munros, is likely to involve months of planning, a dedicated support team to navigate and carry the essential energy-bars and emergency gear, and then a campervan, a cook and a bicycle or two.

Last year, thanks to the pandemic, saw an explosion of records broken and new FKTs established by elite runners, both male and female. This book recounts the stories of several of the most challenging.

Of the 13 chapters, one recounts how in July local runner Ian Stewart established a new FKT for what his wife Laura dubbed the Cairngorm Parkrun, one continuous expedition on foot linking all 58 Munros in the Cairngorm National Park. He started on Mount Keen and reached his Cairngorm summit finish at 2am some five days and 22 hours later, having covered 261 miles, climbed almost 67,260ft and sleeping for just 31 hours, mostly as short naps. Although paced on occasion by 'visiting' friends, it was an impressive accomplishment by any reckoning but one of many such in this book.

The Dartmoor Round chapter is intriguing because the relevant FKT was broken several times during the summer of 2020. The route covers 28 tors, 13,000 feet of ascent over some 75 miles and includes much bog and a haz-ardous crossing of the River Tavy. During July several runners clocked plus or minus 16 and a half hours, but controversy ensued: was the finish on the summit of Sheepstor or the bar of the nearby Royal Oak Inn?

Other chapters cover further prodigious feats, including the RAF officer who in 1980 had run the Three Peaks, linking them by bicycle, in just under two days and who now in 2020, at the age of 73, repeated the trip in a trifle over twice that time. The Land's End to John O'Groats record is well cov-ered. Apparently it's known to runners as the LEJOG and has been done in just over nine days. Elsewhere it's explained that to complete the Munros correctly one must kayak or swim the crossing to Mull.

Ally Beaven, a well-travelled Orcadian, is part of this scene. When not running, either with an FKT objective of his own or in the support team of a mate with an FKT objective, he can be found running the bar at Glenmore Lodge, the Scottish National Mountain Training Centre in the Cairngorms. He writes well and light-heartedly, spelling out the enjoyable agonies that his subjects endure, and which those of us who have an inkling of what is involved can appreciate. Nevertheless, a glossary explaining the parameters of, say, the Bob Graham or the Charlie Ramsay Round would have been useful, while a brief FKT table of the routes described would not go amiss. This must surely be an inspirational book for both aficionados and those in-terested in the power of mind over matter, but I wonder what Mr Naismith would make of it all?

John Cleare

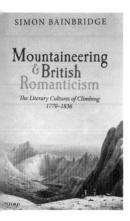

SIMON BAINBRIDGE

Mountaineering
& British
Romanticism

The Literary Cultures of Climbing
1770-1836

OXFORD

Mountaineering and British Romanticism
The Literary Cultures of Climbing 1770-1836
Simon Bainbridge
Oxford University Press, 2020, pp300, £60

'Mountaineering' as a leisure activity was first named by Samuel Taylor Coleridge in 1802 and 'cragsman' as a recreational rock climber used by Sir Walter Scott in his 1829 novel *Anne of Geierstein*, as opposed to the 'craigsman' sea fowler in his novel *The Antiquary* (1816). Simon Bainbridge's argument, from his careful discussion of the evidence in this book, is that 'it was during the Romantic period, rather than in the Victorian period, that mountaineering was established as a leisure pursuit in Britain.' Not only is the evidence embedded in a wide range of literature of the period beyond the well-known poetic examples, but diaries, letters, journals, journalism, 'tour' books and guidebooks reveal 'processes in which gender and indeed class identities were challenged and negotiated, questioned and qualified.' It is Bainbridge's alertness to these distinctions, in a carefully structured book that makes such fascinating and often surprising reading.

Because the origins of British mountaineering have been thought to be Alpine and Victorian, historians have tended to pass quickly from the early and apparently isolated texts of Coleridge's descent of Broad Stand and Wordsworth's climbing to the raven's nest in *The Prelude* straight to the Victorian era. Along the way there has been a tacit acceptance of John Ruskin's and Leslie Stephen's view that 'the Romantic response to mountains was defined by an imaginative, transcendent sensibility.' On the contrary, Bainbridge demonstrates that scientific enquiry, like that of de Saussure in the Alps, had its parallels in Romantic period ascents; that bodily experience and achievement is represented in this writing alongside the imaginative; that the role of imagination itself is more complex than supposed transcendence; that the elevated summit view challenges the picturesque; that Burke's sublime is displaced by real fear of falling; that group ascents, of mixed sex, countered the assumptions of lonely male Romantic epiphanies; that Wordsworth offered the imperative to 'climb every day' as a 'correction' to 'Despondency'; that 'British mountaineers are the inheritors of Swiss liberty' in Wordsworth's political publication in response to the war with France; and that George Mallory took Keats to Everest in 1824! (Okay, read 1924.)

But the chapter on women and mountaineering is a revelation. Bainbridge begins with the fact that by 1798 a satire called *The Lakers* by James Plumptre could feature 'Veronica', dressed for an ascent of Skiddaw in an Alpine 'green veil' and 'her gown fantastically drawn up.' In 1775 an anonymous woman writer gives an account of a party with at least two other women ascending Snowdon. Among those who followed, Bainbridge's roll-call of the ten women named in written accounts is impressive. Aside from Dorothy Wordsworth with her friend Mary Barker, and novelist Ann Radcliffe's popularising account of her ascent of Skiddaw by pony, there are some remarkable stories in this chapter, including those of 'singular females'. In 1825 Ellen Weeton climbed Snowdon as part of a 25-mile solo walk, often walking away from the popular paths in order to avoid meeting men and so getting a reputation in the valley for rashness and irresponsibility. At one point she inevitably comes across a 'gentleman and his guide'. The latter shouts directions. 'I was quite deaf […] I knew the way perfectly well, for my Map and my Guide had been well studied at home.'

On the other hand Sarah Murray's solo accounts revel in being observed in places that some men find hard to access: 'On my return from the promontory I met four travellers, males, not very active in body, who came tumbling down the banks, with fright and dismay, that made me smile.' Smiling even more must have been 'the lady of fashion' who, in the words of Murray's 1799 book, 'left on purpose a bottle of whiskey on the summit' of Ben Nevis in order to drop this information 'before some Highland men, as a piece of carelessness'. Sure enough, one of them 'slipped away, and mounted to the pinnacle', to both the lady's and Sarah Murray's amusement.

Perhaps typical of the revisions and reversals in this book is Thomas Wilkinson's 1805 description of the three Smith sisters of Coniston with whom he made 'an engagement' to climb Helvellyn. But, fearing snow and ice, he reneged on his promise to take them up on the appointed day. When next he met them he found that they had 'shod their staffs with iron' and gone up without him. He commiserated 'in the language of pity for cold fingers and toes. They ridiculed my effeminacy, telling me that they had all three made the summit without a guide, and that they were so delighted with their excursion, that two of them repeated their journey the next day.' Here is mountaineering for fun, with skill and confidence, well before the Victorian era and on Britain's wild mountains. Ten years of research have produced a radical, revisionary and rewarding book that restores the Romantic period to its place in the British 'literary cultures of climbing'.

Terry Gifford

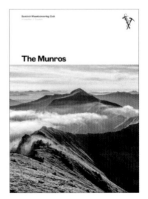

The Munros
Scottish Mountaineering Club: Hillwalkers' Guides
Rab Anderson and Tom Prentice
Scottish Mountaineering Press, 2021, pp384, £30

Hunkered down in the lee of a boulder on Ca Whims, it's time for a snack and coffee. Less than a kilometre east rises the unspectacular summit of Tom Buidhe (957m) of which this lunch spot is but a knobbly protrusion. I've arrived here from Glen Clunie over Càrn an Tuirc (1019m) and Tolmount (958m). So yes, I'm Munro bagging.

It's an admission I would have been reluctant to make not many years ago. Climbers have tended to view Munro baggers and hillwalkers in general with a superior disdain. But age mellows us. I know of a good half-dozen climbers – Kalymnos hot rock and Cogne ice types – who are now busily ticking off Scotland's 3,000-footers. Confinement to these shores by Covid restrictions has provided a respectable excuse.

But we're late starters. There are 282 Munros listed in this latest Scottish Mountaineering Club guide, down a couple on the previous (third) 1999 edition. Amongst Munro anoraks (was the term ever more appropriately applied?) there is an inevitable question: 'how many more have you got to go?' It's one I can only guess at. Until recently, the Highlands have been, for me, primarily a winter destination; hills offering a fun ski descent, irrespective of whether they surpass the coveted 3,000ft mark, have been the focus. The best have been skinned up repeatedly over the years while nearby Munros too bare or bouldery have been ignored.

Nor am I a meticulous record keeper. From sporadic diaries and notebooks I reckon I've 'ticked' about 100, which means (sticking to round numbers) that at my current rate and performance I'll be pushing 100 years old before that final celebratory summit. I'm not ordering the champagne just yet.

Nevertheless, I'll keep plugging away, subject always to Ms Sturgeon's increasingly authoritarian manoeuvres with Covid-pretext travel restrictions. Often in the last year or so words of Hermann Hesse have come to mind: 'Nothing on earth is more disgusting, more contemptible than borders.' Yet politicians feast on them. Half an hour from home, passing Gretna, there it is, 'Fàilte gu Alba'. Listen to the dominant voices from Holyrood and you'd be forgiven for wondering just how 'welcome'.

I'm straying though. For the moment the vital document to carry north is this splendid, extensively revised and updated guide to the Munros: a passport of sorts I suppose, but a passport to pleasure, and maybe just a little temporary pain. On the subject of pain – and for most of us of mature years that word screams knees – this 2021 guide puts more emphasis than its predecessors on the use of bikes for long approaches.

A good example is the ascent of Càrn an Fhidhleir (994m) and An Sgarsoch way out in the west of the west Mounth. Few Munros are this remote. To take in both summits from the NTS car park at the Linn of Dee is a round trip of 42km. According to timings given here, including 810m of ascent, that's an 11-hour day on foot, but just 7h 30m if a bike is used to the ruin of Geldie Lodge. Think of that as a saving of 3h 30m of pounded knee cartilage. I'd be hobbling well before the Linn of Dee hove into sight.

The guide notes that arriving at a standard bike time is more difficult than it is for walking, however those given for approaches in the Cairngorms are certainly close enough. The 1999 edition, edited by Donald Bennet, offered no bike times at all, merely stating that for the two Munros above 'a bicycle is a great help'. Quite so.

Another improvement in the matter of timings is that the new guide acknowledges the sometimes-wearying return journey and gives a time and

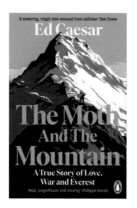

The strange fate of Maurice Wilson, while a footnote in the history of Everest, was always a poignant human story for climbers. The reaction of the men who discovered his body in 1935, Charles Warren, Eric Shipton et al, was not dismissive or critical. They understood only too well the nature of obsession, the inexplicable challenge of the mountain they all faced. Despite the gulf in experience and knowledge, who were they to judge? Wilson's reputation as one of those reckless oddballs the English seem to produce so effortlessly made him an easy subject for the newspapers. Learning to fly so you can attempt Everest? Mad! Yet the general public quickly forgot. The ascent of Everest in 1953 rekindled interest in the mountain, and in the aftermath journalist Dennis Roberts wrote a book about Wilson: *I'll Climb Mount Everest Alone.*

That book was, as *New Yorker* writer Ed Caesar observes 'corrosively wrong' and hamstrung by a deal Roberts cut with Wilson's friend Enid Evans, one third of a unusual but nevertheless contented *ménage à trois* she shared with Maurice and her husband Len in their Maida Vale apartment in the early 1930s, shortly before Wilson's great adventure. If Roberts wanted material for his book, there would be no mention of any of that. Worse, Enid's view of Maurice Wilson was distorted. Her lover left out anything from his already colourful life story that might disturb and consequently Enid didn't know her lover as well as she thought she did. Ed Caesar's great skill is to put the story back on an even keel and tell it with such pace and élan that his book *The Moth and the Mountain* is an absolute delight, full of energy and sympathetic to his subject's complex, moody nature.

height gain for the whole day – there *and back* – not just the time and height gain to the summit(s). Though you could probably make a fair stab yourself at estimating the return leg, it's good to have a reminder that at the top the job is only half done. It also speaks of the attention to detail that has been poured into a book that is simply bigger and better than its predecessor.

Authors Rab Anderson and Tom Prentice have clearly spent days and days tramping the hills, checking route changes – new ATV tracks for example – and taking photographs. There has been a wholesale change of illustrations, many of which are superb. Gone is out-dated clothing and also much of the snow. The book has a less wintry feel than Bennet's edition, with the hills looking much like their everyday selves, and as you are likely to encounter them in these globally warmed times.

Just browsing through is a pleasure. The double page photos that begin each section – the book adheres to the 17 groups of summits as originally designated by Sir Hugh Munro – are sumptuous. As the eye is drawn in, the mind is saying, 'If this is Munro bagging, count me in!' Outstanding, though it's hard to choose, is Rab Anderson's shot of Slioch, buttresses snow-dusted above a frigid Torridon moor-scape. And then, opening the final section, 'The Islands', comes Robert Durran's wonderful shot along

Recovering Wilson's correspondence helped, sold to German author Peter Meier-Hüsing by Roberts, and Caesar tracked down Wilson's grand-nephew who had a box of documents and photographs to share. He captures Wilson's early years in Bradford, his aspirant working-class father's move to the suburbs, recreates Wilson's military service and the devastation the Great War wreaked on the family's prospects, prompting in Maurice a restless dissatisfaction so many of his generation shared. Most impressively of all, Caesar fills in the missing years Wilson spent in the Antipodes, the two marriages, of which Enid knew nothing, his moderate success and the shadow of depression that was never far away. He's also good on the incoherent, new-age worldview Wilson developed, a mix of Oxford Group philosophy, dodgy Blavatsky-inspired Buddhism and Gandhi-style fasting.

With the background firmly drawn, Caesar launches into the story of Wilson's improbable adventure, how he scanned through the kit list of Hugh Ruttledge's expedition and bought a Gypsy Moth, which he rechristened Ever-Wrest. You're actively cheering as he thumbs his nose at the imperial establishment that tries to stop him on his journey, but the truth is that despite all the headlines and talk, he dies alone of cold and exhaustion with the real test still ahead. One question Caesar doesn't answer, perhaps because it is likely unanswerable, is why Wilson took such pains to learn to fly but didn't bother to do any climbing that would prepare him for the rigours of Everest. Recommended.

• *The Moth and the Mountain,* by Ed Caesar, is out in paperback, published by Penguin at £11.

the Cuillin, taken from Sgùrr Dearg with Sgùrr na Banachdaich and Sgùrr a' Ghreadaich cutting into a pale sky. If I'm reading the shadow aright, this is an early morning shot, the rising sun turning the Black Cuillin to red. It must be three decades since four of us scampered along the full traverse (quite likely the best day's 'bagging' you can get). Pouring over Section 17 whets the appetite to go back and savour these fine summits just one or two at a helping.

The route maps too are more detailed than the 1999 edition, drawn from out-of-copyright mapping supplemented by on-the-ground observation. A further innovation is the inclusion of section-by-section Munros Tables at the back of the book, and even a list of the Furths: the 34 summits of over 3,000ft in Britain and Ireland furth (outside) of Scotland. It's something to refer to, perhaps, in the event of further border closures.

Alongside the Tables is a blank column headed 'Date climbed' Maybe I'll get round to filling that in one day. It will never be complete but publication of this inspirational guide to arguably Scotland's finest asset – The Munros – has provided a powerful stimulus for the journey.

Stephen Goodwin

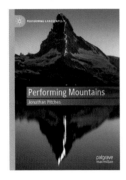

Performing Mountains
Edited by Jonathan Pitches
Palgrave Macmillan, 2020, pp306, £100

Looking back, from the beginning there was a remarkable amount of performance in the International Festival of Mountaineering Literature's 21-year history. At the first festival Ed Drummond spoke his poems whilst ascending his 20ft tripod. We had a play that was performed on a climbing wall, Ian Smith dressed in drag to read a winning entry to the *High* writing competition, Rosie Smith's band played Tom Patey songs, there were new songs from Moira Viggers, a moving monologue from Steve Ashton and the sound of the Canadian Rockies performed by Sid Marty. Joe Simpson's performances were always dramatic, especially in wanting to pick a fight with the organiser for the lack of bar. Some thought that Jim Curran dropping papers and re-shuffling them was deliberate empathy-inducing drama. Johnny Dawes performed an answer to an exam question set by the audience: 'My first time'. Hard to forget his twinkling glance at the audience as he was led off to write his answer by a female student invigilator: pure Dawes impish performance.

When I was a kid in Cambridge on Rag Day the CUMC would peg their way up the pavement on Kings Parade in crowd-pulling horizontal climbing. Surprisingly, the sport of Extreme Ironing was not invented until 1980 by Tony Hiam in the Yorkshire Dales, although Albert Smith would surely have incorporated it, if he'd thought of it, in his *Ascent of Mont Blanc* shows at the Egyptian Rooms in London in the 1850s. Of all these examples of 'performing mountains' only Albert Smith's is discussed in this ground-breaking book by the professor of theatre and performance at the University of Leeds. And, yes, the famous Leeds Wall features, not least in the delightful irony that it was demolished to make way for the author's office (and a performance space that in 2018 hosted a tribute to Johnny Dawes).

The book begins by pointing out how little the study of cultural practices feature in academic mountain studies (4% of 2,500 researchers listed by the Swiss-based Mountain Research Initiative). This is at odds with the explosion of popular interest in mountain arts, although even here films, then books, dominate. This book is pioneering in studying all forms of hybrid mountain performativity from vertical dance (using harnesses and ropes) to participatory skywalks (constructed exposed walkways 'performed' on for social media sharing). Following 'Part 1: Mountain Studies Meets Performance', 'Part 2: Mountains in Ritual, Drama and Site-Related Performance' establishes the international reach of Pitches' research, from Remembrance Day on Great Gable to the site-based arts festival at Persepolis, Iran, where a plan to blow the top off a mountain for dramatic effect was apparently only averted by the budget. Part 3 moves from 'Mountains in Microcosm: The Artistry of Training in the Studio and on the Wall' to 'From Mont Blanc to the Matterhorn: Deep and Dark Play in the Alps' in which

'Eiger watching' is discussed as an example of 'dark tourism' in an 'acting-spectating dynamic' underpinned by 'the notion of "just near-enough"'. Just as Pitches is critical of environmentally damaging installations and practices, he is aware of the limitations of his own terminology: 'it ceases to be play – deep or dark – when things go wrong'.

I had thought at first that the intermittent six 'Handrails' were a mistake. In these Pitches gives a brief account of the ascent of a mountain in the 10-year course of his family collecting Wainwrights on Lake District holidays. The focus of each narrative reflects in a modest way the theme of adjacent chapters: the pull of a summit, little rituals, training, family dramas: 'Site, Light and Dark Memory Put to Rest'. By the end I'd found them a moving reminder that alpinism is not so far away from the discipline and commitment of achieving a more modest mountaineering goal. But two performances I witnessed at Pitches' 'Performing Mountains' conference at Leeds in 2018 illustrate the two problems for this book that are unavoidably intrinsic to its project.

The first is to convey in words the affect of performance. Kate Lawrence re-staged her vertical dance titled *Roped Together* (2011) with her rigger and co-performer Simon Edwards. It is impossible to capture the subtle and moving expression of a dramatic narrative by two hanging dancers, as he controlled her rope and she expressed her relationship with him as a climber. Secondly David Shearing's *Black Rock* was a multi-sensory performance commemorating the 30-year anniversary of Johnny Dawes' ascent of *Indian Face* on Cloggy. Impressively immersive and imaginatively conceptual as this piece was, for me it could not come near the embodied artistry and seriousness of Dawes himself performing on rock. What does come close is Dawes' own verbal arts. He once said to me (as he must have done to others), 'The thing about gritstone is, it's all one hold.' The performativity implicit in those four words – 'it's all one hold' – is both profound and scary. The expression of what is in his head, in his spirit and in his body is a mere residue of its performance in a route he named *Braille Trail*. So subjectivity of response, such as mine to Black Rock, is a limitation that is recognised and embraced by Pitches in his evocation of performances in this book.

Priced for research libraries, *Performing Mountains* brings to centre stage the role of the Alpine Club Library. For those researching the culture of mountaineering and of mountains this landmark book will be essential reading, not least for its bibliography. For everyone else with access to Inter-library Loans this is an amazingly rich, diverse and thought-provoking study of a neglected aspect of international mountain culture.

Terry Gifford

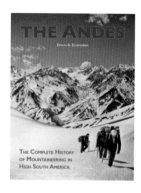

The Andes
The Complete History of Mountaineering in High South America
Evelio A Echevarría
Joseph Reidhead & Co, 2018, pp828, £60

I'm one of those guys that prepares for more climbing trips than he actually takes. In 2002, Benny Bach and I were prepping for our third trip to South America, this time Bolivia. If memory serves, we'd put a map of Bolivia on the wall and threw a dart at it. Regardless, as soon as the objective was set – the Cordillera Quimsa Cruz – it was time to write to the 'master', Evelio Echevarría.

Evelio Echevarría, who sadly passed away late last year, was the master of information, statistics, history and trends of mountaineering in the Andes: not just his Chilean homeland, but of the *entire* continent. Starting in the late 1950s, the Santiago native sent in scores of reports to both this publication and the *American Alpine Journal* about both important and obscure ascents in the 7,000km-long mountain range. Editors at both journals became hugely indebted to Echevarría, who contributed probably a decent percentage of all the reports ever published about this still somewhat untouched mountain range. His was a quiet genius and his steady stream of reports filled in the spaces on the South American map.

Echevarría promptly wrote back to me with instructions on approaching Bolivia's Cordillera Quimsa Cruz, the main parts of the range, and decent objectives. He had suggestions for a variety of things, including transport and certain peaks in the range. It was surprising how well versed he was in a range that was a long way from his homeland. It was an impressive dossier.

In 2018, he put his more than a half century's worth of research into his life's work: *The Andes: The Complete History of Mountaineering in South America.* This book is a mind-boggler if you're a nerd for facts, figures, altitudes, and dates. At its 828-page heart, it's a door-stopping compendium of data on the mountains of South America, with information on who climbed what and when and how. The big sub-sectors of history are all in there: ascents by indigenous peoples, ascents by explorers, ascents by colonials, ascents by later generations, ascents by women, and on.

Perhaps what pleased me most about this book were the vast swathes of stories about European climbers' activities in South America, the kind of stories many Europeans and North American readers might not normally see. And, thankfully, Echevarría puts all those explorations and ascents into the context of what was happening in Europe at the time. Far beyond Whymper and Humboldt and the handful of others we're all familiar with, Echevarría links certain European events (notably the World Wars) to ascents of mountains, walls and towers in the Andes.

When the book came out and having corresponded with Echevarría for more than two decades, I decided it was finally time to meet the great man

The late Andean encyclopaedist Evelio Ecchevarría at home in Colorado with his son Felipe. *(Cameron M Burns)*

in person – hell, he lived just five hours' drive away in northern Colorado. I rocked up to his place, a modest suburban house in Loveland, Colorado, and was greeted by Echevarría and his son Felipe. We settled in for a two-hour grilling by the writer.

How did he know so much about all these mountains? How could he cover so much terrain in person? Apparently, Echevarría took on the Andes bus route by bus route over the course of five decades. His normal on-the-ground approach to research was simple: fly to a country's capital city, then start taking buses up into the hills. The bus routes he chose typically ended in a tiny village or outpost, oftentimes a mine, where few humans lived and surrounded by high peaks. Then he'd just take off into the wilderness with a backpack, a stove, a tent and some food. He climbed dozens of unclimbed peaks – walk ups – just through simple searching. He told me he never considered himself a real climber as he never became proficient with the tools of mountaineering, and rather considered himself more of a peak bagger. Clearly, he was an explorer. He said he made around 100 first ascents of mountains in the Andes. The only person with more first ascents is likely Johan Reinhard, the anthropologist famous for exploring Inca burial sites over decades.

The Andes illustrates Echevarría's intimate mastery of these mountains. The book severely lacks any design bling and comes with a text-heavy presentation, but there are enough photos, maps and delightful little sketches to keep you entertained and reading for the sheer fun that mountain literature can be. But it's the massive amount of data that will bring any Andean climber into this book and prompt them to return over and over again. Each little (or big) sub-range has been represented with every scrap of information Echevarría could get his hands on. It's a wonderful legacy to a humble yet tenacious mountaineer who liked to share one of the world's great ranges.

Cameron M Burns

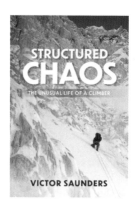

Structured Chaos
The Unusual Life of a Climber
Victor Saunders
Vertebrate Publishing, 2021, pp192, £24

From the outset Victor Saunders is keen to point out that his latest book is about embracing paradox and a search for 'what really matters', on and off the mountain.

The action starts with a perilous bus journey as the author attempts to reconnect with his childhood in Pekan, Malaysia. From 'the lush Malaysian jungle' his father shipped him off to a brutal 'bleak Scottish boarding school … heartless, horrible and cold', where this small, myopic, asthmatic 'brown-skinned' boy was hopelessly out of place.

In 1969 he discovered climbing and it changed his life. Back then, 'climbers dressed as appallingly as cavers' and the scene was small. London had just one climbing shop and the assistant, the late lamented Tony Wilmott, advised the keen, inexperienced youth to: 'Go to Avon Gorge and ask for someone to climb with you.'

We soon learn that beneath the understatement and light-hearted tone there lies a steely determination. His insatiable passion and drive for adventure now spans more than five decades, climbing snow, ice, rock and rubble, from Scotland to the Himalaya. He's a brilliant raconteur: open and playful, even in the most desperate situations. The prose is tight and energetic and his writing evokes time and place wonderfully. I savoured each and every chapter.

Towards the end of the book, Saunders is living as a mountain guide in Chamonix. For most of the book, however, London is his base and he captures the drive and ambition of the 1980s scene here beautifully. He shares his passion for the capital's architecture as he seeks out popular bouldering haunts, such as the Camden canal system.

It's here that he meets 'East End miscreant' Stevie Haston. They forge a solid relationship and hatch a plan to tackle the Eigerwand in winter. Working as an architect, Saunders' training consists of walking everywhere on tiptoe and pinch gripping a briefcase in each hand on the way to the office.

Saunders has guided clients to the summit of Everest at least six times, though he barely mentions this. Instead, the writing mainly focuses on pioneering alpine-style routes on lesser-known Himalayan peaks or in small teams on bigger mountains.

His partner for a two-man attempt on Nanga Parbat in winter is Raphael, an eccentric enthusiastic Dane, someone Saunders had helped rescue from K2 a few years earlier. The expedition is brutal: day after day at -25°C. 'As planned we gave our bodies hell,' Saunders assures us. The quirky exchanges these two offbeat characters share each morning in the tent obliquely reveals their most intimate hopes and fears.

The long and frozen road. Mick Fowler on Spantik in 1987, a friendship rekindled in *Structured Chaos*. *(Victor Saunders)*

Structured Chaos is full of strong, 'pig-headed', driven characters. Sometimes the tension from the climbing encounters spills over. After the Eigerwand, Haston lifts the author off the ground, Saunders observing how 'the veins on the side of his neck swelled and wriggled like caterpillars ... I understood I was about to come to some real harm.' In another episode he ends up in a boxing ring with his regular climbing partner Mick Fowler.

But we sense that it's among these people and through these adventures that Saunders finds fulfilment and comes to realise that 'what really matters' is, in Colin Kirkus' phrase, 'going to the right place, at the right time, with the right people'.

It's difficult not to admire the achievements though. Reunited with Fowler the pair are still exploring desperate new lines on big unclimbed Himalayan peaks. Not bad at 72 and 65 years old respectively. Clearly this journey with those 'unspeakable friends' with 'their impossible beliefs' is not finished just yet.

Andy Cave

Never Leave The Dog Behind
Our Love of Dogs and Mountains
Helen Mort
Vertebrate Publishing, 2021, £9

'All my life, I've been terrified of dogs.' That's a sentiment I share with Helen Mort. I share, too, the genesis of her fear: an attack by a dog on a farm. Like her, I've gone out of my way to avoid dogs, interacting only with those belonging to friends and, like her, I have a scattering of memories of dog-related incidents which left me bitten, panicked and ever after fearful.

What I also have in common with her, this author I have never met, is an obsession with high places: 'the complete happiness' she describes at being in the mountains is mine too. And so I came to this book with curiosity: how could dog and mountain combine to elevate the experience of climbing, walking or simply being among peaks? How do dogs inhabit these wild places and what can we learn from that juxtaposition, or, rather, triangulation of dog, owner and mountain?

In Helen Mort's hands we learn a great deal: the 13 essays that comprise the book are painstakingly researched and wide-ranging. The rich weave of subject matter is threaded through with the intimacy of personal experience and liberally salted with forays into poetry, philosophy, history, spirituality and the supernatural with never an intellectual toe in the water but always signposting new directions of exploration into the relationship between dogs and mountains, those 'theatres of risk, drama and heroism'. There is no slide into intellectual dryness: the lyricism of Mort's writing and her passion for the subject matter carry the reader along the physical and emotional journey in which she is engaged. Her finely honed sense of place transports the reader to the mountains she so joyfully inhabits, describing dawn light as 'an egg cracked over the Cumbrian mountains.'

Mort's affinity with dogs began when she volunteered to be a dog walker and so met her whippet, Bell. Taking her into the mountains opened up new perspectives for Mort, initially an awareness of the duality of dog behaviour. The devoted domestic pet became an independent explorer with a 'cool disregard' for abandoned hunting forays, able to move easily between human perceptions of the range of animal behaviours.

Interviews she includes similarly broaden our understanding of the many-faceted nature of the relationship between humans and their dogs. Chris Bonington believes that while climbing partnerships, thriving on competition and fuelled by ego and ambition, always come to an end, a dog continues to give unquestioning devotion. As Mort puts it: 'With a dog, you are never alone again.' The other side of the coin, of course, is the severity of loss. Lucy Creamer describes the death of her beloved dog and climbing companion Kodo as 'horrendous, like losing a child.' There is, too, a sense of liberation, derived from taking dogs to hills and crags, a feeling that their owners can

The poet Helen Mort, and friend. *(John Houlihan)*

absorb the unbridled pleasure they derive from roaming the outdoors.

Mort's 'curious, questing' approach leads her to meet, among others, search-and-rescue dogs, St Bernards, ill-treated dogs rehabilitated in the mountains and notable dogs from history, but her meditations always return to the central idea of how dogs help us connect with mountains. Alongside this steady narrative pulse is a much more intimate juxtaposition with her 'attempt to make sense of a chapter of my own life.' She writes openly about her obsessions and addictions, difficulties past and present, and observes them as she does her dogs, simultaneously deeply rooted in her consciousness but almost from 'an alien perspective'. This is most evident when she writes about her unborn child who, like the dogs she loves so much, leads her to a new way of making sense of what she sees in the landscape before her. The 'necessary unselfishness' she has learned when taking her dogs to the hills and crags will be mirrored in the responsibility she has to shoulder when her child is born.

Five pages of notes, a bibliography and further reading extend the spirit of exploration. Mort's preparation and research for writing this book have clearly been meticulous. But she clearly wanted her response to her subject to be instinctive, too and it's her experience of falling in love with a dog that sings out of every chapter of the book. She has 'let my thoughts roam, like a dog on a fellside, following my instinct.'

Val Johnson

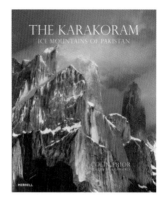

Now in his early 60s, Colin Prior made his reputation in the 1980s with his richly lit panoramic images of Highland mountains, but his path to the mountains was convoluted. Born in Glasgow, Prior left school uncertain about his future and for a while worked as an operations manager for the same international welding company as his father. A growing interest in scuba diving led him in his early 20s to experiment with underwater photography; this was his route in to taking pictures for a living. After a spell as a photographic technician on a North Sea oil platform, he established his own business and has rarely looked back, although the industry, thanks to digital photography and the Internet, is now less lucrative than it was when he started. He put away his panoramic cameras in 2021 and in recent years his work has concentrated in a more detailed way on his passion for nature, although still with his same feeling for light that was a hallmark of his earlier work. Last year he was given the Scottish Award for Excellence in Mountain Culture.

As he became well known Prior was able to balance personal projects with commercial commissions like the four years he shot the British Airways calendar. His latest book, *The Karakoram: Ice Mountains of Pakistan* has been, quite obviously, very much a passion. Shot over a quarter of a century, Prior was first inspired in his mid twenties by his discovery of Galen Rowell's book *In the Throne Room of the Mountain Gods* (1977) in his local library. One picture in particular stood out for Prior, of the Trango Towers, and while they are obviously photogenic, the intensity Prior achieves in this book with his images of the same peaks is striking. Like Rowell, Prior zeroes in on the golden hour at

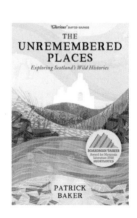

The Unremembered Places
Patrick Baker
Birlinn, 2020, 228pp, £9.99

We all have them, those moments when making a journey in the wild we come across a man-made feature that's inexplicable; a few chiselled stones perhaps, that suggest they were once part of a building but without logic as to why they are where they are, miles from anywhere, miles from any other hint of habitation. Or there's a half-hidden cave, a burial mound, a deserted bothy in which we sense a kind of unease, as though something tragic once happened there.

The wilder the country, the more we scratch our heads and wonder.

Not all of these unremembered places are remote and hard to find, but each one has an atmosphere of its own that has become woven into folklore. A number of them have written histories recording events from long ago before men and women went a-wandering for the simple pleasure of being somewhere different. Delve into their mysteries and you discover the sunrise and sunset. Although Rowell's work can seem, to my eye, and from today's perspective, sometimes overblown, Prior catches the austerities of the Karakoram, as well as the grandeur and beauty. He captures, in fact, the spirit of the range.

He's helped in this by balancing sumptuous colour shots with stunningly reproduced duotones, three of which are reproduced in this edition of the *Alpine Journal,* on the cover and the endpapers. I'd also mention in particular a landscape shot of the Trango Towers across two pages captured as a storm clears, leaving the mountains plastered in fresh snow. It's phenomenally sharp and perfectly reproduced, the threads of cloud still clinging to the face capturing that sense you have looking up at a potential challenge in less than friendly conditions, that paradoxical blend of beauty and threat. Alongside the landscapes are a series of portraits of some of the locals he's met along the way. It's good to include an indigenous human touch, although if the book has one flaw it's that these images are too large, their scale jarring somewhat with that of the mountains. The range of ethnic origins in the faces, however, is a good reminder of this region's long and complex human history.

The conventional wisdom is that picture books no longer sell but if you have a passion for mountains in general and the Karakoram in particular you will want this book. Prior has included notes from each of the trips he made pursuing his interest and there's an essay on photographing the Karakoram from historian Mick Conefrey. The man Conefrey concentrates on is Vittorio Sella. Every photographer who has gone to the Karakoram since has had their efforts compared to the man Conefrey correctly identities as the world's greatest mountain photographer. Most have been found wanting but you sense that Sella would have given a nod of approval to the best of these.

• Colin Prior's *The Karakoram: Ice Mountains of Pakistan* is published by Merrell at £50.

brutality of centuries past when drovers and uneducated labourers endured unimaginable hardships, existing in atrocious conditions because there was no alternative. For them it was often a case of shiver, starve and die.

Scotland is peppered with such places, and author Patrick Baker's journeys among them form the thread of this fascinating book. His curiosity is infectious, as travelling on foot or by canoe he explores remote (and not so remote) places, questions their existence, digs into their histories and tells their stories with an honest prose that creeps into the reader's emotions. No wonder *The Unremembered Places* was shortlisted for the 2020 Boardman Tasker prize.

Kev Reynolds

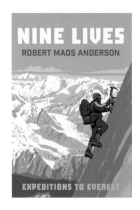

Nine Lives
Expeditions to Everest
Robert Mads Anderson
Vertebrate Publishing, 2020, pp204, £15

It was 1984. A bunch of Norwegians in Mrs Davie's Hotel, Rawalpindi were about to drive away up the Karakoram Highway, but first they had a small problem to solve. They had just bought the kitchenware needed for base camp including a nested set of five aluminium cooking pots, except their dictionary had supplied the word for 'kettle' rather than 'pan' and now, instead of cooking pots, they had a lovely set of five tea kettles in five sizes from a massive three litres to a dinky one-cup. The leader, Hans Christian Doseth pointed at the kettles.

'Ah, so, we should say pot not kettle?'

The Norwegians went off to make a hard new aid route on Trango while we headed off to Hunza. Doseth was slated to climb with Robert Anderson on Everest's west ridge the following year but sadly he was killed on descent from Trango. This seems to have been the first of many tangential connections I had with Anderson. The following year, I was attempting to climb Rimo I in the eastern Karakoram when Steve Venables dropped his rucksack with most of our bivouac kit. We were six days up the climb at 7,000m with no stove. Three years after that Steve went on to make one of the most remarkable ascents of Everest on an expedition led by Anderson. In the years since I have bumped into him in Europe, Nepal (we shared neighbouring base camps in 2010), Antarctica and most recently in 2019 in Pakistan. He is still at it, and still loving it all. The opportunity to review this book was an offer I could not refuse.

Over a period of 25 years Anderson was obsessed with climbing the Big One and this book is about that obsession. (In addition to his obsession, Robert must also have amazing secret powers when it comes to raising money for expeditions. Perhaps this is the Everest Effect. Lesser mountains do not seem to be very attractive to potential sponsors.) Its scale is illustrated by the list of expeditions the book covers.

1985 West ridge, turning round just 250m from the summit.
1988 Kangshung face, when Stephen Venables reached the top, doing, as Reinhold Messner said, 'a very hard thing, but you were lucky.'
1990 Super-couloir (meaning the Hornbein Couloir Direct, or Japanese Route), retreating from 7,700m.
1991 Anderson Couloir start to the north ridge, solo to 8,200m.
1992 North ridge, the standard route from Tibet, turning back at 8,200m.
1993 The Great Couloir to 8,410m.
1995 The Great Couloir again, this time to 8,100m.
1999 North ridge in winter stopped by the mountain at 7,000m.

2003 South Col route guiding to the top.
2010 South Col route guiding to the top again.

When you look at these nine expeditions list, it's clear that no one on Earth has a greater personal experience of so many different aspects of the mountain. Perhaps because of his intimate knowledge of its geography, Robert, skimps a little on physical descriptions in his writing. The photographs help in this respect, but a scattering of maps would have clarified most of the locational questions that the average reader, lacking this knowledge, might ask.

Otherwise, the writing is fluid and engaging; it's a fun read. You are led seamlessly from expedition to expedition. The stories are studded with short passages of internal reflection, bordering on free writing (it used to be called stream of consciousness in my day), which gives an excellent insight into his mind-set. The reader will feel very much present as Robert contemplates the deceptive and hard choices between ambition and staying alive. The stories also demonstrate his obvious compassion for his companions, which I think is a good thing. If you want to know what goes through the mind of a man obsessed with climbing one mountain for half a lifetime, then I can wholly recommend this book.

Victor Saunders

Obituaries

'Yosemite Falls', Constance Gordon-Cumming, May 1878, watercolour, 64cm x 50cm. *(Courtesy of PBA Galleries/Justin Benttinen)*

In Memoriam

The Alpine Club Obituary	Year of Election (including to ACG)
Albert Chapman	2004
John Cheesmond	1973
Inge Cochlin	1992
Evelio Echevarría	1959
Prince Philip, Duke of Edinburgh	Hon 1955
Dave Fisher	1951
Gerald Franklin	Assoc 2013
Egil Fredriksen	1997
Alan Harris	Asp 1981, 1987
Hamish MacInnes	Hon 2009
Peter Page	1980
Peter Robson	1971
Anne Sauvy	1975
Doug Scott	1962, Hon 2011
Crispin Simpson	1968
Geoff Templeman	1980
Jeremy Whitehead	1969

An obituary for Claude Davies, who appeared on last year's list, is included in this edition.

Albert Chapman
1935 - 2021

Albert Chapman was born on 7 April 1935 in Keighley and died peacefully on 17 March 2021 at the age of 85. He will be remembered for his sense of humour, his warm hospitality and his significant contribution to the Yorkshire Ramblers' Club over his 66 years of membership.

A Yorkshireman, Albert grew up in Oakworth, near Keighley and was educated at Keighley Boys' Grammar School before joining the public works department at what was then Bingley Urban District Council. He gained experience with a local road-resurfacing contractor before setting up Chapman Ryan Ltd in 1972, a successful contracting business in road reinstatement and resurfacing. Affable and gregarious, he got on well with his customers

Albert Chapman.

and suppliers, and he proved to be a very capable organiser, with a talent for spotting potential problems and nipping them in the bud. He married his first wife Jill and they brought up two children. After they divorced, he married Sammy, with whom he travelled widely and shared many adventures including visits to India and Nepal.

Strong business performance in the late 1970s allowed Albert to purchase Scar Top, a remote dilapidated Dales farmhouse with a cracking view across the dale to Ingleborough. He completed an ambitious restoration and the house became his and Sammy's spiritual home for over 40 years. Renowned for their generous hospitality and his wife's sublime cooking, Scar Top served as the base for a quick ascent of Whernside, often accompanied by one of Albert's dogs; he had a succession of Newfoundland dogs and an Irish wolfhound. He kept a dozen Highland cattle at Scar Top and was a member of the Highland Cattle Society.

Albert loved the mountains. Never interested in team games as spectator or player, he was introduced to the hills by his grammar school's walking group, which took pupils to the Dales and Lake District. In 1955, at the age of 20, he joined the Yorkshire Ramblers' Club to further his outdoor ambitions. An enthusiastic supporter of club meets across the UK and Scotland in particular, he climbed many of his first mountain summits in the company of more experienced YRC members and regularly attended annual Alpine meets.

He seemed to thrive on no sleep. After a night in the Dix hut he wrote: 'Sleep is not a companion of mine at an Alpine hut; I merely pass the night and listen to the snores of my chums!' He ascended many of the classic Swiss summits and climbed in the French Alps and in Austria. Latterly, in 2005, he climbed Samgyal Peak (5814m), a summit in Ladakh, and his last Alpine summit was the Gran Paradiso in 2006, aged 70 and during a YRC meet.

Albert served the YRC in a number of official capacities and always had ideas to take the club forward. His devotion to it could match that of any; no task or duty was too much. He was instrumental in pushing for improvements to the two club huts. He became president in the year 2000, which was cursed with the foot and mouth crisis. He introduced a bike ride to the club's programme, although a wilder idea to have a club triathlon withered on the bough.

In later years, enthusiasm for mountaineering gave way to an interest in trekking, a particular passion in Albert's life. Starting in 1985, he led, joined or accompanied treks to the Annapurna area, Mustang, Upper Dolpo, Kangchenjunga, Jugal, Rolwaling and Khumbu, Langtang, Bhutan, Sikkim, Ladakh, the Mongolian Altai, Hunza, Bolivia, Morocco's western Atlas and South Africa and made trekking a firm component of the YRC's meets programme.

One of his trekking highlights was the expedition to Nanda Devi Inner Sanctuary co-led by John Shipton, Col Narinder 'Bull' Kumar and Steve Berry in 2000. In his book about the trip, Hugh Thomson observed:

> *Albert Chapman also cheered me up. He was the doughty President of the Yorkshire Ramblers' Club... Like many Yorkshire institutions, the Ramblers' were fond of their reputation for plain speaking, toughness and humour, and Albert was a suitably eccentric President. For today's climb he was wearing a fetching pair of bright orange paisley trousers and a floppy hat. At one point, he turned to me as I was struggling on a difficult section over some slabs: 'Did you know, Hugh, that if you heat up a George Formby record, it makes a lovely fruit-bowl?' By the time I had finished laughing, I was on the other side.*

After a lifetime of mountaineering and trekking, Albert was elected to membership of the Alpine Club in 2003 at the age of 68. He was proud of his membership, regarding it as a fitting accolade to his accomplishments on the hill and in wild places. He was a regular attender at Club dinners and enjoyed reminiscing with other members.

Albert never really got over the untimely death of his wife Sammy six years before his own. His family, friends and fellow YRC members will remember his infectious enthusiasm and boundless energy and love of the Himal. He will be sorely missed.

Mick Borroff

John Cheesmond
1937 - 2021

John Cheesmond.

John was born in 1937 and brought up on North Tyneside. He started climbing while still at school and continued at Newcastle University where he studied geography. He joined the Crag Lough Club in the late 1950s and the Fell and Rock Club in 1958. He was elected to membership of the Alpine Club in 1973. After graduating, he taught for three years in local schools before moving into the early days of climbing instruction, working at White Hall in 1962 and taking over from Joe Brown as chief instructor in 1966.

In the 1960s, John climbed regularly in the Alps, with ascents of the classics of the day, including the *Comici-Dimai* route on the Cima Grande, the Salbitschijen and the *Route Major* on the Brenva. His report on his climbs in the Dolomites (*FRCC Journal,* 1962, pp244-8) is an evocative time capsule of the age. It is a pity he did not write more. He was also very active on British rock, doing first ascents of the direct start of *West Sphinx* on Wainstones, and with Joe Brown, the first ascents of *Sinistra* on Clogwyn Du'r Arddu and *Blind Pew* on Gogarth. In 1971 he joined with friends on an expedition to Nepal travelling overland via Iran and Iraq. On the way out he managed to get left in Kabul, when his fellow climbers drove off thinking he was in the back of the lorry.

In 1969 he moved to north Wales becoming the principal of Ogwen Cottage, Birmingham's outdoor centre, until 1972, when he moved to Scotland, working at Dunfermline College of Physical Education and running diploma courses for students in outdoor education. He still found time in 1975 to take part in an expedition to the Karakorum, climbing the 6,460m Pyramid Peak in the Siachen region. Around this time, John also completed an external master of education degree at the University College of North Wales. His final thesis was on the development of outdoor education in Edinburgh's education authority.

He married Joyce in 1983 and they spent many years climbing Scottish hills together. In 1987, Dunfermline College was amalgamated with Moray House College of Education and John became the head of the diploma courses working with Nev Crowther until he retired in 1992. In 2000, Nev Crowther, John and Pete Higgins published 'A History of Outdoor Education at Dunfermline College of Physical Education and Moray House College and Institute of Education, Edinburgh, 1970-2000', detailing the contribution of these institutes to outdoor education and the training of teachers in the field.

In later years John's main activity in the mountains was skiing, both ski mountaineering and downhill. He held a BASI Level 1 ski instructor's award. In his seventies he became a keen cyclist spending several weeks with groups, cycling Alpine passes, including the Route des Grands Alps from Lake Geneva to Nice. He and Joyce also had many cycling tours in Europe covering long distances. Back in Scotland, he finished his Munros in 1997 and his Furths, those English, Welsh and Irish mountains over 3,000ft, in 2000. John had a lifelong love of mountains. He was an accomplished mountaineer, had an encyclopaedic knowledge of climbing and first ascents and an enviable collection of climbing books, including many first editions. With his mixture of intelligence, humour and modesty he will be fondly remembered, and missed, by his many friends.

Kate Ross

Inge Cochlin
1942 - 2020

Inge Cochlin.

Ingeborga Krystyna Cochlin (née Doubrawa) was born in Stanisławów, a town in the Ukraine then part of Poland. After the Soviet invasion of Ukraine in September 1939, when Stanisławów was returned to the Ukraine, her family had to flee into Poland, eventually settling in Warsaw. She spent her teenage years pursuing her love of mountaineering in her beloved Tatras mountains. Her first experiences of this beautiful Polish mountain range were with her father Emile and brother Ronald; they would spend large periods of the school holidays walking, scrambling and rock climbing on some of the most challenging routes in the Tatra, scaling the likes of Rysy (2501m), Jarząbczy Wierch (2137m), Kościelec (2155m), Kozi Wierch (2291m), Kasprowy Wierch (1987m), Giewont (1895m) and the formidable Mnich (2068m). They also completed the Orla Perć, a challenging trail that crosses many of the Tatra high points and includes via ferrata to help move up some of the trickier parts of the route.

Inga soon joined the Polski Związek Alpinizmu (PZA) through which she made many lifelong friends, some of whom went on to form the core group of climbers who led the great Polish Himalayan winter expeditions of the 1980s. Later she became secretary of the club and helped in the organisation of many of these climbs. It was with the PZA that she went further afield, heading to the Caucasus in Russia, although her impressive ascent of the highest point in Europe, Mount Elbrus (5642m), was marred by a tragic accident in which one of the climbers was killed and the rest of the group, including the Russian minders, had to be airlifted off the mountain by helicopter.

Her love of the mountains continued when she moved to London in 1969 and met her husband Peter Cochlin, with whom she enjoyed a wonderful 50-year marriage and a family of two children. They spent every Easter in north Wales and using Capel Curig as their base, explored the wild valleys and stunning mountains of Snowdonia, sowing the seeds of adventure in their children who themselves have gone on to have a long relationship with the hills. Many winter holidays were also spent in the French and Italian Alps, creating treasured memories discovering these great mountains.

In the 1980s, Inga's Polish mountaineering friends began to set some spectacular records in the climbing world, with Andrzej Zawada leading a phenomenal series of winter first ascents in the Himalaya. Inga worked in the background in London, helping Zawada raise funds, find sponsors for the expeditions and offering hospitality to him and his colleagues when they needed to come to London to discuss plans with interested parties. Later on Inga helped to arrange lecture tours in the UK for Zawada and others, occasionally acting as an interpreter for those whose English wasn't particularly strong.

At around the same time she became associated with the Alpine Club (to which she was elected in 1992), the beginning of almost 20 years of involvement in the translation, writing and photo credits of many Polish language climbing articles, helping bring these great climbs to the attention of the English-speaking community. These included the first winter ascent of Everest in 1980 (*AJ* 1984, pp50-9), the expedition that saw Jerzy Kuckuczka and Andrzej Czok successfully climbing Dhaulagiri (8167m) in winter without oxygen, the first winter ascent of Cho Oyu (8188m) by Maciej Berbeka, Maciej Pawlikowski, Zyga Heinrich and Jerzy Kukuczka. Jerzy climbed all 14 8000m peaks, all but one by new routes or in winter. He was awarded an honorary Olympic silver medal at the Calgary winter games of 1988, all recorded in Inge's tribute (*AJ* 1990, pp32-4).

The Polish expedition successes continued with Wanda Rutkiewicz, Inge's old climbing partner from her time in the Tatras, where the Polish climbers developed their resilience for these challenging winter climbs. Wanda also relied on Ingeborga's translating work to bring her Himalayan achievements to the world. This included her ascent of Everest in 1978, being the first Pole as well as the first European woman to reach the summit and also her climb to the top of K2 (8611m) in 1986, becoming the first woman to reach the summit. In Inge's words, (*AJ* 1993, pp321-3), 'Wanda's main attributes were extreme powers of endurance, intelligence, determination, ambition, and passion for the mountains. Those were the characteristics that made her such a brilliant Himalayan climber.' Her life came to an end when she disappeared near the summit of Kangchenjunga in May 1992

Inge's support was also crucial at that time for the introduction of well-known Polish climbers to the Alpine Club, inviting them to stay at her house when they visited the UK, and taking them to meetings with publishers to ensure their work was fully recognised by the climbing world. The tremendous work that Inga put into bringing the achievements of the great Polish climbing community of the 1980s will remain for future generations, but it was her great generosity, kindness and loyalty to family and friends for which she will be most remembered. She will be greatly missed by all who knew her.

Peter & Danny Cochlin

Claude Davies
1938 - 2019

Claude Davies.

Claude was known to some as the author of the first climbers' guide to the Anti-Atlas in Morocco whilst others will know of him as the regular partner of Joe Brown on many great climbs in north Wales. They made a superbly balanced team with Claude the second who inspired his leader and best friend by his attention to detail especially in matters of safety. He was a multi-talented individual who achieved much in his professional life at the same time as being an enthusiastic golfer, fly-fisher (he and Joe were members of a syndicate that held beats on the Tweed, just east of Coldstream) and, above all, a mountaineer and rock climber.

He was educated at Salford Grammar School where he teamed up with Colin Andrews, the two of them taking to the crags of Llandudno's Great Orme for the dubious purpose of collecting birds' eggs. Fortunately, this led to an interest in rock climbing for its own sake. At that time Claude's best friend was Albert Finney, the Oscar-nominated actor and winner of BAFTA awards, who did not share his interest in such adventurous pursuits. They died within a few months of each other. After school he graduated in civil engineering at Manchester University.

Pete Turnbull recalls a tragic incident in 1953 that he believes had a profound effect on Claude and his whole approach to climbing. Pete, as part of one of Sid Cross's ad hoc Langdale rescue parties, participated in the recovery of a body following a fatal accident on the south-west face of Gimmer Crag. The victim had fallen almost the full height of the route after the rope was cut on a sharp flake, landing close to where Claude was watching. He was required to give evidence at the inquest in Ambleside.

Claude joined the Cromlech Club in 1954 at the age of 16 and remained a member until 2013, serving on its committee for some 17 years. He also

In later years Claude joined Joe Brown on exploratory holidays, first in Spain then the Anti-Atlas of Morocco.

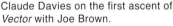

Claude Davies on the first ascent of *Vector* with Joe Brown.

joined the Climbers' Club, becoming its treasurer and later vice president. Like many others he served his climbing apprenticeship on the gritstone crags of the Peak District before moving on to recording new routes mainly in Snowdonia where his tally was in excess of 50. Initially he climbed with a variety of friends, often as leader, but subsequently seconded Joe on a sequence of impressive routes, many becoming very popular classics amongst which *Vector* stands out, (*CCJ,* 2011, pp78-81). *Vector* continually changes direction as it seeks out the line of least resistance. Its perfect name comes from Claude who at the time of the first ascent was studying vectors for an exam.

Claude was a regular visitor to the Alps, usually with his wife Betty and their two boys. Nigel remembers childhood adventures with his father on idyllic campsites such as the one at Vicosoprano. With such luminaries as Ian McNaught-Davis, Jo 'Morty' Smith, Allan Austin, Trevor Jones and Les Brown, as well as Joe himself, Claude climbed a variety of routes such as the south-west face of the Dent du Géant, south face of the Tour Ronde, north face of the Königspitze, the *Yellow Edge* on the Cima Piccola and the *Cassin* on the north face of the Piz Badile. On the latter he and Morty stopped to assist two Germans, one of whom was seriously injured. They were only able to continue when the Germans were lifted off by helicopter.

Further afield he had two trips to Kenya, making an ascent of Mount

Kenya as well as doing a fair amount of rock-climbing in the Rift valley. Claude spoke fondly of two trips to the Wind River range in Wyoming where he greatly appreciated the unspoilt wilderness and 'backcountry' climbing of the Cirque of Towers. He made classic climbs such as Mitchell Peak's north face and Pingora's north-east face. Pete Turnbull remembers evening meals being supplemented with fresh trout caught by Claude and Joe.

I got to know Claude (and Joe) well when for one winter holiday in the early 1980s my wife Marjorie and I shared accommodation in Benidorm with Les Brown. We teamed up with them in various combinations exploring the mountain tracks of the Costa Blanca hinterland, which invariably involved treating the hire cars (thankfully they were old) as if they were off-roaders. Claude was the ringleader in this, never fearing the glutinous mud or the potentially sump-wrecking rocks we encountered all in the search for new crags or even just to get to a favourite mountain restaurant in double-quick time.

We were soon drawn into Joe and Claude's culture of keeping discoveries secret and not recording routes. Every now and then Claude would put together the accumulated knowledge and draw a map indicating the location of the various crags that they (it was usually them; they had much more time than us) had discovered. One particular obsession of theirs was the Castellets, a serrated knife-edge ridge some five or six kilometres in length with many sections involving technical climbing and a few airy (hairy?) abseils. Because of its length the completion of the ridge required many days and several holidays; the problems involving getting off the ridge and then returning for the next section were often quite formidable. A few of their routes eventually appeared in the Rockfax guides to the area and many years later Claude produced a mini guide describing all the routes that were done in this period. It was never intended for publication but he circulated it amongst his friends.

I am not sure how long this lasted but I certainly remember that by 1992 they had moved on to another idyll and each winter we were regaled with tales of a new climbing paradise in Morocco. Claude and Joe had started exploring the Anti-Atlas region near to the essentially desert town of Tafraout in the wake of Les Brown and Trevor Jones who had visited the area as a substitute for an Easter holiday in Wadi Rum, cancelled *force majeure* by the Gulf War. From then on, the hotel of Les Amandiers at Tafraout became the base for forays into the impressive mountains of the Jebel el Kest massif. So began a remarkable and significant period in British climbing, featuring a quite elderly bunch of grandparents. For more than 20 years they, with an expanding group of friends including Pete Turnbull, Derek Walker and Chris Bonington, developed many of the quartzite crags of the massif that were readily accessible from Tafraout, establishing the town as an important centre for traditional multi-pitch climbing. (The granite boulders in the immediate vicinity of Tafraout were ignored in the main.)

Early retirement allowed Claude to spend increasing periods of time at Les Amandiers and it could be said that he was the presiding spirit of the team. He revelled in driving up the exciting un-metaled roads that gave relatively easy access to many of the crags. Claude's growing knowledge of the area along with the establishment of a new routes book in the hotel enabled him to produce *Climbing in the Moroccan Anti-Atlas,* (Cicerone, 2004). On retiring I joined them. Fitting in was made easy by Claude who knew all the staff of the hotel by name; British climbers were honoured guests who stayed for extended periods rather than one or two nights as did most of the visitors. The availability of the new guide inevitably attracted more and more climbers who made repeat ascents of the team's routes, some even pioneering routes of their own. New crags continue to be discovered especially on the north side of Jebel el Kest with the result that the Anti-Atlas is now a major attraction for climbers from all over Europe.

Claude was a consultant structural engineer who became a partner in the very successful company Shepherd and Gilmour that built hospitals, schools and bridges in the north of England. Maybe it was his civil engineering expertise that led to his involvement with the Old Man of Hoy TV extravaganza (1967) when he rigged up a cable from the summit of the stack to the mainland along which Hamish McInnes did a Tyrolean traverse. His professional advice was given freely to and much valued by the Climbers' Club with its large portfolio of old huts that constantly need attention. My experience of Claude was that he was extremely risk-averse (probably essential given his responsibilities) with a forensic eye for weaknesses. One amusing illustration of this was in Spain when I was admiring a large and, to me, impressive 10m wall of recent construction. However, Claude explained its defects to me and, with considerable relish, predicted its early demise. The following day, much to my amazement, this beautiful wall had collapsed becoming nothing but a heap of rubble.

Claude's last visit to Tafraout with Pete Turnbull in 2010 marked the end of his climbing career. He continued to play golf and died on 31 August 2019 after a short illness. He was laid to rest in the beautifully situated grounds of St James' Church in Taxal, Derbyshire where he was born.

I am indebted to the following without whose considerable help the writing of this obituary would not have been possible: Betty and their son Nigel, Barry Grantham, hon secretary of the Cromlech Club and Pete Turnbull.

Mike Mortimer

Evelio A Echevarría
1926 - 2020

Evelio Abundio Caselli Echevarría, who was born in Santiago, Chile in 1926, was professor emeritus of Colorado State University. He climbed and studied amongst the Andes and the Rocky Mountains for some 65 years and researched both ranges, chronicling their known – and frequently unknown – histories from ancient times to the present. His own research activities included exploratory mountaineering. Both his academic and mountain books

Evelio A Echevarría.

and publications have appeared in several countries between 1950 and today. He was elected a member of the Alpine Club in 1959, and much of his research and mountain travel has been described in his prodigious contributions to the *Alpine Journal* since then.

After high school Evelio served with the mountain artillery and ski troops until 1947. Then, in 1953, he migrated to the United States to work at the ski resort at Sun Valley, Idaho. He later travelled to San Diego, California where he married and embarked on a teaching career in foreign languages and world history. He eventually became a full professor at Colorado State University and retired, retaining emeritus status, in 1997.

His own climbing history spans the late 1940s to 2014. He made over 100 documented first ascents in South America, and named many mountains both in South America and the US. For decades, while living in the US, he journeyed to South America approximately 60 times to climb and gather research for his hundreds of articles, books and source guides that were appeared in publications around the world. His climbing was not focused on technical ascents but rather on peaks that had not previously been climbed, on gathering information and researching Andean legends and folklore for his written projects on the history of South American *andinismo*.

These climbs and research culminated in his 2019 magnum opus, *The Andes: The Complete History of Mountaineering in High South America* [Editor's note: see Reviews in this edition of the *Alpine Journal*]. The climbing history of these mountain ranges began in the late Stone Age and has covered a span of more than 15,000 years. *The Andes* is a climbing history that spans this timeframe, documenting the ascents of thousands of adventurous souls of all epochs: from unknown cavemen, hunters, Indians, grave-diggers and miners to explorers, scientists, surveyors, artists and, of course, modern climbers. This magisterial book is the outcome of over 30 years of tireless research into the history of the Andean mountains.

As Evelio explained, many of us do not fully appreciate the scale of the Andes, the longest mountain range in the world. With its highest summit just under 7,000m, the range is over 6,000km long: the distance from London to India. Many mountaineers dream of climbing above 6,000m in their lifetimes, but Chilean and Bolivian miners have permanently inhabited a station at that height on the Uturunco and Aucanquilcha mountains. The highest roads in Europe and North America are lower than the highways that lead to La Paz (3622m), the capital of Bolivia. A Peruvian railway tunnel in Galeras crosses the Andes at 4,816m, nine metres higher than Mont Blanc in Europe. A non-asphalted highway, also in Peru, not far from the tunnel in Galeras, reaches 5,056m. But unusual Andean traits do not end there. The island of Tierra del Fuego in southernmost Chile carries more ice than all the Alps of Europe.

Evelio Echevarría was a man of incredible generosity, modesty and integrity. He was able to recall the heights in feet and metres of any high mountain in South America and the US and was an insatiable scholar of world history. His upcoming book (tentatively scheduled for 2021 release) on 'summit archaeology' (a term he coined himself) researches and describes the epic story of prehistoric ascents in the world's highest mountains. It will be published by Reidhead & Co.

One of the greatest South American mountain scholars and a major contributor to the records of the Club has passed.

Feilpe Echevarría

Prince Philip, Duke of Edinburgh
1921 - 2021

Prince Philip, Duke of Edinburgh.

His Royal Highness Prince Philip, the Duke of Edinburgh, died, aged 99, at Windsor Castle on 9 April 2021. He had been an honorary member of the Alpine Club since 1955. Probably his best-known contributions to outdoor adventure were the founding the Duke of Edinburgh's Award and being the inaugural president of the World Wildlife Fund (WWF). His passing was marked by voluminous media covering, often verging on the mawkish. It is not the intention of these notes to add to this, but merely to record his contribution to mountaineering in its widest sense.

In 1933, aged 12, relatives sent the Prince to the Schule Schloss for boys in Germany, where he met the man who had a seminal influence on his life: the headmaster, Kurt Hahn. This school was a testing ground for Hahn, who would later found the Outward Bound School in Aberdovey, Wales, and later the worldwide Outward Bound Trust.

Hahn believed that the 'awkward' teenage years could be eased by fostering physical fitness, initiative, imagination, craftsmanship, self-discipline and compassion. When Hahn, a German Jew, fled to Britain later in 1933, he founded Gordonstoun school in a stately home in Morayshire, and ran it in a similar fashion to the Schule Schloss. There was an emphasis on learning mountain and sea rescue, activities which Hahn believed encouraged teamwork and compassion. Philip became one of the first pupils at Gordonstoun. 'You were meant to suffer,' he (half) joked, later. 'It's good for the soul.'

In 1956, helped by Kahn and John Hunt, Prince Philip founded the Duke of Edinburgh's Award, a set of challenges initially for boys, extended to girls in 1958. Participants gain bronze, silver and gold awards by volunteering for community service, learning physical skills and going on an expedition, such as a mountain trek or a sailing trip. Over 2.5 million awards have now been awarded to people in more than 140 countries and territories. The Duke saw the awards as a sort of self-help scheme for growing up.

Sixty years ago, in 1961, the WWF was founded, and the Duke of Edinburgh was asked to be its voice as its first president. He held the position of president until the day he died, latterly as president emeritus.

The Duke was patron of the 1953 Everest Expedition, the 1955 Kangchenjunga Expedition and many others. In his foreword to Charles Evans' *The Untrodden Peak* (1956), the Duke wrote:

> *It was from start to finish a great adventure by a band of enthusiasts. With the support of their hard and skilful Sherpa companions, they tackled and overcame one of the most difficult problems in the Himalayas and, quite evidently, enjoyed almost every minute of it.*

On the return of the 1953 Everest Expedition a surge of public interest saw the publication of John Hunt's account *The Ascent of Everest*, a national lecture series, and film *The Conquest of Everest* gained significant acclaim and raise £100,000 in capital. From this, on the 3 February 1955, Sir John Hunt announced the establishment of the Mount Everest Foundation (MEF), its aim to encourage the 'exploration of the mountain regions of the Earth'. The Duke became a patron and trustee from the launch. Details of the origins of Outward Bound, the DoE Scheme and the MEF are discussed in Hunt's *Life is Meeting*, 1978, Hodder and Stoughton, and *The First Fifty Years of the BMC* (1997).

Many great events of the club have been celebrated honoured by a royal presence, starting with Everest climbed at the Royal Festival Hall in November 1953 with the Queen and the Duke. The Duke attended the 1955 Winter Dinner, celebrating Kangchenjunga at which he accepted the offer of honorary membership and, with the Queen, on 29 May 2013, at the Royal Geographical Society, 60 years to the day of the 1953 Everest ascent. The centenary of the formation of the Club was marked on 9 December 1957. His message to the assembled guests of the 150th anniversary dinner at

Lincoln's Inn is reproduced in the report in the *AJ* 2008, p158.

At a meeting with dentists, way back in 1960, he said he was well versed in 'dontopedalogy, the science of opening your mouth and putting your foot in it, a science which I have practiced for a good many years,' and he continued to practice, often amusingly and, I think for many of us, making us realise that behind the official presence was a real, warm, intelligent and often well-informed person.

The country has been fortunate that the Queen has had a steadfast partner throughout her long reign and through many family sadnesses, even tragedies. Many organisations have benefitted from the Duke's support and sense of duty, perhaps none more than the great outdoors, through his support of his awards scheme, the MEF, Outward Bound and the WWF. Our Club has been enriched and honoured by his membership.

Roderick A Smith

David Fisher
1927 - 2020

David Fisher.

David Robin Fisher died on 1 July 2020 in Vancouver, Canada, at the age of 92. He began his climbing career as a prominent member of the post-Second World War generation of British climbers then immigrated to Canada where he became a highly influential figure in the Alpine Club of Canada (ACC). Henry Hall, proposing David for membership of the American Alpine Club, described him as a 'died-in-the-wool mountaineer' but David's legacy is nonetheless as much about his behind-the-scenes work on behalf of the climbing world as it is about his own climbing exploits.

David was born in London in 1927. An energetic and adventurous child, he seemed destined for a life in the mountains. In the decade following the War he climbed continuously in Wales, the Lake District, and Scotland, including winter climbs on Ben Nevis and in the Cairngorms. In this period David completed his military service (1946-8), which was spent mainly in Germany in the Army of Occupation. In spare time he also took gliding lessons from ex-Luftwaffe pilots, paying with cigarettes. He started climbing

Marnie Gilmour, centre, and her future husband David Fisher.

in the Swiss Alps in 1947, his first outing being up the Matterhorn with the guide Emile Perron. He also joined trips to Tasch in 1947 and Kleine Scheidegg in 1948 that the AC sponsored as a way to encourage a British climbing renaissance, many climbers having been killed during the war.

After his military service, David attended Magdalene College, Cambridge, where he was an active member of the Cambridge University Mountaineering Club (CUMC). David was one of the first undergraduates – along with Cambridge's Roger Chorley and Chris Simpson – to join the Alpine Club, in 1951. Summers were spent on classic routes in the French Alps, often in the company of George Band, Roger Chorley, Ted Wrangham, Geoffrey Sutton, and Ian McNaught-Davis. These included the south-west ridge of the Aiguille du Fou, the Aiguille de Roc and Roc-Grépon traverse, the *Ryan-Lochmatter* on the Aiguille du Plan, the complete traverse of the Aiguilles du Diable, the first British ascent, with John Streetly, of the east ridge of the Dent Du Crocodile in 1952), and the traverse of the Meije. On a more whimsical note, in 1953 David was on the first party to summit the Three Peaks within 24 hours, climbing Ben Nevis, Scafell Pike, and Snowdon, with Ted Wrangham's Jaguar helping speed things along between peaks, the same Jaguar in which David was Ted's co-driver in the 1954 Monte Carlo rally.

David liked speed. John Brownsort recalled travelling to north Wales with him on David's motorbike. 'He was very safe but I on the pillion was terrified. I remember powering through Oxfordshire villages at dead of night hanging on like grim death.' Ian McNaught-Davis told an amusing story from those days rock climbing in Wales: 'Dave really saved my life when I fell off Clogwyn D'ur Arddu. I fell through the air the full length of the rope, which was about 120 feet long. I remember hearing someone screaming as I fell at ever increasing speed. I automatically thought that Dave had lost his nerve but it turned out he hadn't and it was me making all the noise. Anyway, we both got away with it.'

The major expedition of David's Cambridge years was to Rakaposhi (7788m) in the Karakoram of Pakistan in 1954, an expedition awarded the Mount Everest Foundation's first ever grant of £1,000. The other members of this CUMC party were George Band, Roger Chorley, Ted Wrangham, George Fraser and the leader Alfred Tissières. This was in effect two expeditions, if you include the 44-day drive from London to Rawalpindi, with many curious places and people navigated along the way. As recounted in Band's book *Road to Rakaposhi,* the Cambridge climbers survived a cornice breaking and managed to open up the route that would ultimately lead to the summit but were themselves denied the first ascent due to bad weather, having to descend in a snowstorm. Mike Banks and Tom Patey made the summit in 1958.

In 1955 David left Britain to see the world. His last contribution was to organise the packing for that year's Kangchenjunga expedition, when George Band and Joe Brown made the first ascent. In gratitude for his work, David was presented with a mounted piece of rock from the summit. This was to be emblematic of David's climbing life: not always making the summit himself but being rewarded for his invaluable support to those who did.

After crossing the Atlantic on the Queen Mary, David headed to Alaska to join an expedition led by Brad Washburn, thanks to an introduction from Charles Evans. The goal was to complete the survey network for a large-scale map of the Denali region. This trip included a first ascent by David and Brad of Mount Dickey (2909m), a mountain that has one of the tallest rock walls in the world at about a mile high. David and Brad stayed in touch for decades and a series of Washburn's famed black and white photographs of Alaskan mountains always found a place on the wall as David travelled from home to home.

David landed next in Toronto, Canada, where he began his civil engineering career with Proctor and Redfern and in 1956 became a founding member of the reformed Toronto section of the ACC, which had been dormant for over 20 years. He met his future wife Marnie Gilmour at a climbing social event. Marnie knew that David had fallen for her when he volunteered to carry her pack to a high camp when they were together at the ACC's 1956 mountaineering camp. They were married in June of 1957.

In the fall of 1956 David led the first climbs, with Marnie and another climbing couple, on a major rock face in what became Bon Echo Provincial

All the talents. The 1954 Rakaposhi team, photographed at base camp in the Kerengi valley. From left to right: George Band (1929-2011), first ascent of Kangchenjunga and president of the Alpine Club; George Fraser, Winchester and King's College, Cambridge, who drove back from Rakaposhi with Band, and disappeared near the summit of Ama Dablam in 1959; David Fisher; Gen Mian Hayaud Din (1910-1965), chief of staff of the Pakistani army who perished when the inaugural PIA flight to London crashed on landing at Cairo airport; Ted Wrangham (1928-2009), landowner, local politician and netsuke collector; Roger Chorley (1930-2016), Gonville & Caius, Cambridge, accountant, public servant and president of the Alpine Club; Alfred Tissières (1917-2003), the distinguished molecular biologist who worked with James Watson at Harvard.

Park. As chair of the Toronto section (1960-3), David was closely involved in leasing the land and building the cabin that created the base for what remains a prized North American climbers' cliff: Mazinaw Rock. For a celebration of his 80th birthday, one of his climbing friends from the Bon Echo days, Jim White, praised David as a tireless servant of the ACC from the largest to the smallest of scales: 'the table that Dave designed and built for the cabin at Bon Echo has been in service for 44 years and is as sturdy now as it was when it was first put together.'

Beyond rock climbing in Ontario and the Shawangunks, David attended every ACC general mountaineering camp in western Canada between 1956 and 1972 bar three that coincided with his wedding to Marnie, the birth of their first child and the death of Marnie's father. In this period he also had two seasons (1961-2) in the Cariboo mountains of British Columbia that included five first ascents.

After 1972, the focus shifted away from ACC camps to adventures with Marnie and their three children, including a 1973 season in the Rockies that involved hikes and climbs from stays at several ACC huts; regular trips to the Montreal Section's Keene Farm hut in the Adirondack mountains; a 1976 season in the Yukon that also involved an elaborate float plane expedition into a remote mountain range in the Northwest Territories and a trip to Europe in 1977 which introduced the children to the French and Swiss Alps. When the children were older, David returned to some outings of his own, including a 1978 climbing trip to the Peruvian Andes and a 1984 ACC trip to hike over the Chilkoot pass from Alaska into the Yukon and paddle down the Yukon river.

In 1964 David began an intense eight-year period on the ACC board, culminating in being president from 1970-2. He played an instrumental role in modernising the club, with a new constitution and by-laws. During his time as president he oversaw the relocation of the ACC clubhouse from Banff to Canmore, Alberta. In a letter from Marnie to David's parents penned after the end of his presidency, she wrote: 'He is still very involved with the building of the clubhouse and keeps getting calls from Banff and Calgary about various problems that arise. He is really the only one who has all the details involved at his fingertips.' Mastery of detail was David's strength.

A major highlight of David's life was his coordination of the ACC's 1967 Yukon Alpine Centennial Expedition (YACE), which demanded everything of his extraordinary skills as a planner, organiser, and mountaineer. Perhaps the largest single expedition ever undertaken in the history of mountaineering, it involved 250 climbers and 26 first ascents in dramatic and remote regions of the St Elias range in Yukon Territory. It consisted of three phases. First was the first ascent of Good Neighbour Peak (4791m) on the Yukon-Alaska border, by a combined Canadian-American team in celebration of the joint centenaries of Canada's confederation and the US purchase of Alaska. The second phase targeted 13 unclimbed mountains in what was dubbed the Centennial Range, the highest mountain named Centennial Peak (3755m) and the remaining ones named for each of the 10 provinces and two territories that existed in 1967, attempts on all of which were made from three separate glacier camps. The third phase was a mountaineering camp located beside the surging Steele glacier. Lord John Hunt, leader of the 1953 first ascent of Mount Everest, was present for a fortnight at the Steele glacier camp. The expedition is memorialized in the book *Expedition Yukon,* edited by Marnie.

David maintained lifetime memberships of the AC and the ACC, was an early member of the Alpine Climbing Group, and had lengthy memberships in the Climbers' Club (1951-2006) and the American Alpine Club (1956-1983). In recognition of his many contributions to the ACC, David was awarded the Silver Rope for Leadership in 1958, the Distinguished Service Award in 1970, and the A O Wheeler Legacy Award in 1993, among other recognitions of his service.

In 1989, David retired and moved with Marnie to Canada's west coast so they could live in a maritime climate and be closer to long-time climbing friends. They had a variety of adventures in their senior years, as well as annual trips to the family cottage in north Wales, where they and friends continued to get out for hikes and scrambles on the peaks. David also never lost contact with his British climbing associates, enjoying visits and climbs with them in Canada, as well as meeting up regularly in the UK. Reunions he attended included a gathering for the 50th anniversary of the Rakaposhi climb and the dinner for the 150th anniversary of the AC. David was a great friend to climbers everywhere.

Andy & Lynne Fisher

Gerald Franklin
1928 - 2021

Gerald Franklin.

Gerald Franklin had a modest record as a hill walker but was a tenacious historian of the Tuckett family of Frenchay, Bristol. His connection with mountaineering was evidenced by his interest in Frank Tuckett, one of the great figures of the Golden Age, a pioneer mountain scientist and vice president of the Alpine Club 1866-8.

Gerald was born into an army family in Richmond, Yorkshire on 10 June 1928 and had an itinerant life following his father's postings. He was never settled for long during his schooling, eventually himself joining the army in the immediate post-war period. He spent most of his service in the Far East.

His working life was spent in the gas industry as an area manager in the south-west. His interest in mountaineering involved many summers travelling hut-to-hut over passes and easy peaks in Austria. Later he, and his wife Jill were awarded length of membership medals of the UK section of the Austrian Alpine Club.

Gerald married Jill in 1969 and they shared a long and happy marriage. For 15 years they spent several months in New Zealand each year, where they transcribed the New Zealand journals and letters of Frederick Tuckett (1807-76) held by the University of Otago, Dunedin. These he turned into a book, which has been of great benefit to researchers. Frederick led an extremely active and interesting life as a surveyor, in the course of which he participated in the early development of Dunedin.

The rather complex interrelations of several Quaker families – the Tucketts, the Fox family of Wellington and the Howards of Tottenham – are laid out in a family tree by Rosemary Greenwood great-grandaughter of Francis Tuckett in *A Mountaineering Heritage*, (*AJ* 1994, pp169-81). Geoffrey Howard, nephew of Frank, provided an account of his memories of being part of this remarkable family in 'A Mountaineering Family' (*AJ* 1945, pp134-44).

In 2013, the local museum at Frenchay organised events to mark the centenary of Frank Tuckett's death. The Alpine Club offered to help with material from the Club's collection and a team led by Hywel Lloyd helped by Gerald put on a highly successful exhibition. This event led to Gerald becoming an associate member of the Club in 2013, of which he was extremely proud.

Gerald's output was huge and detailed, covering mostly the Tuckett and Fox families. He began transcribing all the original material he could find. His dedication and hard work led to the production of booklet after booklet, on subjects as diverse as the Tuckett girls' holiday in Falmouth, Frederick Tuckett's travels in Europe and New Zealand in the 19th century and, of course, the family's many Alpine journeys. Much of his work can be found on the Internet: the Frenchay Museum and the Frenchay Tuckett Society have details. Gerald's contributions to both organisations will be missed but gratefully remembered.

Alan Freke & Roderick A Smith

Egil Fredriksen
1942 - 2020

Egil Fredriksen.

Egil Fredriksen was born in 1942 in Oslo. Although he was a born artist, the door to the Norwegian Academy of the Arts was narrow and Egil did not have the patience to wait. Instead, he became a skilled engineer and led a number of major projects, both in Norway and abroad. Together with Kari, he built a home in Røa and had three children, Kristin, Cecilie and Eivind. But life and love are unpredictable. On assignment in St Petersburg, an older Egil fell helplessly in love with Nadja. She returned with him to Norway and became a support and joy to him into old age.

As a young man, Egil was an active diver. Later, he converted to rock climbing and quickly became a safe and good athlete in another dangerous sport. His efforts and commitment to climbing peaks led him to leadership in Kolsås Climbing Club and later in the Norwegian Alpine Club. In the latter he was chairman of the board for 14 years and did a great job for the club. For this he was proposed as an honorary member but his election was not yet confirmed before his death.

In recent years, Egil had been active in an anarchist group of retired mountain people who humorously call themselves the Norwegian Geriatric Climbing Company. In that context we were able to enjoy his warmth and friendship. Egil never bragged about his own achievements but was exceptionally generous in giving recognition to the rest of us. He regularly brought something good to the joint coffee gathering, and he surprised most of us with an oil-painted portrait. The cancer to which he succumbed was discovered too late for him to be cured. He died on 9 August, aged 78. Many of us miss his warmth and his never-failing attention and concern for those who were fortunate enough to be close to him. His happy laughter resonated at the climbing wall. When we close our eyes, we can still hear it.

Ralph Høibakk

Alan Harris
1920 - 2020

My father, Alan Harris, fell in love with mountains in his teens, when he went walking on his own in Norway during May 1939. My early exposure to this passion was a trip when I was five or six up a cold foggy Italian mountain, when we were living in Rome – possibly in the massif Gran Sasso d'Italia. In a local paper interview in 1988 he said he'd been climbing mountains for 50 years: 'It's just a hobby. I'm not one of those who hangs on by his eyelids.' Quite an understatement – the paper did describe him as a mountaineering enthusiast.

Alan Harris.

Alan was born on 14 December 1920 and died on 17 July 2020, aged 99. From October 1946 until he retired in 1980 Alan worked for British European Airways (BEA), later British Airways (BA), working his way up from management trainee to senior manager. He ended up in the airline business as a result of his wartime service in the RAF. Having trained as a navigator in South Africa, he was preparing to fly bombers over Germany when, by chance, he was seconded to civilian flying with BOAC. He started active duty in January 1944, navigating flying boats out of Poole harbour to Gibraltar, Cairo and the Persian Gulf, then, from 1945, as the war progressed, further east to India. That change probably saved his life and led to him having a fatalistic streak.

Alan's passion for mountains continued throughout his life, especially when he had more time, both before and after retirement from BA. As a member of the BA walking group he went up Mount Kenya, to the Dolomites, the Pyrenees and all over the British Isles. David Barnard, a fellow BA walker, wrote after Alan died: 'His energy, sprightliness, sense of humour and remarkable resourcefulness in every situation saved the day on many of the excursions.' Another BA walker, Andrew Heighton, recalled: 'one particularly memorable occasion was in the Italian Dolomites when our descent was foiled by the steeply rounded nose of a melting glacier – and we had only ice axes, no crampons. To continue was infeasible – would have been a very long and extremely fast and uncontrolled slide which would certainly cause injury. After the usual discussion about options, Alan set off traversing between crevasses – quite scary. We followed till we reached shade and safe snow, even as the light started to fade.'

Alan walked in the Himalaya, New Zealand, California and elsewhere but his spiritual home was Monte Rosa in the Italian Alps. He and my mother Alison first went mountain walking there in 1973. They had decided to walk round Monte Rosa, influenced by Freya Stark's *Traveller's Prelude: An Autobiography* (J Murray, 1950), which talks about her time there, and by Robinson, who knew the area. They made two trips that year. On the first, Alan said, 'we were absolute greenhorns in the Alps'; by the end of the second, 'we had almost become mountaineers.' This was the start of many Alpine walking trips, from the Alpi Maritime to Triglav in Slovenia.

Alan visited Monte Rosa over a dozen times, the last three with my wife Margaret and me. After our first visit together in 2010, he said, 'Life began again in 1973, with Monte Rosa!' In 2012, at 91, Alan led a group of family and friends to the Rifugio Zamboni-Zappa (2066m) for lunch, across a glacier and its moraines and steep paths. On our last visit, in 2014, Alan was no longer able to do that part of the walk or manage the chairlifts but was still intoxicated by the mountains.

Alan was a member of the Italian Alpine Club (CAI) from 1974. This proved to be of enormous benefit in 1989 when he and a friend were stranded overnight near Monte Rosa, and helicoptered to safety the following morning – at no charge. Alan's account (*AJ* 1991, pp126-8) appeared as 'A Night in a Hole in the Ground'. Another walk in Italy in 1990 was recounted in 'Days in the Alpi Apuane', (*AJ* 1992, pp125-31).

He was elected a full member of the Alpine Club in 1987. That trip to Norway in 1939 was the first expedition on his list supporting the application for membership. His proposer was a family friend, W L 'Robin' Robinson, for whom Alan wrote an obituary (*AJ* 1993, pp337-8). Between 1973 and 1985 Robinson accompanied my parents on nine mountain holidays in the Alps.

Alan loved walking, not only in the mountains. He completed the whole of the South West Coast Path in his seventies and eighties and the West Somerset Coast Path at 90. He was active in the Dorset Ramblers, surveying footpaths and rights of way. He was also a zealous theatregoer, music-lover and bookworm, gaining an Open University degree after retirement. He was politically active – a lifelong socialist, trade unionist, campaigner against nuclear weapons, for the natural environment, better state education, and for much more.

Alan lived a long and full life. Mountains were his inspiration but he inspired so many people with his enthusiasm, positivity, and sense of humour.

John Harris

Hamish MacInnes
1930 - 2020

The Old Fox of Glen Coe has gone to earth. He was 90 and had been ill so his death was hardly unexpected, though still not easy to accept, for Hamish was an institution. To both mountain-goers and the media, he was indeed The MacInnes of Glen Coe. As one senior Alpine Club member put it: 'It seems that the very cornerstones of British post-war climbing have vanished into history.'

Tall and lean with a gravelly voice and a sharp sense of humour, Hamish was a singular man, a bit of a rebel perhaps, at times even a tearaway who scorned red tape and its purveyors but knew how to enjoy himself. He was also a polymath: an inventor, a brilliant innovative engineer, an explorer, a photographer, a filmmaker, a teacher, an author, a novelist (of whodunnits with a Highlands flavour), and a well-read intellectual who collected classical music and sang Irish rebel songs. Oh, and a powerful mountaineer of world renown.

Our friendship dated to 1959; he'd come south to lecture driving his souped-up Traveller – the fastest Morris Minor in Britain he claimed – and we hit it off when he discovered I was a photography student who drove a 1937 Aero Morgan. We had a meal together and planned a trip to Peru and while it never happened we became friends and thereafter a trip to the Highlands was rarely complete without a visit to Hamish. He dabbled in performance cars, which he was able to repair and tune himself, and he eventually graduated to E-Type Jaguars, of which at one time he owned several. He drove fast on empty Highland roads and, always a practical fellow, once told me with a chuckle that his deep freeze was always well stocked with road-kill venison.

Hamish was an ideas man with a roving mind and free with his advice. After his head injury on the Dru in 1958, and only too aware of the discomfort of the miner's helmet then available, he prescribed a specific make of stout gamekeeper's flat hat, its crown padded with a thick layer of a special industrial wadding. He even told me where to obtain the stuff. Its efficacy was confirmed when in 1960 Smythe and I survived a serious stone-fall barrage on the Charmoz. Years later when I complained that the then state-of-the-art pile jackets were never long enough, he pointed me at a little old lady in Peterhead who made them to measure for fishermen at half the price; mine did me proud to over 7,000m and it's still going strong. For many years Hamish and his wife lived in Allt-na-reigh, a single-story cottage and barn, once the local roadman's abode, on the roadside halfway down the Glen. A small wind turbine stood behind the building while a clever hydroelectric system harnessed the burn in the steep gully behind where also stood, hidden from prying eyes, the bothy of the Rannoch Club.

Hamish was born in Gatehouse of Fleet, Kirkcudbrightshire but a Highlander by descent and proudly British. His father was a veteran of the First World War and the Shanghai Police. By the end of Second World War the

An eye for design. Hamish MacInnes in the workshop where he revolutionised ice climbing and perfected the MacInnes Stretcher. The calendar reads: 'It could only be a MacInnes axe.' *(John Cleare)*

family were living in Greenock. As a teenager Hamish displayed a precocious mechanical bent and actually built a legally roadworthy car. He also persuaded a friendly neighbour, an experienced climber, to take him to the mountains on his motorbike and teach him enough of the basic techniques to enable him to climb the Matterhorn aged 16. Later, using his own bicycle, he roamed the Arrochar Alps and fell in with the hard men of the Creag Dhu with whom he climbed serious routes on the Cobbler and elsewhere, and although never a formal member of the club, for many years was often associated with its doings.

When the army fortuitously posted him to Erwald in Austria during his national service, he found himself billeted in the home of an elderly guide. These were happy days and he would slope off climbing at every opportunity, sometimes with a group of Munich climbers (among them a couple of young SS veterans), with whom he climbed several routes in the Dolomites. Thus it was that he first encountered pitons, and with his engineer's mind eagerly embraced the techniques of aid climbing, useful experience as it turned out, although back in Scotland he was for many years to endure the rather scathing sobriquet 'MacPiton'.

Returning from one climbing trip with badly frostbitten fingers, a serious military offence, he steadfastly refused the army's then standard cure – the knife – thus compounding the felony, but by the time a court martial had been organised the fingers had healed, as he knew they would. The MO was not amused. Hamish retained his streak of stoicism and disdain for authority throughout his life.

Another incident from this period pointed to his future. Hit by rock fall high on the Zugspitze, one of his two German companions, a woman, suffered a traumatic head injury. Slinging her on his back, Hamish abseiled to safer ground below the tourist cable car, which the conductor, having seen the accident, had halted. Then, still carrying the casualty, he climbed the tall support pylon to reach the gondola where a neurosurgeon happened to be among the passengers. The woman survived. Years later he wrote:

> *On an exacting rescue one lives at a higher pitch than usual when risks must be taken that would not normally be contemplated. Only too often it is a fight for life: there is nothing more satisfying than the successful evacuation of a critically injured person on a highly technical rescue …*

Back in Scotland MacInnes was soon noticed as a bold, even cunning performer on both rock and ice and he started to amass a prodigious number of first ascents throughout the Highlands and Islands, continuing to do so for almost 40 years. Notable in 1953 were first winter ascents of formidable *Crowberry Ridge Direct* and *Raven's Gully* on the Buachaille, surmounting the crux of each bootless in stockinged feet and belayed by the then aspirant Chris Bonington. *Raven's Gully* was then the hardest winter route in Scotland. In 1957 he made his seventh and finally successful attempt on the fearsome *Zero Gully,* the first grade V on the Ben, partnered by Tom Patey wearing 10-point crampons and Graeme Nicol in nailed boots. Hamish was using his Austrian 12-point crampons. By now he was armed with the famous 'Message', an all-steel hammer-pick made for him by a friendly welder. The tool was inspired by his recovery of three climbers killed on an early *Zero Gully* attempt when their wooden axe-shaft belays snapped.

For many years the first winter traverse of the Cuillin Ridge had tantalised ambitious Scottish climbers, a commitment involving some 3,000m of ascent over eight miles and demanding rare weather conditions. Over the years Hamish had made several fruitless attempts but in 1965 he struck lucky and with Tom Patey, Davie Crabb and Brian Robertson completed the expedition in two hard days. Patey described it as 'the greatest single adventure in British mountaineering'.

Hamish had been instructing for the Mountaineering Association for a couple of years when he moved into Allt-na-reigh in 1959 with his new bride, Catherine, a climber and GP to whom he remained married for 11 years. From there the highly successful Glen Coe School of Mountaineering was born in partnership with Ian Clough, also a Glen Coe resident, providing in due course useful employment to some of the best climbers in Scotland, men like Dougal Haston, Rusty Baillie and Allen Fyffe.

Meanwhile Hamish did not neglect larger mountains. Soon after the *Raven's Gully* ascent he bought a £10 immigrant's passage to New Zealand where he met up with Johnny Cunningham, a Creag Dhu chum, and set off for Nepal where, visa-less, permit-less and on a shoestring budget, they planned to attempt Everest using supplies abandoned the previous autumn by the Swiss. Reaching base camp in July 1953 they found their efforts pre-empted by Messrs Hillary and Tenzing, but they did reach 6,700m on still-virgin Pumori close by.

He was back in New Zealand in 1956 where his exploits, including his first ascent of Mount Cook's Bowie ridge are still remembered, before setting off for the Karakoram to join Mike Banks' team attempting Rakaposhi (7788m). The following season he attempted the Eigerwand with Bonington before setting off to hunt yeti in Lahaul. Back in the Alps, the first British ascent of the *Bonatti Pillar* on the Dru in 1958 proved an epic. Climbing with Whillans, Bonington and Paul Ross, and joined by two Austrians, Hamish's skull was fractured by a falling rock. Fighting continuously to remain conscious, Hamish endured four bivouacs and a storm to complete the climb. Hence the flat cap. On the Grandes Jorasses in 1959, partnered by Whillans, John Streetly and Les Brown, he climbed the Walker Spur, just hours after Robin Smith and Gunn Clark had, unknown to them, made the first British ascent. These were milestones in British alpinism and Hamish was elected to the ACG in 1960 and was later the Group's president. However, when the SMC conferred honorary membership ten years later there were several objections that he was a 'professional' who used pitons and manufactured ice axes.

Another measure of the man was evidenced in 1961 during his first of his two visits (the second in 1970) to the Soviet Caucasus. Climbing with George Ritchie and two Russians and carrying food for a planned three days, he traversed Shkhelda (4318m), an expedition demanding sustained rock and ice climbing for – in the event – 13 days along an unremitting pinnacle ridge, continuously above 4,000m somewhere described as a cross between the Dolomites and the Himalaya. Always sparse, Hamish lost 20lb on the climb. While he enjoyed a good dinner, Hamish could be frugal with mountaineering rations. When in 1966 we set off together to film the Matterhorn north face, I discovered Hamish had filled any spare space in my car with packets of cornflakes. 'Unappetising maybe, but filling and lightweight,' he explained.

Ever restless, MacInnes made some two dozen expeditions over the years, typically low-key adventures, often with friends like Brown, Whillans, Chouinard and others, not always chasing summits but as likely hunting for yeti or prospecting for Inca gold. One more publicised trip in 1973 set out to climb the 550m prow of Roraima, the so-called 'Lost World' mesa astride the Guyana-Venezuela frontier where the problems, beside difficult aid climbing, involved battling the unpleasant fauna inhabiting this vertical jungle.

Hamish also returned to Everest, twice in 1972, first with Scott and Whillans as *Gastbergsteiger* on Herrligkoffer's abortive south-west face expedition, then in the post-monsoon slot with Bonington's British attempt. Three years later he was Bonington's deputy leader on the successful climb, but was avalanched and forced to descend to lower altitudes with damaged lungs.

Hamish MacInnes prospecting new ground on Buachaille Etive Mòr. *(John Cleare)*

Not merely a man of action, MacInnes was a fine photographer and cameraman, though tragically much of his early archive was destroyed in a fire at Allt-na-reigh. He made numerous films for various Scottish television channels and the BBC. Best known nationally were the live BBC broadcasts from the Matterhorn's summit, which we made in 1965 (*AJ* 2015, pp177-84), from the Old Man of Hoy in 1967 (*AJ* 2017, pp197-208) and from *Spiders Web* on Craig Gogarth in 1970, where his engineering prowess enabled us to use large colour television cameras from the most unlikely eyries.

His reputation for 'cliff-side engineering' grew, especially after 1974 when we worked together on Clint Eastwood's *Eiger Sanction*. After a climbing fatality early on in filming, Hamish flew out to take charge of safety. He forbade work on the Eiger unless the freezing level was right. The spectacular fall he devised for the naive but ever-trusting Eastwood, safely executed above the Eigerwand's 1,000m drop, appeared so frightening that none of us real climbers would have happily repeated it. Hollywood claimed it was the most difficult stunt ever filmed. Thereafter Hamish was in demand by film and television producers to arrange hazardous stunts and he was instrumental in such productions as *Highlander* with Sean Connery, *The Mission* with Robert de Niro and *Five Days One Summer* for Fred Zinnemann, and even a Monty Python film shot virtually in his Glen Coe backyard.

His lasting legacy however is his less publicised contribution to mountain safety for which the outdoor public are deeply indebted. Working in the drafty workshop at Allt-na-reigh, Hamish developed his famous Message into the world's first all-metal ice axe, which went into production in the mid 1960s and must have saved a few lives. Its successor, the Terrordactyl, with a radically inclined pick, allowed and inspired an incredible advance in winter climbing standards. On Everest in 1971 our prototype 'Terrors' were pooh-poohed by the expedition's European prima donnas. By contrast, during his 1970 Caucasus foray, Hamish's Russian hosts had been so impressed by his first ascent of Pic Shchurovsky's daunting north face, made possible only by their use, that within a year they were marketing their own copies.

More important perhaps was his founding in 1961 of the Glencoe Mountain Rescue Team, which he led for 30 years. Along with the team, he developed new methods of working with the police and RAF and navy helicopter crews, techniques now applied even in Cornwall. A helicopter pad graces the large garden at his self-built house in the lower glen. Personal experience prompted his invention and development of a revolutionary range of mountain rescue gear, notably the lightweight MacInnes Stretcher which folds so it's portable, is sturdy for cliff lowering and can trundle across bog and moorland on a single bike wheel. Used by the military, it sells widely abroad. Such developments were complemented by his definitive *International Mountain Rescue Handbook,* published in 1972 and in print ever since. With Eric Langmuir of Glenmore Lodge, Hamish set up the Scottish Avalanche Information Service in 1993.

After a fact-finding exchange with Swiss mountain rescue organisations, Hamish and Catherine founded the Search and Rescue Dog Association, which ran its first annual four-day course for dogs and their handlers in Glen Coe in the winter of 1965 and has been going strong ever since. Commissioned by a national magazine to photograph the exercise, I was concerned to find my then fiancée being buried in a bivy bag in a snow grave in a high corrie and then abandoned. But we both trusted Hamish enough to know she would eventually be located by the dogs and 'rescued', all in a good cause. I was impressed and despite much initial scepticism dogs have proved their worth many times. Today search dogs can be called on from Dartmoor to Durness. As his close friend Tom Patey wrote:

> *Deceased on the piste, or deranged on the schist,*
> *Maimed on the mountain, marooned in the mist,*
> *Dead or dismembered, the victim is found*
> *By Hamish MacInnes' Merciful Hound.*

Besides *Climb to the Lost World,* covering the Roraima expedition, and his several self-published novels, Hamish's best-known books concern mountain rescue: the *Handbook* is mentioned above, there was *Call Out,* describing adventures with the Glencoe team, *The Price of Adventure* and *The Mammoth Book of Mountain Disasters.* Not surprisingly, with his encyclopaedic knowledge of Scotland's mountains, he also tried his hand at guidebooks, his revolutionary, two-volume *Scottish Climbs* was published by Constable in 1971 and *Scottish Winter Climbs* 10 years later. Essentially pictorial, each route was described by several full-page black and white photographs – unfortunately poorly reproduced – with a few brief words of route description. They were much criticised and it took another 30 years and digital reproduction before the photo-guide format came of age.

Having given up serious climbing by his mid eighties, and settling down to a more relaxed lifestyle, an inept diagnosis of the effects of an acute urinary infection led to his enforced incarceration in a psychiatric hospital. Fifteen months later, after several escape attempts, the diagnosis was overturned and Hamish returned home embittered by a disgraceful episode, only to find his memory had vanished. To reboot his mind, as it were, he immersed himself in his extensive archives, his thousands of photographs and his hundreds of feet of film, re-reading the books he had written, in due course successfully reconstructing his past.

Indeed, much of this archival material was included in *Final Ascent*, a 90-minute pull-together of his life by BBC Scotland, a fascinating if jumbled miscellany of film rushes and photographs hung round his own commentary. Initially shown north of the border in 2019, it was screened nationwide the following year. It proved to be his obituary.

'My regret is I wasn't born in the 1880s,' he told a friend, 'when you could go and explore – that would have been a good time to live.' So it seems appropriate that Hamish's favourite poem was James Elroy Flecker's 'The Golden Road to Samarkand'.

> *We are the Pilgrims, Master; we shall go*
> *Always a little further; it may be*
> *Beyond that last blue mountain barred with snow*

John Cleare

Peter Page
1944 - 2020

No expedition of whatever discipline should ever take the field without a 'Peter Page', a member wholly devoted to the cause: selfless, resourceful, courageous, humorous, fit and strong, compatible, completely dependable and ready to get stuck in no matter what. That was Peter, a truly good expedition man. I believe there was not a vindictive or ungenerous molecule in his spare frame. He was born in Rotherham on 4 November 1944 and passed away in his beloved Exmoor on 30 April 2020.

His love for the mountains stemmed from attending an Outward Bound course at Ullswater in his teens. Later he joined the army and was commissioned into the Royal Engineers (RE). He was posted to the Junior Leaders Regiment RE in Dover and took the

Peter Page.

opportunity to take a Junior Leaders climbing course in north Wales. In due course he served as an Instructor at the Joint Services Mountain Training Centre at Tywyn, where he met his climbing partner, Harry Beaves, who was also on the staff there. By chance they met up again later on in Chamonix. Peter had driven there on holiday, in his campervan, accompanied by his wife Babs and his son Gary, aged two. Harry was in between postings.

Their first route was the Mer de Glace face of the Grépon. Having spent the night in the somewhat Spartan bivouac hut, they set off next morning in fine weather. But progress was painfully slow leading to a very cold and hungry night out on a ledge. The summit was gained mid-morning next day and a horrible descent down the notorious Nantillons glacier they finally met up with Babs and Gary mid afternoon. Their adventures were not over. Having driven through the Mont Blanc tunnel, camped in Val Veni and successfully climbed Le Trident, they missed the last cable car down from the Torino hut having failed to recall that Italy was one hour ahead of France. An epic five-hour descent followed, Gary hoisted on Peter's shoulders, Harry carrying two rucksacks, Babs following gamely, stumbling through brambles and over boulders.

In 1973 Peter was a member of the Army Mountaineering Association (AMA) Expedition to Himachal Pradesh in India. One of the team's aims was to establish the high-altitude capabilities of members for the forthcoming 1976 expedition to Everest. It was a big party, 27-strong. The Menthosa group had to cross over the Rhotang pass, which, because it was early in the season, was still snow-bound and impassable to vehicles. So, we had to cross on foot, carrying all the loads. Moreover, there were neither porters nor mules available at Khoksar on the northern side of the pass to carry all the expedition's gear and supplies the four days journey to Udaipur and thence to Menthosa. The rickety bridge over the wide river at Khoksar looked too risky for Peter, so with three others he built an aerial ropeway across the Chenab river to ferry all the loads and themselves across. Time and again my diary recorded, 'worked like a Trojan with Pete to get all the loads sorted out and weighed.' Peter was always in the thick of things, working cheerfully away and was a member of the team that made the second ascent of Menthosa (6443m) on 5 June.

Peter more than earned his place on the successful Joint AMA/Royal Nepalese Army Everest Expedition in the pre-monsoon season of 1976. Working hard and unselfishly as always, he spent most of his time on the mountain, with four others, keeping the notorious Icefall route open. This was crucial to the expedition's success. In Babs' words, 'he found the whole experience very fulfilling.' This was typical of the man: selflessly getting on with the job, at times a dangerous one, without drama or demanding attention.

After 1976 Peter enjoyed many summer holidays walking and climbing in the Alps. He and Gary climbed Mont Blanc together; with Babs they circumnavigated the Mont Blanc massif. He and Babs walked and climbed extensively in the Dolomites, in Babs' words, 'did a little via ferrata in the Dolomites north to south and hut to hut, experiencing the First World War tunnels and workings within the Dolomites.'

Peter was awarded the MBE for his work on the NATO exercise Spearpoint in 1980. After leaving the army he retired to a village near Dulverton, in Somerset, managing woodland. Back to nature and wild country, his beloved Exmoor and the Brendon Hills.

Jon Fleming

Peter Robson
1926 - 2020

Peter Robson.

Peter Robson was an academic and scholar; he leaves behind a large corpus of sophisticated analysis of economic integration, in books and research journals, including his classic work, *The Economics of International Integration,* first published in 1980 and now in its fourth edition (2002, Routledge). A world authority in his subject, he was one of the leading Africanists of his era and made important policy contributions to economic development in Uganda, where he filled several senior advisory roles for the Ugandan government, as well as in many other countries, including Papua New Guinea, where he was deputy director of their Institute of National Affairs.

Peter was born in Berkhamsted on 21 May 1926. He gained a BSc and MSc in economics from London University and an MA from Cambridge. He held academic posts from 1950 onwards, at Sheffield, Queen's, Belfast and Cambridge Universities, before a long spell at the University of Nairobi (1962-8), where his academic and administrative abilities were quickly recognised and rewarded early, with a chair in economics and the deanship of faculty. In 1968 he was appointed professor of economics at the University of St Andrews and made emeritus on his retirement.

In 1949, Peter married Mary Isobel Tye, a statistician by training, and beloved wife and mother, who died in St Andrews in 2009. They had three children: Christopher, an internationally renowned wind instrumentalist, taught at the Glasgow School of Music, played bassoon with the Scottish, Swedish and Israeli Chamber Orchestras and died tragically in a paragliding accident in 2003; Colin Michael, a translator; and Gillian, a lecturer at Melbourne Polytechnic University.

He was elected to membership of the AC in 1971 just after publishing *Mountains of Kenya* (1969, East African Publishing House), enthusiastically reviewed (*AJ* 1970, p316). The book unfolds a marvellous panorama, about 100 mountains greater than 2,100m, plus a separate account of routes on Mount Kenya.

Little is available on his mountaineering activities after the early 1970s. He was a keen sportsman, with a strong competitive streak, and kept very fit. Until late in his years he was capable of a ferocious game of squash. His loves were alpine climbing, skiing and yachting; as well as his membership of this Club, he was also a member of the Royal Highland Yacht Club.

Peter was, according to a former colleague, 'reserved with an urbane manner at work but with a lighter side in social settings, particularly when his wife Mary was present.' His research and its spinouts to consulting and policy advice were his prime concern, which inevitably took him all over the globe. He had polished manners and a patrician, yet friendly demeanour, evoking mandarin-like wisdom and deep learning. He died in Catalunya on 20 October 2020, aged 94.

Roderick A Smith & Gavin C Reid

Anne Sauvy-Wilkinson
1934 - 2020

Anne Sauvy at Zermatt.

Anne was very proud of being a member of the Alpine Club and claimed she was the first foreign woman to be elected in her own right following the rule change admitting women. She greatly admired Club traditions – its West End premises, its formal dinners with diners dressed in *le smoking* – see her affectionate portrait in her short story 'The London Dinner' – and remained attached to the values of the Club, in particular that it was the sole national institution in the world to have preserved the cultural and physical heritage of the history of alpinism in its archives, library and art collections.

Anne was born 5 March 1934, less than a month after me, only child of Alfred Sauvy, the highly distinguished economic demographer and his wife Marthe, née Lamberet. She herself had a very distinguished academic career: for many years she lectured at the École Pratique des Hautes Études, one of the major university research establishments in France. She specialised in book history, and was a mine of information on bibliography, publishing and the stationers, often obscure, frequently eccentric, of 16th and 17th century France. Her research is highly regarded: she had all the stubborn drive and determination of the true scholar, and she wrote with admirable focus and clarity. She was interested in workshop practice in her chosen period, in typography and iconography; her book *Le miroir du cœur* (1989), for instance, is a beautifully illustrated history of images of the heart, religious and lay, across four centuries.

But in spite of professional success, Anne had been bitten by mountaineering from an early age. Her *carnet de courses* starts in 1947 when she was 13, and a year later, following a CAF collective to the Couvercle, she wrote 'It's wonderful, I'm scarcely tired: *je sais que je peux faire de la montagne.*' In July 1951 she records her first route with a night at a hut and that winter, ski touring. Summer 1952 marks the first of the serious routes with the *Arête*

Short Stories about Mountains and Mountaineers by
Anne Sauvy

THE GAME OF MOUNTAIN AND CHANCE

In its review of *The Game of Mountain and Chance*, Le Figaro said how 'Anne Sauvy, unlike so many mountaineers, has a sense of humour.'

Forbes, and not long after, her first forced bivouac, on the Requin: the infamous *dortoir des Anglais!* On 3 July 1953 she did her first Aiguille Verte (the first of three ascents), two weeks later the first of two ascents by the Bionnassay north face, followed shortly after by the traverse of Mont Blanc descending by the Tacul to the Requin hut, the first of eight ascents of the mountain she so loved. There is an amusing story attached to this ascent, which I think she did with a *guide marrant,* an unqualified, illegal guide. On the train she recounted to some friends how she'd kept it secret from her parents back in Paris, but was overheard by some teacher who promptly told her mother, so she had to admit the truth when confronted back home. But her father was secretly proud of her.

Unfortunately, Anne's enthusiasm for climbing was leading to trouble: at 20 she married her first husband, a brilliant climber considerably older than she, the only person to whom Armand Charlet gave 20 out of 20 on the guides' course for ice technique, but infamous for his foul temper. This became evident on the *Couturier Couloir* when she was pregnant and she decided that climbing with him and maternity were incompatible. She did have a short spurt of doing good routes with friends while he was away on national service in Algeria in 1956; that included doing the *Voie Normale* on the Pointe Walker with a guide, but after that nothing until after her divorce.

She really started again in earnest in 1967, notably with the *Kuffner (Frontier Ridge)*, Les Écrins, and even the Dolomites, and marked the turbulent summer of 1968 with a new set of diaries, which include full accounts of her climbs. With two young daughters in her charge, however, she decided only to climb with a guide. But what guides! Claude Jaccoux, whom she had first met on the benches of the Sorbonne, Christian Mollier with whom I had served my Alpine apprenticeship along with Ron James, and who was responsible for introducing us one evening in 1970 when they were organising their programme for the Grand Paradis north face which I was planning to do it with Adrian Burgess, and later Pierre Leroux of Makalu fame who inveigled her to write his biography which she simply entitled *Guide* (1989).

Although every weekend in her student days she made the long walk in from the railway station to join her group at their Les Serrures bivy, and later bought a house near Larchant on the edge of the Forêt de Fontainebleau,

One of the illustrations from Anne Sauvy's *Carnets des dessins.*

bought a house near Larchant on the edge of the Forêt de Fontainebleau, Anne was a pretty hopeless rock climber. Inevitably she had to do some routes when the weather dictated and even ventured once to the Dolomites (1968). Likewise, while adoring ski touring (she was buried in an avalanche while crossing the Vercors a month after we got married), her technique was still pretty basic, stemming and stem christies. It was the big, long classic snow and ice routes of the time that she adored. She was *'la nana des faces nord'* as her friends described her.

One of her first entries in her new *carnet de courses* is the Brenva and her account serves well to illustrate both Anne's outlook on mountaineering and the quality and patience of her guide. Anne always believed in looking elegant when she went climbing and on arrival by cable car across the Vallée Blanche to join Claude Jaccoux, already at the Torino, her papers were checked by a group of police and customs officials (no tunnel, no EU then) who patronisingly remarked it was doubtless to do the Dent du Géant. She had the satisfaction of seeing their jaws drop when she said, no, she was going to the Fourche. And that was the moment when she recognised that her climbing was not the usual variety for a girl: *'Et j'avais pris conscience que je faisais de la montagne d'une autre façon quand même que la plupart des filles.'* Her description of the route with increasingly bad weather looming, and her fury with Claude in his drive to keep moving – she compares him to the CRS, the French national police rescue service – is honest. It was only when she saw his relief after they got off the Maudit (which she'd insisted on summiting) and Tacul that she understood the pressure he had been under. While they'd got back to Cham that afternoon, all the other guides had gone over the summit and had a harrowing time just making the Vallot: Claude was singled out for special mention at the guides festival a few days later for his handling of the situation.

That ascent marked a new period of powerful climbing and was followed by the Ciarforon – like me later she missed the Midi cable car down – the *Gervasutti* couloir (Tacul), Nadelhorn, Lenspitz, Aletschhorn and the traverse of the Weissmies. In the following three years she added *inter alia* another *Couturier* (1969), a joyful one this time (I literally followed in the party's steps the following day when doing the *Whymper*), the Matterhorn, the *Migot* (Chardonnet), the Grand Paradis north face, the Grande Casse north face right-hand route, and an exciting *Sentinelle Rouge* on the Italian side of Mont Blanc, again with Jaccoux; then the north face of the Ebnefluh linked with that of the Aletschhorn, the *Couloir Barbey* (Aiguille d'Argentière) and the *Norman-Neruda* on the Lyskamm.

I was involved in these last two. As a result of an exchange of letters concerning the Grand Paradis, I'd asked her if she could find me somewhere to work when not climbing. She did, in the Belvédère, a converted old hotel where Anne found me a room to rent just below her own flatlet in the eaves. After my partner Martin Harris (my first Alpine season with him) went home, she invited me to join her with Jaccoux for the rather obscure *Barbey*. Plans to go to the Bregaglia in early September fell through when Claude injured himself and so instead she recruited a team of four, herself with the experienced Jean-Claude Droyer and me with a 17-year-old Jean Afanassieff. Jean-Claude, after an attempt on the left, struck towards the icy rock rib which Anne hated, whilst I managed to avoid it on the right, despite Afa's protestations, until almost the final pitches. After that work called. Anne returned to Paris and me to Oxford, where she came over for a visit mid term. I proposed when picking her up at the airport and in December we married. A whirlwind romance!

Unfortunately for Anne this marked a decline in climbing opportunities, as she had several miscarriages and we lost our son just after birth, resulting in a series of gynaecological disasters. She did have various attempts at trying to restart her climbing and at least we did a 4,000er together, the Bishorn, but she overstrained her joints training. A quack in Chamonix infected her knee and she was in excruciating pain for six months. When eventually she was operated on, two attempts at a graft failed to take. It was the end of her climbing.

Yet Anne had more than one string to her bow. From a young age she was highly creative: she had a talent for humorous drawing but above all an ability and desire to write. When only 13 she started a daily diary in a tiny notebook – one page a day – that she kept religiously until her death. And I have found a countless mass of papers, all of which exhibit a talent almost Mozart-ean in the way she could set down her thoughts without correction or afterthought. In 1982, she gave free rein to this creativity, with the publication of her first collection of short stories, *Les Flammes de pierre*. *Alpine Journal* readers will recognise the reference to the arête in the Mont Blanc range: Anne had chosen, quite naturally, to focus imaginatively on mountaineering.

Her writing is lucid and compelling, often culminating in a hint of menace: in 'Le rappel', an abseil is quite literally interminable; in 'La Fourche', Faustin has sold his soul to the devil to become best climber in the world, and the devil collects his due. The collection won the prestigious *Prix de l'Alpe* and was published in English, under the same title, in 1991 (earlier, in 1983, in German as *Steinerne Flammen)* – and Anne's career as a writer was set for success in France and in the English-speaking world, and beyond. She would publish two more collections of short stories, *Le jeu de la montagne et du hasard* in 1985 – published in English as *The Game of Mountain and Chance* in 1995 – and *La ténèbre et l'azur* in 1991 (*Darkness and the*

Azure, 1999). Her focus, in all that she wrote, remained mountaineering, and perhaps above all Chamonix. Her only full-length novel, *Nadir* (1995), so far untranslated, is the story of a single Chamonix day – victories, emergencies, rescues; her *Chamonix d'un siècle à l'autre* (2001) is a *pot-pourri* of reminiscences and fantasies and dramas set in the valley and told with a delightful touch of humour; her *Secours en montagne: chronique d'un été* (1998, translated into English in 2005, as *Mountain Rescue, Chamonix-Mont Blanc: close observation of the world's busiest mountain rescue service*) chronicles a season spent, at their invitation, shadowing the Chamonix mountain-rescue service, the Peloton de Gendarmerie de Haute Montagne (PGHM). Anne's graceful command of language, allied to her intimate knowledge of the setting, mean that it is difficult to think of a more nuanced, more engaging, more harrowing account of mountaineering triumph and tragedy. The quality of her writing, and the elegance of the translations, mean that her climbing fictions are unusually authentic, fed by her own experience, and particularly readable.

John C Wilkinson, with Jane Taylor

Doug Scott
1941 - 2020

In a career spanning six decades, Douglas Keith Scott was recognised worldwide as one of the greatest mountaineers of the post-war era. The statistics speak for themselves: over forty expeditions to Central Asia, countless first ascents all round the world, the first British ascent of Everest. But what made Doug special was not the height or difficulty or number of ascents. No. For him what mattered was *how* you made those ascents.

Doug and Guy Lee in a snow cave under the south face of Koh-i-Bandaka, in 1967. *(Alpine Club Photo Library)*

Like all the best people he was a jumble of paradoxes: tough-guy rugby player fascinated by Buddhist mysticism; anarchic hippy with a deep sense of tradition; intensely ambitious one day, laid back the next. He was as egotistic as any climber, but was also demonstrably generous and compassionate, admired universally for his philanthropy. In his Himalayan heyday he resembled a beefed up version of John Lennon; in latter years, presiding over his gorgeous Cumbrian garden in moleskins and tweed jacket, he looked more like the country squire.

Born on the auspicious date of 29 May, he grew up in Nottingham, the eldest of three brothers, and started climbing at 13, inspired by seeing climbers at Black Rocks when he was out walking with the scouts. The bug took hold and he developed into a strong rock climber and alpinist. Throughout his life he would defend staunchly the British traditions of free climbing, but he was also fascinated by the aid-climbing pioneers of the eastern Alps and by Californian big-wall culture. By the early 1970s he was publishing regular articles in *Mountain* magazine, and what an inspiration they were, illustrated with his superlative photos. I remember particularly his piece 'On the Profundity Trail' describing an early, and first European, ascent of Sala-thé Wall with Peter Habeler. There was also an excellent series on the great Dolomite pioneers – research for his first book, *Big Wall Climbing* – and a wonderful story of climbing sumptuous granite on Baffin Island with Dennis Hennek, Tut Braithwaite and Paul Nunn.

For an impressionable young student, dreaming of great things, this was all inspiring stuff and I lapped it up. But it was only much later, when Ken Wilson published Doug's big autobiographical picture book *Himalayan Climber* that I realised quite how *much* he had done in those early days. As well as Yosemite and Baffin Island, there were big adventures to the Tibesti of Chad, to Turkey and to Kohe Bandaka, in the Afghan Hindu Kush. And closer to home there was his visionary ascent of the giant over-hanging Scoop of Strone Ulladale on Harris. Now of course there is a free version. Back then, filmed in grainy black and white for television, it was a visionary demonstration of aid-climbing craftsmanship, complete with copperheads and Rurps: the art of Yosemite granite transferred to Lewisian Gneiss.

All the while, Doug had been working as a schoolteacher in Notting-ham. I have no idea whether he planned all along to give up the day job and go professional, but it was Everest that made that possible. The lucky break came in the spring of 1972, with an invitation from Don Whillans and Hamish MacInnes to join them on Karl Herrligkoffer's European Ex-pedition to the south-west face. The expedition failed, but in the autumn Doug was back, this time as part of Chris Bonington's first attempt on the face, defeated by the bitter post-monsoon winds. It was two years later, in India, during the first ascent of Changabang that a message came through announcing a suddenly free slot in the Everest waiting list for the autumn of 1975. With little time to prepare another Everest blockbuster, there was talk at first of a lightweight attempt on the regular *South Col* route but Doug was instrumental in persuading Bonington they should go all out for the south-west face. *That* was the unclimbed challenge. Why repeat a well-trod-den route when you could be exploring the unknown?

The rest, as they say, is history. I can remember the palpable excitement at the end of September 1975 when news came through they had done it. It seemed inevitable that Doug should have been chosen for the first summit push with Dougal Haston. In a team of big personalities, he was the biggest personality of all. Perhaps, like Hillary, who had reached the top on Doug's 12th birthday in 1953, he wanted the summit more than the others; in Bon-ington's eyes he clearly had that extra something, that sheer bloody-minded strength, determination and ability to push the boat out.

The BBC stated in its obituary notice that Scott and Haston 'got into difficulties' in 1975. Complete piffle. Supremely confident, they made an informed decision to continue right to the summit, even though it was almost dark and the oxygen was nearly finished. On returning to the South Summit and seeing how dangerous it would be to continue down in now pitch darkness, they agreed very sensibly to bivouac right there, higher than any other human being had ever previously spent a night, and wait for the morning. It amazes me to this day that Doug was not even wearing a down jacket, yet still managed to avoid frostbite. 'The quality of survival', as he put it, was exemplary.

Success on Everest was achieved on the tip of a beautifully constructed – and by all accounts very happy – British-Nepali human pyramid. Even its architect, Chris Bonington, seemed at times slightly embarrassed by the sheer scale of the operation. Both he and Doug realised that the way forward lay in scaling things back down. For Doug, surviving a night in the open, without oxygen, at 8,750m above sea level, opened a huge door of possibility. Ever curious, he could now really find out what humans might achieve at altitude.

To my mind, his finest climb was Kangchenjunga in 1979 with Peter Boardman, Joe Tasker and, initially, Georges Bettembourg. It was only the third ascent of the mountain, and the first from the north. For Doug the historian it was a vindication of pre-war predictions that the north col might be the best way to the top of the mountain. Ropes were fixed judiciously on the lower, technical face. Up above, they cut loose and went alpine style, without oxygen. Messner and Habeler had already shown it was possible to climb to the highest altitudes without oxygen but they had done it on well-known ground with other climbers around should things go wrong. This was a big step into the unknown and Doug's photos of the summit day are some of most evocative mountain images ever made.

It would take too long to list all his other Himalayan achievements but it's worth mentioning some themes. What was impressive was the way Doug was always re-thinking expeditions. It was his idea to transfer the concept of the extended Alpine summer season to the Himalaya, with loosely connected teams roaming far and wide on multiple objectives, with the family sometimes coming along too. It was he who introduced new young talent to the Himalaya, bringing Greg Child's big-wall expertise to the beautiful Lobsang Spire and east ridge of Shivling, and Stephen Sustad's stamina to the gigantic south-east ridge of Makalu. They didn't quite pull off their intended traverse of Makalu with Jean Afanassieff but, my goodness, what a bold journey it was.

In fact, despite several attempts, Doug never did quite reach the summit of Makalu, nor Nanga Parbat, nor K2. But that wasn't the point. He didn't give a damn about summits for their own sake: unless they were attained in an interesting, challenging way, they held little appeal. Or he might just decide that the omens – or the *I Ching,* or his particular mood that day, or whatever – were not right, as happened in 1980, when he left the slightly exasperated

Boardman, Tasker and Renshaw to continue on K2 without him.

When the mood *was* right there was no stopping him. Amongst all the climbs I would most love to have done (and had the ability to do), the first ascent of The Ogre in 1977 must be the most enviable: HVS and A1 rock climbing on immaculate granite, 7,000 metres above sea level, at the heart of the world's greatest mountain range – the Karakoram. Less enviable was the epic descent with two broken legs. Another visionary climb was the 1982 first ascent of the south-west face of Shishapangma with Alex McIntyre and Roger Baxter-Jones, beautifully executed, with acclimatising first ascents of the neighbouring peaks of Nyanang Ri and Pungpa Ri, in the process scouting out a feasible descent route, before committing to Shishapangma itself, discovering the most elegant direct route to any 8,000m summit.

Several of my friends have been on expeditions with Doug and knew him better than me. I only climbed with him once, when we were both speaking at an Alpine Club symposium at Plas y Brenin. We were not on until the afternoon and it was a beautiful sunny morning – far too good to be shut indoors – so we sneaked off over the Llanberis Pass for a quick jaunt up *Cenotaph Corner*. Doug said the first time he had done it was on his honeymoon. It was now 1989, so he must have been 48. Middle aged, but definitely still in his prime. He led with powerful ease and then suggested we continue on the upper tier of the Cromlech, up that brutal creation of his old mentor Don Whillans – *Grond*. In the absence of large cams to protect the initial off-width, he grabbed a large lump of rhyolite, explaining cheerfully, 'this is how we used to do it, youth,' shoved it in the crack, hitched a sling round it and clipped in the rope. As soon as he moved up the chockstone flew out of the crack, narrowly missing my head, but Doug carried on regardless, blithely calm, assured and fluent, supremely at ease with the rock.

There were other meetings. I once had the unenviable task of having to keep Doug confined to a strict timetable dovetailing with the arrival of the Queen for an Everest anniversary. Conversation, like his lecturing – or indeed his expeditioning – could be enigmatic, discursive, elliptical, often veering off the beaten track into un-trodden side valleys, but always with an undercurrent of humour. And never pulling rank: he was a humble, approachable man, happy to talk with anyone. The meeting that made the biggest impression on me was in 1987 in the village of Nyalam in Tibet. It was the end of an expedition and we had just put a new route up Pungpa Ri, which Doug had climbed five years earlier. Also staying at the Chinese hostel were members of Doug's current team who had been attempting the north-east ridge of Everest. Doug himself turned up later, back from a gruelling road journey from Rongbuk across the border to Nepal, then up to Solu-Khumbu, then all the way back across the border to wind up the expedition in Tibet. The reason? A young Sherpa man who had been helping his expedition had been killed in an avalanche near base camp during a huge storm two weeks earlier. Doug had taken it on himself to travel all the way to the man's family in Nepal, to tell them personally what had happened and to ensure that they received financial compensation.

Sunset and evening star. Doug Scott on the summit of Everest at 6pm on 24 September 1975.

That empathy with the people of Nepal came to fruition in his remarkable charity, Community Action Nepal. There was a precedent in Ed Hillary's Himalayan Trust, but what I like about CAN is that it does not concentrate its efforts exclusively on the most popular region of Solu-Khumbu, but also has projects in other regions such as the Budhi Gandaki near Manaslu. Most impressive of all is the way Doug financed it over the last two decades. At an age when most people in his position would be happy to rest on their laurels, perhaps accepting the occasional lucrative guest appearance, Doug travelled the length and breadth of the country on gruelling lecture tours – often only just out of hospital, after yet another operation on the old Ogre

Returning to Heathrow in 1975, flanked by Haston and Tut Braithwaite, with Pertemba Sherpa and Chris Bonington.

injuries that had come back to haunt him – pouring all the proceeds into his charity. Lecture fees were topped up by sales of Nepali crafts and auctions of Doug's most classic photographs. Doug the auctioneer was a force to behold, as he mesmerised and cajoled audience members into donating ever more astronomical sums for a signed photograph.

As if running a charity were not enough, Doug also managed in recent years to complete his fine history *The Ogre* and finally to publish *Up and About*, the long-awaited autobiography for which Hodder first paid an advance in 1975. His history of Kangchenjunga has just been published. For a man who had once been a bit wary of institutions, he made an enthusiastic and much liked Alpine Club president. He also stood for election to the BMC presidency, asking the journalist Steve Goodwin to help with his manifesto. Steve phoned me in despair to say that the opening paragraph was all about Doug's compost heap. I too have a profound relationship with my compost heap, and I can see exactly where Doug was coming from. But in the shiny corporate world of modern convenience climbing this wasn't going to be a vote winner. Doug did not get the presidency: a great loss to us all, in my opinion. He was a man of principle: visionary and adventurous, but in some ways quite conservative, rooted in traditions that he valued. One of those traditions was the notion that if we climbers are going to spend our lives doing something that has no ostensible practical purpose, then it is important *how* we carry out that pursuit. And for Doug, if I have understood him correctly, paramount in that 'how' were notions of curiosity, personal responsibility, risk and a willingness to embrace – even seek out – uncertainty.

It is always inspiring to see someone happy in their work. Despite the frenetic pace he set himself and his devoted third wife Trish, Doug seemed in recent years to have achieved the kind of contentment that many people only dream of. He had a genuine sense of purpose and an assured legacy. He was a man who seemed at ease with himself. He will be missed hugely here, in Nepal and all round the world, but most of all by Trish and by the five children of his first two marriages. I feel honoured to have known him and glad that if I should ever have grandchildren I will be able to tell them, 'I climbed *Cenotaph Corner* with Doug Scott.'

Stephen Venables

Chris Bonington writes: It goes back to the late summer of 1961. Don Whillans, Ian Clough. Jan Duclosz and I had just made the first ascent of the Central Pillar of Frêney on the south side of Mont Blanc. By pure chance Doug Scott had just reached the summit from the north side. We were famished but Doug shared with us what he had and that night, when we stayed in the Vallot hut, he cooked us a meal.

In the 1960s, whilst on lecture tours, I often stayed with him at his house in Nottingham and we would go climbing around the Peak District. He was a key member of many of my most important expeditions and we have shared some of the most harrowing and tragic experiences of our lives.

The south-west face of Everest was a huge challenge. It had already defeated four strong expeditions but I believed I knew how to overcome it. It was essentially a matter of logistics, of having the right team and enough carrying power to put two people on top of the mountain in that narrow window of opportunity when the weather was right for a summit bid. That pair was Doug Scott and Dougal Haston. Our first attempt in 1972 failed. We ran out of time, were overtaken by the bitter winter winds and cold, but learnt a great deal, which we were able to put into practice when Doug and Dougal made it to the summit in the autumn of 1975.

In the meantime we had some great trips together; in 1974 making the first ascent of Changabang, one of the most beautiful peaks in the Himalaya. It was a snatched opportunity, just before our big expedition to the south-west face of Everest. I had been invited to join an Indian-British expedition to the peak and Doug, Dougal and Martin Boysen joined me. It was a wonderful fun expedition.

In 1977, The Ogre was Doug's expedition and concept. I think he invited me as thanks for his inclusion in the 1975 expedition and the opportunities it had opened up for him. The Ogre could not have been more different. There was no formal leader. Just six of us, Doug and Paul Braithwaite, Clive Rowland and Mo Antoine, Nick Estcourt and myself, as pairs climbing with each other, no high-altitude porters, no cook staff at base camp. It ended up as a major epic after our successful ascent, with Doug breaking both legs on a fall on the first abseil from the summit, having to crawl back down the mountain, roped to us because we could not have carried him. I shall never forget it. He never complained, even though it was a long and complex

Dick Renshaw, Doug Scott, Peter Boardman and Joe Tasker en route to K2 in 1980. *(Alpine Club Photo Library)*

descent. Not only that, but he took an active role in our decision making all the way down to the point where we could get a rescue helicopter in, to carry him back to the nearest town.

The following year we went to K2, to attempt an unclimbed line on its west face. It ended at an early point with the tragic death of Nick Estcourt in a huge wind slab avalanche which also very nearly claimed Doug's life.

He moved to Cumbria in in the 1970s, buying a house just above Pasture Lane a few miles from our home at Nether Row. We climbed together frequently on our local crags and I became involved with Community Action Nepal, the charity Doug founded and for which he worked tirelessly, giving hundreds of lectures a year, all the profits going to CAN. I had the title of patron and took part in as many as I could when persuasively requested by Doug.

I felt hugely privileged to be invited to witness Doug's wedding to Trish in 2007. After moving around Cumbria for some years, after their marriage they bought Stewart Hill Cottage and did what he achieved with all his houses, transforming the house and garden into an exquisite, warm and friendly home.

Paul 'Tut' Braithwaite writes: Late May 1972. A letter from Doug Scott. 'Eh up youth, do you fancy a trip to Baffin Island to do a route on Asgard with Paul Nunn and my mate Dennis Hennek? We leave in 10 days. I knew you'd be up for it so I've bought the tickets. Keep the weight down, looks like we are going to have to carry it at the other end. Oh, by the way, you owe me £750 – pay me when you can. See you at Heathrow if not before. Best, Doug Scott.' This invite from Doug was to be the first of so many over the following 50 years.

I first met Doug at the Nottingham Climbers Club (NCC) annual dinner, held at a venue near Kilnsey in 1965. It was a boozy affair that nearly ended badly in fisticuffs. Our paths crossed many times during the following year or so and we climbed the occasional route together. One that I remember in particular was an artificial route up the Central Wall of Malham Cove. The in-situ bolts and rusty old pegs were in dreadful condition and Doug being a big lad caused me some consternation on the flimsy aid. We climbed together about 20ft apart. I soon realised his capabilities as he coasted up the route carefully so as not to overload the gear. This was a skill he perfected and demonstrated on many occasions in the UK, the Dolomites and the big walls of Yosemite.

Doug was equally talented on steep ice and his beloved gritstone cracks. Back in the day, he would have been described as a good all-rounder, a coveted title at the time. Doug's skills and strength would later serve him well in high mountains around the world in places such as Nepal, Pakistan, Tibet and Alaska, where he excelled and became one of the world's leading high-altitude mountaineers. His remarkable achievements and many awards, including his most cherished, the Piolets d'Or Lifetime Achievement Award, are all well documented.

I was fortunate to accompany Doug on some these trips to the world's highest mountains plus many more to less challenging regions. These fond memories remain as vivid as if it were only yesterday. There was seldom a dull moment, whether climbing or, in more recent times, lecturing. It was always an adventure where full commitment and dedication were called for. Fun and usually a bit of mischief were always thrown in. 'Be prepared for constant change,' was Doug's mantra. For family and friends, life with Doug could be challenging, demanding and at times, difficult to comprehend. He always pushed a little bit further and demanded a little bit more.

When in the mountains, Doug was at one with himself and the surroundings. He somehow appeared to belong and was completely at home. He embraced the elements and all the discomfort and misery that went with them. Buddhism was a huge influence in Doug's life and maybe it helped him in those inhospitable situations. He also had a very unique and special way of bonding with local people, gaining their friendship and trust with ease. His approach was quite simple: he was direct, respectful and honest.

Doug was of course the founder of Community Action Nepal (CAN). He worked tirelessly over the years to improve the lives of people living in the high mountain regions of Nepal. The earthquake in 2016 had a devastating impact on these people and Doug redoubled his fundraising efforts to aid in the rebuilding of so much that had been destroyed. Schools, health posts, porter shelters and in some cases whole villages and communities were swept away. Many of them were past and current CAN projects. Doug undertook long, tiring lecture tours along with hands-on oversight of the rebuilding works in Nepal. His commitment to the project began to take its toll but his stock answer when asked how he was coping was: 'Mustn't grumble, we have lots to do.'

Doug had a passion for writing and devoted much time to cataloguing his adventures in *The Ogre, Kangchenjunga* and his autobiography *Up and About.* In later years, he developed a great love for gardening and together with his wife Trish created a wonderful and inspiring garden around their home in the Northern Fells of the Lake District. Well-tended lawns, flower and vegetables beds sported an abundance of produce. Doug was very proud of their handiwork and would insist on taking any visitor to the house on a garden tour. One generally left with a goodie bag of veg and of course the constant reminder, 'It's all organic you know. No chemicals on this land, youth.'

The garden boasted a recently installed freshwater pool filtered naturally by reed beds and plants, a croquet lawn and a boules court, among other delights. Without doubt, the highlight of any visit to Stewart Hill was sitting around the large kitchen table with family and friends enjoying one of Trish's amazing suppers plus the odd glass or two. Life has seldom been better than those days and evenings at the Scotts'.

Doug's life was truly remarkable, full to the brim with energy. He was a good and close friend. I'll miss the random phone calls, the travel and times on the crag, in the mountains and on the road raising funds for CAN. Most of all I'll miss our friendship and laughter.

Crispin Simpson
1930 - 2020

Crispin Simpson.

Crispin John Stephen Moncreiff Simpson, known variously as Crispin, Stephen or Pin, was a research chemist, first at the National Physical Laboratory, then from 1969 until his retirement in 1997 at Wadham College, Oxford. He died on 28 November 2020, aged 90.

He was elected to the Club supported by Edward Pyatt in 1968 on a strong record in the Alps. While his participation in the Club through meets or written reports was limited, he visited Noshaq, Afghanistan in 1974 with Eric Roberts. This was followed by a trip to the Nanda Devi Sanctuary in 1977, also with Eric, with three peaks over 6,100m climbed. Roberts, aged only 33, was killed in an avalanche on Annapurna in 1979, which left Stephen to seek new expedition partners. His next expedition, led by John Jackson, was with the Gorphwysfa Club, the small group based on Oxford University and north Wales, in 1981. His three subsequent trips to the Himalaya were more trekking than climbing, the last of these in 1998 when he climbed Island Peak. He also had a trip to the Tien Shan area in the late 1980s.

Stephen lived in Kingston Bagpuize, west of Oxford, and in later days suffered various accidents on hazardous cycling commuting trips. He worked in the Department of Physical Chemistry, had many international connections and a steady stream of publications in quality journals. He was made an emeritus fellow of Wadham on his retirement but seems not to have played a particularly active role in college life.

Mountaineering colleagues paint a consistent picture of a fine, if idiosyncratic, all-round performer: strong, fit, and determined to get to the next peak, and the one after that. The abiding memory is of Stephen striding into the distance, leaving lesser mortals trailing in his wake. Some, perhaps many, saw him as taciturn, a man of few words. But spending time with him revealed another side – a keen wit, a sense of fun, and an ability to produce apposite literary quotes.

His approach to the mountains was characterised by enormous vigour and determination. He took little interest in the mechanical side of the sport and had no interest in the devices that fill the rucksacks of most modern climbers to aid their safety. His energy was such that he sometimes found it difficult to accommodate the more modest pace of lesser mortals. He was, in essence, an eccentric, hair-shirt sort of fellow who would have gone down well with Tilman.

I leave the final word to the Gorphwysfa Club chair, Professor Sir Brian Smith:

He joined our expedition to the Himalayas in 1981 near the mountain of Nanda Devi. We experienced atrocious weather. Being trapped in a small tent on the edge of a glacier for many weeks exhausted Stephen's patience. One day he vanished from the campsite to the great concern of his friends. He later told us that he spent a few days living in a remote cave occupied by goats and goat herders. Nevertheless he, with John Rowlinson, made the only successful ascent of Berthartoli Himal South (6315m), the only mountain summit achieved by the expedition. Stephen's company was always stimulating. His originality offered a rewarding view not just of mountains but of life in general. We and the club will miss him greatly.

Roderick A Smith (with Joyce Simpson)

Geoffrey Templeman
1929 - 2020

Geoffrey played a vital role in the smooth running of the Alpine Club for many years. He was not in any sense a mountaineer, but he loved mountains and mountaineering literature. He was loyal, devoted to the Club, would turn his hand to whatever needed doing and was always regarded as a sound brick in its structure.

Geoffrey William Templeman was born on 28 March 1929 in West Wickham, Kent to William and Dorothy. An only child, he attended Bromley Grammar School from 1940 to 1946 and then went on to the School of Architecture, Surveying and Building where he gained a diploma in surveying. After national service from 1952-4, he became a member of the Royal Institute of Chartered Surveyors in 1957.

He worked as a surveyor for local government starting out in the local county council offices, moving to the housing department of the Greater London Council and his last position before semi-retiring was as assistant director of the Arts and Recreation Department with the GLC.

Snowdonia was his first love. As a young man he and his friends from college spent all their free time in north Wales. It was here he met his future wife, Rhiannon, but with the sudden death of his mother following on from the death of his father, their wedding was brought forward to February 1954 and they started married life in his parent's house in West Wickham. Julian was born in 1955 and Bonnie in 1958. The family spent most holidays in Wales climbing Snowdon, Cnicht, Moel Hebog, Tryfan and the Moelwyns among others, and also holidayed in Switzerland, Austria and Italy.

Even before his election to the Club, Geoff helped as editorial assistant to the *AJ*, from 1977 onwards. He took on the job of assistant editor from 1980, stepping down only in 2007. From 1978 (i.e. again before membership) until 2006 he was also the obituary editor for the *AJ*. From 1986 to 1990 he chaired the House Committee which managed the South Audley Street premises and, when the time came to move from there to Charlotte Road, he managed the sale and disposal of the very many unwanted items that had accumulated over the years, as well as physically helping with the move. At some point in the early 1980s he took on the job of assembling and writing the Club's newsletter, which he did until the early 1990s. He wrote many obituaries and book reviews when members contributions were not forthcoming. His review of Joe Simpson's *Touching the Void* (*AJ* 1988, p279) could only have been written by someone steeped in the history and literature of mountaineering.

In a letter proposing his membership of the Club, Edward Pyatt, then editor of the *Alpine Journal*, wrote:

> *While his snow and ice mountaineering record is inferior to that usually demanded of candidates, he has maintained a lifelong interest in climbing and has had extensive experience in this country and of some minor mountains*

Geoffrey Templeman with Doug Scott.

*abroad. His real claim to consideration lies in his record of service to the Club,
one which almost certainly surpasses that of any previous candidate who has
sought admission on these grounds.*

Geoffrey was elected in March 1980. In 1989 when he was 60, Geoffrey
joined several members of the Alpine Club trekking in the Annapurna foothills of Nepal, thus achieving a lifelong ambition.

My father loved animals, the outdoors, gardening, climbing and conservation of the countryside. He was a member of the National Trust and
the Snowdonia National Park Society. He was also an avid book collector,
mainly of mountaineering books, and he also enjoyed repairing old books.

Dad was a very softly spoken, gentle man, kind, thoughtful and consider-
ate to others. Always willing to help out at school fetes and the local horti-
cultural society events. He loved jazz and would often be found tapping his
feet to the likes of Jelly Roll Morton whilst reading the paper.

In short, Geoff was the sort of member that every club needs and treas-
ures. He will be sorely missed by those grateful members who remember
him.

Bonnie Penfold (with Mike Esten)

Jeremy Whitehead
1931 - 2020

John Jeremy Whitehead was born in Buxton, the second of three brothers. He was educated at St Bees in Cumbria and subsequently at Corpus College, Cambridge. He became a schoolmaster and taught physics at Monkton Combe School in Somerset. A lifelong bachelor, he retired while still relatively young and devoted much of the rest of his life to mountaineering, climbing and ski touring, home and abroad, summer and winter, just as much as finance and transport would allow. He resided for the last 30 years in Garstang, which was conveniently situated for climbing and walking in the Lake District.

He taught physics at Monkton between 1955 and 1978 and is remembered with affection by many old boys for his enthusiastic participation in sport and as an officer in the school cadet force, which he led on adventurous training trips to the mountains. He left for a year's sabbatical in 1978, which turned out to be his early retirement from teaching. His very active mountain year in the Alps, Nepal and Peru was described in his article, 'On Curves of Freedom', (*ABMSAC J* 1980, pp19-21). During the year he trekked and climbed in the Himalaya, returned to the Alps for the winter including the Haute Route with Les and Barbara Swindin and then went with Alan Rouse to Peru and the Cordillera Blanca where they climbed Nevado Huascaran (6768m).

He was a member of the Alpine Club for 51 years and was also a long-standing member of the Climbers' Club and the Fell and Rock Club; in summer he often coordinated the joint AC-CC-FRCC Alpine meets. He also belonged to the local Preston Mountaineering Club where he was chair for three years. In winter he was an active ski-touring member of the Eagle Ski Club and the Alpine Ski Club and a member of both for more than 50 years.

Jeremy was the ultimate amateur in the traditional meaning of the word. He will be remembered particularly as a ski mountaineer and he relished nothing more than leading a group of friends. His ability to read the snow in winter and his awareness of the mountaineering situation were impressive. His summer activities were no less extensive and he felt no need for excursions to be comfortable. The maxim that 'it doesn't have to be fun to be fun' applied to Jeremy who was at ease in all weathers and circumstances.

Jeremy started climbing at St Bees and was introduced to rock routes by Rusty Westmorland, his first climb being *Kern Knotts Chimney* in 1947. Always one for remembering anniversaries he repeated the climb 50 years later with the Preston MC and with equipment appropriately restricted to big boots and a hawser laid rope, although he later confessed to having a few wires hidden in his cagoule in case of need.

From 1973-83 Jeremy led ski tours for SCGB, frequently with Jim Roche and Fred Jenkins (obituary, *AJ* 1996, pp317-8) plus countless tours over decades for the Eagle Ski Club. Jeremy acquired an encyclopaedic knowledge of the French Alps in particular by simply going there and doing it.

However, despite the extent of his exploits, summer and winter, he was very reticent about publishing any account. Indeed, SCGB companions would despair at extracting from him even the shortest of written reports, which were necessary in order to obtain funding for further years. He relented somewhat in the late 1980s when he 'published' his guide to ski touring in the French Alps in two volumes, each about 2cm thick, comprising removable sheets held together by clip-fasteners as an A6 sized book. It was a milestone in being the only compendious guide to the French Alps in English, remarkable for its accuracy and honesty in that any routes that the author had not actually completed were marked as such, carrying a warning that some information came from other sources. He declined suggestions that it be published commercially and only produced copies at home in small numbers for friends. The AC Library has wisely retained a

Jeremy Whitehead.

copy of this significant work despite it being out of date. He was also a careful photographer and always ensured that he had a good photographic record of his trips to take home and ponder over until the next trip came along. Fortunately, his indexed collection of over 6,000 images has come to the AC Photo Library where it will remain as a record of his many achievements that he failed to record in writing. He did however edit a comprehensive manual for ski mountaineering, *Alpine Ski Touring and Ski Mountaineering Handbook* (West Col, 1990).

Jeremy's climbing career suffered a temporary setback in the early 1990s when he had a heart attack on his way up to an empty unguarded Alpine hut. His companion rushed back down to the valley to alert the rescue services and next morning Jeremy was helicoptered out. Just a few months later he was back on the crag and, although he carefully avoided the big hills for a further year or so, he continued climbing on low-lying British crags up to VS standard.

It was with the Eagle Ski Club that Jeremy made many of his later ski tours. After year 2000 and by then in his seventies, he still led at least two ski tours each season in the Alps with groups from the Eagle and the ASC.

Over the years he gathered a number of similarly inclined tourers of a senior age who joined him on many trips. Jeremy did the research, contacted the huts and led the tours. For special anniversaries he continued what had become a personal tradition. Having an April birthday meant he spent most Aprils skiing in the Alps. The objective was to skin up a 4,000m snow peak on the day. In 2006, his 75th, the Breithorn was chosen and duly ascended. Of course, this was routine for Jeremy who already counted 13 different 4,000m ski summits under his belt, the first having been the Gross Grünhorn in 1964 for his 33rd birthday. Come 2011 and it was time to mark his 80th. Organizing a party of nine, Jeremy first led them from the Mantova hut to the summit of Piramide Vincent (4215m) as a warm-up and two days later, for the actual birthday, ascended the Ludwigshöhe (4341m). The big day was subsequently in speeches by the Italian hut guardian and with cake carried up in the rucksack of one of the party. Another member noted that though Jeremy was by then quite slow uphill, he was still a very competent downhill skier in good and bad snow.

In 2015 Jeremy had a stroke and was hospitalised for several weeks. However, he got over this quickly and decided that in view of the stroke and age he should start looking at five-year intervals for the special birthday ascents. By then the numbers available and able to accompany him had reduced so it was a party of two that made the 2016 attempt for his 85th. The Allalinhorn was chosen, having a summit not too far from the highest lift, but strong winds and icy temperatures prevented the final part of the ascent. Undeterred, Jeremy announced that the weather was sure to be better in Zermatt and headed for the Breithorn. Sadly, conditions were much the same as in Saas Fee and that option was also abandoned.

Nor was that the end of it. He continued to make ski trips to the Alps with friends in both the ASC and the ESC on club meets and tours for the next three years. In a conversation during that period about a future trip, it was suggested that March or later would be better for seniors but was abruptly corrected by Jeremy who said that he could not wait that long and was already organising something for January. His last trip was an ESC meet in Gargellen in March 2019, shortly before his 88th birthday.

Outline plans were in place for skiing in 2020 when in August 2019 he had a serious stroke from which he did not recover, dying on 31 July 2020 in his 89th year. Jeremy undoubtedly lived a full life in the mountains and on ski tours many of which he led in his own inimitable manner. He will not be forgotten.

Simon Devivier

John Moore writes: I knew Jeremy Whitehead and encountered him sporadically in the mountains for nearly 40 years. Jeremy was an unusually private person and in all that time, although he was notoriously talkative, I never heard him speak about anything except mountaineering, ski mountaineering, rock climbing and mountains. It is difficult to write an obituary that contains insights into personality based on personal knowledge of character and opinions of such a personally reticent man. Jeremy was close to the definition of an obsessive in the most sympathetic use of the word. He was a lifelong bachelor with no obvious social interest beyond his mountaineering activities. He apparently enjoyed classical music, though he never spoke of this.

Many SCGB and Eagle Ski Club members who would not be competent to ski tour guideless, owe their experiences to Jeremy's self-styled 'amateur guide' status. He was of his time and many of the things he did in terms of leading parties of novices on serious alpine ski tours would be unwise in these bureaucratic and litigious days. Sensibly he retired from leading serious tours after miscalculations and incidents began to occur during his outings.

Jeremy continued to take part in Alpine Ski Club day touring meets in the Alps until his last meet at Reschenpass on the Austrian-Italian border in spring 2018. Even there he asserted his independence by leaving a party which had 'run out of steam' in a whiteout, to attempt the summit alone – a sign of the wilful aspect of his character. This characteristic was shown by his reputation for never staying with someone else's party but frequently 'jumping ship' to make his own way up or down. However, he was a martinet in making members of his own party follow everywhere in his footsteps.

In belated appreciation, a friend and I invited Jeremy, then in his 70s, to tie on with us for the Portjengrat traverse. He acquitted himself superbly in a rope of three that was climbing fairly quickly. Jeremy also tied on when I climbed *Central Buttress* on Scafell and *Tophet Bastion* on Gable with Peter Kaye.

Jeremy was a law unto himself in terms of his tour leading but he helped many to enjoy and engage in ski mountaineering through his personally guided tours on behalf of the Eagle Ski Club. He was a remarkable and memorable character, much talked about by his friends and acquaintances and that is a compliment in itself. Jeremy was one of those members of the mountaineering community for whom the hills are everything and who devoted himself with monkish commitment to his credo.

Alpine Club Notes

'Alphubel, Täschhorn and Fee Glacier from the alp below the Längfluh',
Hilda Hechle, watercolour, 38cm x 53cm. *(Alpine Club Collection)*

Jan Morris (1926 - 2020)

Many of my generation, but very few who are younger, will remember 2 June 1953 for watching the Coronation on an impossibly small black-and-white television screen, in a room crowded by many others. I recall little of the ceremonies; indeed was rather bored by the pomp and circumstance, but I clearly remember the excitement generated by the newspaper announcement in the morning that Everest had been climbed. That it had been climbed on 29 May and here we were reading the news in Britain was remarkable given the slow communications of the time. And for many of us, that news was the catalyst that started our own mountaineering.

We owed the breaking of this momentous news to James Morris, assigned to the expedition by *The Times*. On 30 May, after hugging Hillary and Tenzing in congratulation at 6,700m in the Western Cwm, he made a tiring descent in fading light to base camp, shepherded by Mike Westmacott. From there runners were dispatched to Namche Bazaar and the news was radioed to Kathmandu, in code.

Snow conditions bad stop advanced base abandoned yesterday stop awaiting improvement.

This, as he explained in *Coronation Everest* (1958) translated as: 'Hillary and Tenzing reached the summit, all are well.'

Jan Morris, born James on 2 October 1926, died aged 94 on 20 November 2020, the last of the western team of 1953 to pass away.[1] Before Everest his career is summarised as a chorister at Christ Church Cathedral School, Oxford, Lancing College, a soldier in the Queen's Royal Lancers, then a return to Oxford as a mature undergraduate, before starting his working life on *The Times*.

In the years that followed what was often called the scoop of the century, Morris had a remarkable life, not in mountaineering, but as a journalist and author. Working for the *Manchester Guardian*, he uncovered proof of collusion between France and Israel in the invasion of Egypt. In 1961, he reported on the trial of Adolf Eichmann, memorably echoing Hannah Arendt's phrase 'the banality of evil'.

With his hands in his lap, blinking frequently and moving his lips, Eichmann reminded me irresistibly of some elderly pinched housewife in a flowered pinafore, leaning back on her antimacassar and shifting her false teeth, as she listened to the railing gossip of a neighbour.

Perhaps the most remarkable event of her long life was the long process of transitioning from man to woman, one that began in publicly in 1964 and led to gender reassignment surgery in 1972 in Morocco, candidly

---

1. At the time of writing, Kanchha Sherpa, one of the expedition porters, is still alive. In 1952, aged 19, he ran away to Darjeeling where he worked for Tenzing Norgay's family and won himself a place on the team of porters for 1953. See kanchhafoundation.org.

Jan Morris says something funny to Charles Wylie during the Everest 40th anniversary celebrations at Pen y Gwryd. *(Ed Douglas)*

described in *Conundrum* (1974). As one of the first public figures to talk and write freely about this, and the various legal complexities she faced, Jan Morris was more than courageous.

Many will regard her *Pax Britannica* trilogy as her finest work. *Heaven's Command*, *Pax Britannica* and *Farewell the Trumpets* tell of the rise, climax and decline of the British empire.

> *Mine is an aesthetic view of Empire, and there is no denying that as the flare of the imperial idea faded, and the nation lost interest, so its beauty faded too. It had not always been a pleasant kind of beauty, but it had been full of splendour and vitality, and when the Empire lost its overweening confidence, its providential virtue, its forms became less striking and its outlines less distinct. My book* [Farewell the Trumpets, 1998], *therefore, is sad without being regretful. It was time the Empire went, but it was sad to see it go.*

There are so many other books, *Trieste and the Meaning of Nowhere* (2001), *Venice* (1960), *Hong Kong* (1988), *Oxford* (1965) are just four examples, all held in high regard. *Ariel, A Literary Life of Jan Morris*, Derek Johns (Faber & Faber, 2016) will prove a useful guide.

Her writing is so good one often re-reads a sentence several times, savouring the words like fine wine. She's not to be rushed. In interviews towards the end of her life, she repeated her desire that, above all else, kindness might characterise our interactions with others. May it be so.

Roderick A Smith

An advertisement for John Buckingham from Whymper's 1897 guidebooks.

Goodbye Arthur Beale

It supplied ice axes to Ernest Shackleton, the flagpole for Buckingham Palace and rigging for escapologists but the closure in June of Arthur Beale's on Shaftesbury Avenue, with its teal shop front and gold lettering, had a particular resonance for members of the Alpine Club. The company could stretch its origins back to the 16th century and the sign outside its premises proudly announced 'Yacht Chandler, Established Four Centuries'. The Alpine Club knew it first as Messrs Buckingham and Sons, before Arthur Beale took it over. The closure of such high-profile premises, because of Covid-19, would inevitably not go unremarked and as it happens the offices of literary journal the London Review of Books is not far, and contributing editor Jeremy Harding took the opportunity[2] to dwell on the shop's unique appeal, including the role played in its success by the birth of alpinism and the need for reliable equipment.

> Rope was central to the company's success. In the 1860s, the Alpine Club decided to investigate 'what kinds of ROPES, AXES and ALPENSTOCKS will be found most safe and useful for mountain work'. The Alpine Journal reported in 1867 that ropes were the object of 'a large number of experiments' by the club to find out whether they could withstand a weight of twelve stone dropped and checked at five feet. Most of the braided samples and 'many most carefully made twisted ropes gave way in such a manner as was very startling to some of our number, who had been in the habit of using these treacherous cords with perfect and most unfounded confidence.' Only four passed the test, 'all made by Messrs Buckingham and Sons'.

> Three Buckingham ropes survived more arduous tests and it was with pleasure – even a touch of relief – that the report's authors went on to list the merits of the winners, 'which are now made by Messrs Buckingham expressly for the Club' and identified by 'a red worsted thread twisted in with the strands'. 'Expressly' didn't mean 'solely', of course: Buckingham and Sons weren't about to keep this success to themselves. Advertisements in the newspapers promptly announced the company as 'the only maker of the celebrated Alpine Club Rope, which is almost exclusively employed by the leading mountaineers of the time ... Beware of fraudulent imitations.'

Happily Arthur Beale continues online and options for new premises or a pop-up Christmas shop are being considered.

---

2. J Harding, 'Short Cuts: Nautical Dramas', London Review of Books, vol 43, No14, 15 July 2021.

Forza Italia

What are the ties that bind the Alpine Club with the Italian Alpine Club (CAI)? First, a common interest in mountains and the desire to protect their environment. Second, as the world's first mountaineering club, the AC inspired the founding of the CAI. Quintino Sella from Biella led the first ascent of Monviso, a group composed exclusively of Italians, on 12 August 1863. On his return to Verzuolo, their departure point, he told his fellow climbers about his desire to create an Italian Alpine Club. They were: the brothers Paolo and Giacinto Ballada of Saint Robert, Giovan Battista Abbà of Verzuolo, Giovanni Barracco of Crotone, and Raimondo Gertoux and Giuseppe Bodoino of Casteldelfino. This ambition was reiterated three days later in his official report of the climb, published in *L'Opinione*:

Elia Watson's painting of Monviso.
(Alpine Club)

In London an Alpine Club was founded, that is, of people who spend a few weeks a year climbing the Alps, our Alps! There you have all the desirable books and memories. There you can read the descriptions of each climb: without Mathews' accurate description I do not know if we would have been able to climb Monviso. In Vienna, too, an Alpenverein was founded. Could nothing like this be done by us? I believe so.

On 23 October 1863, in the Castello del Valentino in Turin, Quintino Sella founded the Italian Alpine Club aiming to 'promote mountaineering in all its manifestations, knowledge and study of the mountains – especially those of the territory where the social activity takes place – and the protection of their natural environment.'

English interest in Monviso, or Monte Viso, dates back at least six centuries. The writer and poet Geoffrey Chaucer (1342–1400) set a famous tale in *The Canterbury Tales* in the Mount Vesulus area and the Po valley. At that time Monviso was the only mountain in the Alps to be identified by its own name ('Vesulus', meaning, 'mountain that can be seen from afar'); this was a name used by Virgil in Aeneid at the time of emperor Octavian and mentioned by other writers of the time.

British interest in the mountain itself started in the 1800s. In 1839 the Scotsman James Forbes explored the lower reaches and first described the round trip of the mountain. Further information was provided from climbs made in 1854 by A P Whately and H T Jenkinson. John Ball, in 1860,

Left: Quintino Sella, founder of the Italian Alpine Club, in 1883. *(Museo Nazionale della Montagna, CAI Torino)*

studied possible routes of ascent and identified as easier the climb on the south face. In the same and following year Edward Whymper, future conqueror of the Matterhorn, tried in vain to reach the summit.

The first ascent to the summit of Monviso was made in 1861 by Englishmen William Mathews and Frederick William Jacomb with guides with guides and brothers Jean-Baptiste and Michel Croz, using information from Forbes and the Irishman John Ball, a founder of the Alpine Club. The second expedition to Monviso was again English, led by Francis Fox Tuckett in 1862. In 1882 W A B Coolidge made daring climbs on various faces of the mountain and did the first ascent of the north face in 1882, starting from the glacier that now bears his name.

King Victor Emmanuel II of Italy, struck by these English mountaineering efforts, awarded the title of Knight of Saints Maurice and Lazarus, prestigious honours from the Crusades, to William Mathews, Francis Fox Tuckett and John Ball in 1865, and to Edward Whymper in 1872. English women were equally enchanted by Monviso. At a time when women mountaineers were rare, the English Isabella Straton and Emmeline Lewis-Lloyd made the second female climb of Monviso in 1871: the first women to climb to the top were the Italians Alessandra Boarelli of Verzuolo and Cecilia Fillia of Martiniana in 1864.

Over the years, the AC and the CAI have taken different paths: the first has maintained a selective character and has a membership of around 1,500. The CAI welcomes all mountaineers who apply for memebership, without special requirements, united by an interest in the mountains and protection of the environment. The association currently has 322,000 members in 509 sections. Members are mostly Italian. The Saluzzo section of the CAI, founded on 15 July 1905, is called 'Monviso' in honour of the mountain that was fundamental in the constitution of the national CAI and currently has about 1,300 members.

Despite the different characteristics of the two associations, links between the Alpine Club and the CAI have been consolidated since 2011, when John Town and Adèle Long, representing the Alpine Club, participated in commemorations for the 150th anniversary of the first British ascent. The subsequent joint Italian-British climb to Monviso was the first of similar initiatives that have continued in subsequent years, with climbs and explorations carried out in friendship both in summer and winter, at Monviso and the surrounding mountains, in the Varaita, Maira, Grana and Gesso valleys.

Above: The combined AC and CAI team at the Sella hut. *(Phil Jardine)*

Left: Adèle Long and Rick Allen at the Sella hut. *(Phil Jardine)*

The chief link between the two clubs was Adèle Long, editor of the Club's newsletter for several years, who has a passion for Monviso; in 2014, on the occasion of the 150th anniversary of the first women's ascent, she represented Britain on the climb to the summit, with her companions Amanda Graham, Caroline Phelan and Rya Tibawi. Among the climbers from the Saluzzo section of the CAI were Laura Maero and Laura Borello.

During 2020, a week of joint climbs was planned in the Monte Rosa group, under the official patronage of the of the national CAI. The original programme provided that the CAI of Saluzzo would welcome the British by carrying out with them the annual group climb, this year organized with the aim of Castor, on 25 and 26 July. During the week, small groups of members of the CAI of Saluzzo would be joined by the English, in further climbs on Monte Rosa. The Covid pandemic led to a reduction of available places and the need for distancing in huts, reducing the participation of Italians, but did not stop participation. On 24 July, at Gressoney La Trinité, 12 Italians met with as many Britons.

The members of the CAI of Saluzzo were part of the Italian group: Carlo Gagliardone, Silvia Perona, Paolo Allemano, Livio and Elena Perotti, Claudio Rinaudo, Norma Martina, Loris and Paola Civalleri; also the members of the CAI of Cuneo: Sebastiano Cagnassi, Francesco Panzone and the guide Michele Perotti. Alpine Club members were: organisers Malcom Townsley and Adèle Long, Derek Buckle, Nick King, Nick Simons, Andy Wigley, Jon Halliday, Phil Jardine, Lili Mulvany, Gordon Chisholm and Rick Allen, the latter awarded the Piolets d'Or for the first ascent of the Mazeno ridge of Nanga Parbat in 2013.

In the evening there were presentations, informal speeches, a nice exchange of tributes (the Italian ones offered by Peirano Sport and Alp) and a dinner, offered to the English by the president of Saluzzo Franco Galliano. The Italian-English group next day went up to the Sella hut, and the following day climbed Castor in glorious weather. Later the climbers divided: while the Italians descended to the valley, some English continued to the Ayas hut, others to the Rossi and Volante bivouac to do the traverse of the Breithorns. Others descended to Gressoney, to go back to the Gnifetti. On the remaining days of the week, the British climbed many peaks of the Monte Rosa group and climbed the walls of Arnad.

Livio Perotti

Alpine Club Library

The year had barely begun when the Covid-19 pandemic struck the UK. Government regulations meant that, like every other library, we were forced to close our doors to personal visits by both AC members and the general public from March. Nevertheless, we put protocols in place so that our librarian, honorary librarian and keepers could continue to come into Charlotte Road on a part-time and Covid-safe basis to provide as good a service as possible under the circumstances. Telephone and email enquiries continued to be dealt with and postal book requests and returns continued to be processed, albeit at a somewhat slower pace than normal. So, I think it is fair to say that while Covid-19 significantly affected our year it did not dominate it. I would therefore like to express my sincere thanks and those of all the Library trustees to everyone concerned for all their efforts to keep things going during this difficult period.

Also early in the year, Neil Cox gave us notice that he wished to step down as our treasurer and as a trustee after three years in those roles. However, before stepping down Neil was instrumental in securing a £25,000 grant from Hackney Council in June 2020, as part the coronavirus small business and retail, leisure and hospitality grant fund. Again, on behalf of all the trustees, I would like to express my sincere thanks to Neil for all his work, not only for securing this very welcome grant but also for simplifying our accounts, generally putting our financial house in order over the past

Barbara Grigor-Taylor, the honorary librarian, Beth Hodgett the AC's new librarian (centre) and Philip Meredith, chair of the ACL Council.

few years and in mentoring his successor up to the end of the year.

Knowing in the spring that Neil would be stepping down in the autumn allowed us to seek a new treasurer from amongst the AC membership over the summer. We received a number of expressions of interest, but we were very pleased to be able to appoint Alan Henderson to the position with effect from the ACL AGM in October. Alan has a degree in accounting and finance from the University of Glasgow and 15 years experience in banking and commercial finance. Just as importantly, Alan is also a very active climber. He is clearly on the ball, because almost his first act after appointment was to jet off to New Zealand for three months of travelling and climbing before the second lockdown restricted international travel. Since his return, Alan has overseen our annual accounts and return to Companies House for 2020, as well as applying for additional coronavirus support grants for the ACL and AC, pertaining to the Nov-Dec 2020 lockdown period, in collaboration with the AC hon treasurer.

They say that bad news comes in threes, and in the autumn Nigel Buckley told us that he was resigning as ACL librarian to take up a position in the library at Balliol College, Oxford. This was a real blow, because I think it is no exaggeration to say that Nigel has transformed the efficient working and support for members by the Library since his appointment, as well as cementing a seamless working relationship between the Library and the AC Office. Nigel has been a delight to work with during his time with us and it is a genuine pleasure to thank him for all his work on our behalf. The good news is that Nigel is not being completely lost to either the ACL or the AC; he is remaining in post both as secretary to the ACL Council and as the keeper of artefacts. So we look forward to continuing to work with him for many years to come.

In November 2020, we set about the daunting task of finding a replacement librarian. We received a total of 27 applications, which we whittled down to a longlist of seven, all of whom were interviewed online. This was reduced to a shortlist of three who were invited to visit Charlotte Road to be shown around and interviewed face to face. We were unanimous in agreeing to offer the position to Beth Hodgett. Beth has an MSc in visual, material and museum anthropology from Oxford and is currently pursuing a PhD, based between Birkbeck College, London and the Pitt Rivers Museum, Oxford, researching the photographic archive of the archaeologist

O G S Crawford. As well as a number of academic publications, she also has experience of organising exhibitions and conferences, and of public engagement and outreach. Beth commenced the role on a part-time basis in April 2021 and full time in September, when she has completed and submitted her PhD thesis. Almost from her first day, Beth had to set about the task of organising the phased re-opening of the library following an internal review, establishing a click-and-collect service so members can order books in advance and collect them contact-free, as well as the option to book in-person library visits on two days per week, with Covid protocols in place.

After a relatively quiet year during which the number of enquiries was well down on previous years, presumably due to both national and international travel restrictions, activity is now starting to pick up. So, we are all looking forward to fully re-opening the Library in September 2021, after our annual summer closure when Beth will start working on a full-time basis.

AC Collections Database

I would like to remind readers that the library is much more than just books. We use the term as a catch-all, since the Alpine Club Library actually houses and takes responsibility for all the Club's collections, comprising over 30,000 books, magazines, journals and expedition reports; 40,000 photographs and slides; around 700 paintings, prints and drawings; the Alpine Club document archive; and the collection of around 300 mountaineering artefacts. Most of these items are now listed on our Koha cataloguing system. This enables cross-referencing between all items in the database and thus allows for a simple and user-friendly search facility that can be accessed via the library page of the Club's website at *www.alpine-club.org.uk/ac2/ ac-media/library.*

Visitors

Not surprisingly, visitor numbers were much reduced over the year because we were unable to host any after mid March 2020. Nevertheless, in January Nigel and Barbara arranged an exhibition on Leadership, Resilience and Overcoming Obstacles for a group of boys from Hoe Bridge School, Woking, with Victor Saunders giving a lecture on the same topic. In early March, Nigel arranged an exhibition and lecture on the history of the AC for the Rockhoppers Mountaineering Club.

AC ClubCasts

After March 2020, it was no longer possible to hold the normal bi-weekly AC lectures in the Lecture Hall at Charlotte Road. As a result, Nicholas Hurndall Smith, Nigel Buckley, Sherry Macliver and Michael de la Rue initiated the Alpine ClubCast series: short lectures and presentations shared on the Zoom platform. These proved to be extremely popular, often with around 150 members from all across the UK and abroad logging on to view them. Even larger numbers of the general public logged on to view them on Facebook. Importantly, a library archive of all the past lectures, now

'The Matterhorn' with dramatic sunset colouring, from the exhibition
'Alpine Nunatuks'. *(Fi Bunn)*

more than 20, has been produced, with each presentation edited and made
available on YouTube.

Exhibitions
Sadly, we were only able to mount a single art exhibition in the lecture hall
at Charlotte Road during the first few months of 2020 before the first lockdown. This was a visually outstanding exhibition of photographs by Fi Bunn
entitled 'Alpine Nunataks', featuring the glacial islands of the Valais region.
All the other art exhibitions planned for 2020 by Simon Pierse, keeper of
pictures, had to be postponed because we were unable to admit visitors to
the Clubhouse. Simon now hopes to mount these exhibitions during 2022.

In spite of this hiatus, we were not idle and have great plans for exhibitions
during 2021. An exhibition of books, maps and documents on pre-1921 surveying of routes to the Himalayan peaks through Sikkim was displayed in
the theatre in March 2020 to coincide with a lecture on climbing in Sikkim.
This led to plans being formulated by Barbara for a major exhibition in 2021
to commemorate the 1921 Everest reconnaissance expedition and the 1922
and 1924 climbing expeditions. Barbara has spent a huge amount of time
throughout the year researching and identifying original pre-1925 Everest
material in the AC Collections for the exhibition, and writing an accompanying catalogue.

The result of these endeavours is 'Everest: By Those Who Were There'.
This amazing exhibition celebrates the centennial of the 1921 reconnaissance of Mount Everest and the first attempts to reach the summit in 1922
and 1924. It uses the words of the expedition members themselves to tell
the story, from the first suggestions to tackle the mountain made in the 19th

century to the successes and failures of the first expeditions and final tragedy of 1924. Through the climbers' diaries, journals and letters, through their artworks and photographs, and from their clothing and equipment, visitors to the exhibition gain new insight into how these men thought and what they accomplished. Barbara was ably assisted in putting this exhibition together by Nigel Buckley, keeper of artefacts, Bernie Ingrams, keeper of photographs, and Glyn Hughes, honorary archivist. Much of the material in the exhibition has either not been shown before or will be shown for the first time in a century. The exhibition opened on 27 July until October 2021. We hope that Club members and the public will take advantage of this rare opportunity to experience 'Everest: By Those Who Were There'. It provides a wonderful opportunity to celebrate the work of the Alpine Club and the Alpine Club Library in preserving and curating climbing history, and the Club's key role in the first expeditions to Mount Everest. The Everest centennial exhibition is accompanied by a comprehensive catalogue reproducing every item shown, a compelling publication and already a collector's item in its own right.

The year 2021 also marks the centenary of the Pinnacle Club. With the benefit of a Heritage Lottery Grant, the club has been able to preserve its heritage through digitising and cataloguing its photograph and film collection, and creating an oral history. Celebratory events are planned throughout 2021, including a joint Alpine Club-Pinnacle Club exhibition to be held at Charlotte Road in November and December.

Art UK

Art UK is a cultural education charity that enables online access to UK art collections that are not normally on public view. The ACL has now been a member for two years. Initially we put 70 of the best pictures from the AC Collection online through Art UK. Janet Johnson has now selected more of our best pictures so we have increased that number to 99: the limit for our current category of membership. As well as viewing the pictures, AC members and the public can purchase prints in a range of sizes from the Art UK shop. This not only provides a resource for members but also a valuable source of income for the Library to use for restoration purposes. If our involvement continues to be successful and income from sales increases then we will consider upping our membership category to the next level, which will allow us to display up to 299 pictures, close to half of the total AC collection.

Please visit: *artuk.org* for more details, to view the pictures and to purchase prints.

Books

Because the ACL is an active library, we continually enhance the collection by attempting to obtain all interesting new books published on climbing and mountaineering. Success requires considerable effort, and involves negotiating with publishers to obtain either complimentary or heavily discounted

Above: 'Sunset from Mont Blanc' (1873) by Gabriel Loppé, the last oil painting to be added to the AC collection on the Art UK database.

Below 'Monte Viso' by Elijah Walton, among the images from The Watercolour World database of the AC collection.

copies of newly published books. Occasionally we have to pay the full price. Luckily, the year saw strong sales of duplicate books from the regular lists produced by Barbara.

The income from this not only helps to fund the purchase of new books but also the funding of substantial conservation and restoration projects for books, photo albums and archives. So, the duplicate book lists provide AC members with a great opportunity to buy historical (and sometimes rare) mountaineering literature at very favourable prices while simultaneously helping to enhance and preserve the collection.

Pictures

Throughout the year, Simon Pierse, keeper of pictures, has been working with The Watercolour World (TWW) to digitise works on paper from the Club's picture collection. TWW should not be confused with Art UK, although the two online databases are, in fact, the brainchild of the same person: Fred Hohler. The aim of TWW is to create a searchable database of topographical watercolours that depict locations around the world. The focus is on paintings made before 1900 when photography became the major documentary tool. The idea is to show how watercolours contributed to recording the changing world in which we live.

In February 2020, using a state-of-the art portable scanner, Simon worked with Ambrose Robertson and a volunteer from TWW to scan around half of the Club's works on paper. Some of these images are in sketchbooks and have rarely, if ever, been seen outside the collections before. Since the

Craftsmen making boots for the 1953 Everest Expedition at Robert Lawrie's, from the recently acquired Lawrie Archive.

scanner can handle work behind glass, it was also possible to scan some of the largest framed watercolours in our collection and to tile them together into a single image. This work is of immense importance to the Club. So many of our previous digital images were taken from slides and have a colour cast. Of particular value are the many sketches and watercolours of glaciers in the collection. In the context of global warming, they bear testimony to the speed of climate change over the past 150 or more years. Unlike Art UK, TWW does not sell images and the images on their website are not downloadable. However, TWW has provided the Club with full, high-resolution images that we can use and sell to generate much-needed income for the maintenance and conservation of our painting collection. We had hoped to scan the remaining watercolours by early 2021 but this has had to be postponed until after the Library fully re-opens.

Images of all pictures from the collection that have been digitised to date can be viewed at *watercolourworld.org/collection/alpine-club.*

Photographs

As for other parts of the Collections, the coronavirus lockdown meant that physical presence in the AC Photo Library was suspended from mid March 2020. Nevertheless, we were able to respond to email enquiries where requested images were already scanned or held in our database.

The list of archived films was revised and updated. Climbing films by Leo Dickinson and Eric Jones have been donated and added to the archive. A list of potential photographs for the forthcoming AC Everest centennial exhibition was produced. Additionally, we have provided images for an article on the Duke of Abruzzi in the *Himalayan Journal*. Sue Hare has been working with Thames & Hudson on a book and exhibition project on mountain photography. She also expects to provide material for the Alpine component of non-profit Macromicro's project 'On the Trail of the Glaciers', once it is able to restart.

Scanning of the Frank Smythe slide collection presented by his son and of the Mike Westmacott slide collection has been completed thanks to the efforts of Peter Payne. Jeremy Whitehead's extensive photo collection has been delivered to Charlotte Road, and Loreto Bonington has kindly donated Ian McNaught-Davis' mountaineering slides that relate to the British Soviet Pamirs Expedition in 1962.

Artefacts

We had planned to complete the task of photographing the entire Artefact Collection during 2020 but Covid-19 lockdowns put paid to that aspiration. We aim to complete that task when it becomes possible to allocate space to lay out material and allow a photographer to work in the Clubhouse. That task has now become a little larger because we have had new artefacts donated to the collection during the year. Robert Lawrie, the famous maker of mountaineering and climbing boots, donated an archive of photographs and examples of their products, the first of its kind in the AC Artefacts Collection.

It is also worth noting that our keeper of artefacts felt compelled to contact National Geographic when he saw that they were using an image of the wrong ice axe in an article featuring Sandy Irvine. The original and correct Irvine ice axe is held in the AC Collection.

Archives

For obvious reasons, there have been far fewer visitors during the past year than in normal years but the level of enquiries has held up. Without access to the physical archive our ability to respond promptly has been affected.

Accessions have also been fewer than normal but include letters written home from the Alps after an early ascent of the Jungfrau and a diary from Bill Tilman's expedition to the Langtang Himal in 1949. This was one of the earliest expeditions to the Himalaya after the Second World War and the diary was from Peter Lloyd, president of the Alpine Club. Since Tilman's own diaries ended up in a library in the US Midwest, material from other members of this expedition is of particular interest.

Among the Club's own records is a complete collection of newsletters and circulars sent to members since the foundation of the Club to the present time. The items issued up to 1967 were bound into three massive volumes each weighing several kilograms. Although the contents were well

The sorry state of the Matthews Monument in its current location outside the old Hotel Couttet in Chamonix.

preserved, the bindings had deteriorated badly due to the weight of the contents. We therefore commissioned our excellent conservator, Cyril Titus, to rebind the first volume and make a strong storage box to conserve it. This work has been a great success, and Cyril is now working on rebinding and conserving the other two volumes.

Monuments

Like other areas of work, the Covid-19 pandemic had a frustrating impact on efforts to identify and conserve the monuments of the Alpine Club in all but one area. There is a growing enthusiasm amongst members to ensure the objects representing our heritage that lie dotted around the Alps are not forgotten or allowed to fall into disrepair.

Bill Roberts contacted us to ensure that the grave of John Emery did not fall into obscurity. Emery died on the Weisshorn and is buried in Zermatt not far from the grave of the unknown mountaineer. He participated in the ill-fated Oxford University expedition to Haramosh in 1957 and was gravely injured by frostbite. Nevertheless, he continued climbing until his death in an accident in 1963.

Raymond Peto is buried somewhere in Interlaken according to William Newsom. Peto was a very significant member of the Club in the inter-war years. The location of his grave and the manner of his death are currently a mystery yet to be solved. John Allen wrote to Charlie Burbridge, the keeper of monuments concerning the grave of Richard Harris, a member of the ACG who succumbed to hypothermia near the summit of Mont Blanc in 1966. He is buried in Chamonix and his grave will be visited once the pandemic allows.

The grand project at present remains the movement and conservation of the Mathews monument in Chamonix. It is fitting that the monument should be moved to the Parc Couttet on the other side of the terminal moraine on which the old observatory stands because progress has been unavoidably glacial. The mayor of Chamonix is a strong supporter of the project and the opportunity it presents to reinforce the connection between the town, the Alpine Club and British alpinists more generally. Hope remains it will be in its new setting by the summer of 2021. The picture of the monument illustrates the current setting that this monument endures.

Mathews was an important and humble figure in the Club. His contribution was recognised by members not only with the construction of this lasting memorial but by the fact it was the bishop of Bristol who wrote the inscription, making subtle reference to the way in which Mathews supported his brother who became a founding member of the AC. Later he went on to write what was then the definitive history of Mont Blanc.

The keeper is not just interested in past monuments but future ones too. Doug Scott made an unparalleled contribution to British mountaineering and it is fitting that some lasting memorial be established which will join the long list of great lines he pioneered. Peter Holden has suggested a memorial in Doug's hometown of Nottingham; another option is something in the Lake District, possibly at Doug's local pub, The Old Crown. It may be fitting to achieve both to recognise the contribution Doug made to the nation and the contribution he made to the AC.

The keeper is very grateful indeed for the enthusiasm with which so many members regard the monuments. It has certainly helped to sustain him during this great incarceration and he hopes very much to be able to continue his work in visiting and conserving the last resting place of members throughout the Alps in due course.

Philip Meredith

Boardman Tasker Award 2020

The award attracted 22 entries in 2020 from five countries including the UK, the USA, Ireland, Canada and New Zealand. This was the first time in six years that entries fell below 30 but the complexities of Covid-19 made publishing unusually challenging in 2020. The judges were Katie Ives (chair), David Canning and Michael Kosterlitz and they selected five books for the shortlist:

Patrick Baker for *The Unremembered Places: Exploring Scotland's Wild Histories* (Birlinn), a lyrical exploration of Scotland's regions of 'rumour and folklore' that makes for a compelling argument for a greater examination of 'wild histories' beyond the most well-trodden narratives of adventure;

Emily Chappell for *Where There's a Will: Hope, Grief and Endurance in a Cycle Race across a Continent* (Profile), a book that transcends the genre of sports memoirs with prose that deftly captures the physical and psychological intensity of ultra-distance cycling;

Peter Foster for *The Uncrowned King of Mont Blanc: The Life of T Graham Brown, Physiologist and Mountaineer* (Bâton Wicks), an intricately researched biography of a Scottish mountaineer whose contributions to climbing history on Mont Blanc and other mountains have long deserved a close look;

Peter Goulding for *Slatehead: The Ascent of Britain's Slate-Climbing Scene* (New Welsh Rarebyte), an in-depth history of the climbs and characters of British slate that is also a meditation on the nature of obsession and on the persistence of wildness the post-industrial world;

Jessica J Lee for *Two Trees Make a Forest: On Memory, Migration and Taiwan* (Little, Brown), a poetic and deeply moving account of Taiwan's mountains, waters and forests that interweaves the author's experiences of hiking with recollections of political, cultural and family histories.

With Covid-19 making a live event impossible, the award ceremony moved online with an excellent virtual author's event conducted once again by Stephen Venables. The winner was then announced as Jessica Lee for *Two Trees Make a Forest*. Commenting on the winning book, chair of judges Katie Ives said:

> *Lee's book is one that expands the topography of adventure, pushing at the very limits of storytelling. Her journey takes place through overlapping landscapes of summits, mountain legends, political conflict, exile, natural disasters, memories, imagination, immigration and longing-like multiple interwoven paths in a forest and like the numerous possible futures for mountain literature itself.*

> *Back in 1987, during an international festival for mountaineering literature, the climbing writer Dave Cook had pointed out the need to make room for more varied voices, including those of women and people of colour. He'd also urged adventure writers to seek sources of inspiration beyond the narrow formulas of escapist tales, to acknowledge the 'interconnections' between experiences in the mountains and the rest of life, and to reassert 'some of the values of humanity and fellowship against the imperial colonisation of the hills.'*

> *Today, despite all the challenges of pursuing writing in our era, emerging authors from many diverse backgrounds are increasingly producing narratives that help mountain writing grow in creative and original shapes – beyond what even Cook might have imagined possible. Among such books, Two Trees Make a Forest represents a work of both literary merit and bold vision. Lee's story, David Canning explains, is 'Beautifully written, and it successfully progresses the genre of exploration writing into new territory.*

Katie Ives' full speech is available at *www.boardmantasker.com*.

Ed Douglas

Contributors

ALTON C BYERS is a senior scientist and faculty at the Institute of Arctic and Alpine Research (INSTAAR), University of Colorado at Boulder. His first visit to Khumbu was in 1973 as an undergraduate student of geography.

ROBIN CAMPBELL has held every office in the Scottish Mountaineering Club for which administrative competence is not required, including a long stint as editor in the 1960s and 1970s, and as archivist since 1997. Retired from a desultory career as an academic child psychologist, he now wastes his time and money in collecting and studying old drawings and watercolours, particularly those depicting mountains before they were trampled into familiarity by the boots of mountaineers.

JOHN CLEARE has been a freelance professional photographer for over 50 years but a climber for rather longer. Business and many expeditions have taken him all over the world, while he has several dozen books, several films and live TV broadcasts, more than a few new routes and several virgin summits to his credit. An ex-vice president of the AC and an ex-president of the Alpine Ski Club, he lives in remote Wiltshire.

MARGARET CLENNETT became the Pinnacle Club's archivist after moving to a spacious house in mid Wales in 2004; she had a spare room that needed filling. Nowadays, researching the club's history and the lure of her large garden conspire to reduce the time she spends on the hill.

ROB COLLISTER is a retired mountain guide who lives on the edge of the Carneddau in north Wales but still enjoys leading ski tours in the Alps.

LEO DICKINSON is the foremost adventure filmmaker of his generation and a leading adventurer in his own right, having BASE-jumped with peregrines, flown over Everest in a hot-air balloon and climbed hard north faces in the Alps, including the *Philipp-Flamm* on the Civetta. In 1970 he persuaded Yorkshire TV to commission a film of his ascent of the north face of the Eiger. He has made more than 50 films and won prizes at every major adventure film festival. The author of three books, his photography has appeared in *Life* and *Geo* magazines.

PETER FOSTER is a retired consultant physician. He has been a member of the Alpine Club since 1975.

TERRY GIFFORD was director of the annual International Festival of Mountaineering Literature for 21 years. Former chair of the Mountain Heritage Trust, he is the author of *The Joy of Climbing* (Whittles, 2004) and *Al Otro Lado del Aguilar* (Oversteps Books, 2011). Visiting professor at Bath Spa University's Centre for Writing and Environment and *profesor honorífico* at the University of Alicante, he celebrated his 70th birthday appropriately on *Wreckers' Slab*.

LINDSAY GRIFFIN lives in North Wales, from where he continues to report on developments in world mountaineering. An enthusiastic mind still tries to coax a less than enthusiastic body up pleasant bits of rock and ice, both at home and abroad. He remains the world's leading chronicler of mountaineering achievement.

J G R HARDING, a former AC vice president, no longer climbs but still writes about mountaineers and mountaineering. The article on Freda du Faur is one of a trilogy featuring some outstanding women climbers. John's mountaineering autobiography *Distant Snows* (Bâton Wicks) was published in 2016.

ALAN HEPPENSTALL was born in Newcastle-on-Tyne and now lives in Cumbria, after moving up from the south in 1978. Having gained a degree in Italian and French at Oxford, he worked for seven years for the British Tourist Authority, including three years in Rome. As a member of OUMC he climbed widely in the UK and enjoyed several seasons in the European Alps.

MÁREK HOLEČEK is one of the world's leading mountaineers as well as an author and documentary filmmaker. In 2018 he won the Piolet d'Or with Zdeněk Hák for the difficult new route *Satisfaction!* on the south-west face of Gasherbrum I, completed on his fifth attempt having suffered bad frostbite and the loss of a partner on previous expeditions.

MARTIN HOOD works for an international organisation in Switzerland and is a member of the Academic Alpine Club of Zurich. He is the translator of *One Hundred Mountains of Japan*, a collection of essays by the Japanese mountain writer Fukada Kyuya.

GLYN HUGHES is a some-time hon secretary of the Alpine Club, but now carries out the equally important roles of honorary archivist and barman: or as the AC quaintly puts it, 'chairman of the Wine Committee'. In 2014 he took on the near-impossible task of following Bill Ruthven as honorary secretary of the Mount Everest Foundation.

ADÈLE LONG is a retired medical researcher. Although a latecomer to the world of rock and alpinism, she has been fortunate enough to climb or ski on six of the seven continents, bagging a handful of first ascents along the way. During Covid-19, she has been less active on the hill and more occupied with the Pinnacle Club's centenary heritage project and the Alpine Club's Women Rise Up! project. Normality may, or may not be resumed in 2022.

JOHN MOORE comes from Weardale in County Durham. A geologist and retired Imperial College academic, his research interests are rock and ice deformation, orogenic mountain building processes, remote sensing and mining with sketching, history and languages as hobbies. He has ski toured, climbed, explored and worked in Britain and the Alps for 60 years, as well as Europe, Nepal, China, Arabia, Africa and America south and north.

DONALD ORR is a member of the Scottish Mountaineering Club and recently retired from a career in theology and fine art, which does beg questions. He now spends his time climbing and writing, and being irresponsible with his grandsons. His writings on mountaineering and the mountain environment have contributed over the years to the *Scottish Mountaineering Club Journal*.

SIMON RICHARDSON lives in Aberdeen. Experience gained in the Alps, Andes, Patagonia, Canada, the Himalaya, Caucasus, Alaska and the Yukon is put to good use most winter weekends whilst exploring and climbing in the Scottish Highlands.

C A RUSSELL, who formerly worked with a City bank, devotes much of his time to mountaineering and related activities. He has climbed in many regions of the Alps, in the Pyrenees, East Africa, North America and the Himalaya.

VICTOR SAUNDERS was born in Lossiemouth and grew up in Peninsular Malaysia. He began climbing in the Alps in 1978 and has since climbed in the Andes, Antarctica, Papua, Rockies, Caucasus and across the Himalaya and Karakoram. Formerly a London-based architect, he is now an IFMGA guide based in Chamonix. His first book, *Elusive Summits*, won the Boardman Tasker Prize. In 2007 he received an honorary MA from the University of Stirling for services to Scottish mountaineering.

MARCELO SCANU is an Argentine climber who lives in Buenos Aires. He specialises in ascending virgin mountains and volcanoes in the Central Andes. His articles and photographs about alpinism, trekking, and mountain history, archaeology and ecology appear in prominent magazines in Europe and America. When not climbing, he works for a workers' union.

RODERICK A SMITH began his fascination with mountains following the first ascent of Everest in 1953. He has travelled to the Himalaya,

Svalbard, Greenland, Arctic Canada, Japan and the Alps but always returns to his favourites in the Lake District. A lifetime's enjoyment has not been hampered with overweening ambition, but he is proud of his first ascent of a peak in the Stauning Alps and that he can still enjoy climbing and skiing at a modest level, despite the onset of decrepitude.

NICHOLAS HURNDALL SMITH is a climber and classical singer based in London. Having helped reinvigorate the Club's climbing activities, he is now on the committee, working on the aspirants' programme, Women Rise Up! and the Alpine ClubCasts to boost the approachability of Alpine and expedition climbing. He loves nothing better than a day at an esoteric crag in Cumbria or the traverse of an Alpine 4,000er.

THOMAS VENNIN spent a few years working hard in computer development before experiencing, like a midlife crisis, an improbable love at first sight for alpine literature. Nights haunted by the madness of mountaineers awakened his desire to write, first in a blog and then on the *Alpine Mag* website. Since 2018, Vennin has been a regular contributor to *Montagnes* magazine. If he willingly leaves the vineyards of Bordeaux for the trails of the Pyrenees, he tries to avoid putting on a harness and high altitude.

ERIC VOLA is a French climber who lives in Chamonix and Marseille. He spent three years at University College, London, and climbed in the early 1960s with Chris Bonington, Nick Estcourt, Don Whillans and other Brits. In recent years he has translated British mountaineering books, including a selection of Chris Bonington's best stories and Andy Cave's *Learning to Breathe*.

IAN WALL worked at Plas-y-Brenin in the 1960s. Since then he has climbed extensively throughout the UK, the Alps and in Norway. He was involved with the first round of the Kendal Mountain Film Festival in 1980. He has led treks in Africa, Ladakh, Tibet and Nepal, where he now lives and acts as an advisor to the Kathmandu International Mountain Film Festival, Kathmandu Environmental Education Project and in developing and training the Nepal Mountain Leader programme working closely with the Nepal Mountaineering Association.

NOTES FOR CONTRIBUTORS

The *Alpine Journal* records all aspects of mountains and mountaineering, including expeditions, exploration, art, literature, geography, history, geology, medicine, ethics and the mountain environment.

Articles Contributions in English are invited. They should be sent to the Hon Editor *The Alpine Journal*, Alpine Club, 55 Charlotte Road, London EC2A 3QF, UK. (**edward.douglas@btinternet.com**) Articles, including images, can be sent as an email attachment, on a disk or memory stick. File-sharing services are also acceptable, by prior arrangement with the editor. With files created in Microsoft Word please confine formatting to italics and bold. A typical article is 2,500 words **and may be edited or shortened at the editor's discretion**. Longer pieces should be discussed with the editor.

The Alpine Journal is unable to offer a fee for articles published, but authors who are not AC members receive a copy of the issue of the *Journal* in which their article appears.

Maps and diagrams These should be well researched, accurate and show the most important place-names mentioned in the text. If submitted electronically, maps and route diagrams should be originated as CMYK .eps files in Adobe Illustrator, Freehand or similar ensuring embedded images are at 300dpi resolution and CMYK. Hard copy should be scanned as a Photoshop compatible 300dpi tiff at A4 finished size. This can be arranged through the editor if required.

Photographs Image files should have unique names or serial numbers **that correspond to the list of captions** appended to the article, as a separate document, or in an email. They should be large jpgs or tiff files. Captions must include the photographer's name. Colour transparencies should be originals. Pre-scanned images should be **300dpi** Greyscale or RGB, tiffs or maximum quality jpegs at A4 final size or larger.

Copyright It is the author's responsibility to obtain copyright clearance for text, photographs, digital images and maps, to pay any fees involved and to ensure acknowledgements are in the form required by the copyright owner.

Summaries A brief summary, listing team members, dates, objectives attempted and achieved, should be included at the end of expedition articles.

Biographies Authors are asked to provide a short autobiography of about 50 words, listing noteworthy highlights in their climbing career and anything else they wish to mention.

Deadline Copy and photographs should reach the editor by **1 February** of the year of publication.

Index

'From the Payer-Hütte', Hilda Hechle, 1929?, watercolour, c25cm x 35cm.
Ortler group, north side. *(Courtesy of Thomas Smallwood)*

Index 2021

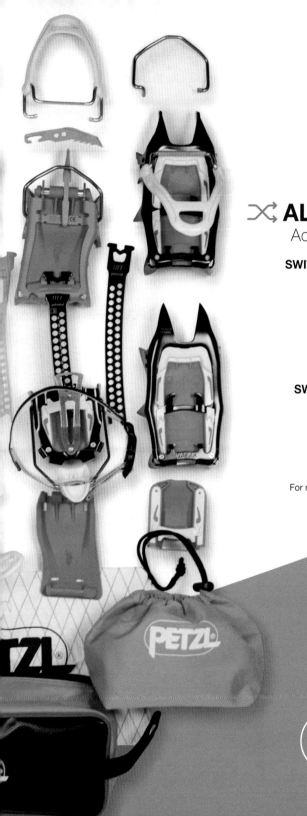

⤢ **ALPEN**ADAPT
Adapt to any ascent

SWITCH FRONT SECTIONS
for flat glacier
or technical ice

SWITCH BINDINGS
for approach shoes
or mountaineering boots

SWITCH HEEL SECTIONS
for tough and durable
or fast and light

For more information, visit petzl.com

BMC INSURANCE

INSURANCE YOU CAN TRUST

www.thebmc.co.uk/**insurance**
0161 445 6111

John Crook, Koyo Zom, Pakistan
Photo: Uisdean Hawthorn